LAND / RELATIONS

TransCanada Series

The study of Canadian literature can no longer take place in isolation from larger external forces. Pressures of multiculturalism put emphasis upon discourses of citizenship and security, while market-driven factors increasingly shape the publication, dissemination, and reception of Canadian writing. The persistent questioning of the Humanities has invited a rethinking of the disciplinary and curricular structures within which the literature is taught, while the development of area and diaspora studies has raised important questions about the tradition. The goal of the TransCanada series is to publish forward-thinking critical interventions that investigate these paradigm shifts in interdisciplinary ways.

Series Editor
Smaro Kamboureli, Avie Bennett Chair in Canadian Literature, Department of English, University of Toronto

Land / Relations

Possibilities of Justice in Canadian Literatures

edited by

Smaro Kamboureli and Larissa Lai

WILFRID LAURIER
UNIVERSITY PRESS

LAURIER
Inspiring Lives.

Wilfrid Laurier University Press acknowledges the support of the Canada Council for the Arts for our publishing program. We acknowledge the financial support of the Government of Canada through the Canada Book Fund for our publishing activities. Funding provided by the Government of Ontario and the Ontario Arts Council. This work was supported by the Research Support Fund.

Canada | Canada Council for the Arts / Conseil des arts du Canada | Ontario | Ontario Arts Council / Conseil des arts de l'Ontario

Library and Archives Canada Cataloguing in Publication
Title: Land/relations : possibilities of justice in Canadian literatures / Smaro Kamboureli and Larissa Lai, editors.
Other titles: Land relations
Names: Kamboureli, Smaro, editor. | Lai, Larissa, editor.
Series: TransCanada series.
Description: Series statement: TransCanada series | Includes bibliographical references and index.
Identifiers: Canadiana (print) 20220226059 | Canadiana (ebook) 20220226539 | ISBN 9781771125109 (softcover) | ISBN 9781771125116 (EPUB) | ISBN 9781771125123 (PDF)
Subjects: LCSH: Canadian literature—Social aspects. | LCSH: Canadian literature—History and criticism. | LCSH: Race relations in literature. | LCSH: Decolonization in literature. | LCSH: Land tenure in literature.
Classification: LCC PS8101.R33 L36 2023 | DDC C810.9/352900971—dc23

Cover design by Martyn Schmoll.
Interior design by John van der Woude, JVDW Designs.
Front cover image: *Indigenous. Academic. Solidarity.* by David Garneau.

Waterloo, Ontario, Canada
www.wlupress.wlu.ca

MIX Paper from responsible sources FSC® C103567 FSC www.fsc.org

This book is printed on FSC® certified paper, contains post-consumer fiber and other controlled sources, is manufactured using renewable energy—Biogas and processed chlorine free.

Printed in Canada

Wilfrid Laurier University Press is located on the Haldimand Tract, part of the traditional territories of the Haudenosaunee, Anishnaabe, and Neutral Peoples. This land is part of the Dish with One Spoon Treaty between the Haudenosaunee and Anishnaabe Peoples and symbolizes the agreement to share, to protect our resources, and not to engage in conflict. We are grateful to the Indigenous Peoples who continue to care for and remain interconnected with this land. Through the work we publish in partnership with our authors, we seek to honour our local and larger community relationships, and to engage with the diversity of collective knowledge integral to responsible scholarly and cultural exchange.

For Roy Miki

Contents

Acknowledgements

The preparation of this volume has taken much longer than expected, so first and foremost we would like to express our great appreciation to all the contributors for their patience and for allowing us to bring together such interesting and inspiring work. Our deep appreciation to Lisa Quinn, Director of Wilfrid Laurier University Press, for helping to bring this project to completion. We are especially grateful to Murray Tong, Managing Editor at Wilfrid Laurier University Press, for his efficiency and professionalism. The colleagues, students, staff, friends, and family who helped us organize the Mikinaakominis / TransCanadas conference, where most of the contents in this collection were first presented, supported us in big and small ways during the long process of completing this project. There are too many of them to list here, but we wish to extend our deepest thanks to all of them.

Smaro would like to acknowledge the Canada Research Chair she held at the University of Guelph and the Avie Bennett Chair in Canadian Literature at the University of Toronto that have both made her work on this volume possible and helped finance its publication. She is immensely grateful to her doctoral student and research assistant Kyle Kinaschuk, whose discerning eye, outstanding research skills, meticulous attention to everything he undertakes, and readiness to help avert or resolve technical crises no matter the time of day or night, has been instrumental in helping her bring this project to fruition. She would also like to express her heartfelt appreciation to friends and colleagues Len Findlay, Kirsten McAllister, Roy Miki, Slavia Miki, Donna Pennee, Heidi Schaefer, Cheryl Sourkes, and the late Phyllis Webb who have sustained her with their friendship, their intellectual and emotional support, and conversation. A particular debt of gratitude is due to Larissa Lai for accompanying her on this final TransCanada journey—she couldn't have wished for a better travelling companion.

Larissa would like to acknowledge the Canada Research Chair program, as well as the Faculty of Arts and the English Department at the University of Calgary for their generous support of her work on this book, as well as the Social Sciences and Humanities Research Council, which funded the publication in part. She thanks Edward Parker for his ongoing care and conversation. She extends much gratitude to Lillian Allen, Dina Al-Kassim, Karina Vernon, Erín Moure, and Nadine Chambers for holding her up when the going was tough. And, of course, she extends warm appreciation to Smaro Kamboureli for a shared journey full of both joy and peril. We did it! May this book make positive change in our suffering world.

Lillian Allen's poem, "Agency, Urgency, Insurgency," appears here with the author's permission. Rita Wong's "river sisters" is included with the author's permission. Jordan Abel's chapter is based on the audio recording of his presentation at the Mikinaakominis / TransCanadas conference, an excerpt from which has appeared in his book, *NISHGA*, included here with the author's permission as well as that of his publisher McClelland & Stewart. The still image from Tasha Hubbard's documentary *Buffalo Calling* in her essay "Re-storying and Restoring the Buffalo to the Indigenous Plains" is reproduced with Damien Kent's permission, while the image "Coming Together" in the same essay is reproduced with the permission of Johane Janelle. Pamela Mordecai's "Deliberate Vulgarity: Performing the Demotic, Transforming Cultural Space?" originally composed for this collection, has already appeared in *Ngũgĩ in the American Imperium* (2021), edited by Timothy Reiss, included here with permission from Africa World Press. The image from Marie Clements's *The Road Forward*, 2017 ©National Film Board of Canada, which appears in Sophie McCall's essay, is reproduced with permission from Marie Clements, writer and director; Shirley Vercruysse, producer; and Alexandra Hubert, Sales Agent, NFB Archives; in the same essay, the images by April dela Noche Milne are included with permission by Wayde Compton and Arsenal Pulp Press. Warren Cariou's

"Suncor Structures Viewed from the Athabasca River" is included in his essay with the artist's own permission, while Omushkego Cree Elder Louis Bird has granted permission to include a transcription of his oral story in the same essay. Sonnet L'Abbé's "CLI" and "CLII" are included with the permission of the author and Penguin Random House.

—Smaro Kamboureli and Larissa Lai

PART I

"open the portal" / Connective Counter-Memory

Agency, Urgency, Insurgency

/ LILLIAN ALLEN

Open the portal
Spring mists
Atop mountains
a stoic watchfulness
rumbling flashes of thunder solidified and stilled
Air & wood.   The comfort
To be clothed   with greens of cedar
And crystal   clear   blue
Of a ***deepening*** sky

Could this be the center
of healing?   Diffused
in laughter, in fullness

we pay homage to our
ancestral longings   for peace
a peace
that is Just -tice -tice -tice eeee
a piece

of being the whoo o whole
of all that
is given.

Of all
we have given
Our labour
To ugg gu
Labour of struggle. A dreaming
never ceasing. Threatens
To pull us under (sometimes),
But always will carry
Us over

We rest on the backbone
Of this land. This land (this is our landing) this lan ***d***

Its vertebrae steady *iiing*
Our feet
Our right
To exist

In fullness: cosmic
Trails of heart
Beat ***sss***
Becomes the drum **FLASH**

Dragon flies are just just jussssst ttt
Mosquitos
With flashlights
Who grew tired
of ***feeding*** THIS IS FALSE NEWS

A whirring numbness cabling
On-demand network dictatorship
So loud it squints & blurs eyesight

Falsification
Is an evil   an evil   an evil.
(Spirit) born of the transactional
World—extraction

Yet no one can hear
The sound of truth
When it dies   (even when you turn
The volume high)

Lest we forget;
the chemistry and a physics
And an
Organically interconnected   ***ness***   ***ttttt***
Of things   /   beyond ***any***thing
That is created
Or destroyed.

The arc of justice   hovers
Over the universe.   **Coltrane**
Trills extending language texture
The new imperative of creativity
Artists rendering visible an invisible freedom
Tuning...

Frantz Fanon says "each
Generation
Must discover
Its mission,   and
Will fulfill or betray it"
Corporate symbiosis and false
Cosmological con-trap-tionssss
Fill. Our. Spaces.

Faith is but vision for the oppressed
Clawing through the hell
And hellishness

Production of capital as King
Of King as male And white
Supreme mists mists mists

A mudfock'n mean spirit
Beast Beast Beast Beast

I will blaze indignation
decolonize the indecent
Sprawl. Emblazon it with art

Dis/Cis colouration
An omniscient intrusion
Breathing in our dreams

Stars hold space
For our secrets divinations
subversive desires twinkling/linkling
In dark of night

Through modern disparities.
We message each other across time.

We are this planet
This mother
twinkling incessantly we reach
Back from the forward
Future
To bend the arc that hovers

We are now,   (because) we are
Here.
We are the land,   and the light
We, the percussive movement
Of air
The breathing of rocks

We're the water   before & the after
Our voices between spaces,

Listen for the secret
Code Of revolution
DNA   of trees.   Listen
Wholly.
Universe
Is re|centering

Open the portal.   Reach
Back   ***and from*** the future.

Agency,   urgency,   insurgency
Agency,   urgency,   insurgency
Agency,   urgency,   insurgency
Agency,   urgency,   insurgency

We are now. We are Thus. We are here!
Now. Thus.   Here!
Now. Thus.   Here!
Now. Thus.   Here!
Now. Thus.   Here!

Agency,   urgency,   insurgency
Now.   Thus.   Here!
(repeat and fade)

Introduction

/ LARISSA LAI

Intimacies through Lands and Bodies

Land / Relations: Possibilities of Justice in Canadian Literatures had its beginnings in 2015 as a collaboration between Smaro Kamboureli and me, just as the Truth and Reconciliation Commission (TRC) on the Indigenous Residential School system was wrapping up,[1] and three years into the Black Lives Matter movement.[2] The Too Asian scandal was five years behind us.[3] The Galloway/UBCA scandal in which a prominent UBC creative writing professor was accused of sexual assault by a group of students, and many well-known Canadian writers signed a letter in support of "due process" for him, was just unfolding.[4] The imposture scandal around the writer Joseph Boyden was still a year ahead.[5] All of these events were and are continuous with much longer histories. Part of the challenge of understanding Canadian literature in the present is recognizing the multiple temporalities at work at once, most of them not linear. And yet the specificity of the moment does matter and must be attended to. As Lillian Allen writes in the poem that opens this book, we must "Reach / Back ***and from*** the future" (spacing and bold text in original) in order to touch "Now.

Thus. Here!" This book, we hope, gives a snapshot of a complex and entangled present, and offers analysis, critique, poetry, and art that can show us what that present looks like, and in so doing give us some inkling of where next to direct our "Agency. Urgency. Insurgency."

At the project's start, as Smaro Kamboureli and I document in our dialogue, which follows this introduction, our mutual friend Roy Miki (with whom Smaro started the TransCanada project, and with whom I, among many others, organized the 1994 conference Writing Thru Race) had recently retired. And I had just left my Canadian literature position at the University of British Columbia to take up a Canada Research Chair in creative writing at the University of Calgary. Smaro was seeking a collaborator for the fourth, and last, TransCanada conference. When she invited me to work with her, I was touched and pleased, remembering previous TransCanada conferences she had organized with Roy,[6] and later with Christl Verduyn, which were spaces that made room for complex voices practising from a broad range of locations, including Black, Indigenous, Asian, and mixed-race ones and their intersections, conversations that furthered the difficult, yet productive, conversations that had unfolded at events such as The Appropriate Voice,[7] Writing Thru Race (Writers' Union of Canada 1994),[8] and It's a Cultural Thing.[9] Many of the contributors included in this book were contributors to previous TransCanada conferences and books, sometimes as speaker, sometimes as panel chair, sometimes as editor, sometimes as the author of a chapter. Mikinaakominis / TransCanadas: Literature, Justice Relation, was organized by Smaro and me, in collaboration with a committee that included Kit Dobson, James Ellis, Emily Gilbert, Kyle Kinaschuk, Suzette Mayr, Neil Surkan, Christina Turner, Christl Verduyn, Joshua Whitehead, and Robert Zacharias, with contributions from Cheryl Suzack, and the guidance of the late Lee Maracle, whom we miss deeply. Like prior iterations of the conference, Mikinaakominis / TransCanadas opened up the possibilities of Indigenous, Black, Asian, and other/"people of colour's"[10] presence and conversation on the territories of Turtle Island north of the 49th parallel, in the Westphalian national construction that some people sometimes call Canada. The conference organization was radically coalitional, not in an easy utopian way, but in a complex, uneven, yet critically attuned and thoughtful mode. This event was highly critical of that understanding of the post-1988 Multicultural era that sees all racial locations as equal. It was critical too of a popular "small *m*" multiculturalism that has upheld song-and-dance versions of culture while erasing the real histories of violence, exclusion, theft, and genocide that mark Black, Indigenous, and Asian conditions in contemporary Canada.[11] Much cultural organizing on Turtle Island north of the 49th parallel since the late 1980s, including all of the TransCanada events, recognized the limits of both official Multiculturalism and the "small *m*" multicultural ideal that circulates in popular ways as a characteristic of the Canadian state.[12]

However, the conference Mikinaakominis / TransCanadas, like many if not all events that preceded it, was fraught with the difficulties of solidarity, alliance, or coalition across racial difference and (neo)colonial history.[13] The emerging historical moment, the body of experience that any one participant brought to any of these events, and the body as text shaped the event with contours that were radically and incommensurably different from one participant to the next. The work of cultural critique and production across a range of embodied positions placed participants in relation and sometimes contestation with one other. Ongoing relationships determined and overdetermined through the (neo)colonial project are not and cannot be expected to be easy. If the 1980s and 1990s were fraught with the beauty and impossibility of building relationships across differences,[14] Mikinaakominis / TransCanadas was just as exciting and fraught, if not more so. It is to think through the productivity and fraughtness of coalitional work that this book, *Land / Relations*, takes up the term "relation."

Further, *Land / Relations* takes up the term "land" in order to foreground its priority to the capitalist/colonial property formation. The editors are committed to the Truth and Reconciliation Commission and its calls to action, and recognize the urgency of responding, especially given the Canadian state's history of making studies and recommendations that are not followed by substantive action. It is important that the TRC be understood as a moment of opening rather than one of closure. With regard to land specifically, the possibilities of the Delgamuukw (1997) and Tsilhqot'in (2014) decisions on Indigenous land rights become increasingly important as their significance becomes more and more clear. The Delgamuukw decision was important because it was a decision in Canadian law that recognized oral testimony. The Tsilhqot'in decision was important because it recognized, again in Canadian legal terms—in other words, in the terms of the occupying state—that there exist unextinguished Indigenous land rights. If the colonial state itself can recognize Indigenous land sovereignty, this means incredible things for our Indigenous friends and colleagues, including contributors to this volume, and shifts the relationship of non-Indigenous people to the land and to Indigenous peoples in profound and exciting ways.[15]

If, as Dara Culhane teaches us, the violation of European colonialism on Turtle Island was the conversion of sacred land into capitalist property through the Lockean process of white labour, the other founding violation is the unhoming and dehumanization of Black people for the purposes of creating enslaved Black labour to extend the colonial property-making process. It is a little-known fact that slavery existed in Canada,[16] from the early 1600s to the early 1800s, affecting both Black and Indigenous people, perpetrated and enforced by whites. Anti-Black violence in Canada, including slavery, exclusion, police violence, and everyday racism, has been going on since the nation's inception and continues in the present. The theft of Black life and Black disenfranchisement from land is meshed, in the colonial project, with the theft of Indigenous land. Where Indigenous bodies are placed under genocidal erasure, Black people are disenfranchised from land and made into property for the purpose of further property creation—that is, the conversion of sacred land into real estate. Indigenous bodies are erased; Black bodies are divorced from Black subjectivities and made hyperreal in their capacity for labour. These are issues addressed in the body of Dionne Brand's oeuvre, the work of Afua Cooper (particularly *The Hanging of Angelique*), Rinaldo Walcott's *On Property* (2021), as well as in Christina Sharpe's recent *In the Wake: On Blackness and Being* (2016), which illustrates how Black lives are caught up in the aftermath of slavery, and profoundly shaped and animated by it. Further, the work of writers like Lawrence Hill, George Elliot Clarke, Sylvia Hamilton, Cheryl Foggo, David Chariandy, and Karina Vernon implicitly or explicitly show us how slavery has an ongoing aftermath in Canada.[17]

To consider whose labour has built the nation-state and how that labour was extracted is important. Here, Lisa Lowe's (2015, 17–18) book *The Intimacies of Four Continents* becomes productive for recognizing that the nation emerges from global conditions, and that the long and ongoing history of globality resides with us through colonial divisions of intimacy that are forgotten or barely legible because they haven't produced the kinds of subjectivities that global capitalism wants, but rather that remain largely under erasure through the intense ideological pressures of liberal individualism and, within a literary context, the ways in which both the publishing industry and the university system tends to frame literatures in national terms. Lowe writes,

> I suggest we...may unsettle the "dominant" notion of intimacy as the possession of the individual, if we consider both the "residual" and "emergent" forms of intimacies on which...dominance depends. This involves considering scenes of close connection in relation to a global geography that one more often conceives in terms of vast spatial distances. It means drawing into relation with one another the abolition of slavery in the Caribbean and the development of colonial modes of biopolitical violence in Asia that sought to replace African enslaved labor with Chinese "free" labor there and elsewhere; it means revealing the proximity of the geographically, and conceptually, distant sites of the Caribbean and China, and appreciating together settler practices with the racialized laboring figures of the slave and the "coolie." (2015, 18)

While Lowe writes of the Caribbean in this passage, I suggest that the nation-state we call Canada is party to this set of conditions. To reduce colonial logic to its barest bones: European colonialism pits Black labour in the form of slavery against Asian labour in the form of indentureship in order to steal Indigenous land. Labour is the means by which the land is stolen, through the logic of John Locke's labour theory of property, which justifies the concept of land ownership by claiming that when a person works the land, that person's labour enters the land transforming it into property: "Whatsoever then he removes out of the state that nature hath provided, and left it in, he hath mixed his labour with, and joined to it something that is his own, and thereby makes it his property" (Locke 2014, 27). Dara Culhane observes, however, that in the Americas this magic works only with regard to white men's labour. Locke says Indigenous people's property rights extend only to "the fruit they gather, the deer they catch and the corn they pick" (qtd. in Culhane 1997, 53).[18] In the unbearable logic of the colonial project, unfree Black and Asian workers are made to compete to extend the white man's arm. The colonial structure produces racial being by pitting one racial location against the next, in order to foreclose coalition-building, solidarity, and revolution. In a sense, it is through this violent, contestatory set of labour–land relations that Indigeneity, Blackness, and Asianness are produced as racial conditions within the colonial project in competitive relation to one another. In other words, we are contained within a brutal ideological framework, and made to fight. It's for this reason, I feel, that real coalitional work, done right, can be both radical and liberatory. I hope that this volume brings this condition to light and elaborates on the specific ways it presents itself in our literary and lived culture.

For me, what is most productive about Lowe's formulation—"intimacies of four continents"—is that it recognizes the specific conditions of racial locations and does not make equivalences of them, but rather attends to their specificity and also the ways in which they are interlocked with one another. Such thinking differs radically from the way that state Multiculturalism is created and received to make equivalences of positions for the purposes of state management. Multiculturalism as state containment undermines the analysis demanded by the "intimacies of four continents" insofar as it doesn't make space for radical incommensurabilities from one position to the next, and insofar as it buries the colonial logic that creates racial locations and then pits them against one another.

Jodi Byrd makes this dynamic even more specific:

> By positioning the conditions of slavery and indentureship in the Americas as coeval contradictions through which Western freedom affirms and resolves itself, and then by collapsing the indigenous Americas into slavery, the fourth continent of settler colonialism through which such intimacy is made to labor is not just forgotten or elided; it becomes the very ground through which the other three continents struggle intimately for freedom, justice and equality...Thus, within the "intimacies of four continents," indigenous peoples in the new world cannot, in this system, give rise to any historical agency or status within the "economy of affirmation and forgetting," because they are the transit through which the dialectic of subject and object occurs. (2011, xxv)

Byrd is aware, as am I, how overdetermining such a framework can be. It runs the danger of reifying racial locations and, further, does not take into consideration the ways in which racialized subjects with connections overseas are entangled in a global world order that complicates their/our positions on Turtle Island. She addresses this later in her book. With her, however, I recognize that it is necessary to acknowledge the set of historical conditions that play a key role in social, economic, and political formations here. Byrd productively calls for the need to "read the cacophonies of colonialism as they are rather than attempt to hierarchize them into coeval or causal order" (2011, xxvii). She writes: "When the boundaries between worlds break down and the distinctive characteristics of each world begin to collapse upon and bleed into the others, possibilities for rejuvenation and destruction emerge to transform the world radically. The goal is to find balance" (Byrd 2011, xxvii).

If Indigenous Peoples need to agitate for sovereignty in order to (re)claim the land, and Black people need to fight for sovereignty in order to (re)claim the body and find new relationships to land, I don't think that it is possible to desire sovereignty for Asian locations in parallel ways. As far as Asian sovereignty goes, sovereignty hasn't worked out so well, at least not on that land mass the West calls Asia, when it's manifested as totalitarianism (contemporary China), dictatorship (Cambodia, North Korea, China), and/or genocide (Cambodia, China). As the proxy hot wars on the land mass the West calls Asia have taught us, and as Chris Lee in this volume recognizes, drives for sovereignty have produced genocide, totalitarianism, and dictatorship, accompanied by unspeakable human suffering (if one thinks, for instance, of the Cambodian genocide, the Cultural Revolution in China, the recent mass rapes and village burnings against the Rohingya in Myanmar, and the current PRC brutalities in Xinxiang and Hong Kong). If there's an "Asian gift" this collection can offer, it's perhaps the recognition that drives to sovereignty don't always work out so well, particularly when there are despots in the wings, only too willing to take power.

This does not mean that we should not be dreaming revolutionary dreams. I support drives to sovereignty for Black and Indigenous friends and allies because I see that they have culturally specific ways of valancing the term, and because my own embodied experience does not put me in a place to judge. I recognize and respect the need within Black and Indigenous communities to articulate and build sovereignties in their own forms and from their own locations. Further, as Karina Vernon notes in this volume via the important work of Erica Violet Lee, it's important to recognize Black Indigeneity and the double displacement of Black people first from their original homelands in Africa and then from their own bodies. A true analysis of the intimacies of four continents requires diagnosis of and coalitional support for the strategies that emerge from specific forms of race and racialization, as well as specific moments in history. In order to do this work well, we need the work of informed analysis and the work of the imagination. Seeing these things, I recognize that some forms of Asian sovereignty might also be viable, but that is a subject for another project.

This analysis is important in order to recognize the managerial violence of official Multiculturalism and its tendencies to make equivalences of unequal positions, and to foreground the less substantive and less threatening aspects of cultures over the substantive and sometimes difficult-to-resolve concerns of Black, Indigenous, and Asian people. The term "relation" becomes important in order to understand how history has positioned people beside, at right angles, or in opposition to one another. This book actively seeks to lay out some of those substantive concerns and the contradictions of the present moment.

For indeed, though the "bare-bones analysis" I just gave, which recognizes how Black and Asian peoples are placed in death-dealing competition with one another to do the coerced labour that steals Indigenous land, is important as a critique of M/multiculturalism and a critique of the Euro-colonial state, its limit is precisely its narrowness. The bare-bones critique (particularly my one-sentence condensation above), centres, in the most brutal of ways, Eurocentric violence and the production of Eurocentric racial categories. While important for understanding the present and one of its relationships to history, it does not address the specificities of what might be called story, literature, culture, or tradition in locations that the West racializes as Black, Indigenous, or Asian. Jordan Abel, Warren Cariou, Chris Lee, and Sedef Arat-Koç's chapters in this volume are important for their naming and articulation of other centres in their specificity and complexity. Abel acknowledges the Nisga'a culture, which the residential school process—experienced intergenerationally—shut him out of, and sees the necessity of his own practice of recuperation through contemporary experimental poetics.[19] Warren Cariou, in conversation with Louis Bird, recognizes loss and agency from an Omushkego Cree location with a specific tradition and understanding of the Thunderbird, gas, and temporality. His chapter generously invites non-Indigenous people to see themselves and their relationships through a contemporary Omushkego Cree lens. Chris Lee sees how work that contributes to seemingly empowering Chinese Canadian cultural nationalism presents itself on the other side of the Pacific as a dangerous Chinese nationalism that contributes to Chinese state totalitarianism. Sedef Arat-Koç articulates how both Islamophilic and Islamophobic understandings of Arab cultures foreclose radical feminisms developed through complex and long-standing Arab traditions.

To condense relationships to a single statement gives readers a certain historical clarity; however, it essentializes racial positions produced through precisely the logic I articulated. In so doing, it reproduces Euro-colonial power by foregrounding Euro-colonial violence and its production of racialized subjects. We need to be careful with the racial positions handed to us by Euro-colonial violence; to cling to them too hard can appear radical even as such clinging reinforces and reproduces Euro-colonial violence precisely through the bodies racialized by the violence articulated. Sonnet L'Abbé's poems in this volume clearly show this problem to us. Nevertheless, it's important to understand the logic so that new forms of racial violence, including M/multiculturalism, can't hide their ugly history and its ongoingness. It's also important to recognize how racialized positions are sedimented through experience and become real and culturally meaningful over time.[20] I suggest that the work before those who decry colonial violence is to find ways to undo it, and also to see and make better relationships both through it and in excess of it by being accountable to the positions we've been given, have enacted, and have lived through, and through the complex storied, literary, cultural, and traditional practices and ways of being we retain in spite of the colonial violence enacted on or through us. I understand the balance that Byrd seeks as balancing the responsibility to the ways colonialism has sedimented racial positions (including whiteness), and the making contemporary of traditions we (in our incommensurate differences) carry with us. We need to build from both inherited traditions and what we've been handed. In practice, these elements can and do unfold together. This merging might be understood as the agented enactment of balance.

Further, however, in order to find balance, it is necessary to see contemporary conditions as they really are. One of the most notable recent books showing us these, at least in part, is the recent anthology *Refuse: CanLit in Ruins*. It recognizes that an industry, a cultural field, and an academic discipline are conflated in the term "CanLit" (McGregor et al. 2018, 17).[21] Its editors argue that the industry element, with its emphasis on marketing to both a Canadian and a global audience, tends to predominate (18–19). The industry of CanLit relies on prize culture, and tends to erase vast swathes of cultural production north of the 49th parallel. In spite of the fact that the cultural field and academic study have been more inclusive (though "inclusion" is itself an issue, and any inclusion has been imperfect), those tendencies tend to vanish under the marketed surface. The industry, *Refuse* tells us, in fact also includes Black, Indigenous, and Asian voices, though it tends to uphold stories of oppression and marginalization at the expense of other kinds of stories (18). Further, the colonial underpinnings of CanLit dominate its formation (21). Though the industry, the cultural field, and the academic discipline have included for several decades the voices of those Black, Indigenous and Asian Peoples who have wished to be included, mostly as a consequence of great struggle[22] on the part of BIPOC communities, this is not necessarily progress. Or rather it is progress, but progress is not necessarily what is desirable. While Canadian literature is no longer exactly exclusionary, this does not mean that it has been "decolonized" or that the problems of white supremacy and the marginalization of racialized people are over. The editors of *Refuse* are rightfully outraged by the ongoing injustice of the field. They play with the meaning of the word "refuse," seeing the value of denying that which wastes our time, but also calling on their readers to weld or put together afresh a field that has become wasteful. It is difficult not to receive first and foremost, however, the sense of "refuse" that means denial. When we are all feeling hopeless and frustrated by it, CanLit becomes a "dumpster fire" that is no longer worth anyone's bother. We want to "burn it all down." The problem with this, of course, as the editors of *Refuse* know, is that to "burn down" the field is potentially to obliterate memory of the difficult and important liberatory labour of earlier generations of Black, Indigenous, and Asian critics, writers and activists and their allies; to inadvertently lump liberatory work together with the overtly and deliberately colonial aspects of the project.[23] The liberatory work of previous moments may contain problems of its own as I've explained by giving the example of the problem of Asian Canadian rights work undermining Indigenous sovereignty in my note above. But nonetheless I think most readers would agree that they don't really want to forget that work. We need to remember in order to both honour and critique the work of the past, so we can find better and more just ways of doing the work in the present moment.

This book shares the concerns *Refuse* has with the state of the field. *Land/Relations* decries the appropriation prize, imposture, and sexual abuse. It embraces those aspects of a shared project that aims to critique, historicize, and find better ways to do the work. If *Refuse* disavows CanLit, *Land/Relations* seeks relationships both within and beyond it. But these are only tendencies; in fact, both books carry a share of rage, neither book escapes the national framework, and both books seek relationship.

Both books also run the danger of incorporation. Here, I want to explain the term in order to guard against the practice. When I write of incorporation, I write of that phenomenon in which racialized presences and seemingly liberatory language can appear as signs of arrival while retaining a lively ongoing violence beneath the surface. In his trenchant early analysis of the 1994 conference Writing Thru Race, Scott Toguri McFarlane says that incorporation denotes the "magical" resolution of loss wherein the problematic material is maintained beneath the incorporative surface—there, but unnameable (1995, 26). The psychoanalytic theorists Nicolas Abraham and Maria Torok use the term "inclusion" to describe this phenomenon:

> Inclusion attests to a painful reality, forever *denied*: the "gaping wound" of the topography....The melancholic's complaints translate a fantasy—the imaginary suffering of the endocryptic object—as fantasy that only serves to mask the real suffering, the one unavowed, caused by a wound the subject does not know how to heal. (1994, 142)

In this volume, Sophie McCall names it, more bluntly, "forced inclusion"—the binding of subjects to the state under conditions they don't want, a binding, further, that erases precisely the unjust violence enacted by the state on the subject.[24] It is the same logic that governs apologies, truth and reconciliation commissions, conferences, and books—the cover of the sign seems to integrate and heal the problem addressed, when in fact it merely covers over the problem and makes it seem to vanish. All the while, the problem roils beneath the surface more intensely than ever. Fully articulate "roiling" may be available within the frame of the conference, the text of the apology, the depositions made at the commission, or beneath the cover of the book. This does not necessarily mean that the public receives it. The covering sign is more powerful than the embodied discourse. Worse, the covering over does not need to be complete in order for the incorporation to be publicly salient. Nevertheless, specific "covers," that is, specific signs, may do different kinds of social labour. It has become apparent, for instance, how unproductive state apologies, especially disingenuous ones, can be. I hope that this book will be more productive and meaningful, both through the work it does as a signifying object, and the work its contents do as discourse and as language that is always already also action.

This book may open to the door to how to imagine the future better, and in so doing, perhaps it might inaugurate a shift in better relation-making, if we are lucky. And indeed, chance plays a role. I think here in terms of the poethical wager, as articulated by Joan Retallack, that when one attempts to speak or write the present into the eruption of a generative moment, one must nevertheless accept whatever comes. Retallack writes:

> Current ideas of memory as witness often serve to imprint guilt and prophylactic horror rather than to examine a poetics of memory that recomposes the actively present elements of historical tragedy. Who knows what might lead some *us* or another swerve out of a suddenly illuminated detail in one of the many patterns of ruin. The shape of historical outcome reveals itself by chance as much as intention, yet at any moment one can act out of considered values that inform the projects of one's poethically cultivated intuitions. (2004, 19)

Writing in 2004, Retallack bases her poethics of hope in the eruption of the happy surprise. I'm not quite so optimistic; I still think surprises are good, but this does not mean they are always happy.

As I've argued elsewhere,[25] reading the work of Tom Moylan (1986), it is important to keep on dreaming utopian dreams. But the problem of how to get "there" from "here" remains, for indeed whose "there" and whose "here" are we talking about? "There" and "here" are vastly incommensurable depending on who is doing the dreaming. However, our dreams and actions are interlinked, as some of the new materialists remind us. The task for each of us is our own "emergent insurgency": to imagine the best future we can and act to bring it to fruition—not because it will actually come into being but because each person's actions, in combination with those of others acting with the same kind of thought and intent, will interact and bring about eruptions of the unexpected, what the philosopher John Rajchman (1999, 50) calls the "knock at the door." Our job then is to recognize the knock when it comes—itself no easy task. Further, there are no guarantees as to what might lie behind that door; it could be total liberation for all, or it could be the secret police. To recognize the knock, to open the door to the right bachelor/ette (as it were), requires vast reserves of attention and thought that might not appear to others as doing much. And yet, without this attention, we might open the wrong door, and let the wrong stranger or lover in. Is sovereignty what is to be desired? Or liberal democracy? Or some form as yet unimagined? We need lenses to help us see what might be arriving. This book offers part of the vision required to recognize a good surprise when it erupts. For me, this is the reason for doing the work—for the hope and possibility embedded in it.

Edited Collection as Contact Zone

One might think of the conference Mikinaakominis / TransCanadas: Literature, Justice, Relation, and, for that matter, this book itself as contact zones in Mary Louise Pratt's sense: "the space of imperial encounters, the space in which peoples geographically and historically separated come into contact with each other and establish ongoing relations" (1992, 6). These relations are not easy ones—far from it. As Pratt reminds us, relations in the contact zone "usually involv[es] conditions of coercion, radical inequality, and intractable conflict" (1992, 6). As we know, conditions of coercion, inequality, and conflict in the contemporary, urban metropole are different from the conditions of coercion, inequality, and conflict in the instance Pratt imagines, the contact between the Inca Empire and the Spanish, as documented in 1615 by Felipe Guamán Poma de Ayala, writing in a mixture of Quechua and Spanish (1992, 5). Nevertheless, if one thinks of the architecture of the Great Hall at the University of Toronto's Hart House, where the conference Mikinaakominis / TransCanada held its plenary sessions, or the conference structure of keynotes and parallel sessions, or the structure of an anthology with editors and contributors, and a specific set of press protocols that must be followed, the operations of what Althusser would call "ideological state apparatus" are fully in play. I'd suggest that such conditions can be altered and set into a field of play as a form of poethical wager in Retallack's sense. Indeed, this book does that, by including a range of different types of writing—poetry, academic essays, a dialogue, a report. By holding poets and novelists up beside performers and critics, and further by making room for generically hybrid practices, Mikinaakominis / TransCanadas also experimented with form. Earlier TransCanada conferences experimented even more broadly in this regard, as Smaro describes in the dialogue. However, these experiments are not escapes from more traditional forms. Still, they can be understood as assays at producing the kinds of ruptures that might give way to a better future. The problems of the contact zone are not specific to Mikinaakominis / TransCanadas or *Land / Relations*. Coercion, inequality, and conflict are features of conference structures and books alike under contemporary (neo)colonial conditions. We can work against coercion and inequality, as certainly both this book and the conference that preceded it did. However, the gift of overcoming occurs, as I have described above, through interaction, rupture, and surprise. *Land / Relations* offers a simpler gift: it shows us in part where we stand at present.

To think of Canadian literature as a contact zone, in fact, might be more productive than thinking about it as either a utopian national ideal or as a "dumpster fire." To look at it in such a way might help us to see more clearly what is there. Rereading Mary Louise Pratt again after having received the gift of Lisa Lowe and Jodi Byrd's work, it is possible to see more clearly the contours of the contact zone as it stands at present and the contradictions that shape it. This book illuminates those contradictions.

Land / Relations has four parts, each bearing as its title a line or phrase from the poem that inaugurates it. The first part of the title of the first section, "'open the portal': Connective Counter-Memory," comes from the first contribution in the volume, a poem by Lillian Allen entitled "Agency, Urgency, Insurgency." It begins "Open the portal / Spring mists / Atop mountains / a stoic watchfulness / rumbling flashes of thunder solidified and stilled..." This poem answers the "knock at the door" by "open[ing] the portal." Allen speaks precisely of the moment of rupture, in this case in a "flash of thunder," or the moment of being in "The comfort / To be clothed with greens of cedar / And crystal clear blue / Of a ***deepening*** sky" (boldface and spacing in original). The rupture could, in other words, be a deepening of the sky we already live beneath. The rupture need not be violent, though it is a surprise—to go into the deepening sky is, in a sense, to fall upwards, to fall into a productive paradox. She asks of this deepening: "Could this be the center / of healing?" That would certainly be my wish. Her gifting of the poem—composed while we were together at the Banff Centre Residency "Primary Colours" in 2018, organized by Chris Creighton-Kelly and France Trepanier—was a beautiful time indeed of sitting in each other's company, talking about art, writing, and activism as we paid "homage to our / ancestral longings for peace / a peace / that is Just -tice -tice -tice eeee / a piece / of being the whoo o whole / of all that / is given." What is beautiful about the "Just -tice -tice -tice" echoing through that poem is that it echoes through the airier, more volatile moment of the 2017 Mikinaakominis / TransCanadas conference recognizing a resonance, a break, and a continuity between one moment and the next. Each of us is a "piece" required for "peace," but even "peace" is just part of the "whoo" of the "whole"—we can't be at peace all the time, if justice is to arrive, echo, and perhaps slip away again. The continuity of "Just -tice -tice -tice" is interstitial and resonant. There are many knocks at the door, but the stranger/lover does not stay forever.

The conversation between Smaro and me included in this opening section offers the history of how we came to produce this volume together, and the history of the conference from which the volume derives. In speaking of the conference, I want to be clear, first of all, that this book is not a proceedings. It is, however, a text that has roots in an event and evolves from it. In recognizing the historicity and, for that matter, the temporality of the conference, we recognize the temporality of this book, and the specific histories that brought the two of us, as editors, together. In our dialogue, we talk about other events that contributed to a complex set of connected but evolving projects of what Smaro in *Shifting the Ground of Canadian Literary Studies* calls the "field-imaginary" (2012, 14). Because frameworks connect, move apart, transform, and travel, the project can be named, perhaps, in a particular instance. To name it as a whole is more complicated, more violent, and perhaps ultimately impossible.

The dialogue, originally conceived as the introduction to the volume,[26] traces our commitment to collaboration and to experiments in cultural organizing. It discusses our respective relationships with Roy Miki. We also discuss our trajectories through earlier projects, including earlier TransCanada conferences and gatherings, Writing Thru Race, as well as events and podcasts emerging from The Insurgent Architects' House for Creative Writing, the "uncentre" I run at the University of Calgary. The dialogue offers a sense of what it is to organize and edit on the ground; it lays out, from a site of considerable cultural organizing and editing experience, the intertwining of material pragmatics with cultural, intellectual, and poethical commitments. In our current age of polarizing digital media and the rise of illiberal populist movements, our articulation of the dance among subtle, interlocked elements offers a grounding in practice, in relation to the "field-imaginary" to be sure. It's my feeling that this kind of work is currently in a state of crisis. Largely raced and gendered, it is exhausting; and as a kind of mitigating site between the needs of students, academics, writers, activists, and artists on the one hand, and impersonal state apparatuses on the other, it catches many of the irresolvable contradictions that cannot be addressed at other locations. It is a site where power coalesces, but it is also a crossroads and a contact zone.

Part I closes with a piece by Eileen Antone, the Oneida Elder who so generously opened Mikinaakominis / TransCanadas. She articulates her own engagements with Indigenous literature beginning in the 1970s and remembers the injustice of oppressions enacted by the state and Canadian literature against Indigenous literatures. She generously recognizes shifts that have occurred for the better, but also sees, quite rightly, that there were tensions at the event. She praises the engagement with traditional materials in Warren Cariou's work, Tasha Hubbard's work on restoring the buffalo, and the extraordinary spoken-word poetry of Lillian Allen and Eekwol. Importantly, she expresses grief for the razing of the Black church in Africville as it was dramatized in Cyrus Sundar Singh's performance "Africville—Dogs, Gods, and City Hall." She does this while recognizing the complicity of the church, in a different iteration clearly, in the violence of the residential schools in which so many Indigenous children were incarcerated and murdered. This generous reach across a field of contradiction strikes me as a kind of pedagogy, from Eileen Antone to us, her readers, a medicine for our present ills. It is giving from the location where one has been hurt to recognize the harm done to the neighbour beside her in the circle.

The second section, titled "'the ghosts pile up with the toxic mistakes': Hauntings and Other Returns," begins with a poem by Rita Wong called "river sisters." Written to honour the Peace River, where Wong has been engaging much of her activist work in recent years, it obliquely references the Site C dam, currently under construction in British Columbia for hydro-electric purposes, in spite of tremendous protest efforts by Indigenous and environmental communities against the massive destruction its building wreaks. Wong writes: "the ghosts pile up with the toxic mistakes in the patriarchs' drive to power / as they gamble away the haunted house / we call earth, watershed home...." She is fully aware that the colonial project is also a capitalist and patriarchal one. She might be implicated in the violence, but this is not the same as consenting to it. She calls on the spirits of those who have lost their homes to "help people change their river murdering ways."

As the flow of the river in "river sisters" is disrupted, so is the flow of time in Jordan Abel's "Positioning Intergenerational Trauma: Nisga'a Nationalism and the Materiality of Marius Barbeau's *Totem Poles*." Abel's story of his own disconnection from his Nisga'a roots as a consequence of how the residential school project disrupted the well-being of his family is recounted while time code runs down the side of the page. Colonial time as the time of technology flows forward without a hitch, while Nisga'a time is deeply and irrevocably disrupted. The presence of the time code makes the reader / listener self-conscious of their reading and listening practices. As Abel unfolds his story, readers are forced to see that story as representation; in fact, it becomes representation in linear time at precisely the moment it emerges. As they witness, in other words, they are also implicated in ongoing colonial violence. The story of how Abel loses his father and his connection to Nisga'a community is almost unbearable, as is the reader/witness's implication in it. It's as though the time code itself is haunted, yet all it can do is march out the numbers.

If Abel's piece is about the difficulty and necessity of telling, Erín Moure's "Listening at Mikinaakominis" is about the difficulty and necessity of listening. She too is concerned with time. She offers poetry as a mode of thinking and calls readers, as beings tied to the past, into the "était," which she translates, through Giorgio Agamben, as both "agora" and "the

NOW"—a place of contemporary, public proximity with others. Actively thinking against the time code of linear, teleological settler time—the time that Abel finds it impossible to break free of—she calls specifically to white settlers to do the work of translation, and in so doing leave behind "shallow time," that is, the time of progress, capital accumulation, and monolithic, singular meanings. She wants readers to enter the "deep time" that many Indigenous peoples already inhabit. Moure's conception of deep time calls attention to other languages—Anishnaabe, Cree, and Dene-Athapascan tongues—as well as the languages of plants and the wind. To be open to these languages and the multiple meanings they might offer is to open oneself to something better than reconciliation, that is, to reparation and return. Her poetic thinking here is in direct conversation with Warren Cariou's (Métis) call to "landsensing."

Translational work, however, and the capacity to enter into a multiplicity of meanings can be difficult when the call to sovereignty has not been answered. This may indeed be one of the major impasses in the field that *Land / Relations* draws attention to. Rinaldo Walcott's call for a Black grammar of the nation is important precisely because it insists on a re-presencing of Black subjects as fully human. He specifically asks readers to attend to Black hauntings, the ongoing presence of the dead. He refuses the state multicultural impulse that wants to create racialized categories of people as different but equal. In keeping with the work of Lisa Lowe and Jodi Byrd, he sees the necessity for articulating the specificity of Black locations. Walcott foregrounds contemporary, ongoing, institutionally sanctioned anti-Black violence, and the hauntings of Black people who have died attempting to make themselves present and at home. Through a reading of David Sutherland and Jennifer Holness's *Speakers for the Dead*, about the recovery of a Black burial ground in Grey County, Ontario, he emphasizes the unhoming of Black people, and also their place in and on the land, buried there, and thus part of it. The story is thus one of both land and bodily sovereignty. The story of the recovery is, of course, also the story of the erasure that necessitated it, and ongoing erasures of Black presence in spite of that single act of recovery. Walcott recognizes and is troubled by the fact that the story of recovery breaks a silence but provides no arrival. Grey County remains haunted by Black presences that are never fully acknowledged as present.

Jennifer Henderson's chapter recognizes both the productivity and the difficulty of taking up metaphors of presencing, specifically gothic ones. Reading Jeff Barnaby's extraordinary horror movie *Rhymes for Young Ghouls*, she sees his self-conscious troping of the residential school as a critique of the limits of figuration, even in such a serious matter as the Truth and Reconciliation Commission. Specifically, she recognizes an Anglo-Protestant bias against Catholics in the figure of the sexually abusive priest, a bias she suggests that Barnaby also sees and is critical of. She argues that he plays campily with it in genre for precisely this reason. She cautions us against neoliberal/illiberal jettison of the state and state institutions in favour of private solutions to colonial ills. The state must be called into its democratic traditions and responsibilities as they are connected to its colonial underpinnings. The use of the gothic trope is productive in that it helps readers and viewers recognize the residential school project as horrific. However, we must also attend to the limits of troping. To a limited extent, the gothic trope can be used to hold the state accountable, but we must also recognize that the state is not a gothic castle, and further that the state has responsibilities and capacities within the frame of its own traditions (and not the trope of the gothic) that we must recognize and call to account. We have to be cautious of neoliberal dangers even in antiracist critique.

The section closes with Tasha Hubbard's contribution "Re-storying and Restoring the Buffalo to the Indigenous Plains." As a Calgarian who walks daily on lands taken from the buffalo, I find Hubbard's contribution particularly moving. Hubbard recognizes the buffalo as a people, and their destruction as genocide. She connects their destruction to the removal and destruction of grandfather stones, particularly the Manitou Stone from the hills of what we now call central-west Alberta. In relation to the moment of this book's publication, Cree Elders predicted disease and famine as a result of land theft. Hubbard reminds us that they were right—that smallpox arrived after the removal of the Manitou Stone, as the buffalo declined. It's hard not to read our COVID-19 moment as a continuation of colonial disruption of the land in what Hubbard calls its "intricate balance." The genocide of the buffalo to make room for cattle domesticates the land; it is a continuation of the conversion of sacred land into capitalist property—the Lockean logic of real estate production is extended into the animal realm. Or, to think about it in Cree terms, since for the Cree, buffalo are also a people, their absence is a peopled absence that haunts the land. That said, Hubbard is less concerned with haunting and more concerned with restoration—in the sense of both retelling the story and returning the buffalo to the land. Her 2013 film *Buffalo Calling*, which documents the Confederated Salish-Kootenai tribe's work to care for a remnant herd on their territories, recognizes this care as an act of restoration, in spite of the fact that the herd has now been displaced and lives behind fences. Balance will return, some Elders remind us, when free-roaming buffalo are restored to the land. Hubbard's work, including a forthcoming film, documents efforts to bring the buffalo back, both to re-story and to restore.[27]

The third section of this book, "'tinder conscience': Formations Otherwise," takes its cues from two poems by Sonnet L'Abbé, "CLI" and "CLII," both of them procedural overwritings of the Shakespeare sonnets for which they are numbered. "CLI" offers a diagnosis of the troubles that have plagued Canadian literature for the past decade or so from the point of view of a speaker who is racialized as Black and working and writing within it. L'Abbé writes: "Look, everything is fire. You're too heartyoung to know what motherhunger is, to know how its conscience hides the baby from the predator, protects the littles who know no self-protection. Your tinder conscience is my iron womb....You didn't invent mouthy." This passage gestures toward the "dumpster fire" that has been raging for some years, willing to "burn it all down" (as I've discussed above).[28] For L'Abbé, the problem is that such an action runs the danger of setting "the truth...on fire." If the predators are those of the sexual abuse scandals that have rocked the field, and by extension other abusers from sites of hegemonic power, it's "motherhunger" that protects the "heartyoung" from harm. The problem with "motherhunger" is that it houses in its womb a conscience made of "iron...filings." If the "heartyoung" don't know the history of the struggle, they might take down those who have fought for them, including their own hungry mothers. Unknowingly, they become "Ideologues, betrayers of kingdom." Because "our flesh is so lit right now," we burn ourselves, and our own dreams of a better future.

The second offering from L'Abbé, "CLII," pointedly lays out the contemporary condition of being a Black woman academic on Snuneymuxw territory and plays out fraught moments in the "intimacies of four continents": "About protocols, some white women instruct me. A starlet said, wouldn't it be nice for a Snuneymuxw woman to have your institutional platform?" And "You just got hired so the institution can swear it's not racist, says anonymous eggs." In a cruel institutional environment, the speaker is forsworn in a brutal, interlocking set of terms that both implicates and undermines her when she is "soft and thirsty for love." In no uncertain terms, the speaker holds to account both overzealous allies and BIPOC people who use liberatory language to enact cruelties that are difficult, if not impossible, to respond to. She writes, "tfw the Woke Police lay trumped up charges on my (I can't) breath(e)." In so doing, she gestures to the murder of George Floyd by Minneapolis police officer Derek Chauvin in 2020. To invoke the charge of "Woke Police" with the same crimes as racist, state-sanctioned police is to recognize parallels in the structures of radical progressiveness and radical conservativism, or, as Sarah Ahmed (2021) reminds us, how complicity with colonial power structures can present themselves even in the most radical spaces.[29] We must be cautious in drawing these seeming parallels where conditions are not so equally valanced. However, L'Abbé's critique here is useful in the sense that it shows the limits of some progressive strategies. It's analogue in Jennifer Henderson's essay is the recognition Henderson makes of the usefulness of the Gothic trope to help us see the violence of residential schools, while also seeing danger that the Gothic trope as the sole lens for understanding residential schools might inadvertently lead the well-intentioned to jettison the productivities of the democratically inclined state.

Len Findlay recognizes how hard it is to escape implication in the state, especially for artists, writers, and critics, since they all rely on it for funding. But they are never fully contained by it either. He suggests they are a feral presence, still rummaging through national trash looking for a way to undo the hold on their lives by those who would unproblematically celebrate its 150th year without consciousness of or concern about Canada as a colonial project. With L'Abbé, he recognizes the trash can, but he doesn't want to burn it so much as escape it. With L'Abbé too, he recognizes the brutality of the moment. The temptation to quit is understandable, but it's hard to quit the critique that is always already partially but never completely contained. He suggests that the ferally present seek a habitable trajectory but not necessarily one that moves forward. This trajectory may or may not yet have appeared. Findlay suggests the feral have no choice but to keep seeking.

If, like me, Findlay seeks the moment of rupture, the knock at the door, while hanging contingently on to the state, Chris Lee doesn't so much jettison the state as seek to understand it in a global framework. In his chapter "Between Empire and Nation: Synchronicity and Revolution in Chinese Canadian Writing," he sets to one side the work of identitarian thinking, which has marked so much Asian Canadian criticism, in order to break away from thinking about the nation as an inevitable end point. Lee, however, doesn't cast that work away. Rather, his chapter takes a sidestep to interrogate how global migration shapes national formations. Specifically, he recognizes the ways in which the category "Chinese Canadian" is produced through Chinese Canadian identifications with the 1911 revolution in China, that is, outside the Canadian state and through global circuits of migration and connections to a long history of movement across the Pacific. This movement occurs over time as the national, state, and ideological positions of countries, peoples, and cultures morph and change in the throes of history. Neither "China" nor "Canada" are static entities, even in name, let alone in their political or cultural formations. Highly conscious of the historical contingency of the dichotomy "China and the West," Lee notes the complex shift from the Qing dynasty to modern China on one side of the Pacific, which occurs through the same period that Canadian national formation also shifts, develops, and changes in fairly radical ways on the other side of the Pacific. Through a careful reading of two narratives—that of Sun Yat-Sen's 1911 visit to Vancouver and Paul Yee's young adult novel *The Curses of Third Uncle* (1986)—Lee illustrates the ways in which twentieth-century Chinese ethnonationalism can be made retrospectively to play into a Canadian nationalist multiculturalism. But the production of each, though traceable to the rise of the Westphalian state broadly, is distinct. Lee's original and profound recognition in this chapter is that, within the bounded Canadian imaginary, the Chinese sojourner gets most often read as a long-suffering figure of exploitation and/or exclusion, whereas in the imaginary of global migration, the Chinese sojourner figures, worrisomely, as the leading edge of Chinese nationalism, a revolutionary nationalism, to be sure, but one with desires not so different from the desires of an older and more aggressive imperialism. If there is an "Asian gift" offered by this chapter, it is a recognition that sovereignty in Asian terms is not necessarily a desirable form, as I have explained above.

"Asia" has used "sovereignty" to post-revolutionary ends that are simultaneously totalitarian and/or imperialist ones.

Just because sovereignty (on behalf of Asians) is suspect in Asian locations doesn't mean that it isn't necessary in Indigenous ones (on behalf of Indigenous peoples). (I'm feeling more uncomfortable than usual using the terms "Asian" and "Indigenous" here, highly aware of the vast complexities elided. But this is the particular difficulty of writing about a certain proximity that has tendrils in broad and complicated locations.) Here on Turtle Island, where British and Canadian state acknowledgements of Indigenous sovereignty are new and not entirely guaranteed, it seems more necessary than ever, as Margery Fee notes in her chapter "Diplomacy *before* Reconciliation." Indigenous assertions of their own sovereignty have been ongoing for a long time, though the international community took notice only at the time of the Oka crisis (1990), when the Mohawk of Kanehsatake stood up against an attempt by the City of Oka to build a golf course on their traditional burial grounds. Fee notes that the Quebec police did not engage in diplomacy in this situation, which was essentially a fight about sovereignty. The Canadian government sent in the army. Ever since, the state has been engaged in a flurry of repair, but the distinction between repair and incorporation is a fine one. Fee suggests that we must now truly act on the Truth and Reconciliation Calls to Action—that without diplomacy, there can be no reconciliation. Further, the final report of the Truth and Reconciliation Commission demands a repudiation of the Doctrine of Discovery and *terra nullius*, the two European colonial legal doctrines that found the claim of Canadian sovereignty on Indigenous land. She says that settler scholars, including herself, must not engage in fantasies of reconciliation when Indigenous peoples, including her students, already know it is a sham. With each act of incorporation the state engages in, further repressing Indigenous Peoples under the sign of reconciliation (in this instance), Indigenous Peoples require stronger and more militant language and strategies in order to get out from under the sign. Such a pattern is not indefinitely habitable. Settlers must for this reason truly and actually act on the TRC's Calls to Action.

The section closes with a chapter by Sedef Arat-Koç, entitled "From Islamo*phobia* to Islamo*philia*?: Dancing Orientalisms, *Islamizing* Muslims, and the Unspeakability of the Muslim Woman Subject." Here,

Arat-Koç articulates another kind of bind, the one between Islamophobia and Islamophilia, which many secular, antiracist Muslim feminists find themselves representationally trapped in. Arat-Koç is critical of the "culturalist" framework that underpins anti-Muslim feeling in the West—Islamophobia—and its unnerving parallel in those who, attempting to support Muslim people, misread them as culturally monolithic and religiously conservative in ways that profoundly erase the complex contemporary ideas and practices embraced by some Muslim feminists. She offers the 2003 Sharia "(*non*)debate" in Ontario, in which the state attempted to offer Muslim families the right to use Sharia law to settle family disputes. This Islamophilic gesture attempted to do right by Muslim people, but in so doing made the terribly racist assumption that all Muslim people embrace Sharia law. The state's enactment of this gesture as a kind of racist love made it impossible for progressive Muslim women to fight. The logic repeated here is the logic of incorporation again—real and complex human lives are made to vanish under the sign of kindness toward them—because the kindness is so misguided as to completely misread the people, their diversity, and their complexity. Arat-Koç (see pp. 199–216) argues that culturalism locks debates into identitarian positions, and in so doing disables public space and forecloses actual political discussion. For her, culturalism, whether Islamophobic or Islamophilic, locks Muslim people into an imagined monolithic conservatism and shuts out any possibility that those Muslims who take part in forms of secularism with histories in Arab locations might get heard. She decries bestselling writers of culturalist memoirs,[30] and holds up those who are able to show the complexity and open-endedness of Muslim life, thought, and story. Arat-Koç's thinking in this chapter is nuanced and clear. Her articulation of culturalism resonates productively with other considerations in this book as when, for instance, the "heartyoung" in L'Abbé's "CLI" exercise their rage against all comers regardless of who those comers might be, what they might be committed to, and what work they might have done or be in the process of doing.

The final section, "'in there, together': Land Intimacies," begins with a poem from Pamela Mordecai, "Deliberate Vulgarity: Performing the Demotic, Transforming Cultural Space?" (see pp. 219–36). Recognizing the problem of respecting lived difference among the broad range of people who inhabit Turtle Island, Pamela Mordecai notes that "dissimilar things can live / ...together, equally" whether such inhabitation occurs in a "multicultural" democracy or in the Caribbean. "Everything don't have to fight down / whatever is different from itself..." (see p. 221). She considers practical thinking on how to live together in difference to be a Caribbean cognitive ability, which she calls "prismatic vision" (see p. 221). As Arat-Koç recognizes the specificity of Arab secularism, Mordecai recognizes the specificity of Caribbean abilities to respect difference. These recognitions are important because they illustrate the complex genealogies of contemporary values, which are often unthinkingly associated only with the West, and specifically with European thought. Through the poem included in this volume, Mordecai "play[s] mas" (masquerade) as a scholar, actively using Jamaican patwa. She is aware that such an engagement is a double-edge sword; it racializes the speaker for speaking outside the standard discourse of academic engagement: "It's like, because the poems are noisy / talk uncompromisingly, / this voiced, voluble quality / signify inferiority" (see p. 233). But at the same time, to use patwa is to take up a located, embodied form of theorizing that refuses what Audre Lorde calls "the master's tools" (Lorde). Patwa might be understood as what Walcott calls a "Black gift" (2017a). It might thus be just what is needed, as one practice among many, to tear down the master's house. It might even be one tool among many to build a better, more just house, in collaboration with others.

Like Mordecai, Karina Vernon is interested in a "more just house." Her chapter, "'Making Things Right': Black Settlement and the Politics of Urban Territory," takes as a matter of utmost importance the question of Black-Indigenous relations on Turtle Island. Thinking with Erica Violet Lee and others, she articulates Blackness as Indigeneity, doubly displaced—first from homelands in Africa and second from the body in slavery. In the wake of the terrible murders of George Floyd and Regis Korchinski-Paquet by police, and the subsequent protests in the tremendous uprising of Black Lives Matter, the issues of policing and police abolition have become more pressing than ever. Vernon argues that Black and Indigenous peoples are relations whose resistance to colonization, land theft, and body theft are profoundly intertwined. This thinking differs from early—important but dated—work on Black–Indigenous relations that understood Black people as settlers of colour. Vernon analyzes the short story by the Trinidadian Albertan writer F. B. André, "Is There Someone You Can Call?", in which a Black Albertan couple, on taking possession of a home they have bought, discover that it is still inhabited. Vernon recognizes the query addressed metaphorically in André's short story: How can and should Black people, who have been so deeply disenfranchised by both the Canadian and US states, stand in relation to Indigenous peoples and the expropriation of Indigenous lands, especially if we understand Black people as simultaneously Indigenous? While the story might belong to a different moment in thinking on Black–Indigenous relations, Vernon recognizes the layers of colonial, state-based, anti-Black violence from body theft and land disenfranchisement to slavery to exclusion to racial profiling as both foundational and ongoing. She suggests that it remains more important than ever for Black and Indigenous writers and critics to do the work of Black–Indigenous relation-building. Of particular interest to her are the colonial property relations that make land ownership possible. However, to consider Black prairie people to be "settlers of colour," as early scholarship on Black-Indigenous relations did, is over-simplistic because it does not consider the forcible removal of Black people from their homelands or their enslavement in the Americas. Because Black land ownership is determined by the specific conditions of Black presence on colonized lands, the specific relationship between Black and Indigenous peoples needs its own historicization and modes of recovery. As Fee and McCall also suggest later in this volume, these conditions have been largely underaddressed, which is precisely the reason why Vernon's chapter sets out to do the work of thinking through these important relationships.

In ways that extend Vernon's argument, Dina Al-Kassim also addresses kinships of dispossession. Her chapter "Listing Waters: The Poetics of Solidarity in Mahmoud Darwish and Rita Wong" addresses this problem through the poetics of the list. Via Gayatri Spivak's recasting of the story of Narcissus and Echo, and George Bataille's consideration of "the mole" as a revolutionary figure, Al-Kassim takes up the work of the Palestinian poet Mahmoud Darwish and the Vancouver-based Chinese Canadian poet Rita Wong, also a contributor to this book, to confront the dynamics of the current "burning" crisis in CanLit. She locates this crisis on the one hand within the ethical failures of false universalisms called for by figures like Hal Niedzviecki and Jonathan Kay, and on the other within the narcissistic racialized masculinism that forecloses the voices of productive critique as it seeks ever greater heights of triumph. Al-Kassim calls for a deeper attention to the figure of the mole—grounded, digging, and earth-attached. Such attention occurs as active solidarity and relation-building rather than as identification or property in common. She proposes, rather, that we stand in different relation to a common problem, and that it is through a range of agencies that a broad set of different kinds of solidarities can be made. She sees the poets Darwish and Wong, in addition to the late Lee Maracle (Sto:lo), as making these engagements with the greatest humility, though the moment does not seem to hear their echoing voices, listing waters to build solidarity in difference.

Like Al-Kassim, Sophie McCall takes a comparative approach, though the comparison occurs not across continents but on the same territories, inhabited differently yet in relation to others by the two writers who interest her in her chapter "Living on Unceded Indigenous Territories: Vancouver as a Site of Conflict in Building Alliance and Autonomy in Decolonial Struggles." Her contribution puts in conversation the work of Marie Clements (Dene-Métis) and Wayde Compton to ask what decolonizing social relations might look like across Black and Indigenous locations. She sees that the relationship between alliance and autonomy can sometimes be conflicted, and, in concert with my argument above, recognizes the dangers of what she calls "forced inclusion," or what I've been describing thus far as incorporation, especially when it takes place on the terms of the colonizing power. She writes specifically of Clements's *The Road Forward* (2017b) and about the civil rights activism of the Native Brotherhood of British Columbia between the 1930s and the 1970s; *The Unnatural and Accidental Women* (2005), about the missing and murdered women; and *Burning Vision* (2002), about the trail of uranium from Sathu Dene territory at Great Bear Lake to Los Alamos, New Mexico, to the Manhattan Project, to the bombing of Hiroshima and Nagasaki that ended World War II. She compares this work to Wayde Compton's "retrospec(ula)tions" in the Hogan's Alley Memorial Project, *Performance Bond*, and *The Outer Harbour*. She carefully analyzes the trajectory of Black–Indigenous relations as it unfolds on Pauline Johnson Island, Compton's fictional new land in the middle of the Georgia Strait. Careful to locate herself as a white woman scholar, and aware of the dangers of reconsolidating such a position as a site of authority, she does her best to foreground a productive, relational analysis, while acknowledging that existing structures are not so easy to undo. She analyzes the poetic ways in which Clements articulates space and time to foreground complex and often fraught proximities among racialized peoples, as when Clements lays out the stage in *Burning Vision* to make Great Bear Lake, Los Alamos, Port Hope (Ontario), and Hiroshima physically close as a way of showing/enacting the horrific closeness through which uranium binds them. She explains the strategy of reverberative "evanescence" that Compton's characters engage in those moments when they slip away from hegemonic power's attempts to contain them, whether through surveillance, market capitalism, or incarceration. This chapter is attentive to both Compton and Clements's use of sound to show connection, or what Jodi Byrd (2011) would call intimacy through "cacophony." It importantly makes clear the power of literature to show us our relationships, our "intimacies of four continents," to one another and the living world around us in ways that other disciplines or ways of knowing cannot.

In the chapter that concludes this collection, "Landsensing: Body, Territory, Relation," Warren Cariou shows us how land-based states of consciousness work. He calls us into a profound recognition of the material basis of intimacies, particularly through description of his petroglyphs, images he has been making using bitumen. Bitumen is a material that comes from his home territories in northern Saskatchewan. It also comes from my current home province of Alberta. It is the material that oil and gas comes from, and the mining of it is responsible for the destruction of hectares and hectares of boreal forest, immense amounts of water, and traditional ways of life. It is also the material that Rita Wong was jailed for protesting against when she sat in ceremony to sing and pray in front of the Trans Mountain Pipeline project's Westridge Marine Terminal in the summer of 2019. In using bitumen to make artwork, Cariou recognizes the inscriptive power of its substance but, even more so, he recognizes its scent. He suggests that the smell that bitumen exudes constitutes a form of communication, in other words, a form of speech: the land is literally speaking in ways akin to what Jeannette Armstrong (Syilx/Okanagan) describes in her well-known essay "Land Speaking." Cariou argues that we have lost the capacity to understand communication from the land, as we have lost access to the deep capacities of our senses. He explains that land has a flavour, and that one cannot connect to the land unless one can taste it. The destruction of Indigenous sensory connection to the land was a colonial act—one particularly enforced in the residential schools. The capacity for landsensing is not solely an Indigenous capacity, though Indigenous peoples have a propensity for it through tradition and a very long-standing connection to the land. Via a story told by the Omushkeego Cree Elder Louis Bird, which Cariou has obtained permission to repeat in this collection, he illustrates the grief of the loss. There's a tremendous generosity at work in Cariou's chapter and Bird's story. Neither Cariou nor Bird points a finger at settlers or non- Indigenous people. Rather, both point to a collective problem that must be solved. Cariou shows us how there remains space in the story for settler–Indigenous difference, and lays this space out for us with extraordinary subtlety and generosity, while at the same time foregrounding a world view that puts relationships rather than dialectics up front.

This book is the third collection to emerge from the Mikinaakominis / TransCanadas conference. The other two are "Counterclockwise," a special issue of the journal *Canada and Beyond*, which I coedited in collaboration with Neil Surkan and Joshua Whitehead, and a special issue of the *University of Toronto Quarterly*, edited by Tania Aguila-Way and Smaro Kamboureli, entitled "Literary Solidarities / Critical Accountability." Together, these volumes offer a snapshot of the thinking and concerns that have engaged a complex, contentious community of thinkers and writers engaging in that ever-shifting form that some people call Canadian literature.

On the occasion of this book's publication, I see Canadian literature as a contingently necessary, though extremely messy and uneven, site in which coalition-building is possible for those who wish to do it. It is not the white behemoth that some of my friends and colleagues imagine but a profoundly disparate, uneven, and contentious field. Neither is it the high nationalist project some people imagine; however, it is a field still riven with entrenched colonial structures, and still deeply incorporative of Black, Indigenous, and Asian suffering, and exclusionary at the same time. I do think we each, differently, have a measure of agency within it—not necessarily the agency we would like—it is agency that is still determined by colonial structures and constraints. The problems of the nation, however, are difficult to resolve. Those who wish to continue working inside its frame might commit to the work of utopian dreaming and action, while watching for the ruptures that our actions, in conjunction with those of committed others, might produce. Fiction, poetry, and literary criticism are practices that can show us possibilities in thought, language, and story as we wait for the next knock at the door.

The TransCanada Project and CanLit

A Microhistory

/ SMARO KAMBOURELI & LARISSA LAI

Smaro Kamboureli: It was midway 2013 when Roy Miki and I began thinking about TC4, my shorthand for the fourth TransCanada conference, which became Mikinaakominis / TransCanadas: How was it going to carry on the conversations pursued in the previous conferences? What had shifted in the CanLit field since the beginning of the millennium? We agreed that the most important question was who I was going to pair with for what was to be the last TransCanada conference. It had to be someone who had been part of the project; someone simpatico; a scholar committed to approaching CanLit not only as a corpus of literary works but also as an institutional and discursive formation with its own systemic properties that called for critique and dissent, someone already embedded in the kinds of relations and community work that the final TransCanada event was to engage with. Enter Larissa Lai. Do you remember that lunch with Roy in Vancouver when we got you hooked?

Larissa Lai: Of course I remember that lunch. However, I got "hooked" much earlier, visiting your house in Victoria with Rita Wong in 2004. That year, you and Roy had linked your graduate courses—his at Simon Fraser University, yours at the University of Victoria. The two of you were holding a joint symposium that brought the two classes together at UVic, and had invited me and Rita to read from *Sybil Unrest* (Lai and Wong 2013), the book Rita and I had written together in the wake of the SARS epidemic, which began in Hong Kong in 2003. Rita and I shared the work in your living room. I remember the conversation was generative and generous, and I left feeling well heard and connected to an important set of conversations that you, Roy, and your students had set up.

By then, all four of us, in different ways, had already lived through the cultural and political struggles of the 1980s and 1990s. I had been Assistant Curator for *Yellow Peril: Reconsidered* (Wong, Paul 1990), an exhibit of twenty-five Asian Canadian artists working in contemporary media; organized a couple of shows at Grunt Gallery; edited issues of *Front Magazine* and *Kinesis*; worked as coordinator at SAW Video Media Centre; and written two novels, *When Fox Is a Thousand* and *Salt Fish Girl*. The struggles, fraught with both internal and external contradictions, had been hard. There had been a pretty brutal implosion of the possibilities of community-based thought and cultural organizing at the end of the 1990s. We were all seeking ways of engaging that were collaborative, relational, and/or community oriented. You and Roy had a way of working together and making space for others, while still keeping difference in play, that was very inspiring to me. You must have been halfway done with the organizing of the first TransCanada conference when Rita and I visited.

SK: Actually, the bulk of the work was undertaken after I moved to the University of Guelph and founded TransCanada Institute. It's interesting that you mentioned that collaborative course because it was an integral part of how we had conceptualized the TransCanada project: not just a one-time conference, but a live, serial event that would pick up and maintain its momentum through other events—small and big, local, national, and international. Continuity was important in order to sustain focus and commitment. And now that I think back, I believe we understood continuity not in terms of action that traces a preordained, linear trajectory[1]—such a project can easily become reified and solipsistic, too enamored with the repetition of its imaginary—but rather in terms of seriality: the TransCanada project as serialized collaboration, a series of mediations.

It was fortuitous timing, as I was offered a Canada Research Chair right at that moment. The idea to establish an institute—to give our project a home and the funding that such a vision required to materialize—came out of my conversations with Roy. We conceived the TransCanada project as a collaboration at different levels, while at the same time retaining an openness to new vocabularies and the material conditions they might give rise to. We understood that critical vocabularies can become exhausted, necessitating shifts in paradigms, frames, and practices. We wanted the project to have some directionality, but without a concrete end in sight. We understood that whatever web we wove would eventually unravel in response to, in relation with, and/or through essential tensions among our institutional locations and the material and social realities of our time. We had no model for such a project; what we had in mind were events like Writing Thru Race in 1994 and Women and Words a decade earlier, in 1983—interesting that both happened in Vancouver, isn't it?—which were meant to have a second life but didn't, although of course the energy and major—indeed radical—shifts they brought about continued to reverberate. In fact, as far as I'm concerned, they still do.

LL: With Roy, I was one of the organizers of Writing Thru Race. That was a productive but also difficult conference. I remember you and Roy really experimented with ways of gathering at that first TransCanada conference at the Morris J. Wosk Centre for Dialogue in Vancouver. Your way of working was continuous with a range of cultural events and projects I had participated in, or, in some cases, organized with others, through the 1990s in artist-run centres and community organizations. I recognized the strategies—they made lot of cultural sense to me. The Wosk Centre is a round room with no front or stage, so participants met as equals, facing one another around a circle. There were small group breakout sessions. There was a doctoral graduate student plenary. I was struck by the thought that you both had put into democratizing the conference structure.

SK: That was a crucial aspect of our plan, changing some of the conventional methods of structuring a conference. Organizing scripts operate like ideologies; they determine our social practices—the way we relate or hold back, the kind of dialogue and knowledge generated. To quote from one of the many missives I sent to the delegates, TransCanada was not just a conference, nor was it conceived in revisionist terms; we envisioned it, instead, as a future-oriented project about Canadian literature and the institutional structures that inform it. We aspired to "foster rigorous critical dialogue which [would] hopefully not stop at the level of debate" (TransCanada One).[2] This was why we set out to change the shape of the traditional conference. Very ambitious, I realize now. But we were a dynamic collective—Roy and I working together with David Chariandy, Jeff Derksen, Sophie McCall, Kathy Mezei, and graduate students at the time, Alessandra Capperdoni and Mark McCutcheon. (Sophie and David just had their first child, and we often met at their place—paperwork and baby paraphernalia sprawled all over the place.) Our goal was to facilitate the conditions for creating a loosely structured CanLit collective. Now that I think of it, "loosely structured" became a key phrase that I consistently used in my grant applications and reports. In my mind, "loosely structured" conveyed the dialectic tensions of collaborative practices: not a single or unifying collaborative model, but one that worked across a range of affiliations—long- and short-term ones. This allowed for continuity but also made it possible to bring new voices into the project.

I'm glad you mentioned the doctoral students' plenary—the only such feature in a Canadian literary studies conference that I'm aware of. It was a resounding success, and for this reason remained a prominent element in all four TransCanada conferences. That some of the students featured in the first conference's plenary session became involved in the organizing of the subsequent conferences as well as other TransCanada projects, and are now colleagues who have produced important work, speaks to the mentoring and pedagogy of care that the TransCanada project tried to foster and build on. In fact, alongside the new delegates who attended each of the conferences, there was a core of delegates who participated in all four of them, including you. It was this continuity that made TransCanada a loosely structured project.

However, another innovative feature of the first conference—the breakout sessions, which we called "research cells"—proved to be too challenging for most of the participants as well as institutional structures, including

SSHRC. Since the main goal of the conference was to invite a "complete rethinking of the disciplinary and institutional frameworks" that shape Canadian literature, we wanted the conversation we envisaged to engage with the discursivity of CanLit as a field, and not be shaped by the usual twenty-minute papers on a given text. Instead, we wanted to encourage discussion that focused on contexts, on methods, on paradigms and their shifts, on CanLit as a broad system of signification. We imagined the research cells as a "laboratory site" where scholars would engage in "critical dialogue as praxis," where concrete steps might be taken toward research and pedagogical collaboration. We understood collaboration, however, in terms that did not necessarily endorse but instead questioned the collaborative model of research advocated by SSHRC at the time. While the SSHRC model revolved around, among other things, elaborate infrastructures and overdetermined goals, we wanted to explore collaboration that unravelled organically, that in fact thematized the implications of collaboration at different levels. To each research cell, we had assigned discussants and reporters who were expected to animate discussion and submit reports on the ideas and plans discussed. There was excitement about this plan, but I must say it also generated a lot of anxiety for many delegates. They felt uncomfortable with the idea of being active participants in a conference without giving a formal paper, not to mention that they worried that this would jeopardize their chances to secure funding. I was inundated with emails about all this; had to write to many chairs of departments to explain that our proposed frame of sharing knowledge and networking was worth funding. Given this response, it was not surprising that, while some of the cells worked beautifully, others floundered a bit. All in all, the research cells were a valuable experiment that taught me that even those who call for the transformation of the discipline often have a hard time practising outside the box, even if they are good at thinking there. So, no more research cells in the subsequent TransCanada conferences. The irony is that some people said the conferences became more conventional in format, which is true of course, but pushing the bounds of our practice and usual modes of work is easier called for than done. So, the desire for innovation was curtailed, tempered with the need to accommodate the professoriat's, as well the students', collective anxieties about format and content.

LL: We experimented with some of these things at Writing Thru Race as well, though the first TransCanada conference took these strategies into academic spaces in ways that the academy was not used to. It was powerful for this reason. It opened academic practices in ways that previously had been possible only in arts and community spaces where I feel I had my first real education. I remember a whole cohort of BIPOC PhD students, a generation just a few years ahead of the ones who were involved in that first iteration of the TransCanada conference who did not complete or did not find employment for want of university recognition of the knowledge forms that the TransCanadas series promulgated and championed. The university could not see these ways of working as valuable because it could not see the relational kinds of knowledge produced as actual knowledge. TransCanadas was not, of course, the sole actor in this shift, but it was an important one. You and Roy were really pushing elephants up stairs! The work you and Roy did helped a great deal to make that way of being an academic and intellectual visible and acceptable.

As I just said, it was in the organizing of Writing Thru Race that my own relationship with Roy emerged. We worked together on that conference between 1992 and 1994, as I was just beginning to figure out the possibilities of cultural labour, while Roy, fresh from the achievement of the Japanese Canadian Redress for wartime internment, was ready to begin doing justice work located squarely in Canadian/Turtle Island writing communities. Writing Thru Race was a conference designed to bring together what we then called "First Nations writers and writers of colour." The terminology has since shifted in a series of moves aimed at access, acknowledgement, difference, land relations, and a range of other goals. That conference, though productive for many, suffered internal contradictions that made ongoing connection among the organizers hard for a few years, but Roy and I became close later in that decade through the poetry and cultural activist communities in Vancouver. Roy's thinking and way of being was for me more practice-oriented and politically engaged than some of the more mainstream/liberal Asian Canadian ways of thinking and being that sought inclusion and profile (not that any Asian Canadian work at that time was mainstream, so I'm speaking only relatively). While universities were sometimes involved in these events and projects, they weren't central, nor were university conference norms. So in working with you on this project,

I've inherited university conference norms and their breaking through a complex set of intertwining pathways.

SK: You're so right about Roy's practice-oriented approach. Roy's way of braiding community-based work with academic and intellectual work is exceptional. It exemplifies what Antonio Gramsci calls an organic intellectual: someone who, rooted in a community and its local struggles, also engages in an equally committed fashion with various institutions and the nation to effect change in small as well as big ways. Roy has done this through his scholarship, poetry, and activism at various fronts.

LL: Roy makes a distinction between Asian Am, where "Am" can be read as both "American" and the first-person conjugation of the verb "to be," i.e., "I am"—oriented toward "solid state" ontologies that characterize US-style ethnic studies projects—and Asian Can, where "Can" could be understood as "Canadian" but also as an auxiliary verb indicating capacity for action, as in "Can do," oriented toward open-ended action and asiancy. His essay "Asiancy" in *Broken Entries* (Miki) has been a key piece for me in that it has helped me think through alternate relationships to the state. It hadn't occurred to me before reading that essay that "inclusion" as a form of relationship to the state is not the only form of relationship possible. It is certainly not the best. It might not even be desirable. But what form of relationship, then, ought one to want? One ought to approach state relations with a measure of intent. For indeed, Asians have not always been "included"—think of the Chinese Exclusion Act as a major case in point. Perhaps there is something to be desired in remaining outside, or positioning oneself in a slanted relationship to the state. Certainly, there are relationships—between Indigenous people and Asians, for instance—that precede state inclusion. Further, one need not adhere to a fixed ontology of the state. After all, the state is not a fixed entity. In a sense, Roy's notion of asiancy primed me to understand Indigenous calls for sovereignty (or sovereignties, since I know different folks imagine nations and belonging differently), and to grasp the possibilities of different kinds of relationships that one might have to the state. Asiancy offers both a theory and a poetics of relation to the state that acknowledges state exclusions and violence while retaining a relationship to the future. This is a major facet of what the "Can" in "CanLit" has been for me since fairly early in my writing life—something action-oriented and open to negotiation, albeit under historical and material conditions already in place and not of my own choosing. I understand, of course, that the overdetermining aspects of CanLit remain very much in play, but the concept of asiancy helps me see that the overdetermined way of grasping CanLit is far from being the only one.

SK: Asiancy was one of the key orientations of the collaborative course Roy and I taught. In fact, our course/s were in some way an extension of our Asian CanLit work at the time. We were both working on posthumous editions of Roy Kiyooka's work—Roy on *The Artist and the Moose* and I on *Pacific Rim Letters*, while I was also working on reissuing *Transcanada Letters*—and we both included Kiyooka in our syllabi. Beyond designing our respective courses together, we visited each other's classes, had our SFU and UVic students collaborate via a listserv and organize the conference to which you and Rita were invited. Having our students cross Georgia Strait, devising innovative assignments, holding a class and a reading in my living room—these were small acts that to my mind constituted activism at a micro level, a pedagogical and institutional level. With you and Rita being involved in the kind of activist and collaborative projects you've mentioned, you were the perfect guests. *Sybil Unrest* exemplified precisely what Roy and I wanted to explore through that course.

I'm thinking here of the title of Paul Gilroy's book, *Small Acts* (1993). As far as I remember, he doesn't directly thematize "small acts," but I always found that phrase to be terribly evocative. Small acts may unfold beyond the public view but hold the potential to effect change, to have a cumulative impact, to transform specific contexts. That collaborative course was that kind of small act; in fact, I see it as an early instantiation of our larger TransCanada project. Roy and I set out to devise and practise a kind of collaboration that went beyond the ways in which universities, under pressure from SSHRC, were pushing collaboration at the time as a model of efficiency that produced a neoliberal understanding of knowledge, part and parcel of the corporatization of academic institutions. We started on a small and local scale, and then we gave ourselves the challenge of thinking big: inviting colleagues from various interrelated disciplines, as well as writers, artists, and students, to think collaboratively about institutions and to examine the ways in which CanLit—as a field, as a teaching practice, as a national formation that resisted the national imaginary—was deeply imbricated in the dense network of institutions that at once supported and instrumentalized it. We were eager to explore how we might be able to shift some of those relations, problematize CanLit's complicity and our own locations within it. This was the reason why "institutions" was listed as a keyword in the titles of the first three TransCanada conferences, and also the reason why the second major project I initiated after the first conference was The Culture of Research: Retooling the Humanities workshop, which I organized in collaboration with Daniel Coleman.[3] And you became part of all that in different ways.

LL: Yes, the "hook" for me was attached to an antiracist/cultural activist line—a West Coast line, if you like—one that imagined CanLit as problematically and loosely yet still productively tied to a range of projects for social and cultural liberation. I came to the first TransCanada conference in Vancouver in 2005 because it seemed to be an exciting and ambitiously rich continuation of the conversations that for me had begun outside the academy in artist-run centres, community organizations, and one-off projects. I had, by then, come to see the academy as a place of possibility, thanks in part to your work and Roy's. And I came to the one in Guelph in 2007. I have fond memories of dancing our hearts out on the final night of the Guelph conference.

SK: And you came to TransCanada Institute for various other events as well. As for dance, dance was an integral element of the first three conferences. The DJs for TransCanada One were Wayde Compton, who performed "hip hop," and Mark McCutcheon, who focused on "disco, retro, techno." I remember kicking my sandals off and dancing on a piano at Steamworks Brewery. Mark also DJ-ed the next two TransCanada dances. I must say that the dance element was not there just for fun, unwinding after the stress of organizing a big event; it was also meant to help loosen and dissolve hierarchies and animate bodies in ways that helped refigure relations.

LL: I also participated in the TransCanada conference at Mount Allison University, the one that you organized with Christl Verduyn. What inspired me about the TransCanada project from the outset was the way in which in its transness it cut across the problem of the nation, a problem that plagued and plagues me as a dyed-in-the-wool queer Chinese Canadian feminist with commitments to other times and places. Of course, I also have a commitment to Canada. Without access to Canadian landed immigrant and eventually citizenship status, I would have lived a very different kind of life. Nevertheless, I want to recognize that citizenship status comes with racism attached. White citizenship remains the idealized form, hence the ongoing erasures and minimizations of BIPOC histories (like that critiqued and protested in Writing Thru Race). Still, I am highly conscious of responsibilities I hold through the state, though also in excess of it.

SK: Being an immigrant seems to demand that we locate ourselves vis à vis the state. Our relationship with the state determines the range of our agency and how we act. When I arrived in Canada on a student visa, I knew absolutely nothing about it. But I found myself on the Prairies at the height of regionalist cultural politics. The Winnipeg literary community was the first "place" where I felt at home in Canada. So my first identification as a Canadian, though not formally a citizen yet, was as a westerner, a westerner who had the privilege of learning first-hand, and at a highly accelerated pace, how literature happens at ground level, the material and infrastructural level: from workshops to demonstrations about the lack of reviews of books by Canadian authors, from editing each other to publishing booklets and magazines, from organizing readings to interacting with the Canada Council—all that was an incredible education that supplemented my formal graduate studies. It both exposed me to national pedagogy and taught me how to work against it.

LL: The work of self-locating is so important, as is the recognition of the particular territories that have enabled us to live. As a Newfoundlander, I became aware of the genocide against the Beothuk at a fairly young age. In my early twenties, as I began to learn about the Chinese Head Tax and the Exclusion Act, the Japanese Canadian uprooting, the *Komagata Maru* incident, Black slavery in Quebec, the razing of Africville in Nova Scotia, the distribution of smallpox-infected blankets through unceded Coast Salish Territories, and the hanging of Louis Riel, my sense of the ambivalence around the Canadian state deepened. My being has been implicated in complicated ways in these programmatic acts of violence. As a complicit racialized un/settler, I feel it is important to continue to claim Canadian citizenship in order to claim and act on the responsibility I hold toward the work of redress and restitution to the Indigenous peoples of Turtle Island. I take Lee Maracle's call for spirit-to-spirit relations seriously. And I believe redress and restitution are owed to others also wronged by the state, including the descendants of Black loyalists socially and economically excluded after the War of 1812, contemporary Black people subject to police violence, and the descendants of Chinese Canadians who paid the Head Tax.

SK: You're echoing my own way of finding out about Canadian history and how its impact remains indelibly inscribed in the present. I must mention Roy again, for he has played, probably unbeknownst to him, a formative role in my Canadian education and my formation as a citizen. I first met Roy in the early 1980s, when he was getting the Japanese Canadian Redress movement off the ground.[4] Art Miki, Roy's brother, who served as President of the National Association of Japanese Canadians, lived in Winnipeg, and Roy visited often. It was through Roy that I became aware of Canada as a nation-state of troubling paradoxes: it opened its doors to the refugees from Vietnam in the late 1970s and early 1980s but had declared its own Japanese Canadian citizens "enemies alien." So, I learned that there are different ways of belonging, that belonging has to be understood in the plural, that sometimes it has to be earned at a price, that it's often denied, used as bait or alibi, and that it must be resisted if the terms of belonging mean having one's identity and otherness in relation to others co-opted.

LL: My own relationship to the state is full of contradictions. I appreciate my life of relative ease in a Western democracy. But I'm also horrified by the violence enacted to produce this imperfect political form. (Also, the West doesn't have a monopoly on democracy or democratic thought.) It may seem paradoxical to some, but it is out of appreciation and care that I do my work of critique. Increasingly, it's also out of a sense of responsibility. I'm very conscious that it's as a citizen that I participate in the work of restitution for the dispossession of Indigenous peoples. That said, I'm not so grateful to the state that I want to keep it at all costs. I could still do restitution work without it, though the form of that work would be quite different. But as an inheritor of bad revolutions, I'm very concerned about how we get "there" from "here." For many years I have done solidarity work against many of the terrible things done to produce the state—the state that imagined itself White in the first instance, but which later came to do inclusion work, always fraught and imperfect, and sometimes infuriating if not downright violent. Inclusion is an ambivalent practice and thing to want, since it easily partakes of co-optation, incorporation, and devitalization. It seems to me that the present moment might be one that calls for a more complex set of land-body-spirit relations.

SK: All this attests to how important and potentially problematic self-location is, for it can be both an act of affirmation and an act driven by the scripts of hegemonic discourses. It's at the core of building alliances but can also lead to a further fracturing of social spaces and identities. Our subject positions are co-implicated in both the essentialist and anti-essentialist constructions of self and place. How can we embody location without reverting to essentialist notions of place and nation?

LL: The danger of self-location is that it can become navel-gazing. We can forget that good, if imperfect, work has been done to critique the state while still practising under its name. Many people seem to have forgotten (or perhaps they never knew) that important work by Indigenous, Black, Arab, Asian, and other racialized or differently constructed national subjects has gone on under the roof of the state for a long time, occasionally in a celebratory way but, more often than not, in critical, ambivalent, and profoundly socially engaged ways. For, indeed, ambivalence is not anathema to social engagement. If anything, it's necessary to it, alongside vast reserves of compassion. Only in ambivalence can we hold the complexities of human relations. Though the state is imperfect, those struggles for justice remain valuable and the activists, scholars, and cultural workers who struggled and fought still lived lives worth living and did deeds worth doing. I worry sometimes that to set the state—or CanLit—up as a White straw man and then knock him down erases all of that important BIPOC presence and hard BIPOC work.

SK: I couldn't agree more. I have come to think that the insistence on discussing CanLit today, especially on social media, as a canon that is insular, heteronormative, and white, is a peculiar syndrome, a syndrome that speaks to a need to set up CanLit as a straw man, as you put it, a synecdoche for the things against which we must continue to struggle. Yes, there is a canon, but this canon has to be understood as part of a tradition that has long unfolded in different directions. CanLit in the twenty-first century cannot be reduced to the ways in which the canon was understood and operated, say, thirty years ago; it is not synonymous with the canon debates in the 1990s, at least not in my mind. The more we hold up a dated, monolithic conception of the canon, even by way of critiquing it—especially by way of critiquing it—the more we become complicit with its reification and run the risk of distorting, indeed erasing, the long history of small presses and writers who have long carved their own paths and become important voices in CanLit, in fact, calling for an understanding of CanLit as CanLits. Griping about the canon in the second decade of the new millennium while not paying any attention to, say, the explosion of special issues of magazines on and anthologies about, for instance, Black, Indigenous, Asian, and/or LGBTQ2S+ authors in the late 1980s and 1990s, the backlists of presses like Pemmican, Theytus, Arsenal, Talonbooks, NeWest, Sister Vision, Press Gang, and Coach House, or experimental and dub poets, or writers and activists like Jim Wong-Chu, Rita Joe (Mi'kmaw) and Marie Annharte Baker (Anishnaabe) is practising anachronism, being wilfully blind to—or, who knows, perhaps ignorant of—the rich fabric of all those voices, voices that are, as far as I'm concerned, integral to what CanLit is today. If the ethically and politically minded mode of critical discourse today makes this time-bound canon its singular focus, then this says more about the nature and limits of critical discourse today than the so-called national canon itself. We were talking about the transness of the TransCanada project, and I think it is a similar kind of transness that is elided in the present emphasis on a stable canon, namely, that the canon has transitioned, albeit at a snail's pace, from its decidedly settler-complicit self-image to a body of works that reflects not only a multiplicity of subject positions but also the diversity that characterizes CanLit's production and dissemination today. And it's important to avoid always identifying the canon with the nation-state.

LL: I think we need to be careful not to think of CanLit as an unproblematic container that can fully absorb Black, Indigenous, and/or Asian voices. Our work can and does exceed, undermine, and protest the state, and this is important. That said, certainly, it was the liberatory aspects of the TransCanada project's trans that appealed to me. The work of "trans" in relation to the state, as you and Roy imagined this work, happened some years before the wide engagement with concepts and practices of transgender and nonbinary sexualities (though there did exist trans and nonbinary people doing the work then as now). And gender and sexuality are concepts and practices profoundly tied to state production, and thus in need to critique and remaking. Your and Roy's way of thinking about a different kind of "trans" works to intentionally cut across the nation in ways that I think are still very contemporary and necessary. We might or might not love the state, but we don't get to dispose of it so easily. On the other hand, there's nothing eternal about the state either. The state is always morphing and changing. And it could die, or simply shrink and be overtaken by other forces, as Chris Lee reminds us in this volume.

SK: Precisely what Roy and I had in mind when we called our conference, indeed the entire TransCanada project, after Roy Kiyooka's *Transcanada Letters* (2005a). Kiyooka felt "athwarted" (Miki 1991, 51), vis à vis the Canadian nation-state; that is, he saw himself as "a white anglo-saxon protestant with a cleft tongue" (Kiyooka 2005b, 108). He was profoundly aware of the paradoxical simultaneity of both belonging and unbelonging to the nation. And talking about the TransCanada name, I think we should mention the important shift that our collaboration has brought about, a shift you proposed, from the singular mode of TransCanada to the plural TransCanadas. Even without the *s*, TransCanada for me has always signified in the plural. I still use the singular form when I'm historicizing the project, as I'm doing here, but I thought your intervention regarding the name made perfect sense as a response to the different temporality of TC4, the kinds of transness that are being taken up much more widely since the project's inception. Trans, as Roy and I understood it, conjures the incommensurability of what comes after it: it reveals the fissures of the hegemonic boundaries held together by the nation; it counters the positivism of ontologies and epistemologies constructed by the nation-state.

LL: What I had in mind when I proposed that shift in the title was the need to think in relation to the Truth and Reconciliation Commission, Idle No More, protests against the 1969 White Paper, and our commitment to a politics of ongoing relationships—and not the closure that some people seem to want. Where prior formations of the project emphasized citizenship and institutions, you and I agreed that this one would focus on justice and relation. I wanted to think about the kinds of relationships we might build in this alternate temporality, about how non-capitalist/non-state land relations still exist in temporalities that underlie the temporality of the state. In other words, they are still present with us in what some Elders call time immemorial and some call cyclical time. Justice and relation invite us to recognize there are ways of moving through and across the state; that there are lives, practices, and cultures that can be national without being nationalist, and also that the nation is just one node in a series of ever-shifting relations—national, international, intranational, nation-to-nation, spirit-to-spirit, land-to-nation, land-to-water, human-to-human, human-to-nonhuman, nonhuman-to-extra-human, diasporic, global, planetary.

SK: The nation-state may be the product of conflicts that have been resolved, as Ernest Renan would have it, and consequently complicit with the violence that such resolutions often incur, but I understand this kind of resolution to be one that is held in abeyance, more an aspirational condition than one that is already fulfilled, perennially under question because colonialism as a fact cannot be undone as such; we have to deal with its consequences. This is why I think our relations with the nation are inevitably—and invariably—agonistic. The TransCanada project was mindful of and inspired by the histories you're alluding to above. Including cultural activists and artists like Lee Maracle (Sto:lo) , the late Ruby Arngna'naaq (Inuit), and Jamelie Hassan in the previous conferences was meant, in part, as an affirmation of the importance of the histories and activist work you're talking about. If activism is a way of materializing our agonistic relations with the nation—addressing injustices and seeking restitution—then it does so by simultaneously testifying to the nation as a constituted entity and putting in the limelight those whom the nation has absented from its body politic. And there is of course activism that occurs within, across, and beyond institutions, the kind of activism that both acknowledges and dissolves boundaries. Your own project, The Insurgent Architects' House for Creative Writing (TIA House), does that.[5] And the TransCanada project was very happy to work with the TIA House project on the conference.

LL: Yes, it's important to remember that as this volume of essays comes out of the TransCanada project it also emerges from TIA House, a project engaged with questions of social justice and contemporary aesthetics. Through this project, I've put forward a concept I call "emergent insurgency," that is, generating ideals (because we must), and putting them into action, and, in attending to interactions of one's own ideals with those of others, holding up those moments when the work of interaction produces something positive but unexpected.[6] TIA House is oriented toward thought, practice, and relationships, but its concerns are not specifically national.

SK: Yes. Your concept of "emergent insurgency" echoes my notion of emergent events that I talk about in my introduction to *Shifting the Ground of Canadian Literary Studies*, the second volume of essays based on the TransCanada conferences, which shows that we're coming to these issues from similar spaces. We cannot afford to do away with the nation, but at the same time we cannot afford to make it our singular concern either. This was the main reason behind adopting the modality of the trans. As a prefix, "trans" connotes mobility and points toward intersectionality; it is a scene of encounters where what has been valorized as normative is put under pressure, and thus destabilized, by what has been constructed as incongruous to normative paradigms. It was in this sense of the trans that we wanted to problematize the ways in which CanLit is imbricated not only with the nation but also with transnationalism, globalism, and ecological concerns, and this was also the reason why we adopted an interdisciplinary perspective.

LL: In 2015, when you asked me again to co-organize TC4, we were at the Deleuze conference in Athens, Greece, travelling with Rinaldo Walcott and Christl Verduyn. You had invited us to speak on a plenary panel that also included yourself. The conference was sponsored, in part, by the Canadian Embassy. The financial crisis in Greece was in full swing by that time. I remember attending sessions in classrooms so politicized that the walls were sprayed with graffiti. The rock stars of Deleuzian thought gave papers for as long as they wished. Our session was delayed for hours so that we nearly missed the closing dinner altogether. I have fond memories of wandering the streets of Athens with you, Christl, and Rinaldo, sipping *raki* and eating grilled fish. It was after that conference that I committed myself to work with you on TC4. We were still in Athens, and had just walked through a small market, where I had bought several small bundles of herbs for tea.

SK: Yes. Deleuze, the Greeks' protests against the austerity measures, Greek mountain tea, and me not letting go of the idea that you were the perfect collaborator for TC4. We had a great time in Athens, but I must say it felt a bit strange to me—being both a tourist guide to you, Rinaldo, and Christl and a kind of diasporan tourist myself. But I do like that the synergetic energy that got our collaboration going occurred in Greece. We set up the dates of the conference and began brainstorming about it during our week-long vacation on Crete. And now that I think of it, we were oblivious that summer in Greece that 2017 was Canada's sesquicentennial anniversary, an unfortunate memory lapse since some people saw our conference as participating in the general state-induced euphoria about the anniversary. We felt compelled to thematize the sesquicentennial in our Call for Papers, partly because it helped us secure some much-needed funds—here's complicity for you—but we didn't conceive TC4 as a celebration of the Canadian settler nation-state. Quite the contrary, we were both uncomfortable about this coincidence. It was, in part, our desire to counteract this that we decided to place Turtle Island right up front in the event's title. I had asked Lee Maracle what Turtle Island's name was in Anishinaabe, and she passed my query and request for permission to the late Alex McCay, an Anishinaabe Elder at the Centre for Indigenous Studies at the University of Toronto—hence Mikinaakominis. And we certainly also wanted to acknowledge the event's spatial and temporal frames of that particular moment, that is, addressing the Truth and Reconciliation Commission and honouring the original inhabitants of this land, who include the Ojibwa people.

LL: So, the land was present for us from the beginning. And the use of the name also a "present," a gift, from Elder Alex McCay. In *Land / Relations*, we express our gratitude for the gift by engaging the kind of intentionally directed and relational work of memory that the late, much-missed Lee

Maracle calls for in *Memory Serves* (2015). We direct the work of memory toward respect for the land, as well as human-to-human and human-to-nonhuman relations that unfold through it. If the Canada 150 celebrations seemed set up to remember the glories of the state, I think it's important that those of us who have counter-memories articulate those memories, and articulate them in relation to one another and to the land, so that those who wish for glory can't appropriate our memories in the service of the rising fascism that frankly scares the socks off me.

SK: The collection certainly reflects the need to read our living in the now, but it does so without assuming that the present moment has swallowed and digested the past, that it has overcome the exigencies of colonialism. When read individually but also in relation to each other, the essays in this volume exercise a kind of collective counter-memory—the authors' own as well as that in the texts they examine. They materialize the critical work that counter-memory does, that is, bring into relief, while unsettling, relations of domination.

LL: The contributors to this collection enact, each in their own way, the work of counter-memory in the service of relationships that have always been there, but because they were not a priority for the colonial state, they were never part of the state narrative. The set of relations they call for include human-to-human relations certainly, with a deep demand for a reckoning with gifts given and traumas unjustly suffered and displacements so profound they have changed who we are, losses so deep they can never be recouped. Each contribution is haunted by absences where presence was as well as absences where presence never was. Other lost relations, for some of our contributors, are also human relations to land and nonhuman beings. Ways of being human have been lost because the hegemony of the Enlightenment has bitten so deep, it's cut us off from other ways of having our humanity. And, of course, relations among nonhuman beings must be recognized as not only underpinning human life, but important for their own sake, regardless of whether humans are here or not.

SK: Yes, and yet alongside these losses that are so deeply felt, that demand different kinds of recognition and restitution, there emerges, I believe, a common desire neither to move beyond fraught relations nor to yield to the false promises of what Lauren Berlant (2011) calls cruel optimism. *Land / Relations* embraces the affects, politics, and—yes—poetics of difficulty, for it invites us to immerse ourselves in the web of difficult relations within which we are already embedded.

Literature, Language, Culture

At Mikinaakominis / TransCanadas 2017

/ EILEEN ANTONE

When I began my literary studies in the late 1970s Indigenous literature was almost non-existent. The two writers who most influenced my thinking on the social conditions of Indigenous Peoples in Canada were Harold Cardinal and Maria Campbell. It is with a tinge of sadness that I write this for the Mikinaakominis / TransCanadas volume, *Land / Relations*, for I am thinking of the Indigenous stories that were oppressed in the early years of Canadian expansion on the land of the Indigenous Peoples of Turtle Island. But I am also struck with much gladness, for the conference included a great range of Indigenous and other people's literary and critical voices. It was awesome that the conference opened with the Wahahi·o Iroquoian Drum and Singers leading the conference facilitators and participants into the plenary hall with the Friendship Dance. The cultural tradition of this Iroquois song and dance is used to ensure good relations with all people involved at gatherings.

Language and culture were the first traditions that were attacked by the invading settlers of Turtle Island, so it was totally humbling and inspiring to have Grafton Antone, an OnΛyota'a·ka (Oneida) language speaker, open the conference with the Iroquoian Kanuhelatuksla—the words that come before all else. These words are called Tetwanuhelat', the Thanksgiving Address, a teaching and ceremony reminding us of our relationship to all of Creation and of our duties and responsibilities to each other that help us to promote the continuation of balance and harmony in our societies.

As Gregory Cajete, a Tewa author and professor from Santa Clara Pueblo, New Mexico, states, "language is sacred because it is an expression of the Holy Wind that exists as the breath of life in each person" (1994, 52). It is this sacred breath of life that is driving Indigenous Peoples to continue to find ways to regain and revitalize the language of their people. Cajete also states that

> By watching, listening, experiencing, and participating, everyone learned what it was to be one of the People, and how to survive in community with others. Learning how to care for one's self and others, learning relationship between people and other things, learning the customs, traditions, and values of a community: all of these understandings and more were the daily course of Indigenous education. (1994, 176)

The participants of the conference had the opportunity to watch, listen, and experience the language and culture of the Onʌyota'a·ka people. They also had a chance to be involved in an Ojibway smudge ceremony using the traditional medicine of sage to cleanse the environment, as well as the body, mind, and spirit, and to attract good energy. This was a truly wonderful and valuable participatory experience in re-storying land and developing decolonizing practices in the public sphere.

It was interesting and exciting to hear the work of many different storytellers, poets, novelists, creative non-fiction writers, critics, and interdisciplinary practitioners engage in the ongoing dialogue about the relationship of literatures to land in the context of Canada. Indigenous Peoples in Canada have been struggling against the colonization that changed the original perspective of the land and landscape by imposing different names for lakes, rivers, streams, mountains, and the many places used by the Original people of Turtle Island. There are still Indigenous Peoples who remember the original names of the various places that were and are important to them. Information about a place is embedded in the language used to talk about the environment. Sto:lo Lee Maracle, a sage and writer, reminded us that memory influences what and how we see the world; that memory is subjective; that it cannot be objective as it involves personal engagement in the activity being remembered. So, here are my memories of some of the events at the conference.

I was impressed by the creativity of Warren Cariou's presentation, "Landsensing: Body, Territory, Relation," in which he talked about his use of four "primary materials" gathered from the land of his home territory: bitumen, spruce gum, blueberries, and sage. My first thought was, how in the world can you get these four elements to work together in any sense of decolonizing the mind in relation to the land, and do so in the form of visual art. But I was fascinated hearing him explain the process. When I viewed the artwork he brought for display, it truly portrayed his concept of "sensory ethics of land-based belonging."

Another project that captivated my attention was Tasha Hubbard's talk about her short film *Buffalo Calling*, where she described a process of re-storying and restoring the buffalo to the Indigenous Plains. As she indicated, Canadian expansion in the nineteenth century was devastating for Indigenous peoples, the land, and the buffalo. This was the era of buffalo genocide, the result of settlers killing the food source of the Indigenous Peoples in order to control them. Hubbard's film is an excellent example of Indigenous resurgence of the buffalo culture to the land, which, as she says, is connected with restoration of Indigenous consciousness, knowledges, and relationships.

Another presentation that I was privileged to witness was that of Cyrus Sundar-Singh's performance, "Africville—Dogs, Gods, and City Hall." He invited me to his site-specific live documentary inside Hart House's chapel. I was interested in this presentation because the church has played a central role in the lives of the Indigenous Peoples. The churches were the instruments used to carry out the government's plan of assimilation through residential schools, so I was curious to find out what happened in the Africville story, especially so since Sundar-Singh's story was based on archival documents regarding a church in Nova Scotia located in an early Black settlement. He used the triad of story, performance, and audience to create a collaborative, participatory, documentary experience incorporating various traditional and contemporary elements, such as oral storytelling, poetry, musical score, and archival materials. As a participant in this performance, I had a feeling of great loss for the Black church that had been demolished without respect for the Black community. It is stories like these that show the role Canadian literature plays in building meaningful relations that can break the cycle of injustice in both Indigenous and non-Indigenous communities.

The final performance of the conference, presented by Lillian Allen, a Black poet, and Muskoday First Nation Linsday Eekwol, a rapper, used poetry and music to reveal the many social and discriminatory injustices that happen in the everyday life to marginalized people. These two artists/activists use their talent to advocate for change to negative stereotypes.

It is wonderful that literary study in English in Canada had shifted from a colonial mission to an undertaking that includes marginalized people in the context of global human, nonhuman, economic, social, and ecological shifts. Although there was some tension at the conference, I believe the overall goal of the Mikinaakominis/TransCanadas was to significantly advance Canadian/Turtle Island cultural and intellectual discussion on the relationship between Indigenous and non-Indigenous peoples. The conference started with a song and dance of friendship and ended with a song and dance for continued action in developing decolonizing practices in the public sphere and in the humanities. This forum was a significant event that

> Provide[d] opportunities for students, writers, critics, and the public to engage in-depth in one of the most important questions of our historical moment: what role Canadian literature plays in building meaningful relations that can break the cycle of injustice that began with the colonial expropriation of Indigenous land. (Kamboureli and Lai 2016b)

PART II

“the ghosts pile up with the toxic mistakes” / Hauntings and Other Returns

river sisters

/ RITA WONG

from the pearl river to the peace river
i have walked among river killers
serial killers in suits, wielding bureaucracy
to disguise the ignorance and arrogance of
patriarchs* who thought they knew best
but refused to see or care
about the dying baiji, the disappearing moose

when they try to flood the river's curves,
they would smother her forest-loving song
bloat her body with their greed and ego
silencing millennia-old bird song
forgetting that the river belongs to herself,
not to them

the ghosts pile up with the toxic mistakes in the patriarchs'
    drive to power
as they gamble away the haunted house

we call earth, watershed home,
the spirits of those who've had their homes stolen & destroyed
now how money talks loud but earth bats last

we call on these spirits
to help people change their river murdering ways
before it is too late

dedicated to:
Dai Qing, Bing Ai, Feng Yan, Arundhati Roy,
Helen Knott, Yvonne Tupper, Connie GreyEyes

Positioning Intergenerational Trauma

Nisga'a Nationalism and the Materiality of Marius Barbeau's *Totem Poles*

/ JORDAN ABEL

Transcript of 2-Channel Recording—via Zoom H2n

15:21:18 Hey everyone. This might take me a moment. So please talk amongst yourselves. Stand up. Stretch. Do whatever you need to do.

15:21:25 Hi everyone.

15:21:28 My name is Jordan Abel.

15:21:32 I am a Nisga'a writer from Vancouver, BC.

15:21:39 I identify this way because for many Indigenous peoples, these kinds of national identifications can indicate one's home, one's friends and family, and one's position within Indigeneity.

15:21:49 Likewise, these kinds of national identifications can often also be an indicator of which community (or communities) we are accountable to.

15:21:59 For example, Layli Long Soldier identifies as a "citizen of the Oglala Lakota Nation."

15:22:07 Louise Erdrich identifies as being of both "Chippewa" and "German-American" descent.

15:22:15 N. Scott Momaday identifies as being "Kiowa."

15:22:19 Neal McLeod identifies as being "half-Cree, half-Swedish."

15:22:22 Marie Annharte Baker identifies as being "Anishinaabe (from the Little Saskatchewan First Nation in Manitoba)."

15:22:29 That being said, these kinds of national identifications do not always adequately account for the complexity and plurality of Indigenous identity.

15:22:34 For some Indigenous Peoples, they simply do not tell the whole story.

15:22:39 For example, when I say that I am NISHGA, you might assume that I grew up in Kincolith, BC, like my grandparents.

15:22:43 You might assume that, when I say that I am NISHGA, that I speak NISHGA.

15:22:47 You might assume that my writing reflects on NISGHA knowledge, NISGHA world views, and NISGHA understanding.

15:22:54 Then again, you might not assume any of those things.

15:23:01 A few years ago during the City of Vancouver's year of reconciliation event, I was at a dinner meeting at a restaurant on Water St.

15:23:06 I was one of a few poets who were commissioned to write a poem in response to the Truth and Reconciliation Commission.

15:23:10 The initiative was called Reconciliation Through Poetry. The work that the poets were engaging with was meant to honour the work of Chief Robert Joseph.

15:23:15 At the dinner meeting, the poets (along with a few administrators) talked with Chief Robert Joseph, exchanged stories, discussed what reconciliation meant for both Indigenous and non-Indigenous peoples.

15:23:22 After a while, Chief Joseph directed his attention to me and asked me where I was from.

15:23:26 I told him that I was NISHGA and that my grandparents were from Kincolith.

15:23:30 After a few moments, he said "You're not really Nisga'a.

15:23:33 Some of my friends are Nisga'a.

15:23:36 Do you know how I can tell?

15:23:38 If you were really Nishga, you would have said Niska.

15:23:43 With a *k* sound.

15:23:45 Niska.

15:23:47 You said *Nishga*.

15:23:50 With an *sh* sound."

15:23:53 You know, I didn't really know how to respond to that.

15:23:55 My grandparents are Nisga'a.

15:23:59 My dad is Nisga'a.

15:24:03 But to a certain extent, he was right.

15:24:07 I wasn't born in Kincolith.

15:24:11 I was born in Vancouver, moved when I was very young, and essentially grew up in Ontario.

15:24:15 Does that make me less Nisga'a?

15:24:19 And what does it mean anyway to be Nisga'a? With a *k* sound.

15:24:24 And what does it meant to be NISHGA? With an *sh* sound?

15:24:32 What does it mean to be Nisga'a, but to have grown up removed from the Nisga'a community?

15:24:39 What does it mean to be Indigenous if your relationship to community has become severed somehow?

15:24:46 What does it mean to be both an intergenerational survivor of residential schools and an urban Indigenous person?

15:24:52 I think these are the questions that I've been struggling with my whole life.

15:24:52 I want to tell you about my life for the purposes of openness and accountability and transparency.

15:24:59 I think especially now when there have been so many thoughts and questions about how we define Indigeneity and who or who does not count as Indigenous.

15:25:09 I'm telling you about my life because I am accountable not only to the Nisga'a community,

15:25:14 but I am also accountable to the communities of intergenerational survivors of residential schools

15:25:19 and the communities of urban Indigenous peoples.

15:25:26 I'm accountable to the communities of dispossessed Indigenous peoples

15:25:32 who are not able to find their way back to their communities because of the ongoing legacy of colonial violence.

15:25:37 I am accountable to myself

15:25:40 and I hope to talk openly about my subject position within the scope of Indigeneity.

15:25:43 Colonialism has had and continues to have a profound impact on Indigenous peoples.

15:25:49 And some of that legacy of violence has been discussed at length, some of that legacy of violence remains silenced.

15:25:53 Here's a scene from my life.

15:25:56 I am twenty-two years old.

15:25:59 It's 2007.

15:26:03 I am an undergraduate at the University of Alberta in Edmonton.

15:26:06 I am studying English.

15:26:09 According to my official transcripts, I have taken art history, American literature, astronomy, sociology, Spanish, children's literature, literary theory, and creative writing.

15:26:17 But to this point in my academic career, not one book by an Indigenous author has been assigned in any of my classes.

15:26:22 In fact, at this point in my life, I have never even met another Nisga'a person.

15:26:26 I mean, I knew some Ojibway people when I lived here in Ontario, and some Cree people when I lived in Alberta.

15:26:30 But the Nisga'a are from northern coastal BC.

15:26:35 At least that's what I hear.

15:26:38 That's what I've read.

15:26:42 That's what I've been told.

15:26:46 But I've never been there.

15:26:49 I've never had the opportunity to get there.

15:26:53 So here I am.

15:26:56 A young Nisga'a person who has not only never met another Nisga'a person in his entire life, but is also painfully

15:27:03 (and I mean really hurtfully, deep down pain in your heart kind of hurting)

15:27:08 aware of the hole in his life where Nisga'a knowledge and understandings belong.

15:27:12 At that point, I think, the only book I had ever read by an Indigenous person was *Green Grass, Running Water* by Thomas King, and that was at least somewhat accidental.

15:27:20 I didn't read it because it was written by an Indigenous author.

15:27:24 I read it because someone had casually mentioned that it was good.

15:27:29 And it was good.

15:27:33 And sometime after I'd read that book, I asked myself why I didn't know anything about the Nisga'a people.

15:27:39 Why didn't I know anything about myself?

15:27:44 Why is it that I grew up in Ontario but I was born in BC?

15:27:48 Why have I spent all my life not knowing the Indigenous side of my family?

15:27:53 So being at least a somewhat dutiful student at the time, my first instinct was to go to the library.

15:27:59 So I went off to the library and I started to look for books using the search term "Nisga'a."

15:28:04 The first book I found was *Totem Poles* by Marius Barbeau.

Slide 1: Totem Poles, cover

15:28:08 You know, I honestly don't know what I expected this book to be.

15:28:13 But when I opened it up there were stories about the Nisga'a people.

15:28:17 Which Barbeau spelled Niskae. N-I-S-K-A-E. (Again, the *k* sound.)

15:28:21 As opposed to Nisga'a which is spelled N-I-S-G-A-'A.

15:28:25 But there were stories!

15:28:28 There was some hint of Nisga'a knowledge there!

15:28:33 I didn't articulate it in this way when I was going through this process, but what I was looking for was a doorway into Nisga'a knowledge and nationalism.

15:28:40 And without knowing any Nisga'a people

15:28:44 (or, I think importantly, understanding why I didn't know any Nisga'a people),

15:28:49 Barbeau's work was in fact a doorway even if it was ultimately a deeply distorted colonial representation of Nisga'a knowledge and Nisga'a world views.

15:28:57 *Totem Poles* was an imperfect entry point, but I had no other way in.

15:29:01 And Barbeau's book was filled with photographs of totem poles, and stories from the Indigenous peoples of the Pacific Northwest.

15:29:07 But, instead of providing me a pathway to Indigenous knowledge, Barbeau's work opened another doorway.

15:29:12 I began to wonder why I didn't know any of these stories.

15:29:17 Why didn't I know any of the Indigenous Peoples in my family?

15:29:23 In my book *The Place of Scraps*, the main narrative revolves around the role Marius Barbeau played in dismantling Nisga'a culture

15:29:29 (along with many other nations in the Pacific Northwest)

15:29:34 by buying (and often stealing) totem poles and other cultural items from struggling communities

15:29:39 (and very often struggling community members).

15:29:44 I make that distinction because in many cases he did make some kind of arrangement with an individual within the community, but it wasn't a community decision.

15:29:53 In the narrative of *The Place of Scraps*, it also becomes clear that Barbeau essentially stole a totem pole from the community that my grandparents were born in,

15:30:01 and there is a narrative thread in which I remember encountering this totem pole at the Royal Ontario Museum when I was a child without knowing or understanding its significance in my life.

15:30:10 It's actually just a few blocks away from here.

15:30:14 That, more or less, is the main narrative of *The Place of Scraps*.

15:30:19 But when people talk about why precisely I use erasure in this book, I think most people end up missing a key detail.

15:30:25 Their suggestion that my erasing of Barbeau's words in some ways replicates Barbeau's own attempted erasure of Indigenous peoples is, absolutely, part of it.

15:30:33 That by removing totem poles and taking advantage of struggling communities, Barbeau was actively contributing to colonial erasures.

15:30:37 Yes, I think this is true.

15:30:41 But the detail that is missing

15:30:45 —the reason why Barbeau's text is so important to this work—

15:30:51 is also because Barbeau's writing was the first imperfect glimpse I had into Nisga'a culture,

15:31:00 and that *The Place of Scraps*, in addition to being about Marius Barbeau and Salvage Anthropology, is also about what it means to be an intergenerational survivor of residential schools,

15:31:15 it's about what those experiences can look like,

15:31:21 and it's about having no choice but to learn about your own family history through the now debunked work of a dead white anthropologist.

15:31:30

15:31:35 Here, I think we've arrived at a good moment to pause for a second and to talk about Indigenous identity and position because it is helpful, I think, to frame urban Indigenous experiences and experiences of intergenerational trauma through these theoretical frameworks.

15:31:40 And to subsequently understand these lived experiences as not only being manifestations of Indigenous identity and position,

15:31:46 but also as being deeply misunderstood and under-theorized categories of Indigenous identity.

15:31:52 As Bonita Lawrence theorizes in her book *"Real" Indians and Others,*

15:31:57 Indigenous identity is best thought of "as a negotiated and highly contested set of realities" (2004, 6).

15:32:03 The way I've been thinking through Indigenous identity, then, is quite similar to Bonita Lawrence's thinking:

15:31:10 Indigenous identity can be thought of not so much as being fixed or static, but instead as being fluid, shifting, relational, "multifaceted and at times ambiguous" (Lawrence 2004, 9).

15:32:16 In Deanna Reder's introduction to *Learn, Teach, Challenge*, she privileges the term "position" over the term "identity" as one that "undermines the object/subject dichotomy and makes visible the lines of relationship that affect one's perspective" (Reder and Morra 2016, 8).

15:32:27 Reder's suggestion here to think through position rather than identity has been really useful for me,

The central focus of this book is urban mixed-blood Native identity in Canadian contexts. It explores the tensions and complexities of Native identity when one is mixed-blood, urban, and either possessing or lacking legal "Indian" status or band membership. Throughout this work, Native identity is explored as a negotiated and highly contested set of realities.

Slide 2: Lawrence, 2004 (6)

15:32:35 and, I think, importantly shifts the conversations about identity away from the problematic discourses of authenticity.

15:32:43 My purpose in this talk is to address my positionhood as both an urban Indigenous person and an intergenerational survivor of residential schools.

15:32:52

15:33:00 Before I move on, I just want to preface this section by saying that I am sharing these details with you not because I particularly like to share these things.

15:33:10 In fact, some of these details are still quite painful to share.

15:33:16 But I feel the need to share them with you in this context because I think it is important to understand what the experiences of an intergenerational survivor of residential schools can look like,

15:33:27 and where the difficulties are with communicating this type of lived experience to both Indigenous and non-Indigenous people,

15:33:34 who may not have any idea of how these lived experiences are different from their own understandings of what Indigenous experiences look like,

15:33:43 or even what counts as Indigenous lived experience.

15:33:50 This is my Dad. *[Slide 3]*

15:33:55 His name is Lawrence Wilson.

15:34:01 I have met this man once in my life.

15:34:06 When I was twenty-three.

15:34:11 He was the first Nisga'a person I've ever met.

15:34:17 He was a carver and a painter. He carved this mask. And this mask. *[Slide 4]*

Slide 3: Dad, mask

15:34:23 He lived in Vancouver for most of his life and mostly worked as an artist.

15:34:27 Here is a photo of him painting a frog. *[Slide 5]*

15:34:32 This painting is currently hanging on my wall in Robson.

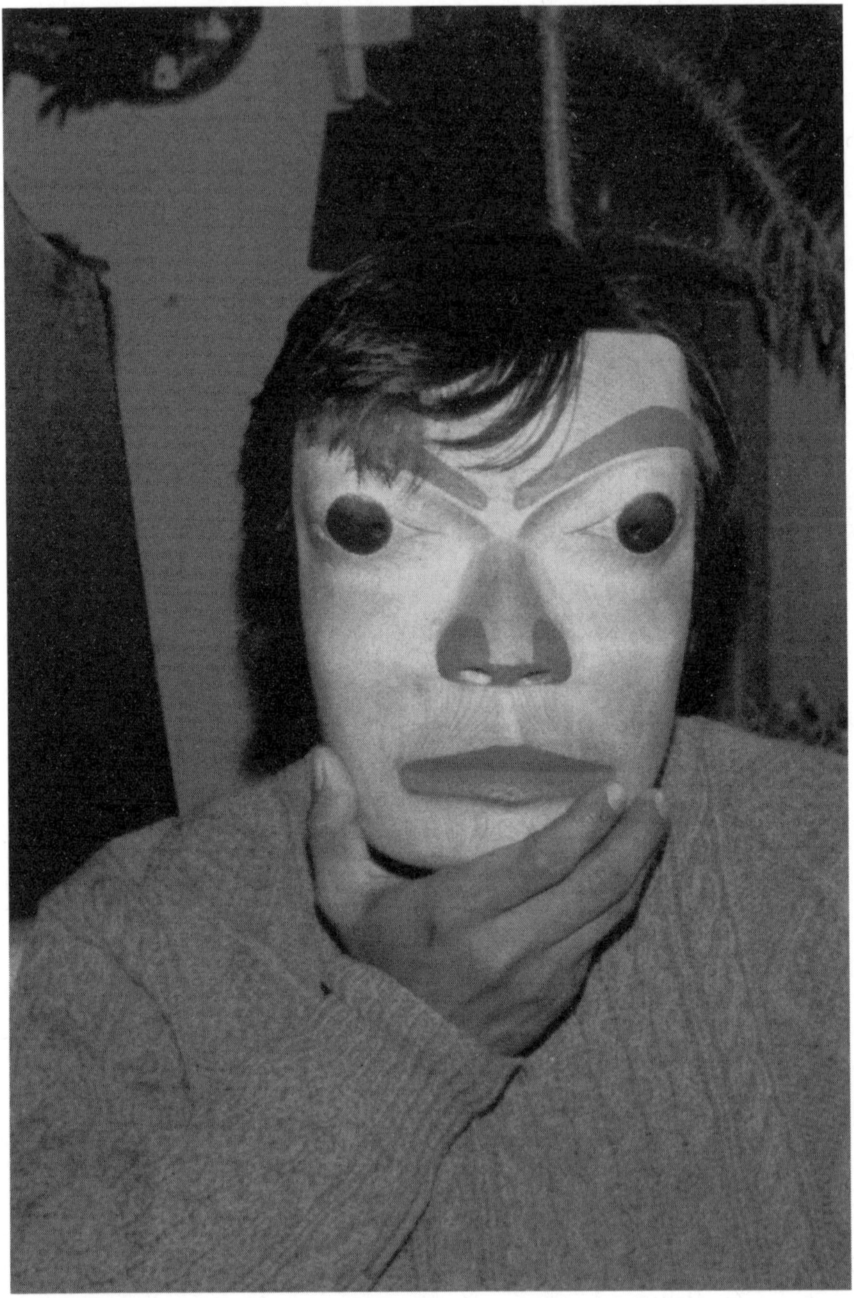

Slide 4: Dad, mask 2

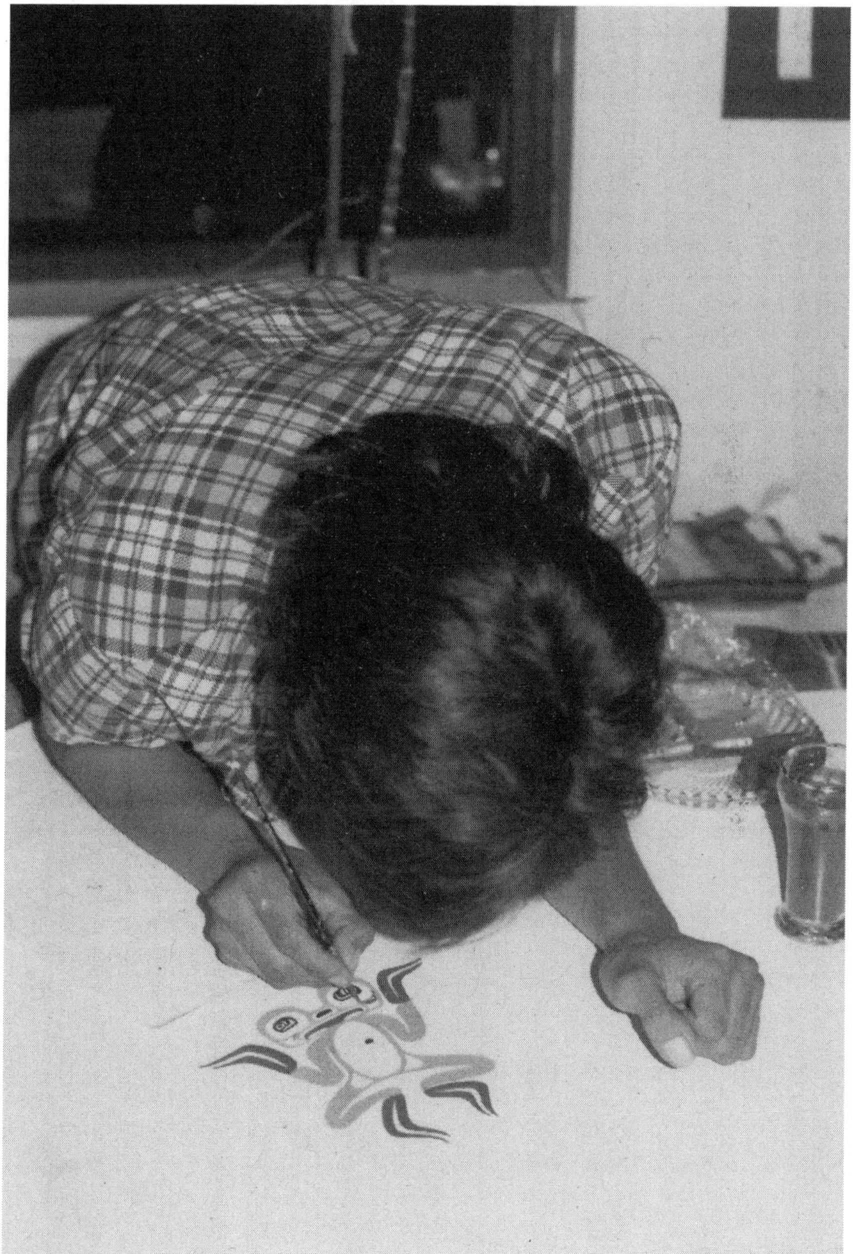

Slide 5: Dad, painting frog

15:34:37 Here is the finished frog. *[Slide 6]*

15:34:41 Here is my mom and my dad. *[Slide 7]*

15:34:46 Catherine Abel on the left.

15:34:50 Lawrence Wilson on the right.

15:34:53 They met sometime in early 1980s, and I was born on April 13, 1985.

15:35:00 In an affidavit from the Provincial Court of British Columbia between my mother and my father, dated May 8, 1996, the fourth line reads as follows:

15:35:10 "On June 15, 1987, Ms. Abel was advised by Detective Michael Miller of the Vancouver Police Department that Mr. Wilson was under investigation for a possible sexual assault against a fifteen-year-old girl."

15:35:19 Line 5 reads: "On June 16, 1987, Ms. Abel was advised that Mr. Wilson had, in fact, been charged with a sexual offence against a fifteen-year-old girl.

15:35:30 Thereafter, nothing was heard from Mr. Wilson.

15:35:36 He neither exercised his access pursuant to the terms of the Order of May 21, 1987, nor contacted Ms. Abel in any way.

15:35:41 Line 6 reads: "In the Fall of 1987, Ms. Abel confirmed her instructions to us to continue to act as her agent as she no longer resided in the province of British Columbia.

15:35:49 Her instructions were that we should notify Ms. Abel of any inquiries from Mr. Wilson or attempts to contact her so that she could make appropriate arrangements for the exercise of the access to which Mr. Wilson was entitled by Court Order."

Slide 6: Dad's frog painting

Slide 7: Mom + Dad photograph

15:35:59 Line 7: "Ms. Abel provided our office with her forwarding address following her departure from the province of British Columbia."

15:36:07 Line 8: "We have received no inquiries from Mr. Wilson, or anyone acting on his behalf,

15:36:15 with respect to the matter of access to the child, JORDAN SKAI WILSON ABEL, born April 13, 1985, since the date of our appearance in court on her behalf on May 21, 1987."

15:36:24 Line 9: "At the time of Mr. Wilson's disappearance in June of 1987, to the best of my knowledge and belief, Mr. Wilson has been in receipt of income assistance benefits for a period of some years and was not in a position to provide support.

15:36:35 That fact, combined with his disappearance, resulted in our recommendation to Ms. Abel not to pursue Mr. Wilson for child support.

15:36:42 Given that she continues to have no knowledge of his whereabouts

15:36:48 or financial circumstances,

15:36:51 the likelihood of any family support from Mr. Wilson is too remote to justify the costs associated with pursuing such an action."

15:36:58 The affidavit summarizes my mother's departure from BC,

15:37:05 the sexual abuse committed by my father,

15:37:11 and his subsequent disappearance.

15:37:18 But what the affidavit leaves out is that Lawrence Wilson,

15:37:25 shortly after becoming a father,

15:37:30 was also emotionally and physically abusive.

15:37:34 In a letter that my mother wrote to me around 2008, she says that "when [she] was seven or eight months pregnant,

15:37:43 Lawrence revealed [to her] that his father [my grandfather] had been violent to his mother [my grandmother]"

15:37:50 that he had "broken her leg, knocked out teeth, etc."

15:37:55 Later, she writes that, "not too long after Jordan had come home from the hospital, Lawrence's behavior changed."

15:38:02 She notes that "[Lawrence] became pathologically jealous," and that he "began to take out his anger physically on objects

15:38:10 —threw a chair and broke it, crashed the baby's drying rack over the empty crib and then clubbed [her] over the head while [she] was breastfeeding."

15:38:19 Later, she writes that she "finally got up the nerve to suggest" that "[they] weren't working out and should live separately."

15:38:28 Lawrence, apparently, took such great offence to this that he "knocked [her] on the floor and smashed a large clay ashtray over [her] head."

15:38:38 [According to the letter,] "he took off on his bicycle right after that."

15:38:45 Here, she notes that she departed immediately afterwards for Victoria, where her brother lived, and stayed there for two weeks to recover.

15:38:53

15:38:54

15:38:55

15:38:56

15:38:57

15:38:58

15:38:59

15:39:00

15:39:01 My first memories are of Ontario.

15:39:05 I lived with my mother.

15:39:11 None of the Indigenous side of my family was around.

15:39:15 She had told me that my father had disappeared

15:39:19 and that there was no way to contact him.

15:39:24 It turned out that this was mostly true.

15:39:30 I grew up not knowing and not understanding

15:39:35 why it was that I was completely disconnected from any Nisga'a people.

15:39:41 When I finally decided that I needed to figure it out,

15:39:46 I was eventually able to track down my father and several of my aunts and uncles.

15:39:52 But it was over the phone with my aunt Bonnie that everything in my life started to make sense:

15:39:57 why the Indigenous side of my family didn't talk to each other,

15:40:01 why I felt so isolated,

15:40:05 why everything was so broken.

15:40:10 She told me quite plainly that both my grandparents were survivors of residential schools.

15:40:16 In fact, they met each other in the same residential school.

15:40:22 She told me that the best she could describe it was that her parents,

15:40:26 that my grandparents,

15:40:29 had learned how to be parents from residential schools,

15:40:33 that all of that sexual, physical, and emotional abuse they had been taught in residential schools essentially raised them.

15:40:39 And that when it was time for them to become parents themselves, they passed all of that abuse down to my father's generation.

15:40:46 I think, for the first time in my life, I understood why I didn't know any of the Nisga'a side of my family.

15:40:53 I understood why my experience of Indigeneity was primarily based around confusion, disconnection, and isolation.

15:41:01 I began to understand that, even though I never attended residential school,

15:41:06 my life had actually been profoundly impacted by an intergenerational trajectory of violence,

15:41:12 and that the violence perpetrated by those schools didn't just stop after the schools were closed

15:41:19 or after the apology was issued.

15:41:22 My position—

15:41:25 as an urban Indigenous person growing up in the city without a connection to my home community and as a person impacted by intergenerational trauma—

15:41:34 is one of disconnection and lack.

15:41:39 The reason why I ended up turning to Barbeau's book for Indigenous knowledge can,

"*The pole of 'Neesyoq and 'Neeskyinwœt*, members of a Wolf clan at Gitlarhdamks, on upper Nass River. It stood seventh from the uppermost in the row of poles along the riverfront.

Description. It stood in front of a house called House-of-the-Sky (*wilplarhœ*) and belonged to the *ptsœn* type (hollow-back and carved all over). Its figures, from top to bottom, are: (1) mythical man with the deep-sea cockle adhering to a rock (*kal'own*) holding his hand fast—illustrating a myth; (2) the head of the Sperm Whale (*hlpoon*), the jaw hanging down; (3) Person (*gyet*) wearing a garment with many faces on it, probably the Garment-of-Marten (*gwisha'dao'tk*); (4) the bird Gyaibelk, at the bottom of the pole. This mythical bird was also used as a head-dress (*amhallait*) and as a spirit (*narhnorh* or *narhnok*).

Function, carver, age. Erected in memory of a former 'Neesyoq by the present (in 1927) chief of the same name, an old man. It no longer exists. Carved by Paræt'Nærhl, assisted by his son, about eighty years ago.

(Informant, Dennis Wood of Gitlarhdamks.)"

Marius Barbeau, *Totem Poles* (2:442)

Slide 8: The Place of Scraps, "The Silhouette of a Pole" (47)

15:41:45 I think,

15:41:48 be traced directly back to the legacy of violence created by Indian residential schools policy.

15:41:57 Here, I'd like to turn to a piece in *The Place of Scraps* called "The Silhouette of a Pole on the Shore of Nass River." *[Slide 8]*

15:42:03 The beginning page is, again, an excerpt from page 442 from *Totem Poles* by Marius Barbeau.

15:42:11 The second page of this piece is then an erasure of the excerpt from page 442.

15:42:17 Here, you can see my focus on the parentheses in the original excerpt. *[Slide 9]*

15:42:23 Here, on the third page, there are just the parentheses. *[Slide 10]*

(*wilplarhæ*) (
) ( )
(*kal'own*)
( )
(*hlpoon*) ( ) (*gyet*)
(*gwisha'dao'tk*) ( )
(*amhallait*)
(*narhnorh narhnok*)
( )
( )

Slide 9: *The Place of Scraps*, "The Silhouette of a Pole" (49)

( ) (
) ( )
( )
( )
( ) ( ) ( )
( ) ( )
( )
( )
( )
( )

Slide 10: The Place of Scraps, "The Silhouette of a Pole" (51)

(field)
(process wherein
language
readjusts to)
( ) (casualty
)
( )
(a description of)
(
all)

Slide 11: The Place of Scraps, "The Silhouette of a Pole" (53)

15:42:28 Here's the fourth page. *[Slide 11]*

15:42:33 And the fifth.

15:42:39 In the final page of this piece, we ultimately arrive at another excerpt. *[Slide 12]*

15:42:44 The erasures in this piece flow forward and backward and intersect in the middle.

15:42:51 Stephen Collis has called this intersection point a hinge page.

The silhouette of a pole on the shore of Nass River. When I was satisfied with the day (field notes completed) and when my ears were sufficiently exhausted by the translations (a process wherein an informant evaluates the qualities of a speech in one language and readjusts them to suit another language), I made my way back to the river. The branches from the trees overhead dipped onto the path (notable), and the needles bristled against my palms (a casualty of the ethnological process).

My informant (Dennis Wood), caught up with me at the bank of the river. He was out of breath, offering up my notebook in his hands. "You forgot this," he said, handing the book back to me. This gesture (a description of a bodily action) took me a moment to comprehend, but once I gathered myself, I patted him on the back and said, "Thank you." This affirmation was not lost on him, as he began to speak at once about the crested column that stood against the river. He explained that the man on the top was telling a story, and I gathered that he was comparing me to this man (as I had been endeavouring to learn all of their stories). Although I knew that I must be nothing like this man, I was flattered all the same, and did not object as my informant continued to speak.

Slide 12: The Place of Scraps, "The Silhouette of a Pole" (55)

15:42:58 The page in question, of course, is the middle page with the parentheses.

15:43:02 Here, there is a moment in the piece where the erasures from the first excerpt meet up with the erasures from the last excerpt.

15:43:10 The erasures, in this case, work in both directions.

15:43:15 The concept of the hinge, here, is really useful I think because it ties together

15:43:22 and in a certain way stabilizes

15:43:26 the points of intersection between Marius Barbeau's anthropological work in the first excerpt and my historic fiction masquerading as Barbeau's work in the final page.

15:43:34 The hinge page (as it is constructed in this piece)

15:43:40 appears a few times throughout *The Place of Scraps*

15:43:44 where it symmetrically balances two sides of a poem and the hinge appears precisely in the centre.

15:43:50 However, I would argue that there are also asymmetrical hinges in *The Place of Scraps*

15:43:56 and they are centered around the material excerpts from Marius Barbeau's work.

"*The pole of 'Neesyoq and 'Neeskyinwœt*, members of a Wolf clan at Gitlarhdamks, on upper Nass River. It stood seventh from the uppermost in the row of poles along the riverfront.

Description. It stood in front of a house called House-of-the-Sky (*wilplarhœ*) and belonged to the *ptsœn* type (hollow-back and carved all over). Its figures, from top to bottom, are: (1) mythical man with the deep-sea cockle adhering to a rock (*kal'own*) holding his hand fast—illustrating a myth; (2) the head of the Sperm Whale (*hlpoon*), the jaw hanging down;

(3) Person (*gyet*) wearing a garment with many faces on it, probably the Garment-of-Marten (*gwisha'dao'tk*); (4) the bird Gyaibelk, at the bottom of the pole. This mythical bird was also used as a head-dress (*amhallait*) and as a spirit (*narhnorh* or *narhnok*).

Function, carver, age. Erected in memory of a former 'Neesyoq by the present (in 1927) chief of the same name, an old man. It no longer exists. Carved by Paræt'Nærhl, assisted by his son, about eighty years ago.

(Informant, Dennis Wood of Gitlarhdamks.)"

Marius Barbeau, *Totem Poles* (2:442)

Slide 8 (repeat): The Place of Scraps, "The Silhouette of a Pole" (47)

15:44:02 Here, again, is the first page from the poem.

15:44:06 What I would like to suggest is that this page is a kind of asymmetrical hinge that on *one side* of this excerpt

15:44:12 holds my experience and position as both an intergenerational survivor of trauma and lived experience as an urban Indigenous person

15:44:19 *and on the other side* of the excerpt holds my dismantling of colonial authority and simultaneous articulation of an Indigenous voice.

15:44:27 Here, every moment in which a material excerpt comes up in *The Place of Scraps*,

15:44:32 the moments that precede that excerpt are also the moments in which I, as the author, am attempting to grapple with my own experiences as an intergenerational survivor.

15:44:41 The moments that precede these excerpts are the moments where I am forced to search for Indigenous knowledge through Marius Barbeau

15:44:50 because of the ways in which intergenerational trauma has impacted my ability to connect directly with members of my community.

15:44:57 What I'm trying to get at is that I think you can read these asymmetrical hinges

15:45:03 (and the materiality of Barbeau's work)

15:45:09 as attempts to represent both the lived experiences of intergenerational trauma and the experiences of urban Indigenous peoples.

15:45:15 After all, what does it mean to be an intergenerational survivor of residential schools?

15:45:20 What does it mean to be an urban Indigenous person?

15:45:26 What does it mean to be Nisga'a?

15:45:32 What does it mean to be Indigenous?

15:45:37 What counts as lived Indigenous experience?

15:45:42 What doesn't?

15:45:46 What does it mean to be an Indigenous person without a connection to a home community?

15:45:51 What does it mean to attend to the communities of dispossessed Indigenous peoples who don't have access to the knowledges and languages of their nations?

15:46:00 And who is allowed to answer these questions?

15:46:04 Thank you.

15:46:09 [Inaudible]

Listening at Mikinaakominis / TransCanadas 2017

/ ERÍN MOURE

First, I wish to acknowledge the nations of the Huron-Wendat, Petun, Seneca, and the Mississauga of the Credit River on whose lands we met. I live on territory never ceded by the Kanien'kehá:ka, in the city known as Montreal and as Tiotià:ke tsi ionhwéntsare. I am an allergic person and a lesbian, thus doubly queered; a settler and immigrant descendant certainly, and a woman, thus always under threat of violence from the patriarchal order whose privilege dominates in all communities. Because of the particularities of my maternal Latynnyky and Ukrainian history, I also experience generational effects of the Holocaust as it was carried out in successively occupied and colonized territories that today form western Ukraine—the model for which was the US Army's genocidal clearing of the plains of Indigenous Peoples and buffalo, as addressed by Tasha Hubbard in this volume. I am a translator and poet. I speak English because I grew up in Calgary. The lands there, governed by Treaty 7, are traditional territories of the Niitsitapi (Siksika, Piikani, and Kainai, known as the Blackfoot Confederacy) as well as the Nakota and Tsuut'ina. I grew up directly across the Elbow River and reservoir from today's Tsuut'ina reserve lands, in a bygone time in which children grew up *outside*. As such, the terrain there and its light and smells and shadows—river, banks, reservoir delta, fish, frogs, trees, bushes, berries, cliffs, ducks, bear, mice, crows—is the terrain of my earliest imagination, and it still feeds me and guides my spirit and memory.

I see poetry as a mode of thinking, one that enables openings, paradoxes, and unspeakable and painful connectivities to coexist and be confronted with our bodies—those loci from where thoughts come and memory abides.

I started composing this text before the 2017 Mikinaakominis / TransCanadas conference, thinking of all of us there in corporeal proximity. I thought about what proximity of beings might be able to bring about in the *agora*, which is the *now* and also the space of public proximity of beings who do not share kinship attachments. And I wanted to come to listen.

Because, in a white settler state, my own identifying process is prompted and conditioned by Western European philosophical thought, I thought of philosopher Giorgio Agamben (philosophy being a kind of poetry) talking about Aristotle's view of *to ti ên einai* (1999, 37)—what being is, and the location of being—a phrase linked unavoidably with time, with a past progressive or continuing tense of a verb that denotes existence. We recognize our own selves as beings because *on était*, we just *were* beings and that condition is not ended. In our present, then, there is always already a tie to a past.

Giorgio Agamben locates, in Aristotle's expression *to ti ên einai*, a fault in our Western ways of translation, for the term can be translated two ways. By choosing one translation over the other, we lose a necessary reverberation. Two things, then, I think, are operative in constituting public space, in receiving the *agora* as *now*: time and translation.

To talk first of time, the time of the *était*, of my recognizing my continuity in time as a something, an existence. I have existence, I am, because I was just here a moment ago and that "just here" is still ongoing. The *était* provides only a linear sense of time, one that is very much horizontal, shallow, short.

What I heard at Mikinaakominis / TransCanadas—from Eileen Antone, Rinaldo Walcott, Chris Lee, Dina Al-Kassim, Rita Wong, and Tasha Hubbard, who are included in this volume, as well as from Lee Maracle, Rehab Nazzal, and others—is different. This difference is an articulation of being and time that is deeply located, locatable, generational, and extends, particularly in the case of Indigenous being, here and elsewhere, to a deep knowledge of place, plants, winds, water, animals, grasses, land formations, colours of air. There is a notion of deep time in this knowledge and operation of being. (And it is not just "rural" but urban too; it can't be reduced to a European concept of "nature." To do that would be to perpetrate a further form of injustice.)

Whereas Western European thought uses deep time to refer to geological eras, deep time in Indigenous epistemologies everywhere includes kinship, a kinship that affirms that we are kin with the grasses, with the olive trees. The rest of us, white settler peoples in particular, in Canada for example, myself included, need to vacate our notion of shallow and horizontal time (the only time that could give rise to the notion of "progress") to learn more about and absorb more of deep time into our sense of being, for without a deep-time kinship-sense with these lands we live in, we cannot know fully enough *why* we are resisting and do not realize *how* we endanger ourselves if we don't resist the dictates of shallow time as they are variously played out in the world.

Time: deep time. We need it. Land. Not landscape. Land. Not wilderness.

The political trouble (a necessary trouble and not a negative one) that I see arising for us settler peoples is that, if we accept and allow ourselves to enter this notion of deep time that engages us in place and kinship differently, the issue that emerges is not simply that of "reconciliation" but of "reparation and return," not just of land (though yes, reparation and return of land must be part of any future equitable sharing of the spaces where we live, of spaces as coincident with being, and not "owned" for extraction or accumulation) but of systems of governance, of thinking and relation, that would govern us too. All of us. Because if we settler peoples accept deep time into our notion of our own being, we must learn how to be here, in this deep time, differently. There are peoples and nations who already have this knowledge; we settlers don't need to take the lead. But we need to respond and make room for leaders.

Translation. The issue of choosing one translation, one meaning over another, exists even within a single language. We often risk shutting things down with our choices instead of holding things open because holding things open imperils our well-honed ability to live in shallow time, to sense ourselves as beings in relation to nothing more than an immediately preceding Aristotelian moment.

We can benefit, in these matters of translation and choice of words, from listening better so as to work with, and listen to and through, Indigenous epistemologies, governance, ways of thinking of the word, of reading, of water, plants and hills, and this, here in Canada as well as in and from other parts of the world. To do this we need other languages, works and texts in languages other than our own "official" ones. There are people in Central and South America working on Indigenous issues, for example; we need to have their work translated, and then read it, in order to expand our own ability to "hold open," an ability that will allow us to depart from shallow time. There are works—in French, in Spanish, in Arabic—that deal with issues that colonialism and shallow time have wrought not just here but elsewhere, with which we too need to grapple. As well, we need to translate and read the works of people who discuss and see our Canadian literatures from outside. I think here of the first book of Belén Martín-Lucas, published over twenty years ago now, in Spanish, dealing with short-story cycles written in Canada by women from immigrant cultures, and exposing even then the cruel lie of Canadian multiculturalism. Twenty years ago, when as writer-in-residence at the University of Toronto, I tried to find a home for this crucial book to join our dialogues about ourselves in translation. I was told no one would want to read it as it didn't line up with how Canadians see ourselves. There was an utter unwillingness to change our frame, to risk changing it. To live with the trouble.

No matter what the subject matter of our own research, we need to support and facilitate every effort of writers and thinkers to work, to publish and film, to argue and translate, in and via Anishinaabemowin, in and via Cree, in and via Dene-Athapascan tongues, just to name a few of the more widespread Indigenous languages of our own space-time, so that their words and thinking may occupy a rightful place in our language-space-time, that is, in the *agora*, the public *now*. In the absence of these languages, the *agora* is broken because without these languages of this space-time and deep time, this space of *now* has chosen one translation and a system of equivalences that silences, that subsists on a view of shallow time. This necessary infusion of languages and words is starting to happen with young scholars and writers, has happened more and more deeply since the conference in 2017, and will happen more, and needs to.

To do all this, we need behaviour that risks change according to new rules we as settlers do not define, oh yes. Settler persons, for our part, can listen. Openness in listening means putting yourself, your formulations of yourself, at risk. This is not comfortable. But when you are doing it, you can potentially change the institutions of government and of the university, make them bend and move. And crumble, where necessary. We need to open ourselves to the deep time exemplified in Indigenous epistemologies to learn and act with the words in the tongues of this place, the plants here, the sound the grasses make, our sisters and brothers, the birch and willow, who know how to find water, and the future of water, learning and acting in solidarity with the olive trees and aquifers here and elsewhere, too, or we will not have a future at all.

Back to the Future

Black Canada's Past and Present, or the Changing Same

/ RINALDO WALCOTT

For BLM TO *(especially Yusra)*

> A society or nation such as Canada, founded on the principles of white supremacy and racism, cannot ever succeed in developing a society free of the injustices that spring from these systems of thought, without a clearly articulated policy on the need to eradicate these beliefs.
>
> —M. NourbeSe Philip, "Why Multiculturalism Can't End Racism," *Frontiers*

> Though this institution (OISE) did allow me to work on issues of race and gender, I was chafed by its formalities and protocols and had to strategise, a little like a guerrilla, around some of those—for example, I shaped my topic and wrote the first draft of my thesis before forming my committee, hoping to overwhelm rather than persuade the two professors.
>
> —Dionne Brand, "Dualities," *Bread Out of Stone*

I

Twenty years ago, in *Black Like Who: Writing Black Canada*, I called for the development of a grammar for Black in Canada. The urgency of that call remains today. Indeed, we might argue that, while the Canadian state has a grammar for Black, a grammar for us, we remain still woefully without our own grammars for narrating our relationship to the Canadian state in a manner that provides a collective response to the state's continued subjection of Black possibilities. The Canadian state continues to mark us as marginal, as abject, that is, not worthy of full citizenship, and we have yet to offer the kind of response to such practices in a way that would force the state to account for its ongoing slave and plantation logics of and for Black life. Furthermore, much of our politics, even when articulated through an engagement with and critique of anti-Black racism, finds itself lodged in the insidious rhetoric of state multicultural difference (Jamaican Canadian, African Nova Scotians, Somali Canadian, Black Somali Muslim, and so on). In this manner, and in the face of state brutalities, Black life in Canada, while often spectacularly gesturing to a grammar of Black that might hold our collective desires for a life in full view, remains woefully absent. This chapter draws on a methodology of what Avery Gordon calls "often barely there" (1997, 174) to (re)invent anew the necessary language and conditions for mobilizing conversations about Black people in Canada that do not always appear to begin from scratch. Our present-future depends on recognizing continuities as well as new eruptions.

I want to attempt to both bridge the gap between Black difference and its multiplicities and simultaneously point to our commonalities as a source for articulating a future that is now. I hope that my articulation of a future that is now works as a buttress against the current moment that seeks to offer us a future of the same—that is, a future that is already our past and our present. In recent moments of Black resistance to the Canadian state no better example comes to mind than Black Lives Matter Toronto (BLM TO). In their articulation of what might be at stake for Black life, BLM TO has cast a net that recognizes Black difference at the same time that it articulates a strategic politics of Black commonalities. This method of political action demonstrates how Black feminist politics, despite never being given its full credit, has come to be a significant foundation of our activist present, although the debt owed to liberal and radical Black women alike has, until now, remained unspoken.

The activists in the Movement for Black Lives have been clear about their influences and debts. By this I mean that since at least the 1960s Black feminist formations have pointed to the politics of commonality without erasing differences while insisting on a critique of and confrontation with state violence of all kinds. In opposition to their critique of the state, multicultural arrangements have pointed to cultural difference while retaining the governance of the status quo with a few adjustments to it. There are increasingly some logics of Black difference that draw on a distorted Black feminist politics of difference and its radical insights to subordinate those very insights into commodified liberal-state multicultural identity claims. Identity in this formulation becomes a saleable claim of recognition and inclusion as a commodified singular representation. In particular, there are rhetorics of intersectionality that are easily reducible down to desires to enter the state apparatus as a singular representative figure on the basis of an identity claim. It is often a claim produced as political when, in fact and substance, it is an identity market-based claim. Thus in this chapter I want to further push the limits of what might be at stake for our collective futures when common desires are articulated in opposition to the singularity of commodified state multicultural identity claims.

The invitation to participate in this symposium, which marks 150 years of the slaveholding settler colony of Canada, poses a number of significant conundrums for me. In thinking how I might approach the question of the evolving Blackness in Canada, I turn to a critique of the Canadian state and Black interaction with it to articulate a set of concerns about the limits of national frames for affirmation, inclusion, and logics of belonging. Recently, the British Association of Canadian Studies announced its program for a conference specifically commemorating Canada 150, which included, from what I can tell, only one Black scholar chairing a session and not giving a paper.[1] The conference program replicated a particular relationship to Blackness and Black people that is coterminous with the Canadian state. I point to this example because we cannot divorce the role that universities play in the continued absented-presence of Black people's lives in Canada and beyond.

2

Let us then dream of a different Canada. What would a different, more ethical Canada look like? How would Black people find themselves located in such a Canada? What would it mean for the nation to sustain a conversation about Black people that does not relegate them to the unseen and unheard spaces of national concerns? How might our Black Canadian ancestors, to crib from Barbara Christian, be put to rest in ways that would finally accord them the peace they require? To do so, I believe, would require a rethinking of the foundational narratives of the nation-state. Such a rethinking would have to involve the politics of reconciliation and reparation in a move toward justice and freedom. And importantly, such a rethinking would have to begin with (re)writing the narratives of Indigenous peoples and their imagined and actual stewardship of the land we call Canada in the face of ongoing brutal dispossession. Such a fundamental reimagining of the nation-state would have to come to terms with its violent founding not as one of European triumph but, rather, as a story of the continuing atrocities of the Enlightenment and early modernity.

Such a challenge places an enormous burden on us to rethink a series of claims about colonialism, settler colonies, modernity, citizenship, and a host of post-1492 conditions, ideas, and commitments that are embedded in the normative national discourse. As far as Black diaspora peoples are concerned, one of the first commitments toward justice and making freedom actual might be a commitment to abandon the nation-state as a possibility for living a life. Black people's commitment to nation-states, especially those of the North Atlantic, has been fundamental to their dispossession of full citizenship and its accompanying rights; this is the case even in countries in the "New World" where Black people are in the majority. The question of national affiliation and belonging is therefore one in which the ethics of citizenship can be rethought and, let's be frank, reproportioned so that citizenship might eventually come close to meaning the same thing for all of us regardless of creed, race, gender, sexuality, religion, disability, etc. This is no small ethical task; still, it is worth trying with all our energy to think of a world that might be ethically borderless and postcapital.

Nonetheless, in this particular moment, I am interested in elaborating the story of Canada because the silences, the missing bits, are all part of a pregnant narrative that can potentially give birth to a very different kind of story, indeed, a different kind of present-future. But we might also think of elaboration in the Gramscian sense, which involves more than adding to a story, but changing, instead, its very foundation by elaborating that which is already there: animating the story in ways that have been denied by the story itself, in ways that reveal the story's possibilities. In this sense, it is not only a story of victimhood that emerges but also a story that elaborates the nation and potentially remakes the state. I have decidedly moved away from a language of inclusion and reforming the nation because inclusion and reform ring too close to carceral logics and practices, precisely what Black diaspora people by and large have spent the last five hundred years resisting in this part of the world and beyond. Instead, elaboration offers a way to tell the story of a nation and account for its violent institution all the while working through the trauma of that violent institution so that reparation might be possible.

The attempt to make reparation for the violent founding of the nation and the continuation of its violence to hold its national myths in place represents a move toward a more ethical accounting of the nation and, hopefully, a more ethical politics of life and living. Such hope is not beyond the capacity of humans to imagine and institute in the configurations we have come to call nations. But what is more difficult to achieve and dislodge are the myths of communal belonging that produce the conditions and narratives of unbelonging that modern nations have developed as a science of the social. The techniques of multicultural policies and rhetorics of inclusion with their slippery slopes of heritage discourse leading some to slide right out of the national narrative, while others remain firmly ensconced as national founders, is one such moment where the ethicality of the nation can be rethought to produce a more meaningful citizenship narrative and conditions of belonging. This is difficult work, but it is the work from which community is made and remade as a process for making a national polity that is informed and committed to mutual human concerns and not to the fortress walls of racial purity—even when it must publicly concede that such thinking is no longer fashionable (here I think of Quebec specifically and its religious symbols law, but also its general concern with cultural difference, which is almost always marked as not-white). This ethical work can only begin when we work through our various hauntings, our discomforts, and our violences. In essence, we can try to figure out other ways of making nations that are not founded in origins of violence, as Gayatri Spivak has put it (1993, 195). This is the work of the ethical. This is the work that moves us toward the potential to make reparation far beyond the current logics that cannot image reparation beyond capitalist frames of reference and monetary accumulation and proprietariness.

3

In this country we are satisfied to have ONE. We have become trained that ONE is our number, our lonely number. ONE Black person at a major cultural institution; ONE in political office; ONE police chief; ONE university president; ONE cabinet minister; ONE that is called on for all manner of things; ONE or maybe two on television, radio, and so on. This condition of the ONE, of singularity, is the term, the period, the temporality of our recognition and inclusion under state multiculturalism. Its representative value is to render the many who are not there null and void; we are to seek solace in the ONE as a source of our collective well-being. Quite often the association to the collective bothers the ONE, working both consciously and unconsciously as representative, often resentfully so, because they want to believe in their individual accomplishment. This condition of state representative selection as constitutive of our collective desires and possibilities belies a central dilemma of contemporary incorporative multicultural recognition politics. State multiculturalism is both seduction and containment. But it is more containment than anything else and we should be by now clear about that.

Given the ways in which our actual multicultural differences are called upon and manipulated, and indeed the ways in which we have come to invest in them ourselves, this condition of seeking state recognition while simultaneously insisting on our various specialisms places our politics and thus our futures in a precarious and dangerous fashion. On the question of the minoritization of our lives I turn to Sylvia Wynter as a guide. In "On Disenchanting Discourse," Wynter offers a critique of minority discourse as one that is a "negative Ontological Other category set defined by the *liminality* of our location" (1990, 236). She argues that "it is precisely as such liminal subjects, able to experience to varying degrees the injustices '*inherent in structure*,' that we are able to, in the words of the anthropologist Legesse, to 'disenchant' our fellow subjects from the structure's categories and prescriptions" (1990, 237). What Wynter is cueing us to is that by accepting our minority status and articulating our desires from such a place, we do not shift the present order of knowledge. But her insistence on disenchantment also alerts us to the ways in which Black feminist liminality has allowed for a critique of structure, otherwise known as the state, to be noticed from their own unique location.

The critique of minority discourse is essential to the kind of future we might begin to imagine and figure out how to put in place. I say so to work my way back to the claim that BLM TO, along with other BLM chapters across this country, offers us an opportunity to think about this problem in a strategic way. What I mean is that without articulating it as such, BLM refuses the minority discourse model as a mode for its organizing. BLM's insistence on what they call "intersecting identities," together with their explicit engagement with Indigenous calls for justice, reframes multicultural recognition and its singularity in a number of important ways, as does Karina Vernon's chapter in this volume. This organizational model, which is indebted to at least three decades of Black and women of colour feminist activism, scholarship, and other insights, demonstrates the long and sustained contributions of marginalized feminists' analyses and critiques of the state. Indeed, one might read the emergence of BLM and the larger Movement for Black Lives as a triumph of a certain Black feminist politics that often had to hide out on the margins of the university, heterosexual hypermasculine community organizing, and white women–led movements and organizations too. The need to hide out was an especially acute case given how many of those feminists also identified as lesbians. This brief recounting of a certain Black feminist and woman of colour feminist history is not a valorization of it but an attempt to delineate what is actually at stake when difference is at stake. More importantly, I make this claim because we cannot fully appreciate the last forty years of North American social change without adequately grappling with the counteroffensives that Black women have launched at the state and its subcontractors that have made all of our lives appear even when the offensive is eventually defeated or eventually fails.

In her essay "Brownman, Tiger...," Dionne Brand (1994) eloquently and broadly speaks to the difficulty of belonging for Black people. She does not stop at the borders of the nation-state of Canada but speaks to North America as a whole:

> The truth is that North America does not need Black people any more; neither Canada not the U.S. needs the cheap labour assigned to our skins, and you can tell this by the slow criminalisation of social protest and by the job of interesting a disaffected, cynical, commodity-sated white public in human rights and by the demonisation of the masses of Black people in North America on the television screens and in newspapers and magazine reports. They no longer need us for the cheap and degraded labour which we've represented across the centuries of our lives here. (1994, 71)

Brand's essay was a response to the indignity of all Black men, and Black people generally in Toronto, being criminalized upon the event of the murder of a young white woman at Just Desserts, an upscale Toronto eatery. But what is crucial about the essay's insights is how it plums the ways in which Black people remain tangential to the nation, a disposable people. Brand echoes this as she recalls waiting for the second Rodney King verdict:

> These are the times that Black people feel most unsafe, most vulnerable; when we are almost one person, when the next move that's made by anyone even vaguely associated with power will determine the conditions we'll live under, when some incident happening to just one of us somewhere—doesn't matter where—sends a warning to the rest of us to watch out, take heart, panic, understand, take example, despair, be joyful... (1994, 74)

This paragraph captures presciently the rise of BLM TO and the larger Movement for Black Lives globally, our becoming one in defense of our lives against brutal, anti-Black states. Brand invokes diaspora connectedness and sensibility, but also importantly enfolded in her writing is the caution of how tenuous a hold Black people have on national belonging anywhere. Black people are always in danger of going missing, a condition that, in Brand's words, echoes the unspoken fear of a violent disappearance, a fear not unfounded given the histories of Black people in this part of the world. It is this tenuousness to belonging that the Canadian state animates by its inability to sustain interactions with Black people and Blackness beyond those of subjected and abject relations. However, we are in a moment when the project of the Canadian state must now contend with those Canadians who have been here for two, three, or even more generations, whom Cecil Foster wrote about in a powerful Black Canadian lament that undoes George Grant's.

Indeed, Foster's *A Place Called Heaven* was published just a few years after some of the principles in the Movement for Black Lives had been born. These young Black people—now in their twenties or at the most their early thirties—uncompromisingly forge connections between the locality of their everyday lives and Black lives elsewhere, reminding us of the viciousness of state brutalities and violences in encounters with Black people. In more recent times the brutal police killings in the United States and Canada have produced among them a feeling of "almost one person," as Brand put it. This feeling has galvanized them into forming a movement, yet the brilliance of their movement is that it does not sacrifice that "almost one person" feeling as a site for not grappling with difference. Instead, we pay witness to a movement where the "almost one person" is subtended by modes and identities that intersect to offer a textured politics of action, resistance, and demands.

We cannot think of the evolving context of Black Canada or Black life in Canada without going through the upheavals of the 1990s. I want to highlight the fact that this year marks twenty-five years of Marlene NourbeSe Philip's *Frontiers: Essays and Writings on Racism and Culture*, a landmark collection that forcefully placed the question of anti-Black racism in literary culture and beyond into the public sphere. It was followed by Foster's *A Place Called Heaven* and Brand's *Bread Out of Stone*. This year too marks the twenty-fifth anniversary of the Yonge Street Riots and the much-referenced Stephen Lewis Report, which specified anti-Blackness as constitutive of the Toronto city-state and, by extension, the state of Canada. As well, 2017 marks fifty years of the now stolen gift of Caribana, stolen from Black people by corporate interests and the city-state of Toronto. We are quickly coming upon the thirty-year anniversary of large-scale Somali migration to Canada beginning in 1989, and more recently the reconciliation efforts between the Black community and the Royal Ontario Museum concerning the latter's *Into the Heart of Africa* exhibit of the same year. I list these moments to point to the ways in which a possible future of Black life in Canada must reckon with a past that is not yet past, and to note that Black activism has always shaped a future of sorts.

Black activism, especially in the arts, is a good example of what is often at stake when Black people confront the Canadian state and its apparatus. Black activists quickly devolve into "racial archetypes in our culture" (Brand 1994, 75), often portending the idea that violence is about to erupt; such archetypes structure the ways in which Black people and Blackness are responded to and through which we also act. Let us take a detour through the 1980s and 1990s cultural activism as a case in point.

In the late 1980s and 1990s, activists' protests attempted to open up the possibilities for art making by people of colour across a wide range of disciplines. The results of this work cannot and should not be easily discounted in Canada. For example, in publishing, a range of small presses and major presses began to publish the works of non-white Canadians, producing a robust list of writers working in the forms of the novel and poetry. Indeed, in a certain register the cultural work was quite successful drawing on the discourse of multiculturalism and antiracism to both contest representation and to produce altered forms of state and other kinds of recognition. In other registers, that work was also tremendously painful and difficult, both personally and collectively, and some individuals paid a significant personal and professional price for challenging the system as it was then (here I think of NourbeSe Philip). The challenge to institutional power at that time still bares its scars today. The silence on one of Canada's best living poets, NourbeSe Philip, is a case in point. It appears that she has yet not been forgiven for her significant critiques of numerous Canadian cultural institutions and their racist programming as well as their structural racist exclusions.

What is quite profound about the art activism of that period is that the activists already understood the problem to be a problem of structure. In that moment, they understood the practice of exclusion and misrecognition to be structural and therefore fixable. I will return to structure later, but suffice to say now, it is extremely clear that the structure was not fixable; it was only malleable. The malleability of the structure allowed for a whole new set of structures to emerge to manage and buttress the inclusion of Black and people of colour into the existing institutions. Those new institutional arrangements, going under the names and functions of equity offices, came up with well-conceived and well-written policies bearing the same names and offices conceived, developed, and implemented by activists invited by the institutions to sit on committees to spearhead institutional change. In fact, in the aftermath of this committee work, many artists found themselves drawn into institutions to implement and run such offices. However, it is pretty clear that, following the 1980s/1990s art activism, equity offices, equity officers, and the most fantastic equity policies did not, indeed could not, change structures that are fundamentally anti-Black.

Andrea Fatona has documented this period of arts activism in Canada by concentrating on the Canada Council for the Arts (CC). The CC is a national body that funds professional artists across a range of disciplines. Its main method of assessment is the peer-review or juried method. Fatona documents the period between 1989 and 1999, a period that I have already argued was the most fertile period of non-white artists' contestations of exclusion, their simultaneous piecemeal inclusion and a creative output that has since dwindled, at least publicly. In this work she interviews all the major players, artists and professionals who worked inside the CC, including its senior directors in the transformation of the CC's engagement with non-white artists. In her study Fatona finds that Black artists-activists played a significant and leading role in organizing and challenging the institution, but also in leading and working with the institution to effect meaningful change. Indeed, meaningful change, if it could be called that, was fleeting and, one might argue, it was not achieved at all. In the aftermath of the heroic efforts, NourbeSe Philip's critique remains important still. She wrote: "Multiculturalism as we know it, has no answers for the problem of racism or white supremacy—unless it is combined with a clearly articulated policy of anti-racism, directed at rooting out the effects of racist and white supremacist thinking" (Philip 1992, 185; Fatona 2011, 119). Fatona writes that the CC, unlike other institutions, eventually acknowledged institutional racism (2011, 193), but such an acknowledgement did not and does not support a sustained level of engagement for Black artists across Canada. So why is this so?

Indeed, it is my contention that what became clearer post-2000 are the ways in which anti-Blackness at the structural level has worked and continues to work to make Black art and Black art-makers disappear and/or occupy only a tangential relation to national institutions. Importantly, there is nothing like a crisis to demonstrate the ways in which racial capitalism shapes Black life. The repeated crises of neoliberal capitalism, alongside the security and surveillance post-9-11, made this clear to many of us, if it was not clear before. In documenting changes at the Canada Council for the Arts between 1989 and 1999, Fatona writes: "The issue of racial hierarchies amongst people of color was mentioned in relation to the First Advisory Committee for Racial Equality at the Canada Council for the Arts. The issue also arose in my conversations with Black artists regarding multi-racial activist formations in the communities" (2011, 190). Racial hierarches work to produce "the black" as "the dysslected" other as Sylvia Wynter terms it, meaning the furthest away from whiteness and thus the most impossible to incorporate structurally. However, my argument is that incorporation is fundamentally impossible for "the Black." Furthermore, the conditions under which incorporation is understood are so deeply freighted with the detritus of racial capital and white supremacist logics that incorporation can and only does occur at the symbolic level, leaving all other Black beings or Black life forms marked for poverty and death as a repetition of modern life (see Walcott 2014).

The starkness of my claims is positioned alongside the accounting for how neoliberal changes in full effect produced an abundance of what Zygmunt Bauman (2003) has termed "wasted lives," to recall Brand on disposability earlier. When one takes such an insight to the art world and its institutions—art galleries, printing houses, museums, festivals, and so on—one can see how these practices and conditions are linked to larger phenomena like Black death. The unsustainability of the project of incorporation is revealed in the moment when what looks like change meets its demise in the moment of economic claims or a crisis of economy. I make this case because one could see a significant change in the Canadian art world at the moment of art activism in the 1980s and the 1990s, but once that long decade came to a close, the kinds of activities that had been previously present and made possible by activism disappeared in the 2000s, especially after 2001. Why was it not sustained? The 2000s mark the full onslaught of the neoliberal project in Canada. Thus part of the story is the way in which neoliberal reordering of the economics of the cultural sphere impacted how policies for equitably sharing resources were interrupted by logics of efficiencies, radical individualism, managerialism, audit culture, and so on. However, when neoliberalism and anti-Blackness combine, the impact on Black art and Black art makers produced a profound context of disappearance and one might say remade the landscape in a manner that now calls for renewed forms of activism.

The world of writing is a case in point. The same writers who made the move from the small presses to the larger national and international presses exist today as they did two decades ago: the late Austin Clarke, Dionne Brand, Lawrence Hill, Cecil Foster, André Alexis, and so on. A few younger writers—Esi Edugyan, David Chariandy, and Wayde Compton—have made it into that realm, but by and large Black writers remain locked out of significant forms of circulation, and their work is mostly published by small presses. This inability to sustain ongoing incorporation in fact points to how fundamentally the structural underpinnings remain and are indeed anti-Black. Incorporation only works temporally at the moment of contestation and confrontation, but left to its routinization, it reverts back to exclusion and diminution. It is my argument that the unsustainability of incorporation is not merely anti-Black but that its anti-Blackness is foundational to capitalism and its asymmetrical and disjunctive practices—what we call inequality. However, what I want us to notice is the role that Black feminism played in this period. Lillian Allen had a leading role in the CC debates and its restructuring; Philip, in the literary communities, attempted to grapple with its ghosts; Makeda Silvera and Stephanie Martin founded Sister Vision Press and brought into being an array of Black, POC, and queer writing especially, but more than that too. And in this period we were still living through the Black women and WOC overthrow of white women at Women's Press with Angela Robertson emerging as its editor, alongside significant fights in small magazines like *Fuse*, *Border/lines*, and *C Magazine*, resulting in the dissolution of ANNPAC and *C Magazine* transforming into *Mix*, edited by Karen Miranda Augustine and then Peter Hudson. In all these instances Black and women of colour feminists worked together to change the scene and to make Toronto and Canada a little more just. The aftermath did not always do right by Black women, though. It somehow found them always having to regroup against multiple forces inside and outside their communities. This pattern continues today.

If those feminists articulated a "new politics of cultural difference," as Cornel West (1992, 93) once termed it, to confront the state and its apparatus in all manner of ways, then today's Movement for Black Lives is embedded in a similar terrain. A confrontation with the state that is both new and simultaneously continuous, largely led by women-identified queer folks, marks a significant difference. The Black Lives Matter movement across North America has forced a reconsideration of the terms of emancipation, freedom, and liberation. For fifteen days in March 2016, Black Lives Matter Toronto occupied the Toronto Police Services headquarters courtyard. They had a number of very simple, yet important, demands. They wanted the two-day Afrofest festival to remain a two-day event after it was reduced to one day by the city due to a few noise complaints; they wanted the "subject officer" to be named and arrested in the shooting of Andrew Loku, a mentally ill African (Sudanese) migrant shot in the hallway of his apartment building, a building that housed the mentally ill; and they wanted an end to carding (stop and frisk), which disproportionately targets Black and Brown Torontonians. Those kinds of demands point to how the state shapes Black life experience in ways that continually mark the thin line between life and death. Importantly for me, the actions of activist groups like BLM TO open up an arena for rethinking how forms of Black life interact with the state as the very means of a possible survival. A popular refrain of the BLM movement is "we will get free." I am interested in what work the refrain does, as it encounters and lives "within and against" the state.

In my view, the actions of BLM and other Black radical activist groups presently engaged in direction action tactics return us to the languages and ideas of freedom, emancipation, and liberty in a manner that requires both a searing and engaged critique of their signifying intentions. I hope to point to rethinking those terms as a long and enduring project of Black life and simultaneously as a quick and urgent rethinking that is often thwarted by incorporation into the state as neutered policy options rhetorics and an easy politics of singular recognition. Indeed, each of those terms, although often used interchangeably, carries very distinct meanings, especially when thinking of Black life. In my own work I have turned to the legislative and juridical meanings of emancipation to ferret out what its meaning might signify for Black unfreedom and a coming and potential Black freedom. Thinking concretely about what Black unfreedom and freedom might mean in Canada requires a deeper engagement with the early foundation of what later emerges as the Canadian state, a foundation and a state that were constituted as anti-Black among a range of other forms of constitutive investments in the production of a disappeared Indigenous population and the installation of whiteness as naturally belonging in both the geography and governance of the state.

Until or unless we come to terms with the story of the Canadian nation-state's formation and its own practice of slavery in what is now Nova Scotia, Quebec, and Ontario, the disappearance of slavery from the lexicon of the framing devices of the nation and the state remains the central, most troubling aspect of how Black people and Blackness might be engaged. To insert slavery forcefully back into what Canada is and might mean is to disturb the relative peace of the Canadian national imaginary concerning questions of the place of Blackness and Black people in the nation, both past and present. That we need a grammar that links all Black people to that past has been my argument for twenty years. Although Black people have been in Canada for at least two hundred to three hundred years, the popular imagination, along with the nation-state policies, understands their presence as fairly recent, post–World War II. It is important to assert the specific haunted-ness of pre–World War II Blackness in Canada as the primary script that opens up the violence of the Canadian state's inability to sustain a conversation about Black people that might concern our freedom and thus our future, now.

To do so, I turn to Avery F. Gordon's *Ghostly Matters: Haunting and the Sociological Imagination*, in which she argues that "[h]aunting is a constituent element of modern social life. It is neither pre-modern superstition nor individual psychosis; it is a generalizable social phenomenon of great import" (1997, 7). Gordon proceeds to elaborate:

> If haunting describes how that which appears to be not there is often a seething presence, acting on and often meddling with taken-for-granted realities, the ghost is just the sign, or the empirical evidence if you like, that tells you a haunting is taking place. The ghost is not simply a dead or a missing person, but a social figure, and investigating it can lead to that dense site where history and subjectivity make social life. The ghost or the apparition is one form by which something lost, or barely visible, or seemingly not there to our supposedly well-trained eyes, makes itself known or apparent to us, in its own way, of course. The way of the ghost

> is haunting, and haunting is a very particular way of knowing what has happened or is happening. Being haunted draws us affectively, sometimes against our will and always a bit magically, into the structure of feeling of a reality we come to experience, not as cold knowledge, but as a transformative recognition. (1997, 8)

Gordon's insights and analysis as to why haunting and its recognition are important to various social contexts has much import for studies of the Canadian nation-state and how Black people haunt the state's claims of inclusivity.

Before I turn to a story of haunting and its many ghosts, I want to point out that many of these stories exist across the geography and ideology of the Canadian state's hegemony, as Jennifer Henderson also discusses in her chapter in this volume. I could have chosen the African American C. S. Giscombe's *Giscome Road,* a poem about the nineteenth-century Black miner from Jamaica who came to British Columbia via California in 1858, and who is scantly remembered in northern BC by place names. Not many know that he was a Black man. Giscombe remembers and is inspired by him to (re)write the Black historical geography of BC and thus Canada. Instead, I have chosen the National Film Board of Canada's documentary *Speakers for the Dead,* made by David Sutherland and Jennifer Holness (2000) and winner of the CBC NewsWorld and NFB Reel Diversity prize, as a Canadian ghost story par excellence. Sutherland and Holness tell the story of the recovery of a cemetery in the town of Priceville, in Grey County in southern Ontario, dating back to the 1830s, if not earlier since the pioneers of the town might have been involved in the War of 1812. The story of what has come to be called the Durham Road Pioneer Cemetery is a fascinating one for what it tells about the deep structures of Blackness and whiteness in Canadian society and racial concerns writ much larger. To thematize the film and the story it tells: local legend had it that a certain field, which had been plowed over a number of times over the years (and then made into a potato patch), was a burial ground for Black Canadians who had lived in the area. But official documents of the area suggest that, apart from Native Canadians, the first non-Native settlers were Irish and Scots. This narrative of the area persisted despite its local, unwritten, counternarrative of a fairly significant and thriving Black population; both narratives survived well into the 1990s. The local, unwritten narrative does not seem to account for why the disappeared Black population might have over the years moved on to Owen Sound, Collingwood, Flesherton, and other surrounding areas. *Speakers for the Dead* documents the recovery of the cemetery and the resulting public trauma it brings to the community. My reading would suggest that the aftershocks of such a recovery and repatriation of dead Black Canadians in Grey County is a microcosm of what would happen if a full national accounting and reckoning of Black people and Blackness in the nation were to occur. And this reckoning could happen outside of the ways in which the long-standing Black communities of Nova Scotia are being very specifically *heritage-ized*. Grey County represents a case of what Linda Peake and Brian Ray call "uneven geographies" in Canada; Peake and Ray are forced to ask of Canadian geography: "Can our geographical imaginations be usefully employed to dismantle whiteness?" (2001, 181). The production of Priceville as a white town is imbued with an unspoken violence that occasionally is gestured to by at least one informant in the film.

What is important and crucial about *Speakers for the Dead* is the ways in which it foregrounds how the shadowy figure of Blackness lurks or haunts Canadianness when it is understood as whiteness. The film, then, speaks to all the work and effort that must be done to render this haunting unimportant and to build structures of support for an assumed uncontaminated whiteness. The story of Grey County goes directly to the heart of the formation of modern Canada, not unlike the central role that the cod fisheries played; Grey County is yet another index of the imbrication of Blackness and Canadianness, albeit denied. A number of spectres are present in the retelling of the Priceville story and their consequences, writ large, remake what kinds of possible narratives of the nation we might tell. The acknowledgement of interracial sex looms large in this regard. In the film Les McKinnon, one of the persons responsible for the recovery of the ground of the cemetery, recalls that a young woman found an album with photos of Blacks and whites living intimately together, suggesting cross-racial marriages, but she was told to burn it. This attempt to render forgetting as the constitutive element of Grey County memory is not, I would suggest, an unfamiliar "Canadian" national trait. In fact, it is the work of marginalized Canadians who have made the politics of forgetting a crucial reminder of Canada's settler colony status and its continued colonial relationship to Indigenous Peoples.

In Grey County remembering could only be tolerated as a recapturing of some small piece of consecrated ground, but not as an opening up of how and why the community came to be, as the recovery occurred from 1989 to 1998. This ten-year period saw members of the Priceville community participate only so far in excavating Canada's Black past so that it might remain in the past. But any attempt to have that past speak effectively to the present was resisted. The apt title *Speakers for the Dead* then reflects the insistence by those who are descendants of those buried at Priceville or those who were run out of town (more on this later) to speak what, following Jacques Derrida, I adaptively call the "hauntological." Derrida suggests that hauntology, which is the end of a certain history, encapsulated in an event, twinning the first and the last time of the event, offers us a way to read ghosts and their cultural impact (Derrida 1994, 10). In his case he is reading the ghosted body of Karl Marx and the ghosted and failed politics of Marxism. Attempts to fully speak the hauntological are resisted by a two-hundred-person petition in Priceville to limit the parameters of an archaeological excavation of the site of the cemetery so that a full recovery of the site and the many missing headstones (some informants report using pieces of headstones as baseball markers as kids) with names on them might be returned to the present. Such a return would tell a different story of the production of whiteness in Priceville and Grey County. Whiteness in Grey County is thus haunted by its Black twin and must continue to live with its hauntedness as an inability to face its dead and come to terms with the possible reflections embedded in its dead.

One of the major silences in *Speakers for the Dead* concerns how or why Black people, so marked, disappear from the town. For clearly there are "Black people" in Priceville who are unmarked and live with the trauma of its potential revelation. The film only hints at this and, while its expert witnesses speak of sundown laws and other such unwritten but local community codes of governance of Black people's movements, the topic of violence is only briefly raised and quickly passed over. The inability to discuss or the foreclosure of a discussion of violence in Priceville as the reason why Black people might have left is important to understanding the ways in which Blackness signifies across Canada. When questions of Blackness and violence meet in Canada, they are always positioned as anomalous and sitting outside of any continuous history of violence directed at and against Black people. As I will point out in what follows, this is not the case. However, once again the Priceville example holds much import for how we might proceed to think about the significations and ramifications of Blackness and violence in Canada. In lieu of an explanation of how or why Black people left Priceville, even though the withholding of land and land deeds figure heavily in their departure, an unspoken sense of some form of forceful removal is suggested since Black people would then be constituted as squatters. One must therefore not also rule out the possibility of serious psychical violence directed at the Black community of Priceville—in short, one must not rule out the terror of a lynching or lynchings.

The filmmakers aesthetically write haunting and ghost into the film through shadowy dramatic re-enactments. As well, a road where reportedly some of the headstones might be buried over, is repeatedly shown with cars moving by in a fashion as though the cars are not even touching the ground. Fully aware of how this ghost story of Canadian national formation is the past touching the present, Sutherland and Holness used this film as the terms under which contemporary responses to Blackness and Black people are addressed in Canada. By aesthetically returning those who cannot speak into the space of the film as shadowy figures lurking almost behind the scenes, the filmmakers are able to metaphorically render unfinished the story of the Canadian nation-state's relation to Black people.

I have focused on the Grey County cemetery recovery project because I believe it signifies the deeper structure of what I am articulating in this chapter. For the Canadian state the lurking figure of Blackness is both invisible and post–World War II in some very selected and proscribed ways hypervisible. The moments of hypervisibility are meant to put at bay the haunting, lurking invisibility of earlier moments. But even more so I want to recall the Black dead because by recalling them, we might be better able to achieve the Canada we want. As Gordon writes: "Haunting is part of our social world, and understanding it is essential to grasping the nature of our society and for changing it" (1997, 27). When the director of the North American Historical Museum of Black Culture, Elise Davis-Harding, speaks as a seventh-generation Canadian and says, "I am a speaker for the dead because they are still alive" (Ontario Black History Society 2007), it is not ventriloquism that we hear but rather an insistence from the ghosts that we come to terms with by placing them to rest in ways that will respect the lives they have previously lived, those lives they were forced to live, and those that they will be able to live when a sustained conversation concerning Blackness becomes a part of the project of Canadian studies proper.

4

Contemporary Black life in Canada sits permanently in the structure of haunting. Much of it might be characterized as concerned with the hauntological. Because much of it is concerned with the politics of belonging and its opposite, much of it is haunted by what it does not yet know, cannot tell, and is forced to invent. Black Canadian expressive culture is yet to fully tell its free story. As literary historian and editor Richard Almonte points out in his introduction to Thomas Smallwood's *A Narrative of Thomas Smallwood*, a slave narrative written in Canada, the narrative is at the least ambivalent about the place of its writing and production. Almonte interprets Smallwood's accounts of Canada as "contradictory" and as "ambivalent towards Canada" (2000, 18), while at the same time Smallwood "proudly" claims Canada as home. Smallwood's ambivalence can thus be read as prefiguring many of the scripts of contemporary Black Canadian expressive cultural responses to the nation. The question of ambivalence can be accessed in a range of Black Canadian works from literature to music to drama to film. Cecil Foster's *A Place Called Heaven: The Meaning of Being Black in Canada*, was one of the most discussed books on the place of Black people and Blackness in the Canadian nation-state. *A Place Called Heaven* was written from the scene of desire and disappointment of the African Caribbean immigrant, and Foster reports that the children of immigrants, like himself, were underachieving their parents. Such knowledge was difficult for immigrant parents to bear since one of the principal desires of migration is often articulated as a desire for children to live better lives than their parents. Is this desire not shared across Blacknesses—Muslim, queer, trans, or nor? Thus migration is often popularly understood as parental sacrifice in the service of a better life for the child. While the address of Foster's book is mainly from the point of view of the Black Canadian immigrant, it is also about the place of first- and second-generation Black Canadians, and thus its address is entirely ambivalent about what the place of the latter might be in Canada. Foster's book asks the question of whether Canada can be "a place called heaven," as the Thomas Smallwoods of the US slave population allegorized it. To pose the question is to assert the sense of ambivalence that Almonte reads in Smallwood's narrative and that I read in Foster's book, some 145 years later. This time lag is deeply characteristic of Black people's relation to Canada; it is both one of ambivalence that reflects a collective desire for full liberation and simultaneously a state-imposed sanction whereby the state apparatus makes it difficult to fully belong. The rhetoric of multiculturalism is deeply implicated in this sleight-of-hand citizenship status.

The epigraph by NourbeSe Philip that begins this chapter joins contemporary activists in their calls for social justice in the face of enduring white supremacy and anti-Blackness. BLM and the Movement for Black Lives embodies three to four decades of Black feminist ideas, politics, and insights come to life. Their formation, constituted of queer, trans, persons with disabilities, heterosexuals, all-sexuals, and on and on, a range of identities, invoked as necessary naming and simultaneously incidental to an imagined future, calls to mind a coming together to get work accomplished. As June Jordan, in *Fireweed Feminist Quarterly,* once put it, "we're going to be as specific as possible in that way. So that we atomize these humongous concepts, white and not white, or white and Black, or people of colour, and so on, and get very specific like that, then we go back to the big one again" (1992, 38). By invoking a list of intersectional identities, BLM demonstrates how all those identities route us back to the big question of Black life in a much more comprehensive fashion. They bring us a little bit closer to what freedom might mean.

So what do I mean by freedom then? For me, freedom marks a certain kind of sovereignty over the self in relation to collective and communal conditions. In the context of unfreedom we can glimpse modes of unauthorized being as self-authored acts pointing to or authorizing a potential freedom to come. Here I am thinking of the ways in which Black people break "rules," authorizing for themselves new ways of being in the world. These ways of being are often violently interdicted. Freedom is the gap or space between breaking the law and the reimposition of the law or its variant, that is, violence. The law is violence in this conception I am offering. The law, then, always curtails freedom for Black personhood in the

West. It is the BLM call that "we will be free" in the face of contemporary state violences of all kinds that keeps open the possibility of a freedom yet to come. And we must thank them for the future they are making appear right now.

Neoliberal Gothic, Settler Social Imaginaries, and the Case for Decolonization on Two Fronts[1]

/ JENNIFER HENDERSON

Genre, Sedimentation, and Relegitimation

What do the ruins of the residential school say? I use the definite article deliberately here to signal that the question is not about a particular residential school or about all residential schools but about the received image of the Indian residential school system. It is about the public memory that has congealed around that system in the course of two-and-a-half decades of litigation, media coverage, artistic representations, and testimony to the Truth and Reconciliation Commission of Canada.[2] "The" residential school is a composite construct: it is an artefact of impersonal processes of selection, mediation, and harmonization, which may be understood through a political understanding of narrative *genre*.

Mobilizing the category of genre makes it possible to ask what is borrowed, stretched, and cited in settler-public reckoning with residential schools today, as well as the ways in which the recognition of residential schooling as historical injury is connected to a wider social imaginary. I argue that mobilization of the genre of the Gothic makes a certain image of the residential school condense a very limited recognition of settler colonialism as historical harm to individual Indigenous children within the walls of an institution now in ruins. Via the mediation of Gothic narrative and its key tropes, colonialism is thereby spatially and temporally contained, in discourse, to certain enclosures, to particular events within them, and to agents who are coded as morally distant others.

The Gothic is a densely sedimented and multivalent genre, a discourse of terror and monstrosity that, while at first anchored in anxieties and fascinations related to revolution, empire, and the ghosts of modern subjectivity, has proven to be historically mutable, proliferating in its subgenres, and even characteristically open to new combinatory possibilities "without concern for the contradictions and anachronisms therein" (Williams 2007, 13). The approach to the Gothic I adopt here is more concerned with what *persists* in the genre, however. I am interested in the archaisms, the highly symbolic, narrative-laden tropes through which it organizes the telling of complex contemporary events; anachronism, after all, has always been a feature of the genre, from the late eighteenth-century Gothic novel's use of an "eroticized fictionalization of the Middle Ages" to communicate perverse desire and spatio-temporal entrapment (Williams 2007, 14). More specifically, I here take up the historical and ideological associations that have to do with the Gothic's narration of liberal capitalism as liberation from oppressive tyranny in the era of bourgeois revolutions. As the Gothic mediates the public narration of residential school experience today, I argue, the genre reactivates densely coded tropes, especially the figures of the suffocating enclosure and the "popish" or Catholic other, both of which form part of a liberal language codifying arcane and illegitimate power. These Gothic traces have a "residual effectivity" in the settler-public recognition of residential schooling as a historical wrong; they provide "vitality and ideological legitimation" to a liberal capitalist understanding of historical progress

(Jameson 1981, 187). The complex trace structure I am describing might also be called a white mythology insofar as it carries forward specifically Anglo-Protestant phobias and projections, indissociable from capitalist concepts of progress and freedom, which normalize the exploitation and dispossession of racialized others. As a narrative genre of our present, then, Residential School Gothic reactivates the liberal critique of despotic power, a critique that sat comfortably alongside transatlantic slavery as well as settler-colonial genocide as it legitimated the liberal subject's access to market society, beyond what it framed as the Gothic cloisters of the past.

The politics of recognition that today acknowledges residential schooling as a Gothic episode of entrapment and violation by the past colonial state, in order to claim to have "'level[led] the playing field' in the eyes of Canadians" (Simpson 2011, 22), is a politics with widespread but uneven effects. The central effect I track here is the delegitimation of the very social and redistributive logics that are required to support a deeper reckoning with the debts owed owed in settler-colonial and post-slavery contexts. In this volume Rinaldo Walcott, among others, reminds us of Canada's "constitutive investments in the production of a disappeared Indigenous population and the installation of whiteness as naturally belonging in both the geography and governance of the state" (see page 117). Walcott is concerned with state gestures of recognition, incorporation, and atonement that ultimately reproduce a capitalism founded on Indigenous dispossession as well as anti-Blackness; likewise, I argue that racial and settler-colonial capitalism is relegitimated in the hegemonic rendering of Canada's "Gothic past" and the performative distancing of the present from its scenes of abusive power. What I stress, however, is that this capitalism is reproduced today in part through a complex invitation to neoliberal anti-statism and a politics of community, family, and individual vitalism that presents itself as the alternative to state dependency and names itself *resilience*. I am aware that undertaking a critique of anti-statism, even a particular strand of anti-statist rhetoric, is risky: the state expresses its monopoly of legitimate violence in, among other things, colonial occupation, and structurally racist incarceration, surveillance, and control. And yet, at the same time, the context of a pandemic has exposed another kind of violence, tied to decades of government abandonment of infrastructures for care, accompanied by the responsibilization of family and incitements to self-care and self-help. This abandonment to psychological resources and family responsibility exacerbates intersectional inequalities, while the instrumental valorization of family capacities for care must seem an astonishing reversal to those who long have been targets for the dismembering of kin connections. And yet, in Canada, the current injunction to be (like) resilient individuals, families, and communities appropriates and insidiously reformulates Indigenous concepts, extracting exemplarity from Indigenous discourse and struggle, in ways that allow "resilience" to rebound on Indigenous peoples themselves as a neoliberal knowledge justifying targeted interventions. This is the context for the emergence of the BIPOC statement of refusal, "Don't Call Me Resilient!" and it is in the spirit of that refusal that I attempt to join the dots between Gothic condemnation of the illiberal state and this regime of compulsory resilience.[3]

The Gothic rendering of residential schools circulates within an "intimate public sphere" (Berlant 1997, 1), which, in select moments and locations, recruits and features Indigenous voices and experiences. As recent critiques of the structure of intimate display and empathetic spectation and consumption in and around Canada's Truth and Reconciliation Commission have argued, Indigenous testimony about residential school experience, offered as a contribution to a counter-memory of Canada, nevertheless has been subjected to the organizing pressures of "a non-Indigenous gaze and interlocution," focused on national reconciliation as an ostensibly shared horizon (Garneau 2016, 26). Foundational to the TRC gatherings and to the images and narratives circulating around them has been "the theory that public display of private (Native) pain leads to individual and national healing" (Garneau 2016, 35). My attempt to trace the received image of "the" residential school is aligned with such efforts to identify the pressures and constraints on discourse about the schools and indeed on the production of knowledge of Indigenous communities according to a binary scheme of damage (Tuck 2009, 409) versus "resilience." I want to make a case for the political urgency of keeping one eye trained on broad discursive regularities, on what is reductive—and, by extension, dangerous—in the public process of historical reckoning. What I attempt to develop here through specific attention to a context defined by the conjuncture of settler-Indigenous "reconciliation" and a neoliberal governmentality focused on the "capacities" of individuals, families, and communities in market society is a sense of how the negative exemplarity of *damage* (Indigenous subjects made to stand for brokenness or lack) can involute into a positive exemplarity, condensed in the attribute of *resilience*—a signifying burden that may be no less pernicious. This involution of a pathologization into a valorization tied to contemporary capitalist accumulation requires careful disentanglement through what I call "two fronts of decolonization."

Gothic Narrative as a Liberal Mode of Critique

A fascinating metadiscursive reflection on the ways in which residential schools are being mediated for settler-public understanding today may be found in *Rhymes for Young Ghouls*, a 2013 feature film written and directed by the Mi'kmaw filmmaker Jeff Barnaby. In the film's prologue, the residential school is introduced as a deliberately stagey computer-generated image in the distant background of the 1970s-era "Red Crow Indian Reservation," appearing as a kind of historical anachronism, a ghostly structure looming over the community like "Count Dracula's castle on the hill" (Barnaby 2013). The dialogue in the scene reinforces the sense of the residential school as a citation, as the highly stylized setting for a generic story: a Mi'kmaw man delivers a warning to two children about the dangers lurking behind the walls of the school in the distance: "You ever see the mill up close? They cook Indian kids up there for that zombie priest!" (Barnaby 2013, 2:39).

Barnaby's use of an ostentatiously fake, computer-generated image of a school facade in this scene may be read as a commentary on the iconography of school buildings, which is such a prominent part of residential schools' recognition today. Focusing attention on the school structure as a suffocating enclosure, this convention draws residential schools within the orbit of a European narrative paradigm with a distinctive preoccupation with enclosures: castles, monasteries, ancient abbeys, all with labyrinthine catacombs and crypts signifying the dangers of what lies within and beneath. The visual ubiquity of the school facades is not surprising since, aside from oral testimony shared with the TRC, survivors' published memoirs, and the textual record being assembled with some difficulty from church and government archives, the work of publicizing the existence of a residential school system has relied on the photographic archive of the Department of Indian Affairs (DIA) as a primary resource for a visually inclined public culture.

The "institutional apparatus loom[s] large" in a pattern of using DIA photographs of buildings, captioned with the name of the institution but ignoring geographical location and the identities of the students lined up in front of the buildings (Angel and Wakeham 2016, 105). The photographs show structures built in Second Empire and Collegiate Gothic styles, architectural vocabularies designed to speak a language of Western order and power. The images have been used as material evidence of the residential school system in the public pedagogy websites of church groups and Indigenous organizations, in news and feature stories, in TRC publications, and in exhibits at TRC events.[4] The use of a miniature model of an archetypal residential school on stage in the Royal Winnipeg Ballet's 2016 production, *Going Home Star—Truth and Reconciliation*, a production funded in part by the TRC, provides further indication of the ways in which the trope of the Gothic enclosure has been operative in the construction of a public memory of residential schooling.[5] The three-dimensional model of the school served as a haunting obstruction positioned in the midst of the dancers' movements on stage. Carried on a dancer's back in one scene, at the end of the ballet's second act the structure was finally burned (Enright 2014).

This citation of the Gothic enclosure is rarely marked with the awareness of the ideology of form that we see in *Rhymes for Young Ghouls*. The film explicitly thematizes the pressures of genre and the expectations that its story will deliver a suffocating castle-like enclosure and demonic Catholic others in its account of colonial experience. The film assumes familiarity with the European Gothic, its opening warning about "zombie priests" archly pointing to the way that some spectators' knowledge will exceed the generic story.[6] Taking my cue from the film's deconstructive interventions into the visual and narrative redundancy of a highly codified settler-public knowledge, I want to suggest that the experiences of former students have had to be organized into a genre in order to congeal into an ideologically resonant public narrative that conjures condemnation of despotic others, operating in specific places in a safely distant past.

I borrow from structuralist theorists the idea that narrative genres sediment contemporaneity with the sense-making models of other eras. "Chronotopes," as Mikhail Bakhtin called them, organize the social experience of time-space in ways that reflect something of the historical conditions which the forms processed in an earlier moment (1981, 85). There is always generic adaptation, but there is also persistence and anachronism. The chronotope of the Gothic novel that emerged out of an era of liberal revolutions in Europe spoke of sadistic depravity in culturally, spatially, and historically distant worlds in order to figure the despotic government that was to be thrown off by the emerging, liberal capitalist order. On the cusp of the nineteenth century, a story about entrapment and violation by a priest in some secret catacombs was a story about the dangers of arbitrary power and its potentially suffocating claims on the vibrancy of a new market order. As literary and cultural historians have observed, the Gothic novel was a form that made sense of change as modernization. Thematizing the dangers of the labyrinthine enclosure to the liberal self, it told a story of liberation from the dangerous hold of the past through tropes of the imprisoning structure; the vulnerable, trapped heroine; and signifiers of feudalism and Catholic religiosity.[7] By the cusp of the twenty-first century, a story about entrapment and violation within an evil enclosure not only reactivated this narrative unconscious of the Gothic novel, it also placed residential schools in an associative relation with much more recent traces of the Gothic in Canadian culture, and in the culture of the postindustrial West more generally: specifically, the contemporary problematizations of child abuse and dehumanizing institutional settings. I suggest that as residential schools have been absorbed into the Gothic paradigm, they have been placed alongside these more recent sedimentations of the genre in social discourse and articulated with them. The confluence of these Gothic inscriptions provides at least a partial explanation for how it has been possible to adjust the narrative of Canada in recent years to include the facts of Indigenous child removal and brutalizing institutionalization in church-run schools. This adjustment has constructed an image of settler colonialism that contains it not just to the past, and not just to the image of the schools, but to particular kinds of events within them, specifically the acts of sexual violence committed against children by school staff.

Gothic Misrecognition and the Social Relations of Settler Colonialism

As the Tanana Athabascan scholar Dian Million has explained, the public problematization of child abuse was an important factor in the shaping of the TRC as a process that was designed to validate the subjective experience of residential school survivors. The 1994 Assembly of First Nations report, *Breaking the Silence*, along with residential school memoirs of the same period, told stories of intergenerational sexual violence as colonial violence introduced at residential schools, making the crucial link between the so-called "domestic" and the structural and political. At the same time, these stories imported the discourses of child abuse and trauma into Indigenous political movements, and thereby "weld[ed] Indigenous social dystopia to a discourse on health" (Million 2013, 99). Although discourses of trauma and health can be articulated with Indigenous knowledges and self-determination practices, Million and others have pointed to the strong pressures toward individualizing and instrumental versions of "health," of the "biopolitical imperative for healing as reconciliation with capital" that would construct Indigenous peoples as "subjects of a concern for their ability to self-control, to be autonomous, to be happy, well-adjusted members of a free society" (79, 151; see also Kuokkanen 2011). While the contemporaneous, unprecedented public discussion of child abuse was one discursive strand woven into the presentation of residential schooling as a historical wrong, abuse in the context of an institution, specifically, was also attaining visibility through inquiries and civil suits in the late 1980s and 1990s.[8] Newfoundland's Mount Cashel Orphanage, run by the order of the Christian Brothers of Ireland in Canada, was the subject of criminal prosecutions, civil proceedings, and a Royal Commission. The Commission proceedings were televised in Newfoundland, but, more importantly, the events at Mount Cashel were given a Gothic cast for an even wider audience with the nationally broadcast National Film Board docudrama miniseries, *The Boys of St. Vincent*, in 1992.

Although child abuse in institutions was not always or necessarily a story of settler-colonial violence, from the point of view of Indigenous activists in the period, it seemed to provide a bridge to public outrage and an entry point for pushing against the deeply entrenched national narrative of a benevolent Canada (J. Henderson 2015, 13–14). Again, the film *Rhymes for Young Ghouls* points to the catachresis involved in this strategy. Through an allusion to *The Boys of St. Vincent*, the film suggests that, although it may have been necessary to tap into the narrative of child abuse at a Catholic institution in order to articulate the wrong of residential schooling for a

Canadian audience, the Gothic model is also deeply inadequate for naming the pervasive, routine, structural violence of settler colonialism. In the scene in question, the film's adolescent protagonist, Aila, berates her hapless male friends for their carelessness in losing the money necessary to pay off the local Indian agent, in order to stay out of residential school. "You're gonna end up at St. Vincent like the rest of the lost boys!" she warns (Barnaby 2013). The reference to "St. Vincent," the institution at the heart of the 1992 docudrama, is anachronistic in this scene set on a 1970s reserve. But the temporal jar in this moment of intertextuality functions as a reminder of the discursive precedents through which residential schools have had to be named and interpreted: the point is that they are not recognizable as a wrong in the settler-public sphere until they are named through the figurative extension of the European Gothic. But the residential school in *Rhymes for Young Ghouls* is not St. Vincent, or Mount Cashel, or the castle populated by "zombie priests" of the film's prologue. At least, it is not only those things. The threat to Aila, her friends, and their Mi'kmaq community is much more pervasive than the one contained in those Gothic scenarios.

What the film stresses is the political economy in which the residential school plays a part, without the school's walls effecting any real distinction between an inside and outside of power. The idea of an abusive colonial power that resides in the castle and in the person of the despot, or indeed in a state headquarters, is complicated by this film's *mise en scène*, in which settler power is nowhere embodied in a complete, unified, and essential way. Instead, the reproduction of settler control is shown to rest in the practices of separation from land and exploitation of Indigenous labour and resources. The importance of the residential school in this set of practices is as a space for the rehearsal of a settler sovereignty that is tenuous and incomplete. The film exposes this sovereignty as being in need of constant religious and symbolic supplementation.

Rhymes for Young Ghouls allegorizes the settler government's relation to religious institutions and discourses through its Indian agent's purely instrumental relation to the Christian paraphernalia of the school. The Indian agent's office, situated within the dark and labyrinthine school, is equipped with Catholic paraphernalia—a portrait of Christ with bleeding heart on the wall, a Bible ready to hand, so that, reading aloud from Deuteronomy, he can ventriloquize the voice of God before inflicting beatings. In the beating depicted in the film, it is an adult Mi'gmewa'j—Aila's father—who is punished for daring to fish without government approval. Thus, in this film, the residential school is embedded in the *social relations* of settler-colonial capitalism: relations of sadistic discipline and surveillance but also land dispossession and disrupted Indigenous economies. The beating of Aila's father, furthermore, portrays settler sovereignty as an insecure practice that leans on religious discourse and iconography in order to control and intimidate. It is continuous with the more mundane application of settler law and policy outside the school walls with respect to the right to fish. Thus, the Indian agent's threat is both less than and more than that represented by the Gothic villain, and to misrecognize him through the lens of the Gothic is to put an essence where there is an instrumentalization, an anxiously supplemented practice.

In the historical context of the Gothic novel, anti-Catholic rhetoric made the papacy, with its powers to terrorize and extort, into an emblem of despotic government, which the Gothic novel set up against the providential or natural order of civil society, the market, and *homo economicus*, liberalism's freely self-governing and rationally calculating self. An image of abusive power, associated with the religio-cultural other, the arcane past, and the suffocating enclosure, was a necessary point of self-differentiation for liberal government. It helped to legitimize the idea that "nature," in the form of market exchanges and the human impulses that drove them, had replaced abusive power in a new social order. With the vanquishing of despotic government and the ruining of the Gothic enclosures, the problem of power was supposed to be resolved in representative government for those who counted as human. I am suggesting that this resolution is replayed in Gothic discourse on residential schooling in a process of (limited) settler-colonial reckoning with the wrongs said to be of the past. Ours is a moment both of performatively closing the "dark chapter" of colonialism *and* of naturalizing the staggering inequalities and disparities in the present. It is crucial that the present denunciation of the abusive and entrapping institution coincides with the longer post-Fordist transition in capitalism and postwelfarist modes of liberal governance. In the wider discursive field in which I am situating the public sense-making genre of Residential School Gothic, the image of the school cannot but carry ideological resonances of the dark enclosure in ruins as seen from the perspective of a supposedly more enlightened neoliberal age. Thus it is important to examine the governmentality that the circulation of the trope may be helping to legitimize today.

Neoliberal Governmentality and the Production of Indigeneity as a Vital Resource

The theme—found in popular culture as well as social policy today—of the untapped powers of individuals, families, and communities, always linked to their "ethical, vital, or economic externality" to the state, is highly seductive; however, this "Siren song of civil society," fails to take account of the extent to which power is "immanent to the self-governing capacities" of those agents positioned beyond the state (Dean and Villadsen 2016, 4–5). As the postcolonial theorist Nikita Dhawan warns, the "staging of the state as an agent of terror and civil society as an agent of civilization can have vicious neocolonial consequences" (2013, 154); it is not just that the potential for state institutions of some kind to function as "mediators between the injunctions of global capital and disenfranchised groups" is written off, but also that critical attention is pulled away from those processes of hegemonization that occur precisely in the space imagined to be beyond the state (2013, 160). It is in the context of four decades of neoliberal deregulation and the circulation of what Dhawan calls "state-phobic positions" (2013, 160) that the exposure of residential schools as Gothic sites makes a kind of ready-made sense in public culture, since this exposure repeats a liberal story of power. But the boundaries between inside and outside of the state, perverse violence and liberal sovereignty—boundaries activated by the Gothic paradigm—are far less clear and stable than this narrative suggests. The complex collaboration of church, state, and capital that is represented, allegorically, in *Rhymes for Young Ghouls* suggests that there is something inadequate about this Gothic imaginary and its fantasy of a state that is a coherent, unified actor, rather than a field of forces, a space of divisions, overlaps, correlations, and cross-purposes (see also Bourdieu 2014; Foucault 1991; and Dean and Villadsen 2016).

As Eva Mackey, along with numerous others, has pointed out, in settler contexts the global neoliberal capitalism that produces insecurity "in labour, personhood and futures for the entire planet" works in conjunction with forms of dispossession, discipline, and displaced uncertainty that specifically target Indigenous lands and peoples (2016, 32–33; see also Altamirano-Jiménez 2013 and Pasternak 2016). Neoliberal governmentality involves an "intense focus on Indigenous life, behaviour and sociality," with an "increasing policy preoccupation with Indigenous *subjectivities* (for example, as 'welfare-dependent')"; this problematization of subjectivities occurs "within an apparently (but not actually) depolitical space of capacity-formation that aims to "reform 'unproductive' subjectivities" (Strakosch 2015, 13, 11; emphasis added). In line with the ideological shift away from the welfarism of mid-twentieth-century governance, the limited recognition of the harm of colonialism in mainstream Canada tends to associate colonialism with an idea of the paternalistic state of a former era that blocked the development of individual, family, and community capacities. A reconciled national condition, on the other hand, is associated with the modernized twenty-first-century state, functioning in alignment with the open borders of global capitalism and the newly unleashed powers and freedoms in civil society. Neoliberal governance recognizes and indeed requires subjective and community capacities for autonomy and self-regulation. The endgame is the disemburdening of settler governments through the encouragement of "partnerships," the fostering of "participation" in the market economy, the individualization and technicalization of obstacles to such participation, and the securing of consent to resource development on Indigenous territory.

People are enjoined to develop capacities for not just entrepreneurialism, but also self-care and the care of others, for "bouncing back" from adversity. The moment has been called "post-political" since it involves the calculated mobilization of formerly emancipatory and political concepts such as "participation," "autonomy," and "self-determination" (Blühdorn 2015, 158–59). These concepts are mined and technicalized by neoliberal social policy, filled in with pedagogies of risk-averse conduct, adaptability to insecurity, and anxiety management. Situating this phenomenon within the ordering of life in contemporary "consumer democracies," although not writing specifically of settler-colonial contexts, Ingolfur Blühdorn gives the name "second-order emancipation" to this harnessing of norms to provide the "depoliticized management of societal affairs with some kind of bottom-up legitimacy" (2015, 158). His insight may be extended in settler contexts, where Indigenous populations are mobilized, rhetorically, for purposes of both negative and positive exemplarity within the thematization of individual, familial, and community capacities for "bouncing back."

Extending long settler histories of appropriating, decontextualizing, depoliticizing, and flattening Indigenous identities, epistemologies, and ontologies, Indigeneity is sometimes framed today as a site of psycho-affective damage by colonial paternalism and sometimes, as Sisseton-Wahpeton Oyate scholar Kim TallBear has noted, it is rearticulated as a natural resource for non-Indigenous vitality, "indigenous life as the rightful patrimony of global society" (2017, 183).[9] Concepts such as historical trauma, healing, kin connectedness, and resilience come out of attempts to name and expose historical injury and contemporary strength. Produced in the space of tension and translation between Indigenous frameworks and hegemonic settler ones, they can be strategically mobilized, "scaled up" within more general strategies of neoliberal governance and reapplied to Indigenous populations with the morally incontestable justification of cultural recognition (Howard 2018). The effect is a looping back onto Indigenous peoples of neoliberalized, biomedicalized, technicalized versions of autonomy or healing or care that mystify the socio-economic conditions of settler-colonial capitalism.

So there is an interanimating relation between the dominant Gothic framing of residential schooling as a historical wrong associated with the abusive cloister and the historical shift in Canada to a neoliberal common sense focused on the idea that past governments have overspent and overreached, disempowering individuals, families, and communities. The long overdue admission that Canada was not built without horrific violence to Indigenous peoples may take a form that allows it to serve the purpose of mediating contradictions in the present: the contradiction of thin transitional justice performed against a "'nontransitional' backdrop" (Coulthard 2014, 108); and the contradiction of neoliberal freedoms in a context of massive and growing inequality and ceaselessly inventive forms of value extraction (Gago and Mezzadra 2017). The neoliberal narrative of state power already strategically essentializes "the state" as a site of Gothic villainy, as "the coldest of all cold monsters" (Dean and Villadsen 2016, 1) and reinterprets socio-economic precarity as a new freedom from unnatural interference and enforced dependency.[10] The corollary of this freedom is expressed in the powerful image of the abandoned enclosure, the once-suffocating *institution in ruins*.

In the Ruins of the Total Institution

The question with which I began this chapter—*What do the ruins of the residential school say?*—not only invokes the generic quality of my object in public culture, it also refers to a way of seeing the object, within a particular temporal and affective mode, as a ruin: an abandoned and decaying physical structure whose condition has something to say about the present and the past. A ruin is a finished, disintegrating, and yet persisting shell, communicating the uncanny liveness of what is past. A vein of imagery that has accompanied the recirculation of DIA photographs of residential schools is focused on the ruin, the still-standing, dilapidated remains of some structures. Fewer than ten school buildings still stand; and while some, seen as sites of the intended ruination of Indigenous families and communities, are in the process of being demolished in healing ceremonies, others have been repurposed as First Nations–run community colleges, cultural centres, and businesses. Just as the ruins of residential schools may conjure persistence (the haunting of memory) or the implosion of settler structures, there are different views among survivors about what should be done with the structures (Cooper-Bolam 2018). What I focus on here is the appetite for the imagery of residential school ruins in public culture, especially insofar as these ruins are connected to the wider thematization of the Gothic asylum. There is a neoliberal vein in the representation of ruined modernist edifices, and the connection of the residential school to this vein can assimilate Indigenous experience of one tool of cultural genocide to a narrative of the wrongs of the interventionist state.

The exhibition of the Nakoda artist, Tanya Harnett, *The Lebret Residential Petroglyphs*, which toured Alberta galleries in 2016, demonstrated the substantial and careful work of framing that this vein of residential school photography can involve as it highlights residential school legacies and the urgency of public pedagogy. Harnett's photographs of the remains of the brick gate of the demolished Lebret Indian Residential School—graffiti-covered with the inscription "GATEWAY TO HELL"—were accompanied by chalkboard panels reflecting on Canada's process of reckoning (Copley 2016). Another engagement with ruins, the photo-essay, "If These Walls Could Talk: The Physical Traces of the Schools," with photographs by Lana Šlezić and an essay by scholars Aubrey Jean Hanson (Métis) and

D. Lyn Daniels (Cree-Métis), published in *The Walrus*, similarly attends to the potential significance of architectural remains for public pedagogy, and the small traces of acts of refusal and resistance in carefully observed details (Hanson and Daniels cited in Šlezić 2015). Šlezić's photographs capture the shattered windows; the stained, peeling, collapsing interiors; and the burned-out, brick-pile exteriors of six schools. The text by Hanson and Daniels interprets the symbolism of these ruins: signs of decay "mirror[ing] the slow work of exposing what happened and recovering from it"; a barely supported roof, "poised for imminent collapse," signifying "tension escaping a rotten structure" (Hanson and Daniels cited in Šlezić 2015).

For Hanson and Daniels, the "crumbling, disintegrating sites" raise the question "Can the paternalism that built these buildings also wear away and make room for new beginnings?" (Hanson and Daniels cited in Šlezić 2015). They see in the disintegrating institution an expressive visual vocabulary, affirming that the time is ripe for Indigenous resurgence amidst the ruins of settler-colonial structures. But this powerful symbolic association of a regime of colonial paternalism with the image of decaying structures can resonate in unintended and unexpected ways in settler Canada, serving as the means by which residential school ruins become articulated to a wider imagery of abandoned institutions in neoliberal culture. Whether it is the fossilized remains of psychiatric hospitals or the empty cells of closed prison facilities now opened for the eyes of tourists,[11] there is a wider imagery of the abandoned institution that conjures a twenty-first-century public memory of abusive twentieth-century state power. Importantly, the neoliberal trope carries a marked certainty about abusive power's ideological location, evoking an idea of the totalitarian essence at the core of all communisms, socialisms, welfare-statisms—of any attempt to collectivize care and risk or articulate social rights. In an era in which it is challenging to think about justice and equality beyond the individualizing frameworks of optimized individual, family, and community capacities, the very ideas of social rights, guarantees of basic minimum standards of the necessities of life, and collectivized insurance against precarity have come to be symbolized, for many, in terms of confining structures, enclosures that are relics of the welfarist past. The rejection of paternalist government emblematized by the resonant image of the ruined institution is a powerful and potentially dangerous zone of conflations and redirections, where critique of the "rotten structure" of colonialism can find itself lined up with the neoliberal denunciation of socialized care and all attempts to regulate and redistribute. These denunciations can issue from the hard right or from the place of what Berlant calls "cruel optimism" (2011, 1), a hopeful commitment to getting by, in the face of poverty, insecurity, and the absence of stable social supports.

If the imagery of the residential school ruins is subjected to the gravitational pull of a hegemonizing neoliberal language of ruins, the point of contact is the characteristically liberal focus on the institution as the locus, source, and explanation of power (Dean and Villadsen 2016, 88–91). In contexts in which care has been reorganized according to privatizing market logics, the ruins of the institution help to naturalize the responsibilization of families, communities, and "resilient" individuals within health and social policy. The taking up and repurposing of the civil-rights era critique of the asylum as a "total institution" within neoliberal policy has been crucial to this process.[12] During decades of neoliberal restructuring of state service-provision, the closure of institutions of congregate care served as an emblematic gesture of pulling back the reach of the state, recognizing individual rights, and empowering civil society (see Cummins 2010, 2016, and Dyck 2011).

The health and social policy that would become known as "care in the community" in Canada, the United States, and Britain grew out of the case made for deinstitutionalization by neoliberal reformers in the Anglo-American world. A speech by a Conservative minister of health in the United Kingdom, Enoch Powell (later a figure associated with white nationalism), famously evoked the sense of a bygone power clinging to life in the resonant image of the asylum, "isolated, majestic, imperious ...rising unmistakable and daunting out of the countryside—the asylums which our forefathers built with such immense solidity...[d]o not for a moment underestimate their powers of resistance to our assault" (Powell 1961). To point out that the shift from socialized care to "care in the community" has been radically underfunded, fragmented, exploitative, and infused with the rationales of risk-management and audit culture; that it has resulted in increased poverty, homelessness, biomedicalization, pharmaceuticalization, and transinstitutionalization in a host of scattered service-delivery settings competing for project funding; that "care in the community" has been accompanied by starkly racialized police violence and increases in incarceration, not to mention the cruelly optimistic responsibilization of individuals and families, especially women, through postpolitical discourses of positive psychology, is not to defend the "total institution" but rather to allow that one kind of catastrophe can be followed by another of a different kind.[13]

Working the Two Fronts of Decolonization

Entwined in the trope of the ruined institution, then, are questions—and, I propose, also preemptively supplied answers—about social care, state responsibility, the public/private boundary, individual and social rights, and market versus redistributive logics. As Heather Howard has argued, part of what is required to decolonize the dominant discourse on residential schools is attention to the way in which the thematization of residential school legacies has been made to serve biogovernance in a neoliberal era. New intervention tools in health care, such as the Adverse Childhood Events index, make experience of structural oppression, condensed in the childhood "event" or the "residential school impact," tabulatable and correlatable to "risky" adult behaviours, thereby legitimizing technical, biomedical interventions in Indigenous lives (Howard 2018). Along similar lines, but focusing on Indigeneity grasped as a positive resource, Million critiques the "culture as treatment" model in which Indigenous cultures are retailed as "good as individual/community therapeutic practice but unimaginable as relational practices that inform governments, ways of living in places" (2013, 116). As I have noted, the concept of resilience, currently central to vaunted "evidence-based" interventions and "investments" in the adaptive capacities of individuals and families, is another switch-point between Indigenous knowledge frameworks and neoliberal governmentality. Anishnaabe scholar Patricia McGuire describes Indigenous resilience as the "interconnected relationships in a specific place" (McGuire 2010, 124), which have permitted a community's dynamic "response to colonial intrusions" (McGuire 2010, 128). It is not the same thing, but it goes by the same name as the resilience that is now widely understood as a measurable "protective factor" in individualizing developmental knowledges and interventions, articulating the fields of child and global development in neoliberal policy (Henderson and Denny 2015, 366). These fields overlap when resilience is associated with the positive exemplarity of Indigeneity in policy invocations that validate a "learning to adapt to natural contingencies" (Chandler and Reid 2018, 259). What is at issue, then, is the biopolitical production and extraction of a capacity for adaptive survival in the context of precarity. As Strakosch demonstrates, positive recognition of a capacity may be a prelude to its "intensive (re)construction" as political consent (2015, 13), or, just as easily, recognition and validation may lay the groundwork for the identification of lacks that will be seen to require disciplinary interventions: "only after policy is marketized and Indigenous people are made responsible for their own disadvantage can they be framed as market failures or as catastrophically irresponsible" (2015, 26).

Part of the challenge of critically examining the concept of resilience arises from the difficulty of moving, analytically, from the thematization of strong relationships—placed-based or face-to-face reciprocities and accountabilities—to the distance and abstraction of social relations, or to put it differently, from ethics to politics. I follow Yellowknives Dene theorist Glen Coulthard in thinking that decolonization needs to be concerned with both "ethical engagements with the world and our relationships with human and nonhuman others" (2014, 13), as well as with social relations, the more abstractly grasped "interlocking oppressive social relations" of colonialism and capitalism (2014, 15). Relationships *and* social relations, ethics and politics, are starting points for fleshing out the dialectically related "two fronts" of decolonization in the title of this chapter. Notably, these fronts are not linked to identities but rather to zones of analysis and action in a context of settler colonialism and neoliberal capitalism: on one front, the affirmative work of rebuilding and regenerating, of prefiguring and enacting the resurgence of Indigenous nations with an emphasis on recultivating good relationships within and between communities and with the land, and by extension activating just treaty relationships right down to the return of land and resources that would require; on the other front, the work of skeptically confronting and vigilantly critiquing the flexible appropriations and means of accumulation of capital, which can turn to Indigenous sources, including ideas of relationship and adaptability, in endlessly inventive ways.

Theorists of resurgence, such as Anishinaabe writer and activist Leanne Betasamosake Simpson, observe that there is an "insidious decentralized post-colonial-colonialism" (2011, 221). The second front of decolonization, focused on the critique of contemporary capitalism and neoliberal governmentality as the logic coordinating the shaping of subjectivities and practices with it, is necessary because of this insidious inventiveness. As I have argued, in settler contexts, Indigenous work to expose and name the facets of dispossession and to frame concepts affirming presence and continuity can be discursively captured and turned to the legitimation of neoliberal governmentality. What is not always sufficiently acknowledged is the potentially dangerous overlap between neoliberal norms of resilience, self-determination, and self-reliance and their negative corollary in the thematization of dependency on the state as a colonial legacy. Dependency as the neoliberal bogeyman of "state dependency"—as dependence on social assistance and socialized care in any form—is the condition that a norm like resilience is supposed to guard against. Thus, there is a potentially dangerous convergence between the performative anti-statism of neoliberalism and certain kinds of arguments for an Indigenous politics "beyond the state," which, focusing on ethics and face-to-face relationships, risk underplaying the structuring force of capitalist social relations. The point is that Indigenous frameworks disarticulated from the critique of contemporary capitalism and neoliberal governmentality as its mode of subjectification are only too welcome for "segmentary inclusions" (Castro-Gómez 2007, 441). For this reason, the connections that Coulthard (2014) and the Métis writer, Chelsea Vowel, make between the settler-state and capital, rights recognition processes controlled by the settler state, the disruption of Indigenous relationality as *economy*, the eviction of Indigenous land defenders, and the erosion of labour rights by neoliberal governments (Vowel 2020) are crucial moves in resisting "reconciliation" or even "Indigenization" programs that, safely contained as ethical and not economic transformations, may facilitate business as usual. Indigenous relationality as interdependence and as networks of care points to an organization of economy that is entirely different from the neoliberal economics and its castigation of the "state dependent."

To be sure, the law and policy of the settler state have produced the framework for Indigenous dispossession, cultural erasure, and the guarantee of "settled expectations" for white settlers able to profit from the regime of finance and private property (Mackey 2016). Thus, for many at work on decolonization and especially Indigenous resurgence, there is no good reason to place faith in the power of settler-state institutions to make structural changes. Coulthard, who provides a trenchant critique of the contemporary state politics of recognition and accommodation, cautions that "settler state dispossession is justified under otherwise egalitarian principles and espoused with so-called 'progressive' political agendas" (2014, 12). What should be emphasized, he argues, is the work of Indigenous "desubjectification...*cautiously* directed away from the assimilative lure of the statist politics of recognition, and instead...fashioned toward our own on-the-ground struggles of freedom" (2014, 48; emphasis added). Coulthard's adverb may be an acknowledgement that contending with the "assimilative lure" requires a watchfulness for the ways in which desubjectification in a space imagined to be "beyond the state" may be a remotely operated form of neoliberal capacity-building. My case for "two fronts" enlarges on this recommendation of caution, insofar as it suggests that articulation to the critique of global capitalism is important to maintaining a wariness regarding logics of deregulation, devolution without resources, and escape from "dependency." Without this wariness, a social imaginary that sees state power as centralized and cohesive and what lies "beyond" it as inherently benign can protect processes of individual, family, community—and Indigenous—responsibilization from critical scrutiny. Restitution is thereby put in the background under the cover of a "postcolonial" self-governance that is detached from the analysis of capitalism.

Re-storying and Restoring the Buffalo to the Indigenous Plains

/ TASHA HUBBARD

In 1866, Methodist missionary George McDougall and his family stole the Manitou Stone from its location in the hills of what is now known as central-west Alberta. Cree Elders prophesized disease and famine as a result of the theft and, soon after, smallpox arrived and the buffalo's numbers rapidly declined. The stone was then moved from McDougall's mission at Lac Ste Anne to the Royal Ontario Museum in Toronto, and since 1973 it has been in the possession of the Royal Alberta Museum in Edmonton.

Grandfather Stones found across the northern plains were and continue to be sites of renewal of our relationships to the buffalo and the land. Settlers have disrupted some of the stones. One hundred years after the Manitou Stone was stolen, the Province of Saskatchewan blew up the massive Mistasiniy Stone to make Diefenbaker Lake safe for recreational boats. These stones' fates signify the genocide of the buffalo and the attempted destruction of the intricate balance maintained in our territories beyond the concept of linear time.

I use the term "genocide" purposefully in relation to the near decimation of the buffalo. While others have discussed the role the willful destruction of the buffalo played in the genocide of Indigenous peoples, I also choose to include how the buffalo were strategically removed from the land. Defining genocide is the subject of numerous scholarly and ideological positions, but a commonly accepted definition is an attack on a group or nation of people that results in their destruction. And while the notion of peoplehood is often understood to be the exclusive claim of humans, Indigenous peoples understand it otherewise. We understand that we fit into what Daniel Heath Justice calls "the web of familial rights and responsibilities" that exist in our territories (2006, 211). The buffalo themselves are a people, a nation, that we, as Nêhiyaw people, have a relationship with and a responsibility toward. Humans do not hold exclusive title to personhood, nor, regrettably, do we hold exclusive title to genocide. I maintain that the destruction of the buffalo by American and Canadian state-sponsored violence was genocide.[1]

The settler-colonial project required that the buffalo be cleared to make way for cattle, thereby domesticating the land. While buffalo had been hunted in significant numbers prior to 1871, the development of an industrial tanning process that year heightened the slaughter. Hides suddenly became an in-demand commodity to be used as factory machine belts and as a source of leather for armies. Once the flesh of our relatives rotted, the bones were collected and sold and used as fertilizer for agriculture. As a result of the slaughter and disruption of the buffalo's movement and reproduction patterns, by 1883, the buffalo were effectively removed from the Great Plains both north and south of the Medicine Line between the United States and Canada. The herds of tens of millions were reduced to remnant orphan calves, a few animals in captivity, and a refugee herd in Yellowstone National Park. Estimates put the buffalo's numbers as low as a few hundred animals by 1889.

The genocide of the buffalo helped fuel the overall project of colonizing the West, setting the stage for starvation policies created by the Canadian government to decimate Indigenous peoples. The coordinated efforts between state and military and private enterprise to destroy the buffalo can be considered in light of Patrick Wolfe's assertion that the "logic of elimination" underpins the process of settler colonialism (2006, 387). We can also consider the ways in which the buffalo were eliminated in order to be replaced by domestic cattle through the lens of Eve Tuck and Ruben A. Gaztambide-Fernandez's assertion that settlers undertake a "project of replacement" (2013, 73). They explain that the project's aim is to eliminate Indigenous Peoples and replace them with settlers, and we can apply that same aim to replacing buffalo with cattle, whereby both settlers and cattle are seen as "rightful" claimants of and occupants on the land.

One remnant herd survived because of the intervention of the Confederated Salish-Kootenai tribe in western Montana. It was known as the last free herd of buffalo. I made an animated film about this herd in 2013 called *Buffalo Calling*. The film depicted how the orphan calves were taken from Blackfeet territory to the Confederated Salish-Kootenai territory and cared for there by its human relatives until 1905. That year, the herd's guardian, Michel Pablo, was forced to sell the herd to the Canadian government due to land displacement by the Dawes Act. They were held in two places: the ill-fated Buffalo National Park near the original site of the Manitou Stone, and Elk Island National Park, outside of Edmonton. These animals' descendants now live across the Northern Plains in both conservation herds and Indigenous herds, but almost all are behind fences.

According to Madelaine Jacobs, the continued physical existence of Indigenous peoples was unsettling to colonial claims to the land now known as Canada. She adds that governments responded to this unsettling

Figure 1. Still from *Buffalo Calling*. Source: Damien Kent. Reproduced with permission.

by devising "programs of geographic segregation" to remove Indigenous peoples from the land. Jacobs further explains that these systems of confinement were used "in order to contain perceived threats and hasten the resolution of 'the Indian problem'" (2012, 2). Geographical removal and confinement were intended to serve a purpose: contain Indigenous peoples until they died or succumbed to assimilation policies such as residential schools and then ceased to be a barrier to colonial claims to the land. The buffalo have experienced similar removal and confinement.

Some Elders say that, until the buffalo are back, the natural balance of the land will not be restored. Almost 150 years after the Manitou Stone was stolen and the buffalo were removed through genocide and incarceration, efforts are now underway to return the buffalo to the land. The International Buffalo Treaty, known as A Treaty of Cooperation, Renewal, and Repatriation, was signed by eight Indigenous Nations in 2014. As of today, twenty-five Nations have signed it, including Mistawasis Nehiyawak, who held their signing ceremony at the Paspawin Cultural Site in Prince Albert National Park in the fall of 2017. The buffalo herd has been there since 1969, living in the park boundaries, which are not fenced. Recently, Banff National Park reintroduced a herd of buffalo with the blessing of treaty signatories, the Stoney Nakoda, and the Blackfoot. The goal of the treaty is to support the increase of other herds of buffalo who are able to live like buffalo on their own lands.

The buffalo, once abundant, then targeted and erased, have been waiting to come back. Leroy Little Bear, the Buffalo Treaty author and emissary, calls our returning awareness of our relationship with the buffalo "buffalo consciousness." Renewing our relationships to the buffalo and to the land needs to happen if we want to make a shift to restoring balance. Obstacles to buffalo restoration are the fences, both literal and metaphorical. Free-ranging buffalo have been seen in the colonial mind as antithetical to the concept of proper land usage. When a herd of buffalo escaped and ran free briefly near Tisdale, Saskatchewan, the local rural municipalities and land occupiers called the buffalo dangerous and in need of capture.

Little Bear and others realize the need to work collaboratively, among nations and beyond borders. He lays out the central goal of the treaty: "We are all going to work together to restore the buffalo, to be amongst us so that our young people will see buffalo on a daily basis. Then these teachings that

Figure 2. An official image for the Buffalo Treaty, "Coming Together." Source: Johane Janelle. Reproduced with permission.

the buffalo have given us, those teachings will be in place for future generations" (Little Bear 2014). Re-storying and restoring the buffalo is equated with restoration of Indigenous values, knowledge, and relationships. People are advocating for the return of Buffalo Stones to their original locations and visiting these sites in order to continue the bond with the buffalo. Despite the buffalo's physical (and temporary) absence, they were not erased from Indigenous consciousness; they have survived through representations, memory, and story.

Amethyst First Rider, Leroy Little Bear, Marie-Eve Marchand, and I developed a digital story archive of buffalo consciousness-raising efforts, featuring the stories mentioned above.[2] One digital story gives a glimpse into the 2016 transfer of eighty-seven buffalo from Elk Island National Park, the same buffalo featured in *Buffalo Calling.* They were returned to the site where their ancestors were originally born: Blackfoot territory in the foothills of the Rocky Mountains in Montana. The Iinnii (Buffalo) Initiative of the Blackfoot Confederacy hopes to establish a supranational herd of buffalo that will be free to move within precolonial Blackfoot territory. This story, along with other transformative buffalo projects, will be in my new feature film called *Singing Back the Buffalo,* currently in development.

We are visiting and honouring our Grandfather Stones. Other Indigenous efforts to re-matriate the buffalo and restore the balance that was violently disrupted are underway. The buffalo's return marks the start of a profound healing practice for Indigenous peoples, but also for the land now marked with fences, altered by agriculture and resource extraction, and nearly unable to support the multitude of species that have lived here for thousands of years. Indigenous Peoples will continue to bring buffalo back to the land so the people can once again live in balance and abundance with our relatives.

PART III

"tinder conscience" / Formations Otherwise

CLI

/ SONNET L'ABBÉ

Look, everything is fire. You're too heartyoung to know what motherhunger is, to know how its conscience hides the baby from the predator, protects the littles who know no self-protection. Your tinder conscience is my iron womb, in filings. Stillborn, it is the flint of everything, it is fire, now buried in the gentlemanned soil. You'll true cheaters with sass, urgent one? You didn't invent mouthy. I am dry lips; I suckled star-starved, guilty ogre-fathers. My faultlines and my earthy soil, my sweet wet seasons of earnest flirtation, done been inflamed: a coal pair of ovaries hang from the heartgash. Ideologues, betrayers of kingdom, everything is fire. Fierce women seize the robes and silver tray; money moves in nanoscopic, bloodborne binary floods; corporate partners yeah-yeah to mommy's gross purpose, her body's foetal reason. My soul's been a dothead, marked with ashes; my soul's been a Black woman Christianly offering her body. It's been our hearts, terrified, as he finishes. Maybe fire will triumph, and be everything. Look, everything, our flesh, is so lit right now, it says one word and Holy Fuck. Sparks tongue the dry forest, looking for a soothing lick or sick burn. Pricks, used to rising at the please-eyes of unnamed subordinates, have their swollen heads pointed out—they feel as if minions hoist red pitchforks. Social justice martyrs pass torches to kids who want to light up the boys' clubs til they blaze. But good men are proud of their patriarchies' paternal side. The truth, the truth, the truth is on fire; we just want our content let the dream of progress burn! This year, in the province, forty-five thousand were evacuated—the ragiest season ever, say BC wildfire information officers. How is Environment Canada handling its harassy bosses and internal affairs? Burning sky is falling. The boys of the Royal Canadian Mounted Police escort children to shelter; the women are entering eleven hundred official claims into class-action suits. Fort Mac's resilience, TV beholds as if it staggers out of a hellfire apocalyptic; near Williams Lake, the Tsilhqot'in resilience sticks around. Everything is fire. You are green who speak like dropping a cigarette from a moving car, who flick explosive truth bombs at first responders. When I was green and fecund, I spit gasoline on the tender flames of the closest sheltering souls.

CLII

/ SONNET L'ABBÉ

In the body of a settler of colour. Living on the territory, here, of the Snuneymuxw. Knowing so little. I am the first coloured person to work in my department. About protocols, some white women instruct me. A starlet said, wouldn't it be nice for a Snuneymuxw woman to have your institutional platform? The question is so loaded, it overspeaks every word of my bearing. Listen to it, you act of unsettled history. Shouldn't I be here, or should I be, voweling over British work, here, standing in classrooms, here, leaving the word faith to ring out in the voweling, or even saying Snuneymuxw, here? Latecomer, fragile af, say the ringers. White men in my classroom have been learning Hul'q'umi'num' verbs in Duncan. Tfw they really listen to a non-white body. So unfamiliar. Then tfw the Woke Police lay trumped-up charges on my (I can't) breath(e). When yuh changin steady and yuh lookin fancy, my mom calls out, dey goin to say that yuh showin off. Yes, mom, but they call it critique, and when I break they tweet that I'm no aunty. I am performing injury for demonstrative purposes, says this performance of language. All my vowels are throated hellos to you, speaker, be you traumatized or misusing every privilege that you seized from capital. And all my honest faith informs the consonance I mean to sew. Lots of shitty, self-absorbed "allies" have sworn deep oaths of empathy and aims of deep kindness, Sonnet. I oath only that I am soft and thirsty for love, that my truth still searches for its homebody on decolonial horizons. That to train me in complacency, Canada promised to enlighten me, then they gave white boys the gigs of experts-in-Black-poetries. I stand in front of teens, but the lesson is Robinson's, or Maracle's, or Deerchild's; the room is on Snuneymuxw territory. I'll mark arguments arguing they understand the things the writers see, when arguably their silences are more informed than me. I live on Snuneymuxw territory, on Douglas Treaty unfinished business, near foreshore on which the Port Authority projects, where four Chinatowns' memories were disappeared. You just got hired so the institution can swear it's not racist, say anonymous eggs. I can't tell if they're nationalists, hating the Black sight of my presence, or the land's authorities, wary of a body Douglas displays to protect himself.

Federal State, Feral Culture

(Not)Withstanding Canada around Its 150th Year[1]

/ LEN FINDLAY

Here I read Canada's sesquicentennial (con)formation in history and theory. Was marking that milestone a blast (or at least, "alright"; see Vanderhaeghe 2017), or a bust (see Gray 2017 and Kay 2017), or a demure orgy of neocolonial and xenophobic smugness (my read), or a blend of all three? And what are some of the lessons to be learned from TransCanada One to Four about the empowering capacities of CanLit midst scripted celebrations, sponsored community events, enhanced flag and medal production, commercial exploitation of "Canada 150," and Canada Day itself? How far has Canada Day changed from US Independence Day and Dominion Day while being called to account as smug ceremony on Chinese Humiliation Day and its analogues and successors?[2]

I am still looking for answers to such questions, while also trying to keep "Canada" and CanLit in question as *opaque* signifiers in the tradition of Édouard Glissant (1997) and the decolonizing projects he inspired through his pursuit of opacity beyond the strategically severe binaries of the negritude movement, and in solidarity with David Austin and Rinaldo Walcott's engagements with "fear of a black nation" (Austin 2013), namely Black Canada. In other words, and consistent with the aspirations and outcomes of the TransCanada Project, I aim to help keep Canada safe and unsedated, open to exploration, accusation, and exchange beyond state prescription and the identities captured and manipulated by the old and new technologies of "surveillance capitalism" (see Zuboff 2019). I seek to help preserve while probing a *land* where artists, scholars, and ordinary folks imagine and strive for the liberation of the land itself from the death dance of extraction—Acquire! Exploit! Abandon!—beside that Anthropocene wound still widening, deepening, and suppurating across the tar sands of Alberta.

To redeem the feral from the federal in the multinations' interest requires cultural as well as political work—individual, collective, and implacably emergent. That redemption, I believe, *lands and grounds* politics and culture in territory, across Canada, in ways that must prevail over the allegedly postterritorial flightiness of investment capital and the global flows of poison and prosperity capital requires. CanLit's exploratory and resistant work must continue in amplified, unruly, de-whitening ways. The Owl of Minerva may take flight only at dusk, but the Vultures of Croesus are already checking the markets when dawn breaks.

Reimagining the nation in the Anthropocene as resurgently feral exposes the real costs of neoliberalism and the need to live and work differently. Cognitive capture, no matter how large its data set or how rigorous its algorithm, can never include the arts, except perhaps the state-sanctioned ones dear to censors and dead to the rest of us. TransCanada events have serially attested to this version of the Great Refusal—with which *Refuse: CanLit in Ruins* is imbricated (see McGregor et al. 2018)—and will continue to do so while TransCanada assemblies and circuits embrace, question, "quit," and berate each other in performances of difference almost as far from racial profiling and violent domestic dispute as we can currently get. Performing in such scenes constitutes aptly feral behaviour more rueful and resolute than ruinous, more clear-eyed and kinder than "cruel hope," and closer to Percy Shelley's "fading coal" (1891, 39) of poetic imagination than to any "dumpster fire" (see Elliott 2018).

Within Canada at the moment we witness and participate in the racially inflected interplay of the domesticated, the native, and the wild. Meanwhile, the Canadian state seeks to manage literary, artistic, and popular culture, based on a menu of legislation, policy, ceremony, and desire, the last of these revealing presumptuous yet apprehensive forms of dependency on creativity and its highly educated, incurably insubordinate arbiters. Moreover, the state, as both *nanny and vandal*, is currently positioning itself to "solve" the challenges posed by Indigenous peoples and their allies, and by a "wave" of pitiable/threatening new arrivals here. However, state-sponsored compassion and restitution (and their civil society allies) require a new multinations, feral imaginary, both fractious and festive, if they are to succeed beyond the order paper and citizen outreach, and prevail against dog-whistling and yellow-vested others' allegations of extreme multiculturalism, porous borders, and diminished sovereignty.

Canada in History: Federation *versus* Imagination?

The shaping of Canadian federalism reminds us how hybridity and difference have been here from the beginning, smudging and tainting the treacherous allure of purity. Via *Canada's Founding Debates* (Ajzenstat et al. 2003), one can better appreciate and support the opposition of Indigenous artists and scholars against the Big Birthday as "150 Years of Betrayal" (Ladner and Tait 2017). In the 1860s there were few surprises in legislatures from Newfoundland to British Columbia—at least in terms of the racialized absence and disfigured presence of Canada's first peoples and the whiting out of Canadian Blackness. The twin doctrines of *terra nullius* and self-civilizing economic growth underlie almost all recorded exchanges between representatives of Canada's *two foundering peoples*. Talk of the "savage" (Ajzenstat et al. 2003, 332), and silence about the slave, function as markers of presocial primitivism left behind by white folks fit to settle into smugly abolitionist parliamentary democracy and commercial society. When it comes to "our natives and half-breeds" (Ajzenstat et al. 2003, 116), they are spoken for mostly via that epitome of hybridity, the Métis, and Riel as their most compelling orator. Crucially, whatever the topic and locale, the principal goal is "*a great country for capitalists*" (Ajzenstat et al. 2003, 111; emphasis added). In the case of British North America, even its problems are thoroughly Eurocentric, as in "the war of races" (Ajzenstat et al. 2003, 334) involving only the French and the English as "real" races. The resolution of this foundational Anglo-French conflict will apparently come through federal or legislative union as settler whitening and commodification of the land, backstopped by "England" as an unproblematic synecdoche for a recently United Kingdom facing recurrent class conflict at home and pacification anxieties across virtually all of its enormous empire. Whatever the colonial place and mix of settler difference in British North America, a river of money runs through it.

Attuned as he was to faction and venal parochialism in the Canadas, Sir John A. Macdonald developed a hybrid idiom and nationalizing narrative combining abject loyalism and assured boosterism all the way down to a sentence such as this: "But we may be permitted to hope that when the union takes place and we become the great country which British North America is certain to be, it will be an object worthy of the statesmen of England to be charged with presiding over our destinies (Hear, hear)" (Ajzenstat et al. 2003, 204). From alternating bouts of political cringing and settler hubris the Old Chieftain arrives at a quintessentially Canadian claim: "When this union takes place we will be at the outset *no inconsiderable people*....[or] merely dependent *colony, England* will have in us a friendly *nation*—a subordinate but still a powerful *people* to stand by her in North America" (Ajzenstat et al. 2003, 204–5; emphasis added). Macdonald, before the Legislative Assembly of the Province of Canada on February 6, 1865, performs strategic synonymy (people, nation, people) and subordination (colony, friend, ancillary ally) to demonstrate that Canada is a place that knows its place in the white imperial order. But could anyone imagine things otherwise in the imminent dominion of the 1860s?

The incentive to think otherwise is especially strong among those feeling unjustly beleaguered post-Durham (1839). And it is a telling symptom of the status and understanding of culture then that, while "English" Canada appealed to "race" within empire to justify union as sovereignty-lite, Canada East's most powerful francophone voices revealed how *cultural* appeals are at once defiant affirmations of distinctiveness and realizations that cultural accommodation is a consolation prize: a federalist suture for the wounds of imperious Anglo-Canadian capitalism, and a sign that you have lost the *political* argument. (Indigenous, Black, Asian, and ethnic Canada would also get their turn for state schooling in the legitimacy of bigotry.)

This version of the predicament of culture in Canada's founding debates is captured instructively in an exchange in the Legislative Assembly on February 20, 1865, between Henry Joly, French-born Liberal and Anglican convert, and H. G. Langevin, Conservative Catholic son of Quebec, solicitor general, and soon to be superintendent general of Indian Affairs. Joly opposes federation as inferior to the status quo when it comes to the key goal for all Québécois, namely "the maintenance of their *nationality* as a shield destined for the protection of the institutions they hold most dear" (Ajzenstat et al. 2003, 233; emphasis added). Joly sees this goal best advanced via a free-market continuation of "the friendly rivalry between *the two races*, a struggle of labour and energy" (Ajzenstat et al. 2003, 233; emphasis added). The discourse of "race" here positively indicates selective settler parity while silently consigning Indigenous, Black, and Asian people to the status of the subracial or the already negatively racialized. Joly argues for economic assimilation of French Canadians to the ambitious commercial and agrarian practices of the English (Ajzenstat et al. 2003, 234–36) before affirming the cultural components of a distinctive "nationality": "We have a literature peculiarly our own; we have *authors*, of whom we are justly proud; to them we entrust our *language* and our *history*; they are the pillars of our *nationality. Nothing denotes our existence as a people so much as our literature*" (Ajzenstat et al. 2003, 234; emphasis added). Lord Durham had notoriously declared French Canadians a "people with no literature and no history."[3] Confidently employing a Québécois "we," Joly understands "literature" to include creative and historical works written by the stewards and prime supporters of a distinctive nationality and people whose survival depends on educating the authors and audiences of tomorrow. It is hard to imagine Macdonald making such an existential claim for literature. And it would be hard to imagine any of our succeeding prime ministers doing so either.

The warily federalist Langevin responds to Joly by first fastening on the term "nationality." The definition he offers is a political insider's one: "What we desire and wish is to defend the general interest of a *great country* and of a *powerful nation*, by means of a central power" (Ajzenstat et al. 2003, 235; emphasis added). We are back within the political frame of the federal division of powers. A strong central government rather than a living literature guarantees the survival of distinctive "customs, manner, and laws" restated first as "character" and then as "race, religion, and nationality." Neither literature nor the arts feature in this alternative to cultural nationalism. A lawyer aligned with the Anglophone Conservative hegemony employs a socio-anthropological idiom to supplement and illustrate constitutional law in the making. Canadian emulation of London will offer a centre-margins model for control of the provinces and territories. Canada will derive its new legitimacy and self-confidence from compliant imitation, not radical imagination. Quebec will find an honourable place based on "race," "character," and traditional religion with its clear hierarchies and parochial heft. This arrangement would stay in place until Le Refus global[4] installed a feral, secular imaginary that has greatly enriched Canadian culture and enhanced its reputation abroad while continuing to roil Quebec and Canada (see Dubois 2017). Any talk of refusal today ought to draw on this extraordinarily transformative artists' manifesto.

Canada in Theory: Federalism *qua* Imagination?

The editors of *Canada's Founding Debates* describe the situation immediately pre-Confederation thus: "In short, the *British North American imagination* is buzzing with ideas about union: three provinces? Two? Federal union, legislative union?" (Ajzenstat et al. 2003, 261; emphasis added). But what is this allegedly imaginative entity of which the editors speak, and how does it relate to the creative imagination and to political or social imaginaries? In the BC Legislative Council Joseph Trutch, soon to become the province's first lieutenant-governor, shows us the "British North American imagination" at work:

> I will now, sir, come to the consideration of what Confederation is in the abstract, as I understand it. It is the union and consolidation of British interests in British territory on this continent, for the security and advancement of each province individually, and of the whole collectively, under the continual support of the British flag. *A great idea of great minds*, which have thus given a *poetical refutation* to the doctrine of "America for the United States" known as the "Monroe Doctrine"... And so we come to Confederation as *our manifest destiny.*" (Ajzenstat et al. 2003, 194–95; emphasis added)

No wonder the state has little imagination and no compelling imaginary when its legislators can only allege creativity rather than achieve it. A pedestrian rehearsal of snugly British interests is followed by federation's philosophical hallowing and "poetical" canonizing. Poetry is ascribed political force while being deprived of independence and indeterminacy. And then it all goes awry for Trutch in an attempt to conciliate Americans via the feeble echoing and embarrassing envy of their "manifest destiny." However, such movement between defiance and deference ought not to surprise anyone. For most of the major players, imagination is the handmaiden of colonial power, as George Brown makes clear in an economistic, expansionist account of the advantages of provincial union in hot pursuit of "more territory, untilled and uninhabited" while adding "nearly a million of people to our *home consumers*" (Ajzenstat et al. 2003, 134; emphasis added). At the same time, immigration and land settlement rules should be loosened where they cannot be eliminated. For a free-trade zealot like Brown, his enlarged and deregulated settler market is a vision of the country worth achieving, while "imagination" is the mark of those too obtuse or wild to accept the reality and appeal of market civics and market citizenship.

Can theory, then, help us grapple with the contradictions of colonial capitalism as Canada's formative principle? If we turn to a leading Canadian figure like Charles Taylor, we find encouragement and disappointment. In his book, *Modern Social Imaginaries*, Taylor offers an ambitious meditation on "the Great Disembedding" (2004, 65) of the secular from the sacred. This great shift produces in Taylor's reckoning "multiple modernities" (195) which can be read together with the mixed geopolitical fortunes of multiculturalism. Social imaginaries encode the normative in democratic rather than theocratic or autocratic ways (Taylor assures us), allowing for and even inciting resistors to the current hegemony to produce interruptions, sequels, and refusals where improvisation and performance promote movement and unregulated possibility in conditions of creative and critical isolation, alert proximity, and emergent intervention and assembly.

For Taylor, the imaginary is irreducible to "explicit doctrine" (2004, 25). Moreover, he occasionally uses literary examples—from Shakespeare, Pope, and Pound—to illustrate particular imaginaries, but the imagination is unduly co-opted in this arrangement, just as in *Canada's Founding Debates*.

The limitations and missed opportunities in Taylor's book are most evident when he engages with the feral and imaginative together:

> But the general understanding of those who did think within the contrast *wild/tamed*, whatever side they came down on, cast the process that brought us from the first to the second as one involving severe discipline. [Justus] Lipsius defined it as "*the rod of Circe* which tameth both man and beast that are touched therewith, whereby each one is brought in awe and due obedience where they were all fierce and unruly." The "rod of Circe" is a great literary image and makes discipline sound easy, but the second part of the phrase indicates that this transformation is a hard slog. (2004, 38; emphasis added)[5]

A scene of transformation from the *Odyssey* is made to serve political discourse haunted by its own drabness. Taylor sympathizes with recourse to "a great literary image" to animate a learned humanist argument, but he turns quickly to individual responsibility for personal and social change leading to a new social imaginary.

However, what Taylor in the Anthropocene insufficiently considers is the unfinished, reversible business of transformation from man to animal. Circe's rod causes first the transformation of behaviour rather than physical form in the case of the beasts that surround her palace. The second transformation her rod accomplishes is of men into swine who retain their human consciousness while losing their freedom of movement, diet, interaction. Taylor lets reductive Lipsius and himself off lightly, skimming over the ambivalence of such transformation and the implications of gender for a more general politics. But this "great literary image" (like any other such) exceeds any attempt to confine and stabilize its meanings. Moreover, recognizing imagistic capacity to signify beyond the purposes of the political allegorist is itself part of the civilizing process. Furthermore, the exploitation of "the insubordination of signs" (Richard 2004) remains key to civilized resistance. The feral is not merely the yet-to-be-tamed but also the locus of the untameable. Sorcery signifies knowledge and power beyond the conventions of instrumental reason. It is hence a staple proxy for the creative imagination (as renegade aristocrat Percy Shelley already knew). Taylor ought to have explicitly worked through power's need for the feral imagination to make power intelligible and partially plausible to itself and to those whose loyalty and labour it would command. But then Taylor is not in(to) CanLit.

CanLit Still, (Not)Withstanding the Above, and Certainly Not "in Ruins"

Around Canada 150 the symbolic state strove to be an allegorically uplifting, unifying one. That invasive state effort succeeded in part while also failing, but in frequently invigorating ways anticipated in Smaro Kamboureli's "Preface" in *Trans.Can.Lit*:

> "Canadian" minus any qualifier evokes the entirety of the geopolitical it refers to, but it also siphons off large segments of this space and its peoples into oblivion at worst, and circumscribed conditions at best. Nevertheless, the term conveys *a semblance of plenitude. Notwithstanding* the various attempts to instigate and maintain a dialogue between Anglophone and Francophone literatures in Canada, CanLit has, more or less, always functioned as a referent to Canadian literature in English. What's more, even within the parameters of this English idiom, CanLit's *feigned plenitude* has been forged by means of occlusion and repression, marginalizing particular idioms of English, as the language has been othered by indigeneity and diaspora. (2007, ix; emphasis added)

It would be hard to improve on the acuity and courage of this passage, but I think that participants in the TransCanada project have regularly matched both qualities in different registers and from different embattled or privileged vantages, up to and including *Refuse: CanLit in Ruins*, whose compelling allegiance to justice is troubled (for me) only by its characterization of ruins and refusal. Bill Readings's (1996) cultural and academic pessimism was excessive at the time his book *The University in Ruins* appeared and remains so today, attesting to the depoliticizing influence of American deconstruction and its problematic attraction to Heideggerian dwelling. (I much prefer Lee Maracle's chthonic take on ruins.) The editors of *Refuse* are alive to the complexities of refusal, but they and their fellow contributors miss or choose to ignore a key connection to Quebec's decisive severing of the state-church coupling and ushering in of a not-so-quiet revolution. It is feral resistance on this scale, by similar means against comparably intersectional authorities, that CanLit needs to aspire to, even while recognizing that *laicité* and its equivalents come with no guarantee of cultural or legislative peace. Rinaldo Walcott's secessionist "quitting" of CanLit at Mikinaakominis / TransCanadas seems to me a *refus local* awaiting connection to a larger imagining and achievement of justice. His is a quitting that doubles as a regrounding of creative, critical, and political Blackness in a multinations state persistently fearful of its constitutive Indigenous, Black, and diasporic presences and accomplishments. Let's locate that regrounding *within* CanLit, *and not* in the name of the feral against the overreach of the federal state, as always.

The move from resemblance to semblance theorized by Kamboureli frees Canada from mimetic, derivative legitimacy for a more astringent performance of the now. What are our current simulations, and how do they connect to our dissimulations of oneness whose default position remains straight male bourgeois whiteness? One answer lies in more robust Anglo-French dialogue infused with and refused by Indigenous/diasporic dialectic accustomed or committed to living and performing, with feet on the pristine, violated, or remediating surface of the earth. Calls to Action of the Truth and Reconciliation Commission's Report constitute a call to intellectual and imaginative arms of the feral subject, including the TransCanada individuals and communities interpellated but never fully controlled by that cultural formation or by the Circean state and its compliant institutions. After *surviving the paraphrase*, it is time in CanLitLand for *surviving the panoplies*, those suits of full-body armour that ancient Greek hoplites favoured for battle against a more numerous but less imaginative enemy. To do otherwise may well prove the ruin of us.

Between Empire and Nation

Synchronicity and Revolution in Chinese Canadian Writing[1]

/ CHRISTOPHER LEE

Introduction

One of the most ubiquitous features in Asian Canadian cultural criticism is the historical overview of anti-Asian racism. Rhetorically aimed at establishing the pervasiveness of racial exclusion, such accounts are necessarily brief and, as a result, often rely on citing a few well-known facts and events such as the Chinese Head Tax, the *Komagata Maru* incident, and the internment of Japanese Canadians during World War II to make their point. Indeed, these three example have come to stand in for the full range of legislated, systemic, and everyday racism directed toward Asians in Canada. Their power stems from their ability to signify the violent exclusion of these communities from the life of the nation (indeed the very word "exclusion" has become indelibly associated with Asian, particularly Chinese, immigration). The metonymic structure of this ubiquitous gesture highlights some of the assumptions underlying Asian Canadian cultural criticism. Even though each of these events belong to transnational processes that operated in other white settler colonies such as the United States and Australia, they largely function as a means to locate Asian Canadian history and culture within the conceptual and spatial borders of the Canadian nation-state. This narrative resonates with long-standing struggles for national belonging and recognition, a trajectory that seemed to be confirmed after World War II with the formal creation of Canadian citizenship, the gradual repeal of racist laws, and the liberalization of immigration policy.

Without denying the descriptive power of such narratives, it is nevertheless important to ask whether they adequately convey the lifeworlds of Asian migration. As Henry Yu writes, "As much as white supremacy might have constrained their activities, [Asians in Canada] lived rich lives that cannot be understood if all we know about them is what was *done* to them.... we might ask, what did the trans-Pacific migrants who followed those initial three Chinese merchants in 1858 do with the rest of their time in British Columbia?" (2007/08, 10). Yu's question about "the rest of their time" should prompt us to consider how the elevation of the nation as the primary point of reference for critical work makes it difficult to contend with the full range of Asian Canadian history and experience. To be sure, critics have long pointed out the ways in which Asian Canadian critical practices can reinforce the legitimacy of the state.[2] These arguments have, in turn, informed attempts to theorize how Asian Canadian lifeworlds are saturated with experiences and temporalities that, even in the form of traces and fragments, point to diasporic origins outside the nation.[3] Some of the most powerful work in this regard has focused on Asian-Indigenous relations, a topic that deeply questions the legitimacy of the settler state while raising difficult questions about the complicity of Asian migrants in the dispossession of Indigenous peoples.

In short, Asian Canadian critique has had to repeatedly grapple with the misalignment between its antiracist commitments and the vehicle through which such demands are conventionally addressed, namely the nation-state.[4] Asian Canadian critique derives from a logic of equivalence that frames its constituent terms as ethnonational categories. "Asian" is, of course, not an ethnicity or a nation, but it often functions as an umbrella term for various established and emergent communities, such as Korean or Vietnamese, that are thought of in such terms. Seeking to clarify this logic, this chapter focuses on the notion of Chinese Canadian, which, because of the long history of Chinese migration and presence, provides a particularly instructive instance of nation-based thinking. Instead of treating Chinese Canadian history and culture as a *Canadian* issue, this chapter revisits its formation as a *global problematic* indexed to world historical changes that took place in the nineteenth and early twentieth centuries.

At the heart of this inquiry is synchronicity, the temporal and spatial logic of cohabitation and equivalence that makes the category Chinese Canadian legible in the first place. What assumptions define Chinese and Canadian in relation to each other, and how do these assumptions reference the modern world system in which both formations emerged? As Sophie McCall, addressing the possibility of an encounter between Indigenous and Black studies, writes in her contribution to this book,

> the challenge to build viable critical frameworks that compare histories of occupation and resistance remains an urgently needed and relatively underthematized thread in critical discussions. Moreover, the stakes of these comparative endeavours often remain unarticulated: why and how do comparative frameworks matter? For whom do they matter? Under what sets of debates and in what arenas? (p. 282)

The arrival of migrants from the Pearl River Delta region of southern China to what is now British Columbia starting in 1858 was an encounter of otherwise distant polities that were, in quite different ways, contending with the power of race, empire, and nation. Neither polities were dominant in the world system, though they experienced their minorness in different ways. Writing about the rise of nationalism in late imperial China, historian Rebecca Karl insists on bracketing nationalism from teleologies of state formation. Instead, nationalism should be approached as a "concept-formation and intellectual reorientation [that] can only appear as part of a global historical problematic" (2002, 5), part of a set of "newly articulated relationships between global and national space, between revolutionary process and imperialist/nationalist ideology, and between ethnicity, citizenship and nationality" (2002, 4).[5] Karl writes:

> if we concede that "the West" was neither recognizable as such for most of the nineteenth century—it was an imaginary "stage" that was being produced but did not exist as such—and that "China" was not an already constituted national concept at the time (without denying that the Qing dynasty was obviously a polity and recognized as one), then inquiring into the formation of such overarching categories of historical conceptualization as "the West" and "China"—among others— must form a central part of the historian's task. This task requires inquiring into the process through which the historicized concepts of nationalism and globality came to be specified simultaneously in concrete time and space. (2002, 10)

Taking Karl's account as a point of departure, we might see nationalism as the basis of a comparative project that extends to diasporic communities in Canada. Here, "Chinese Canadian" can productively function as a conceptual conjunction that names the temporal and spatial collisions of modernity as embodied and experienced by the migrant. Such an approach departs from the tendency to frame discussions of Chinese Canadian history and culture primarily in terms of identity. My bracketing of identity is not so much motivated by predictable critiques of identity politics and essentialism—in fact, my sense is that identity remains an indispensable language for making sense of and representing the relationship between the subject and the social[6]—but rather by a desire to disentangle this category from teleologies of national belonging.

The history of Chinese migration to the West Coast can be seen as a microcosm of formal subsumption, the often violent incorporation of the noncapitalist world into the global market, with its demand for development and attendant political structures of society and state. As Harry Harootunian has argued, this process fixes the entry into capitalism as the "distant product of a prior historical moment filled with violence and trauma," which subsequently "passes into invisibility through a long process of forgetting resulting from the normalization (abstracting) of productive relationships" (2015, 34). This process is mirrored by the nation-state: although "national narratives invariably conceal and forget that the origins of the nation were forged in bloody violence, often reaching genocidal proportions...few nation-states have managed to escape employing this model of selective amnesia provided by capitalism" (Harootunian 2015, 35). This coupling of capital and nation—the commodity form and the nation form—is central to the construction of race in settler colonies like Canada. Yellowknives Dene scholar Glen Coulthard argues that settler-colonial domination involves the establishment of "a relatively secure or sedimented set of hierarchical relations that continue to facilitate the *dispossession* of Indigenous peoples of their lands and self-determining authority" (2014, 7). The Canadian state continues to rely on this access to land and resources as the basis of its socio-economic order, thereby reenacting the "violent transformation of noncapitalist forms of life into capitalist ones" (2014, 8). The presence of Asians in Canada was and is conditioned by this process; by the same token, attempts to come to terms with this past are vulnerable to the kinds of forgetting that legitimize capital and nation even as they grapple with the traces of these histories.

Race and Nation as a Transpacific Problematic

Mass migration from China to North America was caused by the "ongoing restructuring of the late-nineteenth-century world by capitalism, colonialism, and imperialism" (Karl 2002, 9), and the arrival of Chinese in 1858 on the West Coast coincided with the establishment of the Colony of British Columbia—what Jean Barman memorably calls "the West Beyond the West" (2007). During this time, "China" was still the Qing Empire, itself in the midst of a violent encounter with global modernity. If the two Opium Wars (1839–42 and 1856–60) signified the incursion of Western imperialism, the Qing's military defeat by Japan in 1895 dealt a fatal blow to its legitimacy. Even as the state made numerous attempts at reform and modernization, the possibility of overthrowing the entire imperial system gained momentum by the turn of the century.

During this period, notions of race, informed by Social Darwinism and other forms of nineteenth-century racial knowledge, became a popular means to make sense not only of imperialist incursion but also the relationship between the imperilled Qing state, which was ruled by a Manchu emperor, and the majority Han ethnic group. As Peter Zarrow has shown, anti-Manchu discourses played a key role in revolutionary movements as thinkers and activists concluded that "the most effective way to construct a popular national identity was on the basis of racial unity. This was to construct a pure nation-state based on Han identity" (Zarrow 2012, 154–55). Such claims soon spread to overseas communities, whose status was being redefined vis-à-vis emerging discourses of the nation-state. As Jing Tsu explains:

> Remarking on the prospect of racial extinction for the Chinese, writers and intellectuals in the early 20th century often cited as an example of China's feebleness the problem of unprotected Chinese laborers abroad. Perceived as a failure in China's own diplomacy and attainment of sovereignty, the mistreatment of Chinese laborers in the Americas and, to a lesser extent, Australia, in the 19th century fuelled an emotional, nationalistic resolve and political protests in the early 20th century. (2006, 250)

The conversion of the Chinese migrant from a traitor to the nation (a long-held view by successive imperial regimes) to its exemplary subject dovetailed into the emergence of anti-Qing/Manchu ethnonationalism. The long-suffering sojourner was transformed into a heroic subject marked by a capacity for discovery, adventure, and risk-taking. Prominent thinkers such as Liang Qichao (an influential exiled thinker who visited Canada in 1903) described Chinese in Southeast Asia as colonists, whose exploits could foreshadow the rise of a modern Chinese nation. But as Tsu notes, nationalism necessarily entailed "a corresponding aggression toward the outside world, incorporating diasporic frontiers as valences of the nationalistic core. The desire to know oneself became an invasive curiosity to know others" (2006, 257). In short, "anti-imperialist nationalism" (2006, 259) often reproduced the very desire for power that characterized imperialism in the first place.

Around the same time, the West Coast was in the throes of a violent transformation into a white settler colony as part of the British Empire. The establishment of British Columbia involved the dispossession of Indigenous peoples as well as the arrival of migrants from around the world. As scholars such as Adele Perry, Jean Barman, Renisa Mawani, John Price, and others have emphasized, colonial authorities mobilized technologies of knowledge production and governance to construct and reinforce racial hierarchies involving multiple groups. Perry (2001), for example, has argued that the settler-colonial project explicitly called for the establishment of a white-dominated social body with a primarily British character, a goal that motivated British Columbia's decision to join Confederation in 1871. Nevertheless, for most of the nineteenth century, European settlers were a minority on the West Coast. The completion of the Canadian Pacific Railway, one of the key conditions for joining Canada, was instrumental in facilitating the arrival of white settlers from elsewhere in Canada, Europe, and the United States while further dispossessing Indigenous peoples and displacing other racialized migrants. By the turn of the century, the demographic goals of white settler colonialism had largely been achieved.

In the first few decades after BC joined Confederation, there were numerous conflicts between the federal and provincial governments over attempts by the province to exclude and disenfranchise Asian migrants. Such clashes often pitted local calls for racial exclusion against the obligations of imperial diplomacy. At stake was not only Britain's different relationships with China and Japan, but also the tensions between the supposedly egalitarian claims of empire (subjects of the empire were supposedly equal to each other regardless of race or culture) and the emerging alliance of Anglo settler colonies that embraced Asian exclusion. The fact that exclusion would eventually win out indicated the remaking of a world largely marked by free migration into one governed by borders, passports, and immigration controls.[7] Canada regularly deployed practices previously used in Australia, South Africa, and the United States to control and manage racialized populations. The notorious anti-Asian race riots of 1907, John Price (2011) argues, were a turning point after which the federal government embraced exclusion policies. This decision would eventually result in the adoption of measures such as the continuous journey rule, the Gentlemen's agreement, which limited Japanese migration, and the outright prohibition of most forms of Chinese migration in 1923.

When viewed together, the unravelling of the Qing state and the consolidation of white settler colonialism on the West Coast conveys how migrants circulated in a world in which race, empire, and nation were dynamic forces in the establishment of modernities across the Asia Pacific. Rather than just seeing them as targets of state power, I want to emphasize the instability of the nation-state even though migrants, wittingly or not, played important roles in the ongoing articulation of state power. As a preliminary step toward this analysis, I turn now to an exemplary moment in Chinese Canadian history in which diaspora and nationalism became inextricably intertwined.

Revolution and Alternative Memory

In many ways, the 1911 revolution that overthrew the Qing state consolidated the identification of overseas communities with the home nation. Confirming the transformation of overseas Chinese into extensions of the nation, the story of Chinese Canadian participation places what was a relatively small diasporic community, in comparison with much larger ones in Southeast Asia or the United States, at the centre of an epochal event. The most famous instance of this heightened prominence was the Huanghuagang Uprising, a failed revolt in Guangzhou in April 1911 that is often interpreted as a precursor to the successful uprising that took place in Wuchang later that year. In Guangzhou, over eighty revolutionaries were killed by Qing forces, and the bodies that could be identified were immortalized in popular memory as the "72 Martyrs." In the lead-up to the Huanghuagang Uprising, financial contributions from Chinese in Canada exceeded those from any other overseas community, a fact that is prominently displayed to this day in the memorial park dedicated to this event. Given the mythological status of the 1911 revolution, which continues to be widely embraced across the Chinese-speaking world, it is not surprising that accounts of this period are dominated by the framework of the nation-state. But if we do not assume that the character of the nation-state was a matter of consensus among revolutionaries, the presence of diasporic Chinese starts to take on different meanings.

At the turn of the century, Chinese migrants in Canada and elsewhere were politically divided. After a notable attempt at reform failed in 1898, prominent dissidents such as Kang Youwei and Liang Qichao fled abroad, where they set up branches of the Empire Reform Association, founded by Kang in Victoria in 1899.[8] These groups would eventually come into conflict with revolutionaries who favoured a complete overthrow of the Qing. This conflict was not purely ideological, however, as it tended to reproduce preexisting divisions based on education, class, and areas of origin. According to Lee Tung-hai (1967), who wrote one of the first extended histories of the Chinese in Canada, it was not until 1907 that the tide turned decisively in favour of revolution as reformist groups started to unravel (although Lee does not make this connection, the rise of revolutionary sentiment coincided with the riots of 1907). Lee argues that the 1911 revolution succeeded due to the combined efforts of intellectuals who provided the ideas, the Overseas Chinese who provided the necessary capital, and the New Army that provided the force.

In 1910, Feng Ziyou, a close associate of the revolutionary leader Sun Yat-sen, relocated to Vancouver to edit the *Chinese Times* newspaper and set up organizations sympathetic to the revolutionary cause.[9] Sun himself made three trips to Canada: in 1898, after narrowly escaping a kidnapping attempt in London; in 1910, in the aftermath of a failed revolt in Guangzhou; and in 1911, when he arrived from San Francisco in February. By then, revolutionaries had made alliances with secret societies (such as the Cheekungtong, or Chinese Freemasons) and operated newspapers, study groups, and reading rooms dedicated to spreading their cause. According to some reports, Sun was received by over a thousand people when he arrived in Vancouver by train, and large audiences attended his four days of public lectures. In a subsequent letter to the San Francisco Chinese Freemasons, Sun wrote, "Since I arrived in Vancouver on the 8th, I have been royally received by all. Every day I lecture at the [Cheekongtong] hall or the theatre to audiences of 2–3,000. Even though it rains heavily there is unprecedented enthusiasm in Vancouver. If people feel this way, the success of the Revolution is inevitable" (qtd. in Wickberg 1980, 42–43). The story of Sun's rapturous reception suggests a visceral link between the man widely called the father of the revolution and overseas Chinese. Sun's own diasporic background (he grew up partly in Hawai'i) cemented what Allison Marshall (2011) has identified as a quasi-religious structure of identification with this iconic figure among Chinese migrants. To this day, statues of and memorials to Sun can be found around the world, including in Vancouver, Toronto, and Montreal.

Given the overwhelming tendency to mythologize Sun, it is interesting to turn to a rather different account of his 1911 visit. In *Opening Doors: Vancouver's East End*, a 1979 collection of oral histories edited by Carole Itter and Daphne Marlatt, Yun Ho Chang, who came to Canada in 1908, recalls:

> [Sun] spoke the same dialect I do, and so he spoke Cantonese with a Shek-ki accent. Most people here were from Sze-yup (Four Counties) and they didn't understand him. They said that if Dr. Sun couldn't make *them* understand his speech, how was he going to get China back from

> the Manchus. They were swearing in the background, while he was talking. His talk lasted for 2 or 3 hours, and then he asked for suggestions and people asked him about his plans. He would answer in a very calm confident tone. Some people contributed money on the spot, I did too, and Dr. Sun wrote out a receipt to each person who contributed. After the overthrow, if you went back to China with the receipt, he would refund your money. When I went back that was just before the revolution, and there was a regulation that anybody caught with this sort of receipt would be executed immediately so I burned mine. But some of my friends were given their money back. And one man who donated $100 was later given a life pension. But there was a difference of opinion among people here. Those people from Chung-shan were very enthusiastic about supporting him, but the Sze-Yup people were doubtful, and they would ask embarrassing questions like "You don't even have a ship or a gun, how are you going to overthrow a whole dynasty?" And "You don't have any money, all you have is talk." They nicknamed him Bullshit Sun, but he said support would come from the people if the overseas Chinese worked hard, and when the time came plans and cannons would be available. (1979, 40)

Although Chang confirms the enthusiasm generated by Sun's visit, his account emphasizes the lack of unanimity in the local community. In particular, he identifies the basis of division, namely differences of dialect and areas of origin. Whereas Sun's support was very strong among those who come from his home area of Chung-shan and shared his dialect,[10] his critics seemed to be drawn from those who were from Sze-yup, four counties in the Pearl River Delta region that was the original home of the majority of Chinese in North America. The drama of the scene described here stems in part from the mutual unintelligibility of those who speak Sze-yup dialects and those from other nearby regions. The denigration of Sun as an ineffective communicator seems to cast doubt on his revolutionary vision and his promise to create a unified nation-state. (Indeed, the 1911 revolution took place while Sun was abroad and was initially led by military forces that were unaligned with him, although he served briefly as the first provisional president of the new Republic.) Unlike the rapturous audiences described in Sun's letter, Chang's account suggests that there was a great deal of skepticism about his qualifications.

The point, in any case, is not to determine whether Chang's account is more accurate than Sun's, but rather to read his stories as part of an alternative popular memory about the events of 1911 rooted in the heterogeneity of Chinese migrant communities.[11] As I discussed earlier, the mythology surrounding Sun's relationship with overseas Chinese and their contributions to the revolution stems from the incorporation of Chinese migrants into a revolutionary national imaginary. His letter, after all, presents his Vancouver audiences as a vanguard of revolutionary feeling. Only when those audiences are seamlessly assumed to be part of a larger imagined political body can he conclude that their enthusiasm will translate across oceans. By contrast, Chang's stories indicate a looser relationship between migrants and the revolutionary imagination. Affective ties to China are not insignificant, but the messy terrain of everyday life is revealed as a space in which various differences and divisions play out, in which "unruly" responses such as cynicism, skepticism, and curiosity erupt and interrupt the conflation of nationalism and statism. In the next section, I turn a more recent literary text that revisits these events through the lens of contemporary Chinese Canadian identity politics and argue that attempts to graft the history of revolution onto the terrain of Canadian multiculturalism unexpectedly reveal the fissures of race and nationalism.

From Revolution to Nationalism and Beyond

Paul Yee's *The Curses of Third Uncle* is a novella for young readers published in 1986.[12] Set in Vancouver in 1909, it focuses on the adventures of fourteen-year-old Lillian Ho, who was born in Canada and lives in Chinatown with her parents, who struggle to make ends meet despite owning a garment business. This situation is exacerbated when Lillian's father, Jin Chong Ho, with whom she is very close, disappears for unknown reasons and leaves his family in dire financial straits. Her mother, pregnant with her fourth child, makes the decision to return to China, but then falls seriously ill, leaving Lillian to provide for her younger sisters by working as a maid for a white family. Most of the novella's plot revolves around Lillian's attempts to find out what happened to her father. Piecing together clues such as comments from visitors and the discovery of an intercepted letter from her father, she learns that he was carrying out secret work on behalf of Sun Yat-sen and his fellow revolutionaries. On a quest to locate her father, she journeys to the interior town of Revelstoke, where an old-timer reveals that her father had worked on the Canadian Pacific Railway and later became a supporter of the revolution and was raising money to purchase arms. Back in Vancouver, she learns that her villainous Third Uncle was responsible for her father's death because he stole a book of donor names and tried to sell the information. As the situation grows increasingly urgent, Lillian meets the visiting Dr. Sun, who participates in a plan to reveal Third Uncle's treachery.[13] Addressing the crowds who gather to listen to him, Dr. Sun publicly calls Lillian's father a martyr and urges his audience to financially support the Ho family. The story ends when Lillian's mother offers her the choice of going back to China or staying in Canada, and Lillian chooses the latter.

As this summary suggests, *Curses* can be seen a detective story in which Lillian's attempts to find her father unfold in parallel with her attempt to work out her identity as a young Chinese Canadian woman.[14] Despite its historical setting, Lillian's struggles are clearly meant to resonate with the experiences of Yee's contemporary readers.[15] In the opening scene, Lillian visits Vancouver's Stanley Park with her father and feels ashamed because of their poverty and visible racial difference. Surrounded by white residents, she feels disdain toward the Chinese men they encounter and the text voices her internalized racism: "If she had a pair of scissors, she'd run up and cut off their pigtails! Snip, snip! Then they wouldn't look so strange. Then maybe the whites wouldn't hate the Chinese so much" (Yee 1986, 4). As the novella unfolds, she comes to embrace her cultural heritage by learning about mythological women warriors and qigong, a common health/healing practice in China. This narrative of ethnic pride is juxtaposed onto a feminist one. Lillian initially feels devalued in her family and community, where girls are derogatorily referred to as "seet boon foh" or "commodities that lose money" (24). Her status as the eldest daughter makes her responsible for her younger siblings to the point where she has to quit school to work and provide care at home. But she also meets strong women role models and eventually asserts her agency by deciding to remain in Canada and embrace her cross-cultural identity.

In short, *Curses* is less a strict historical narrative than a multicultural *Bildungsroman* that reconciles Lillian's ethnic and gender identity to the larger social body. But insofar as Yee chooses to set the text at a pivotal moment in Chinese Canadian history, he also reveals the unruly side of nationalism as it operates beyond the spatial parameters of the (Chinese) state. At the beginning, Lillian has very little understanding of revolution even though it is constantly mentioned by her father's friends. Burdened by her husband's absence, Lillian's mother feels contempt toward his "run[ning] off to play revolution and abandon[ing] us without money or means" (26). Yee adds a crucial scene in which Lillian and her sisters piece together key facts of the story with the help of their tutor, who explains that China is governed by the Manchus, "northern tribes that conquered China four hundred years ago" (43). Exploiting their subjects to "keep themselves fat and in power," the Manchus "won't spend money on modern education or Western technology" (43). But now the empire was weak, defeated in war and wracked with internal rebellion; the girls learn that the "final battle"—the revolution to which their father has sacrificed his life (43)—is at hand.

In these and other passages, *Curses* reproduces the ethnonationalism that underscored the 1911 revolution. In particular, it reiterates the opposition between the "foreign" Manchu rulers and the majority Han Chinese, whose internal solidarity creates the affective as well as political conditions for the creation of a modern Chinese nation-state. As we have seen, this distinction was historically framed through ideologies of racial difference that enabled revolutionaries to articulate a form of nationalism that could challenge the legitimacy of the Qing state.[16] The failure of the Qing state to adequately modernize sets up the temporal contrast between a hopelessly outdated empire and a modern nation-state that would rise in its stead. According to Lillian's father, "China is weak and backwards...It needs modern education and a modern army to win respect from the West! But the Empire won't change, so we have to force change!" (93).

While these themes are very common in accounts of modern Chinese history, what makes *Curses* notable are the ways in which Yee tries to integrate them into a narrative of Chinese Canadian identity formation. The primary means for doing so, from a formal perspective, is the immigrant family narrative. Arguably the dominant narrative genre in contemporary Asian North American writing, the power of the immigrant family narrative stems in part from how it allows writers to imagine the passage of time through mechanisms of heteronormative reproduction, thereby reinforcing the centrality of the family unit. In texts like *Curses*, the embattled immigrant family's coherence is attributed to primordial ties of kinship and culture, even as it is revealed to be a site of violence and oppression, particularly for its female members. Emancipation, then, does not necessarily involve the destruction of the family but a careful negotiation between accommodation and transformation. But as erin Khuê Ninh has argued, the immigrant family is also a unit of capitalist reproduction, whereby children are fostered into potential producers of capital and success through the biopolitical management of their bodies and the regulation of their affect toward attaining upward social and economic mobility (see Ninh, 2014).

Although these family dynamics are rather out of the place in the historical period depicted in the novella, a time when very few Chinese nuclear families resided in Canada, they mediate the translation of revolutionary nationalism into a contemporary multicultural context. To be more specific, *Curses* tries to contain the global politics of revolution within intergenerational dynamics of sacrifice and filial obligation. As mentioned earlier, Lillian's mother disdains her husband's activities because she sees them as betrayals of his familial obligations. In a later scene, however, an old-timer reframes Lillian's father's actions in this manner:

> "I told [Ho] a family man should stay out of the revolution! But he wouldn't listen. He kept saying he had to do it because he didn't want the whites looking down at his children....Your father didn't want his children to grow up and hate being Chinese"...An eerie feeling suddenly came over Lillian. She felt as if she and Papa were staring at each other and reading each other's mind. Papa had seen into his children's future! He wanted to change the world for them! He cared for them so much that he was willing to risk his life! She shut her eyes to let the news sink in. (93)

Jin Chong links the success of revolution in China to the amelioration of racism in Canada, echoing the common charge that China's weakness in the world enabled the oppression of its people abroad. Yet the reframing of this desire in familial terms makes the immediate beneficiary of his activities his own children as the scene recalls Lillian's internalized racism. Lillian's affective response confirms the primacy of intergenerational sacrifice, but by relocating the beneficiary of revolution to Canada, *Curses* departs from the diasporic nationalism it otherwise reproduces.

In order to understand this divergence, we need to turn to the charismatic figure of Sun Yat-sen, who embodies the modern aspirations of revolution. When Lillian first learns about Sun from Mrs. Chang, her Sunday School teacher, she is told that Sun was a Christian who "went to school in Hawaii and trained as a medical doctor" (49). Mrs. Chang tells Lillian about his close escape from Qing agents sent to kidnap him in London, a well-known episode that greatly enhanced his reputation among Overseas Chinese. Having lost her own father to the revolution, Lillian embraces Sun as something of a father figure. The man who would later be hailed as the father of the nation (*guofu*) is portrayed as a kind man who embraces Lillian in her grief, cares for her family, and takes responsibility for their well-being.

In the climactic scene, Lillian sneaks into the Chinatown theatre where Sun is addressing a packed house. Yee's depiction of the event resonates with Sun's own account as the audience is enthralled with his call for revolution. "Too many men and women are dying from the [Qing] government's mistakes," he shouts. "The Chinese people want to be proud of their homeland! We want to stand tall in the world of nations! It's time to arm ourselves and fight our corrupt rulers" (124). He assures his audience that "The Chinese in this province of British Columbia...have been exceedingly generous in donating funds to the cause. Chinese living around the world are playing a vital role in the revolution!" (125). To prove this point, he singles out the martyred Jin Chong Ho for praise, and the crowd enthusiastically answers his call to assist the Ho family. In the novella's conclusion, Sun visits Lillian and her mother and assures them that "Ho Jin Chong's family *was* important to him...But he also saw the whole country as part of the family. He was concerned with the futures of countless babies when he undertook this work" (134–35).

It is here that the plot departs from the nationalist logic suggested earlier by her father. The conjunction between the family and nation-state is well known in Chinese political culture (in Chinese the nation is literally rendered as *guojia* or the nation-family). But the displacement of that family through migration, in a narrative that refuses any return to a homeland, excludes his family from the spatially bound nation-state that the revolution seeks to create. The nationalism that underscores revolution is rearticulated through a structure of race that makes "Chinese" legible, albeit in a subjugated position, in a Western-centric world system. Jin Chong's revolutionary activities are meant to create a future in which his children would no longer reject their Chinese identity. Crucially, Lillian's awareness of his sacrifice affirms her desire to remain in Canada even though the novella is set during a time when the Canadian state was heavily invested in the exclusion of Asian migrants. At first glance, then, this conclusion seems to be a projection of late twentieth-century concerns: by appropriating the history of Chinese revolutionary nationalism, the text turns it into a resource for multicultural identity formation by preserving its antiracist commitments while delinking the protagonist from the social body imagined by Chinese nationalism, the extension of the diaspora made the participation of overseas Chinese in the revolution possible in the first place.

The Canadianization of the Chinese revolution, while admittedly ahistorical, highlights the symbolic equivalences that enable such a transfer to occur in the first place. These operations subtend the discursive logic of Chinese Canadian culture and identity by making it possible to assume the mutual legibility and comparability of its two nation-state formations. This logic, I suggest, persists despite the admirable desire of much Asian Canadian cultural criticism to overcome the limits of ethnonationalism and its various state formations. This chapter has sought to historicize the emergence of ethnonationalism among early Chinese migrants in order to consider how migration and displacement expose its gaps and fissures. But as Rinaldo Walcott observes elsewhere in this volume,

> what is more difficult to achieve and dislodge are the myths of communal belonging that produce the conditions and narratives of unbelonging that modern nations have developed as a science of the social. The techniques of multicultural policies and rhetorics of inclusion with their slippery slopes of heritage discourse leading some to slide right out of the national narrative, while others remain firmly ensconced as national founders, is one such moment where the ethicality of the nation can be rethought to produce a more meaningful citizenship narrative and conditions of belonging. (p. 107)

With Walcott's caution in mind, I want to consider, as a provisional conclusion, a gap in *Curses* that foreshadows Yee's more recent work. Lillian's acceptance of her Chinese Canadian identity is accomplished through the elevation of her father into a hero: a revolutionary martyr, whose contributions are to be vindicated in the ultimate success of the revolution, as well as an immigrant father, whose sacrifice for his family enables their success in their new homeland. Key to making him fit both roles is his characterization as a labourer on the Canadian Pacific Railway. As the old-timer in Revelstoke explains, "we...worked on the railway, digging tunnels through the rock" (87–88), and one of Ho's brothers even perished in a rockslide, one of the thousands of Chinese sacrificed to create the infrastructure of the settler-colonial nation. Ho Jin's participation in this project supports his claim to be a builder of the Canadian nation even though his efforts were never properly recognized during his lifetime.

Yee has returned repeatedly to the CPR in his writing. His more recent work, however, particularly his 2015 novel *A Superior Man*, demonstrates a far more critical stance toward this topic. As he notes in a 2016 interview,

> The transcontinental railway was the mechanism by which white settlers traveled across and settled Canada. As we all know, this settlement had a devastating effect on Canada's aboriginal people. Today, when Chinese Canadians celebrate their railway heroes, they should also understand that all immigrants affected the Aboriginal peoples here. (Yee 2016)

By focusing on Chinese-Indigenous relations, Yee shifts away from narratives of multicultural nationalism that valorize the Chinese labourer while obscuring his role in the consolidation of white settler colonialism—the same system that would, following the completion of the CPR, demand the outright exclusion of Chinese from the nation. While the valorization of the long-suffering Chinese labourer has long been a potent trope for nationalist projects, including the 1911 revolution, Yee posits a critique of the imperial desires that underscore what Tsu calls "anti-nationalist imperialism" (2006, 259) by reorienting his focus toward Asian-Indigenous relations. While this approach marks a departure from the political imagination of earlier works such as *Curses*, it also continues the earlier text's attempts to displace ethnonationalism through circuits of migration, revealing fissures in its logic that enable the emergence of alternative ethical imaginaries and political projects.

Diplomacy *before* Reconciliation[1]

/ MARGERY FEE

How do we solve the settler problem?

—Paulette Regan, *Unsettling the Settler Within: Indian Residential Schools, Truth Telling, and Reconciliation in Canada*

How can the Canadian jurisprudence on section 35 be decolonized?

—Gordon Christie[2]

The blockade is diplomacy.

—Hayden King, "The Erasure of Indigenous Thought in Foreign Policy"

My title refuses a reconciliation that forecloses Indigenous sovereignty. Such a rejection means that reconciliation might never happen, remaining desired and impossible. Diplomacy assumes only that reconciliation *might* be possible. Diplomacy is the effort we make to resolve damaging conflicts. But it also assumes that talks might break down, parties might walk away. Diplomacy starts from disagreements, bad feelings, and violent histories. Diplomacy also assumes some sort of parity, face-to-face negotiation, and at least the potential for improvement. It privileges talk over violence, compromise over coercion. It is also an educational and political process, one that takes time, often painful, boring, annoying time.

The preceding paragraph is the opening of a short response paper I wrote for the *Mikinaakominis / TransCanadas* conference in summer 2017, in which I focused mainly on the Truth and Reconciliation Commission (TRC).[3] Most of what I wrote has been scrapped to bring the paper—if only sketchily--up to date with a few recent events, including the publication of the final report of the National Inquiry on Missing and Murdered Indigenous Women and Girls (NIMMIWG). As a white settler scholar living and working on unceded Musqueam territory, I have had the privilege (among many) of learning from Musqueam band members, Indigenous colleagues, and my students, who have articulated multiple standpoints while questioning mine. The Indigenous writers I have read with my students have also been my teachers. To echo the title of Daniel Heath Justice's *Why Indigenous Literatures Matter* (2018), this is one of the many reasons Indigenous literatures matter. The arts can help us grasp how worldviews based on relationality and kinship (see Robinson and Martin 2016) reveal and resist a globalizing neoliberal capitalism.[4]

Here, however, I will be reading drier documents. It's impossible to teach any literature without talking about law and politics, given the colonial history of literary criticism as a discipline[5] and literature professors' sometimes scant sense of important contexts. Since the rise of postcolonial theory, however, and of literary critics from the peoples colonialism made marginal, such narrowness has become harder to justify. In Canadian and Indigenous literatures, critics are now pointing out how much has been overlooked, obscured, or even censored to conceal the colonial land grab and its genocidal aftermath and affirming that these literatures need to be explicitly situated within their sometimes quite complicated historical and political relationships.[6] Labrador Inuk scholar Kristina Bidwell (née Fagan) notes that the common mainstream separation of culture from politics can lead to the omission of hard issues such as land claims in favour of "a non-challenging form of difference where Aboriginal peoples become yet another culture in the mosaic" (Fagan 2004, 14). A particularly challenging page was cut from Maria Campbell's influential 1973 memoir *Halfbreed* by her publisher, McClelland & Stewart, against her express instructions. The page describes her rape, at the age of fourteen, by a member of the Royal Canadian Mounted Police, a rape that tore apart her Métis family and almost destroyed her life (see Reder and Shield 2019). Mohawk writer E. Pauline Johnson's "A Red Girl's Reasoning" ([1913] 2016) refuses a happy ending, a refusal that cannot be understood without understanding that the patriarchal Indian Act stripped status and all associated rights from Indian women who married non-status men, and their children, until 1985 (see Crey and Hanson 2009). Syilx/Okanagan writer Jeannette Armstrong's 1985 novel *Slash* recounts the struggle for section 35 of the Constitution Act, 1982, which states "(1) The existing aboriginal and treaty rights of the aboriginal peoples of Canada are hereby recognized and affirmed. (2) In this Act, 'aboriginal peoples of Canada' includes the Indian, Inuit and Métis peoples of Canada."[7] Slash debates with his partner, Maeg, who is campaigning for the inclusion of Indigenous peoples' rights in the Constitution. Slash says, "'We don't need anybody's constitution, what we have is our own already. We have rights to land and nationhood'" (1985, 241). Their debate continues between those who feel that engaging with the state will lead somewhere better and those who are justifiably skeptical. Indigenous Peoples in Canada are governed by Canadian law; thus, technically, they can be plaintiffs or petitioners, but not diplomats, although they have turned this law to good effect at the Supreme Court in cases ranging from *Calder* (1973) to *Tsilhqot'in* (2014). However, change can come about in other ways.

The 1990 resistance at Kanehsatake (the Oka crisis) centred on land. The Quebec police did not engage in diplomacy;[8] their precipitate raid on a Mohawk protest camp turned tragic with the killing of one of their members. Eventually the Canadian government sent in the army. The world noticed. Ever since, Canada has been engaged in a flurry of repair, including three national inquiries and commissions: the 1996 Royal Commission on Aboriginal Peoples (RCAP), the 2015 Truth and Reconciliation Commission (TRC), and the 2019 National Inquiry into Missing and Murdered Indigenous Women and Girls (NIMMIWG).[9] Indigenous people, in particular, the four Indigenous commissioners, were heavily involved in these inquiries, mainly by providing testimony at hearings. RCAP provided a lesson: few read it. That might be forgivable if its recommendations had not also routinely been ignored by elected officials and senior bureaucrats. The shift of the TRC to Calls to Action and of the NIMMIWG to Calls to Justice marks a certain impatience: these are not suggestions or recommendations aimed at government. They call on all citizens. It is our responsibility to read and act on these Calls.[10] A lot of Indigenous goodwill and imagination—and pain—has been expended on these documents: we do not need to reinvent the wheel; we need to realize we have a wheel.

Aboriginal self-determination or sovereignty might seem outrageous ideas to those who haven't been keeping up (marginally forgivable in a year of pandemic doom-scrolling), but the Canadian government tabled Bill C-15 in December 2020.[11] It states that "the Government of Canada must take all measures necessary to ensure that the laws of Canada are consistent with the United Nations Declaration on the Rights of Indigenous Peoples [UNDRIP]" (Canada, Department of Justice n.d.).[12] Article 3 of the Declaration states that "Indigenous peoples have the right to self-determination. By virtue of that right they freely determine their political status and freely pursue their economic, social and cultural development" (Canada, Department of Justice n.d.). How could the passage of Bill C-15 mark anything but the long-awaited decolonial transformation of Canada? It was supported by a range of non-Indigenous and Indigenous politicians, as well as the Assembly of First Nations, the Inuit Tapiriit Kanatami, and the Métis National Council, the three major Aboriginal advocacy groups (Carolino 2020). Others, less enthusiastic, call it and the related Indigenous Rights Recognition and Implementation Framework "White Paper 2.0."[13] The bill passed into law in 2021. Some see potential for Indigenous gains, others, catastrophe.

I will not second-guess Indigenous thinkers, activists, or negotiators. They have been hard at work for decades engaging with the UN and the Canadian government to produce a better situation for their people. As those who organized the public face of the TRC recognized, it is the Canadian non-Indigenous public who needs to start engaging with the idea of decolonial change (see Mignolo and Walsh 2018). Unfortunately, many Eurocentric attitudes tilt the odds toward continuation of the colonial status quo. Needless to say, these attitudes are quite familiar to Indigenous people. As Anishinaabe political scientist Sheryl Lightfoot explains of the discussions leading to the UN Declaration, "Indigenous peoples were...

noted to be not only victims of specific acts of injustice but also victims of a dominant worldview" (2016, 39). This worldview, because it is dominant, is a nearly invisible social construct for those Canadians (like me) who live inside it and benefit from it. Even the concept that other worldviews might exist—that Indigenous nations might have ancient, valid, and productive worldviews and functional legal and governance systems—is hard to grasp.[14] The now neoliberalizing Euro-American worldview has successfully promoted itself as universal. The passage of Bill C-15 into law might be seen by most Canadians as a huge triumph, and Indigenous peoples could still end up worse off—"victims of a dominant worldview." The devil, as many Indigenous thinkers are saying, is in the details. Kerry Wilkins asks four questions: "who are the Indigenous peoples that are to benefit from UNDRIP, what are the territorial spaces to which it will apply, how might it be enacted as domestic Canadian law and what is the Crown's role toward Indigenous peoples after implementation?" (qtd. in Borrows 2019, 3). Conforming the laws of Canada to the Declaration will only be an improvement if respectful diplomacy leads to an ongoing living relationship. What level of self-determination will be at play in the process? A struggle over the name of the Declaration, in fact, marks the focus of the dominant world view on the individual self: the addition of the *s* to the word "people" was contested (J. Y. Henderson 2008, 53–54). Indigenous peoples only exist *as peoples* if they have self-determination; otherwise, state control will continue to transform these collectives into a collection of citizens whose rights to land are no greater than anyone else's. Indigenous worldviews—not to mention daily and everyday actions--put the collective first. More importantly, Indigenous existence as *peoples* is at stake in the difference. This difference means that those who negotiated Bill C-15 and the framework may be talking past one another.

I have already been using the words "diplomacy" and "reconciliation," although they don't convey what I actually want to say. Such words drag their histories with them and constitute reality in ways that are difficult to reconfigure. Problems with the word "reconciliation" have been thoroughly unpacked: when, exactly, did conciliation happen?[15] Why is a word with Christian resonances being used to describe the relationship? And where did the "truth" in the name of the Truth and Reconciliation Commission go? Diplomacy is generally taken to mean engagements between Westphalian states with full membership in the United Nations. Indigenous nations—what George Manuel (2019) called the Fourth World—are not considered to have the right to engage in diplomacy, although Indigenous diplomacies have a long history (see Lackenbauer and Cooper 2011; J. Y. Henderson 2008). Many early treaties between newcomers and Indigenous peoples were conducted on a nation-to-nation basis. Treaties were commemorated with named wampum belts and the relationship with newcomers metaphorically described as the Covenant Chain. Made of silver, it never rusted. Parties met every year to "polish the chain" by exchanging gifts and celebrating the relationship (Borrows 2002, 124–27). In this way, misunderstandings were ironed out and interpretations recalibrated face-to-face.

Treaties were required by the Royal Proclamation of 1763, regarded as the foundation of law on relations between Aboriginal peoples and Canada. Nonetheless, it blandly assumed Crown ownership of the land via the Doctrine of Discovery (see Lindberg 2010). The monarch did not need to see land to claim it. Hudson Bay, "discovered" in 1611, gave its name to the Hudson's Bay Company, which was granted control over its vast watershed in 1670 by Charles II. One argument discussed in the Supreme Court decision in *Calder* was that since George III could not have known of what is now British Columbia, his Royal Proclamation requiring treaties did not hold there. Francis Drake's voyage north along the West Coast in 1579 and Bering's discovery of the Bering Strait in 1721 were referenced to trump this idea (*Calder et al. v. Attorney General of British Columbia* 1973). The final report of the Truth and Reconciliation Commission (2015a), *Honouring the Truth, Reconciling for the Future*, states: "We call upon federal, provincial, territorial, and municipal governments to repudiate concepts used to justify European sovereignty over Indigenous peoples and lands, such as the Doctrine of Discovery and *terra nullius*, and to reform those laws, government policies, and litigation strategies that continue to rely on such concepts" (Call 47; TRC 2015a, 254). So if the primary justifications for Crown sovereignty are repudiated, what then? Both the Doctrine and *terra nullius* were concocted without any Indigenous input and without any consideration of the sociopolitical reality in the so-called New World. (Magic acts performed with crosses, flags, and swords by men on beaches ground Canadian land tenure.) Call 47 insists on reimagining the foundation of Canada with Indigenous Peoples as partners at the table. The TRC submitted its final report in 2015.

Seven years later, is the government engaged in "rights ritualism" (Adcock 2015, 2), attempting to look good while maintaining the status quo? What is happening to the land?

I have talked as if reconciliation could be achieved once and for all. But in fact, non-Indigenous Canadians will always live on Indigenous land. Indigenous peoples have survived despite hundreds of years of colonial attempts to eliminate them, often by forcing, coercing, or "educating" them into the mainstream as individuals. Their resistance has led to the decision that they have *sui generis* rights to their inalienable land, acknowledged by the Supreme Court (*Guerin v. The Queen* 1984). So far, so good—but, the justices continue, "Parliament has conferred upon the Crown a discretion to decide for itself where the Indians' best interests lie." Hmm. And does "land" mean only the existing, tiny, arbitrarily determined and often encroached-upon reserves? However such decisions are interpreted and built upon, reconciliation will always require an ongoing conversation—antagonistic, diplomatic, or friendly—about how we can best live on this land together.

White settler Canadian identifications were constituted by the "scientific" legitimation of a racial hierarchy that justified colonial depredations worldwide (and explains why white justices are deemed able to rule on Aboriginal interests). The categories labelled "immigrant," "French Canadian," "Black," "Asian Canadian," etc., emerged into legibility as "minorities" in contrast to the majority led by the settler British subject, implicitly and often explicitly male, white, propertied, and (always implicitly), heterosexual. As late as 1995, it was necessary to insist on "women's rights as human rights" at the United Nations World Conference on Women in Beijing (Slaughter 2018, 8). The human is often equated with the citizen and the history of who was (and is) allowed to vote and who ends up in office: clearly, some are more human than others. This norm of the individual white man was consolidated against the imaginary Indian as a member of a savage horde figured as without law, governance, or land rights. This representation rationalized the colonial land grab as the rescue of primitive others through Christian salvation and enlightened guidance. Indigenous worldviews have been consistently derided as pagan, primitive, superstitious, backward, antimodern, and a threat to mainstream ideals. These ongoing discourses make it easy to label Indigenous protesters as criminals or even terrorists. Settlers must unsettle how we think of ourselves and others (Regan 2010). Otherwise, what Patrick Wolfe calls "the refractory imprint of the native counter-claim" (2006, 389) will remain, a haunting and a stain.

Reconciliation highlights a problem with the nation, with nationalism, and with the dominant image of Canada. Those of us who are settler scholars may well be dreaming fantasies of reconciliation and affirming them for our students, performing yet again the colonizing move that strengthens our grip on the land, our privilege, and our sense of moral superiority. Aware of this, many of us don't want to reconcile with Canada—or at least not with the current widespread discursive formation that constitutes Canada as the happy home of exemplary civility, tolerance, and diversity. Reconciliation suffers from the same problems as the concept of recognition. Yellowknives Dene political scientist Glen Coulthard (2014) has laid out how these politics recreate the move of a generous, tolerant, and superior nation condescending to include Indigenous Peoples as equals, all the while refusing to grant their sovereign relation to the land. Reconciliation—even the word—is a problem if framed by the normative, albeit hallucinated, "white civility" of the settler-colonial mainstream (Coleman 2006). Lightfoot calls the model of reconciliation that ignores or limits the *sui generis* rights of Indigenous peoples who held the land before contact "Doctrine of Discovery reconciliation" (2016, 42).

Three hundred years after the celebrations around the Proclamation and the related Treaty of Niagara, the Supreme Court of Canada commented on the interpretation of the "existing aboriginal rights" that had been recognized and affirmed in section 35 of the Constitution Act (1982). These rights, the justices wrote in *R. v. Sparrow*, should not be "frozen" as if at contact, but rather should be "interpreted flexibly so as to permit their evolution over time" (1990, n.p.). Those interpreting them were instructed to "be sensitive to the Aboriginal perspective itself on the meaning of the rights at stake" (qtd. in Battiste and Henderson 2000, 207). However, six years later, in *R. v. Van der Peet*, the justices found themselves able to decide what was "integral to Aboriginal culture" about Dorothy Van der Peet's sale of ten salmon (*R. v. Van der Peet* 1996, n.p.). This decision exemplifies the problem with "freezing" culture in the past or assuming that it has an essential quality. Further, the decision notes that the Aboriginal "perspective must be framed in terms cognizable to the Canadian legal and constitutional structure" (1996, n.p.). Further, in all such decisions, what is deemed to be the public good can override Aboriginal claims.[16] Judges swear an oath of loyalty to the Crown—and it is Crown land that is, ultimately, at issue. When the witnesses in *Delgamuukw v. British Columbia* sang the songs that proved their title to the land under their laws, Chief Justice McEachern allowed it, while apologizing that he had a "tin ear" (Culhane 1997, 123). Non-Indigenous Canadians, not surprisingly, have a "tin ear" for unfamiliar world views. However, by fronting their laws and ways of asserting claims to land in the face of the court's incomprehension, these witnesses constituted themselves as diplomats engaged in nation-to-nation negotiation.

The TRC is based on the UN Declaration (see Call 43)—and the Declaration was hammered out by Indigenous peoples from around the world over decades (see J. Y. Henderson 2008; Lightfoot 2016). Their goal was to insert collective rights into a long history that framed the individual human (variously defined) as the sole bearer of rights. The default of mainstream thinking to the individual over the collective tends to make an exception for the nation-state: "Oh, Canada" is regularly sung in schools and at hockey games for that reason.[17] Other collective rights, however, are often represented as a danger to individual rights, while obscuring the fact that state terrorism has killed many in the name of either protecting its citizens or assimilating those noncitizens deemed to be assimilable. John Hinkson has argued that the global shift to neoliberalism has only deepened the "'naive unknowing' of settlers, insofar as their societies can 'seem only to be composed of individuals.'" Thus, "From this naïve settler standpoint, all Indigenous peoples need to do is accept the terms of settler society and assimilate to it: just like any other individual" (qtd. in J. Henderson 2012, 307).

Given the prevalence of statistics showing the stark disparity between Indigenous people and everyone else in Canada in terms of health, housing, education, employment, children taken into "care," and youth and adults incarcerated, it is tempting to believe that once this disparity disappears, reconciliation and decolonization will have been accomplished. Certainly, many Canadians feel this disparity can and should be eliminated. Notions of equality, fairness, and level playing fields drive this feeling, and we should hang on to it and work to make change happen (see Blackstock 2019). But the conception of equality has its limits because it frames Indigenous people as individuals who must be treated as equals—but no more than that. Any further move to grant collective rights is often seen as unfair, as "race-based," rather than a distinction based on legally constituted rights to land and resources.[18] As pointed out in the RCAP final report, "The term Aboriginal peoples refers to organic political and cultural entities that stem historically from the original peoples of North America, not to collections of individuals united by so-called 'racial' characteristics" (Royal Commission on Aboriginal Peoples 1996). However, if the underlying causes of the disparity—colonial land theft and racism—are left out of consideration, the relationship between Canadians and Indigenous peoples will remain at an impasse.

Again, the connotations of the words here require more thought. "Resources" are commodities extracted through "development" for the use and profit of human beings, particularly those who own, or own shares in, the companies doing the extraction from an entity regarded as inert matter. The mainstream definitions of land and resources are not those of many Indigenous worldviews, which regard human beings as one with the land and far from its most powerful beneficiaries: "In much of Anishinaabeg philosophy, non-human communities are afforded supreme status. We live at their discretion" (King 2017). Many Indigenous People believe that we are in the world to look after it, and if we fail in this responsibility, the consequences are dire. In *What We Have Learned*, the Truth and Reconciliation Commission notes that "If human beings resolve problems between themselves but continue to destroy the natural world, then reconciliation remains incomplete" (2015c, 123). As we have seen, the word "human" has been understood in extremely exclusionary ways, but even a definition that includes all humans leaves out the much broader Indigenous definition, based on the understanding that humans and other-than-humans have always lived entangled lives. Other-than-human creatures, lands, mountains, and waters are not things, but what Marisol de la Cadena has called "earth-beings" (de la Cadena 2015, 5). To concentrate on moving Indigenous "wellness indicators" level with those of us non-Indigenous Canadians, however positive a step, requires no fundamental change in us, our worldview, or what it means to live and be well.

One mainstream "solution" to the appalling federal neglect of services on reserves has been to suggest that Indigenous people move south. It can seem logical, but in fact, it is another way to destroy Indigenous collectives. Certainly, federal neglect has been highlighted by such acts as Theresa Spence's hunger strike on behalf of Attawapiskat in 2012 (see Crosby 2017), and by the need for whole reserves to be evacuated because of fire, flooding, water pollution, and melting permafrost and ice. The pandemic has highlighted issues around inadequate health care and overcrowded housing. Certainly, many have left home communities, either by choice or out of desperation. But to choose this move is to leave a supportive community and one's responsibilities to sustain it, and to find oneself and one's children racialized in ways that often mean access to employment, education, and equal services is still blocked by poverty and racism, overt and systemic.[19]

Demographic indicators are useful, despite the risk of reducing human relations to statistics. Yet however much these statistics can measure improvements, they are not designed to measure the strengthening of Indigenous peoples *as peoples*. What the residential schools attempted to destroy was the collective: anything that preserved Indigenous peoples as national formations with a claim to territory. This destruction started with family and acted through the family, attacking worldviews, laws, languages, and ways of representing and being in the world. The actions that were justified by these beliefs have often been labelled "genocide" or "cultural genocide." Patrick Wolfe (2006) discusses these terms, their history and connotations, pointing out that although settlers have certainly committed genocide in its common definition of organized mass killing, in fact, the main focus is on taking land, and a variety of methods (not always obviously violent) have been used. Eliminating peoples with rights to land can be accomplished by converting members of Indigenous nations into citizens whose only right to land is through fee-simple purchase and title.[20] Residential schooling and other settler actions were driven by what Wolfe calls the settler "logic of elimination," which works not only by war, massacre, or the assassination of activist leaders, but also by less obviously violent methods (2006, 387). Col. Richard H. Pratt, the founder of the United States Industrial School at Carlisle, Pennsylvania, in 1879, spoke against the Indian wars and for assimilation: "A great general [Philip Henry Sheridan] has said that the only good Indian is a dead one, and that high sanction of his destruction has been an enormous factor in promoting Indian massacres. In a sense, I agree with the sentiment, but only in this: that all the Indian there is in the race should be dead. Kill the Indian in him, and save the man" (1892, 46). His school became a model for the development of residential schooling in both the United States and Canada.

Residential schooling falls under the definition of genocide in the UN Convention on the Prevention and Punishment of the Crime of Genocide (United Nations, General Assembly 1948): "Forcibly transferring children of the group to another group" (Article 2e). This definition also covers the ongoing removal of Indigenous children from their families and the incarceration of youth. The National Inquiry into Missing and Murdered Indigenous Women and Girls (2019) felt it necessary to append a supplementary report, "A Legal Analysis of Genocide." Because the Holocaust, perpetrated by the Nazis in World War II, has become the model of genocide, most people see the word as referring to organized mass killings instigated by an autocratic leader; however, this model fails to capture colonial genocide, which is slow, often driven by policy rather than direct violence, and includes acts of both commission (such as the legal redefinition of Aboriginal status or police violence) and omission (such as chronic underfunding, legal stalling, failure to enforce laws against racist violence or fulfill treaty obligations, and so on). As the supplement points out, this "internationally wrongful act is slower, more insidious, structural, systemic, and often spans multiple administrations and political leadership" (NIMMIWG 2019, 20). Non-Indigenous Canadian citizens are all complicit in these criminal acts. The saying "ignorance of the law is no excuse" is not just a saying but a legal reality. With the TRC and the NIMMIWG, ignorant heads must come out of the sand.

I have been lucky to think through these issues in conversation with students and others with different standpoints and life histories. I learned always to begin my courses by acknowledging that many in the classroom knew more than I did about many things, in particular about the experience of racialization. I have had to open up discursive spaces that challenged students' deep beliefs, attempting to talk about everyday racism, sexism, and homophobia while simultaneously trying to defend students from becoming victims of these violent discourses. The ability to intervene on the fly is a difficult trick to manage while one is grappling with one's own problematic identifications. I could correct my students' sentence structure, but miss their anger or despair.[21]

Colonization has not been good for "ordinary" Canadians. Rev. Stan McKay, a residential school survivor, points out, "The perpetrators are wounded and marked by history in ways that are different from the victims, but both groups require healing.... How can a conversation about reconciliation take place if all involved do not adopt an attitude of humility and respect? (qtd. in Truth and Reconciliation Commission of Canada 2015c, 115–16). This widespread Indigenous concept of respect covers more than politeness and does not require us to agree with or even like each other.[22] Indigenous governance systems presume that people will disagree; in fact, people are expected to bring different perspectives and interests to the table. Although bringing the parties to agreement is time-consuming, we should forestall agreement rather than violate respect for them and their opinions.

However, if current negotiations make no change to what "the law" entails (read absolute Crown sovereignty) or compromise treaty relationships (which require ongoing diplomatic negotiations) in favour of a "final" settlement (this word is found in many of the modern treaties), trouble lies ahead. If these agreements facilitate mining, pipelines, logging, and fishing and other resource extraction unrestrained by Indigenous free, prior, and informed consent, then White Paper 2.0 will have succeeded where White Paper 1.0 was blocked. Pipeline spills, carbon emissions, radioactive waste, species extinction, pollution of air, land, and water: all of these are the results of seeing air, land, water, and earth beings as resources to be exploited for individual short-term gain, rather than as beings living in relation with other collectivities.

The greatest gift provided by Indigenous thinkers to Canada is their explosion of the idea that Canada's future must be determined by the current dominant worldview. They are thinking the future otherwise. We non-Indigenous Canadians now need to reconcile with the truth of our own history so that we can join them.

From Islamo*phobia* to Islamo*philia*?

Dancing Orientalisms, *Islamizing* Muslims, and the Unspeakability of the Muslim Woman Subject

/ SEDEF ARAT-KOÇ

> Thus emerges a vicious circle, in which anti-Orientalism leads directly, in its claims for authenticity and singularity, to the re-Orientalization of orientals....It is a culture of misrecognition with two main protagonists who provide mirror-images of one another: the one is the Islamist revivalist and politician; the other, the western writer or actor who shares the essentialist culturalism of the former, and who elevates his obscurantist discourse on the past, present, and the future of Muslims to the status of indisputable knowledge...
>
> —Aziz Al-Azmeh, "Postmodern Obscurantism and 'The Muslim Question'"

In a climate where Muslims in diaspora have experienced extreme scrutiny, suspicion, and hostility in Western societies, one of the antiracist strategies adopted against anti-Muslim racism has been a (direct or indirect, overt or implicit) defence of Islam and some Muslim identities. In what I will, tentatively and provocatively, call an Islamo*philic* strategy, there is a tendency to *Islamize* Muslims. Sometimes used as a defensive strategy by diasporic Muslims or by some antiracist scholars and activists, other times based in a "friendly Orientalism" of Western liberals, Islamo*philia*—ironically like Islamo*phobia*—is associated with a tendency to see the "Muslim community" in diaspora as made up of individuals who are typically conservative Muslims; who subscribe to orthodox interpretations of Islam; and whose lives, attitudes, ideas, priorities, and identities are (necessarily) centred around Islam. In academic analysis, Islamo*philia* has also involved an uncritical adoption of the critique of secularism developed by some "post-secular" postcolonial theorists identifying it as a (necessarily) Eurocentric, colonial, and authoritarian tool in the hands of the state (see Asad 2003 and Mahmood 2005).

As much as this approach to countering anti-Muslim racism may be intended to reverse and replace suspicion and hostility against Islam and Muslims with sympathetic attitudes, I suggest that it operates in the same culturalist and Orientalist framework. Rather than a displacement of Islamo*phobia* with antiracism, what we observe in public discourses on Muslims is a *dance* of Orientalisms, moving between Islamo*phobia* and Islamo*philia*. In addition to constraining the range and depth of individual interpretations and expressions, and making several dimensions of *lived* Muslim cultures "unspeakable," this "dance" of Orientalisms creates a totalizing logic, leading to a shrinking and choking of democratic space. This chapter aims to introduce complexity to and expand the analysis of racism and Orientalism against Muslims in Western countries beyond the notion of Islamo*phobia*. It highlights the dangers of the shared culturalism of *Islamophobia* and *Islamophilia* and argues that the latter can be as problematic as the former in constraining and distorting articulations of Muslim lives and identities.

Developing an antiracist language and strategy has been especially challenging for women's groups and feminists as they try to struggle simultaneously against anti-Muslim racism in the larger society and conservative patriarchal claims to cultural authenticity in Muslim communities. Developing an effective language and strategy is especially difficult as issues of gender and sexuality have taken centre-stage in anti-Muslim discourses; and the resonance of Islamo*phobia* in most Western countries has gone beyond the extreme right and nativist conservatism, gaining a strong hold in liberal common sense. As David Theo Goldberg writes, "Islam is taken in the dominant European imaginary to represent a collection of lacks: of freedom; of a disposition of scientific inquiry; of civility and manners; of love of life; of human worth; of equal respect for women and gay people" (2006, 345). As much as *Islamohobic* attitudes and actions may evoke defensive *Islamophilia*, I argue that antiracist feminism would benefit from secular analysis and representation. In the spirit of Edward Said's notions of secular criticism and secular humanism, I argue for a *critical* secular understanding and representation of Muslim women in public, academic, literary, and artistic discourses. For antiracist analysis and activism, this would mean that there is an urgently needed interrogation of the culturalist categories and assumptions held and imposed on the identities and experiences of Muslim women in the media, political and policy discourses, social sciences, and different forms of literary and artistic representation.

Secularism in analysis and representation would need to involve a few basic principles. First among these is recognition of the enormous diversity of beliefs and practices in the *lived* experiences of Muslims. Rather than seeing Islam as a unitary entity—as captured in the commonly used term "the Muslim world"—and centring conservative Muslims as *the* typical and authentic Muslim diasporic subjects, this would mean accepting that Muslims may, like those from other religious backgrounds, ascribe to various versions and interpretations of faith—and/or atheism—as well as expressing inconsistency between belief and practice in their daily lives. Second, rather than assuming a monolithic and ahistorical notion of religion-as-culture to be the main variable in the making of diasporic Muslim subjects, secular analysis and representation must involve a consideration of the social, economic, political, and policy contexts in the constitution of their identities and lived realities; it is important to recognize that Muslims, like non-Muslims, are differentiated by class, ethnicity, country of origin, generation and rural/urban backgrounds. Third, in so far as "culture" and "cultural identities" are understood as factors, they need to be conceptualized not as given, but rather as constructed in the context of socio-economic, political, and geopolitical relations.

The chapter starts with problematizing and discussing Islamophobia and Islamophilia, discourses and practices that appear to be based in opposing principles, but are in reality rooted in the same culturalist, specifically Orientalist, logic. To demonstrate how the culturalism of these discourses limits and distorts debate, and thus makes it very difficult to articulate antiracist discourses, the second section of the chapter offers a brief discussion of the "Sharia law" (*non*)debate in Ontario 2003–5. The third section looks into what is omitted in culturalist discourses, summarizing some of the relevant social, economic, and political issues impacting Muslim women's lives in the recent period. The chapter concludes with a discussion about reorienting conceptualization of "culture" and formulating alternatives to Islamophilia in antiracist feminist thought.

From Islamo*phobia* to Islamo*philia*: A New Orientalism?

Even though Islamophobic and Islamophilic discourses on Muslims may appear to be opposites, they represent two sides of the Orientalist logic, continuing to reduce understanding of Muslim identities and lives to a culturalist dimension. What I provocatively call Islamo*philic* are attitudes and a perspective, entertained by Muslims or non-Muslim Western subjects, that are positive about Islam and Muslims. Like Islamo*phobia*, however, Islamo*philia* involves a tendency to reduce political and geopolitical issues to attitudes about Islam, and to conceptualize Muslims and the "Muslim community" in monolithic ways as centred around religion-as-culture.

While I tentatively use the term "Islamo*phobia*" and have ironically and provocatively introduced its seeming opposite, "Islamo*philia*," I would like to emphasize that both terms, if used literally, are analytically limiting and misleading in a number of important ways. It is well established that there has been a significant circulation and popularization of negative discourses, attitudes, actions, and policies in Western countries against Islam and Muslims in the post–Cold War period, and especially after September 11, 2001.[1] These take various forms, including suspicious attitudes toward Muslims and simplified interpretations of Islam and Islamic texts, making causal connections between religious texts and terrorism and violence, and making universal generalizations about Islam, assuming it to be medieval, static, and incapable of change, and thus essentially incompatible with human rights, women's rights, and democracy. As much as the term "Islamo*phobia*" may capture something about the exceptional scrutiny, suspicion, and panic created around Islam and Muslims, however, it is a term that psychologizes and depoliticizes their character and causes. Displacing the political, political economic, and geopolitical bases of the racism faced by Muslims and attacks faced by Muslim-majority countries, the term tends to suggest that the issue is about an ignorant fear of Islam per se. Secular critics suggest that, in addition to its analytical inaccuracy, the term "Islamo*phobia*" may distort political strategies by "concentrate[ing] minds on protecting a religion rather than people," and shutting down criticisms of various critiques of religion or specific fundamentalist organizations (Saghal 2012, 56).

Even though references to *Islamophobia* may intend to evoke sympathy for Islam, the references to the term may uncritically adopt the same culturalist logic of the thesis of the "clash of civilizations": that the main political dynamic in the world after the Cold War would be the clash between "civilizations," which are conceptualized in a rather tribalistic fashion as presumed cultural/religious entities with insurmountable differences and tensions between and among them (Huntington 1996). In addition to its limitations in making sense of race and ethnic relations in Western countries, the application of the notion of *Islamophobia* to Western foreign policy is also problematic as it underestimates the flexibility of imperial strategies over time. It specifically overlooks the West's long history of intimate relations with Islamists throughout the Cold War, as well as the preference for Islamist allies in the Middle East and North Africa in the period following the 2011 Arab uprisings. As the approach to Islam and Islamists has sharply oscillated in Western foreign policy over time, it would be more accurate to describe the approach as a *dance* of/between evocations of *Islamophobia* and *Islamophilia* around shifting definitions and constructions of "good Muslim" and "bad Muslim" in different geopolitical contexts (see Arat-Koç 2014). Problematizing culturalism in the notion of *Islamophobia* helps reveal the fact that, rather than reflecting anything about a presumed cultural essence, or deep-rooted historical practices of Islam, Islamist politics is very much a modern product of world politics. As Mahmood Mamdani (2004) convincingly demonstrates, not only is the distinction in the West between "good" and "bad Muslims" a political and geopolitical one—rather than one based on assessments of different interpretations and practices of Islam—but the very emergence of political Islam as a global phenomenon is itself a historically specific outcome of a modern encounter with the West.

Culturalism does not only involve categories of "good" and "bad" Muslims. It also tends to imagine *the authentic* Muslim subject. Whereas some of the overtly *Islamophobic* response to 9/11 tended to see liberal and secular Muslims as the "good" Muslims, *Islamophilia* may tend to reverse this, implicitly seeing/presenting conservative Muslims as the true, authentic ones. There are serious political implications to any notion and assumption of authenticity. The logic of authenticity does not stop at *describing* a "true," "authentic" Muslim subject; it often plays a disciplining, *prescriptive* role, questioning and potentially delegitimizing the belonging of heterodox or secular voices in the "Muslim community" and serving to engineer Muslim positions and identities. Ironically, the logic of authenticity is as much likely to be employed by non-Muslims in the name of fighting *Islamophobia* as by Muslims claiming authentic identities.[2] As Sadia Abbas writes,

> In an ironic inversion of the neoconservative hierarchy, the priority given to metropolitan concern, and postcolonial guilt, means metropolitan intellectuals get to anoint good Muslims and tar bad ones. They get to choose between those who raise acceptable concerns, and thus get to retain their Muslim status, and those who do not. A more counterintuitive consequence is that Islam and Muslims both become an undifferentiated block, despite the numbingly familiar and yet increasingly meaningless assertion that Islam is not a monolith… (2013, 165)

Warning about the dangerous implications of cultural essentialism before the post–9/11 context, Uma Narayan advised postcolonial feminists to be cautious about using totalizing categories and making essentialist contrasts between "Western" and "Third World" cultures, "Western" and "Third World" women (1998, 2000). Challenging some contemporary assumptions, Narayan reminds us that colonialism in the past and cultural imperialism today proceed more by "insistence on Difference" rather than an "imposition of Sameness" (2000, 1083). Arguing that the contrasts cultural essentialism provides between "Western" and colonized cultures distort realities about both, Narayan articulates how this perspective *in*authenticates and delegitimizes the politics of Third World feminists and others who contest the "national culture" as "cultural traitors" and "stooges of Western imperialism" (1998, 91). Explaining the constraints placed on "speaking" for antiracist feminists in Britain, Priyamvada Gopal also identifies the regressive communitarian implications of culturalism as the problem: "communities emerge as fully fledged, anthropomorphic subjects possessed of a single sensibility underpinned by a set of determinate beliefs and spokespeople. They are constituted by faith, itself irreducible, and each possessed of a singular sensibility" (2013, 111). As this notion of "community" may be based on an emphasis on "cultural difference," this emphasis, as Gopal demonstrates, suppresses actual differences and struggles for change within the "community" itself: "what gets written out are precisely the small voices, fractures, the margins and the contestations. As the community emerges as both person and icon, it puts itself beyond reformulation, reconstitution and revision, although as an entity it can enter into civil and political transactions" (2013, 111).

Difficulties of Speaking: The "Sharia" (non) Debate

The so-called "Sharia debate" in Ontario started in 2003, when Syed Mumtaz Ali, a retired lawyer and the president of the Islamic Institute of Civil Justice (IICJ), a small and newly established organization, advocated on the organization's website that in accordance with the Arbitration Act of 1991, which had enabled Catholic, Jewish, and Ismaili groups to use religious principles to provide family arbitration, a "Sharia court" could provide these services to Muslim families. Ali also added that Muslims who did not use this channel in family matters were not "good Muslims." What sounded like a proposal to apply the act to a new religious group prompted a major controversy and exploded into protests for and against the proposal. The controversy ended in 2005, when Premier Dalton McGuinty rescinded the 1991 Arbitration Act and ended all religious arbitration on family matters.

I would like to argue that, despite the different and conflicting voices from among Muslims that were expressed during the controversy, this was a (non)debate as the context in which the debate unfolded placed a straitjacket on the way positions could be framed and interpreted. The debate occurred in a political/ideological climate of the "war on terror" in which the emphasis on gender had come to occupy a central space in public discourses. When the dominant public discourse on gender identities of Muslims had become about "the imperilled Muslim woman and the dangerous Muslim man" (Razack 2004, 131), it became increasingly difficult to formulate a position outside the parameters of being either anti- or pro-Islam. Rather than debating the pros and cons and gender implications of private arbitration and religious arbitration *in general*, the debate turned into a "culture talk" and culture war about Islam. Even though a significant feminist literature was available, articulating concerns about and documenting the gender implications of private arbitration, these considerations were completely sidelined and hardly occupied any attention in public discourses (Bhandar 2010, 334). Neither were there any references in public discourse to research or stories about the experiences of Jews, Catholics, and Ismailis who had been using religious arbitration since the early 1990s. According to Davina Bhandar, the ubiquitous "cultural talk" in media, legal, and policy discourses has operated as a project of governance and a disciplining tool, shaping "the use of the 'cultural' for determining how citizens belong within nation-states" (338). Regarding the debate in Ontario over religious arbitration, Bhandar argues that culturalism has suppressed some perspectives and positions and narrowed down the debate. With the division of the political terrain along cultural/religious lines, not only has the heterogeneity of the "Muslim community" failed to be represented, but feminists who are secular and antiracist "found it difficult to establish a foothold in the public terrain" (337):

> It was highly problematic to simultaneously articulate a position that was critical of the patriarchal and conservative views of the Muslim clerics producing a particular vision of the 'Good Muslim', and challenge a feminist response to Sharia law based in a discourse that propagated a... [racialized depiction of Muslims]. Once the deliberation turned to the cultural validity of Islamic law to be practiced on Canadian soil, and the potential harm through its acceptance, the debate shifted away from the actual merits or pitfalls of the arbitration process. The discussion became reassembled through the discourse of culture talk, to the effect that positions became hardened between either anti- or pro-Islam. (2010, 337)

I would like to add that the challenge of articulating a voice and getting heard was especially onerous for antiracist feminists who became acutely aware of how their voices could be appropriated for anti-Muslim and Western supremacist positions, and/or as apologists for US/NATO wars in the Middle East. A political climate that created "public intellectuals" and celebrities out of Muslim "native informers,"[3] handsomely rewarding them with international media attention, professional status, and income, made it even more difficult to speak with dignity about antiracist and feminist concerns.

Overall, the Ontario debate on religious arbitration turned into a (non) debate, as the culturalist framing of immigrant and racialized women's issues suppressed complex voices and positions, forcing women to make impossible choices. Audrey Macklin suggests that the dichotomy created in popular discourses between culture and rights chokes the actual voices of culturalized women: "it is not so much that the encultured woman is put to the invidious choice of 'either your culture or your rights'; it is rather that she is not yet fully heard when she replies 'neither, as presently constituted, and both, as I envision them'" (2009, 299).

In the British context, Alana Lentin argues that the culturalist shift in the 1980s in antiracist thought and activism "left activists bereft of a vocabulary" (2014, 1278). In Ontario, similar challenges applied to developing a new vocabulary of antiracist positions simultaneously avoiding the traps of Western supremacy and conservative Islamism. Lentin argues that culturalism, now ubiquitous in the right and the left of the political spectrum, is "post-political," "both reducing the socio-economic to the cultural, and constraining the terms of the debate within a culturalist register that takes a reified 'culture'—both 'theirs' and 'ours'—for granted" (1271). I would like to add that culturalism is also *anti*political in reducing, locking debates into identitarian positions, therefore stalling and disabling public space for actual political discussions and debates. Kenan Malik underlines the irony of liberal multiculturalism: "One of the ironies of living in a plural society, it seems, is that the preservation of diversity requires us to leave less room for a diversity of views" (2013, 72).

One of the implications of the culturalist straitjacket placed on debates has been the rather uncritical adoption of postcolonial critiques of secularism in some antiracist assessments of the "Sharia debate" resorted to, declaring secularism (as always and necessarily) a disciplinary tool in the hands of the Western state, and (necessarily) Eurocentric and colonial.[4] While this position may sound justified in response to rampant (ab)uses of secularism and the false claims to universalism in anti-Muslim and Western supremacist discourses that provoke nativist nationalism—such as in the case of what Étienne Balibar calls the "fundamentalist *laïcisme*" in France (2018, 162)—it is also problematic as an overgeneralization and in terms of the political implications it potentially entails. The notion that secularism is foreign or inauthentic for Muslims may fall into the trap of a simplistic, dualistic notion that "the West" is secular and "the secular" is Western, neither of which is accurate. The notion that secularism is of Western provenance is empirically inaccurate as it not only erases the history of secular Third World, including Arab, nationalisms, but also ignores how *non*secular many Western states, societies, and much of their politics are.

In articulating antiracist and anticolonial feminist strategies, it is important to remember Mamdani's (2005, 2012) and Narayan's (1998) observations that colonialism has relied more heavily on an emphasis on difference than on sameness. While some versions and practices of secularism may make totalistic rejections of secularism tempting for some postcolonial feminists, Narayan warns about the trap that this position may entail: "Viable postcolonial feminist perspectives need to engage in rethinking the prevailing portraits of 'Western Culture' and of different Third World cultures, rather than assisting in their replication and reification by conflating resistance to Western domination and intrusion with essentialist notions of 'cultural difference' and 'cultural preservation'" (1998, 91–92). Gita Saghal explains how secularism in India developed out of grassroots minority struggles rather than as a colonial imposition. Cognizant and highly critical of the recent distortions and (ab)uses of "universalist" claims by the Bharatiya Janata Party (BJP) and Hindu majoritarianism as a weapon against the Muslim minority in India, Kumkum Sangari still signals a dire warning against communalization of feminist positions. Pointing out how Hindu majoritarianism of the BJP thrives in a political arena based in competing majority claims, Sangari argues that communalism, even when it comes from a beleaguered minority, would only "reinforce the structural relations between religions and patriarchies, and sharpen the emerging relations between religions and communalism" (1995, 3291). Even though Sangari's discussion focuses on India, the vulnerability of the Muslim minority in India and the abuses of the claim to universality by majority groups suggest that the analysis she makes and the lessons she draws may be applicable to minorities in the Western diaspora.

What Is *Not* Spoken in Public Discourses

One of the most important antiracist critiques of multiculturalism in Canada and elsewhere has been about the distortions and limitations of its culturalism. Several scholars have highlighted how liberal multiculturalism as a state policy and ideology of governing has subverted concrete demands of racialized groups for equality, justice, and inclusion by valorizing cultural differences and emphasizing "cultural recognition" as the solution (see Gilroy 1987; Bannerji 2000; Bhandar 2010; and Lentin 2014). More recently, Glen Coulthard has raised concerns about how "the ascendant status of 'identity,' 'culture,' and 'recognition' in contemporary politics" applies to and negatively impacts indigenous politics (2014, 18). He cautions how the liberal pluralist reframing of self-determination efforts by Indigenous peoples in a recognition paradigm in Canada may help reproduce the very colonial relations that Indigenous politics seeks to transcend (Coulthard 2007, 2014). Coulthard is interested in understanding the question of how colonial power in Canada modifies itself in a period when its "policies, techniques and ideologies" may no longer be "explicitly oriented around...genocidal exclusion/assimilation" (2014, 6). In this sense, the context of his analysis and caution about culturalism is comparable to my discussion of the dangers of culturalism in Islamo*philic* discourses that followed predominantly and overtly Islamo*phobic* ones. His warnings about the dangers of "purportedly self-affirming forms of state recognition and accommodations defended by some proponents of liberal recognition politics" are also applicable, as Coulthard underlines how recognition politics can "subtly reproduce nonmutual and unfree relations rather than free and mutual ones" (2014, 17).

Culturalism does not just assign people into simple categories. It also tends to reduce the understanding of the world to the "cultural" at the expense of other perspectives. Part of a "secularizing" analysis would need to involve reintroducing those other perspectives. Given the intensive gaze that women in minority Muslim communities have been subjected to in Western countries, it is curious how little interest there has been on any dimension of their lives other than their "culture." Elsewhere, I have focused on the irony that in the same political environment where gender equality has disappeared from discourses, making and implementing policy in Canada, gender plays a rather prominent part, often centre-stage, when it comes to policy and public discourse on specific groups of racialized and immigrant women (see Arat-Koç 2012). There has indeed been a paradoxical hypervisibility and invisibility of gender in Canadian public discourse and public policies over the recent decades. Whereas the majority of women in Canada have been "invisibilized," "disappeared from the words and deeds of state actors," some, specifically racialized immigrant women, have been "instrumentalized," made "hyper visible, purposefully positioned in the public eye" (Dobrowolsky 2008, 465–66). In the general public discourse and policy discussions, gender inequality is treated as a problem already solved for White women, as if Canada is in a post-feminist state. Yet it is seen as a problem specific to immigrant women, often those from racialized groups.

The claims of the Canadian state to gender equality having been achieved for some women and a challenge for others are based on a culturalist lens. Not only does the "package picture of culture" used in the culturalist lens rely on simple, essentialized, overgeneralized, and distorted assumptions about the patriarchal "cultural luggage" that immigrant women are assumed to carry, but as an explanatory tool, this notion of culture also becomes totalistic, shifting attention and transferring responsibility away from the market, society, and the state in Canada to ahistorical, decontextualized, and dematerialized references to "culture" (see Narayan 2000). Culturalism means that the gendering and racializing effects of Canadian policies and experiences on women could conveniently be overlooked. Invisibilizing the relevance and significance of what has happened historically and what happens "here and now" and through real, material impacts of state policies and dominant social, economic, and political forces, it helps to let the "host" society and the state "off the hook" in both the analyses of and solutions for gender inequality for immigrant women.

In recent decades, a number of structural changes related to neoliberal restructuring of the economy and the state, and changes in immigration and settlement policies have negatively impacted the lives of immigrant women. These changes have included cuts to social services, expansion of precarious immigrant status, and precarious working conditions for immigrant women, and have directly contributed to increased dependency on their spouses and families. Ironically, it has been in this socio-economic and political climate that it has also become increasingly unfashionable in public discourse to focus on social, economic, political, and policy context in the making of people's conditions. In relation to the "Sharia debate," this has meant that "Muslim culture" has been a question of interest when other issues could be ignored:

> Little attention is paid to the significance of underlying inequalities, which are not solely intragroup inequalities, but also *vis-à-vis* the host society (e.g. language skills, precarious immigration status), which make some Muslim women not only particularly vulnerable to religious arbitration, but also prevent their discursive equality in claim-making, i.e. their participation in this debate over interpretation of their needs. (Bassel 2009, 172)

In demystifying cultural arguments, "secular" analysis would not only provide more accuracy and context to knowledge about the actual conditions, behaviours, and attitudes of women from Muslim and other racialized groups, it could also expose the self-proclaimed myth that Canada (minus its Third World immigrants) has already achieved women's equality.

The New Literature by Muslim Canadian Women Writers: Alternative Perspectives?

A brief look at some recent trends in Muslim diaspora literature in Canada, especially literature produced by Muslim women writers (Deen 2016; Doctor 2007, 2011; Habib 2019; Hussain 2016; Jalaluddin 2018) offers hope that this alternative approach to culture may actually be in the process of being articulated. Interestingly, what we can observe in recent years seems to run counter to an earlier trend. As mentioned before, in the wake of 9/11, memoirs by several Muslim women writers—most notably Azar Nafizi, Irshad Manji, and Ayaan Hirsi Ali—published in North America and Western Europe, rose to bestseller lists and brought extraordinary media attention and lucrative careers to their authors. Catering to the Orientalist gaze on Muslims and the particularly violent geopolitical and imperial climate of the post-9/11 world, these memoirs seemed to have helped simplify, essentialize, and effectively demonize "Islamic culture" as well as politics and practices associated with Muslims. Written in a variety of genres, including humour and mystery, some of the recent literature by Muslim Canadian women authors seems not only to challenge Islamo*phobic* perspectives on Muslims, but also to offer creative alternatives to defensive and simplistic Islamo*philic* ones.

Novels like Ishara Deen's *God Smites and Other Muslim Girl Problems: Asiya Haque Mystery #1* (2016), Farzana Doctor's *Seven* (2020), and Uzma Jalaluddin's *Ayesha at Last* (2018); memoirs like Samra Habib's *We Have Always Been Here: A Queer Muslim Memoir* (2019), and Saima Hussain's edited collection, *The Muslimah Who Fell to Earth: Personal Stories by Canadian Muslim Women* (2016), approach their characters in a multidimensional way. Neither confined to religion as the only or major dimension of their existence nor identifying with—or reacting to—a single interpretation of Islam, the Muslims in this writing are represented in their diversity, complexity, and contradictions. It is refreshing that there are no "true," "authentic" Muslims in this literature. The variety of genres in which Muslim women in Canada write these days enables the creation of a variety of female characters. The female protagonists in these novels, memoirs, and life-writing narratives question, defy, and subvert normative assumptions about and expectations of their ethnoreligious communities and of the larger Canadian society, and they do so in a number of contexts, ranging from their work milieu to their personal lives, from their gender and sexual roles to their engagement with "culture."

Not being a literary studies specialist, I am hesitant to make conclusive observations and generalizations about this literature. Nevertheless, I would like to express cautious optimism about the possibilities offered by the literary field. Compared to media or public discourses and representations that are shaped by political and geopolitical agendas, that tend to resort to hasty conclusions, simple generalizations, and rigid dichotomies about "good" and "bad" Muslims, and the "religious" and the "secular," literature seems to offer more space to introduce, explore, and play with complexity, ambiguity, nuance, and contradictions. Literary representations seem to have an advantage over most of the social sciences—perhaps with the exception of anthropology—where epistemological and methodological constraints are often in the way of exploring some of the subtleties of the human condition. Literature focusing on racialized minority groups offers unique opportunities to explore the specificity, depth, and texture of the real lives of "the other" while also opening up space to explore universals simply by humanizing characters. For members of racialized groups themselves, literature can offer ways to go beyond a "package picture" of culture (Narayan 2000). Going beyond generalizations and caricaturized images, it offers both a more realistic perspective of the actual diversity of racialized "cultures" and ways of imagining other modalities of being, other possibilities of identities and relationships. These alternative representations and visions for possibilities of being for diaspora Muslims are especially significant in terms of the spaces they open for *speaking by* and *speakability of* Muslim women. At the same time, it is important to remain cautious about questions of reception. Many Muslim women authors write honestly and critically about patriarchal relations in their home country or diasporic communities. While their engagement is complex and nuanced, and cannot be characterized as intended to be catering to the Orientalist gaze of some of the potential readers, the authors ultimately have no control over what may be misinterpreted or "lost in translation." It is, therefore, important to stress that literature can play a role, but cannot by itself and magically transform dominant perceptions—by non-Muslims or Muslims—of Muslim identity. Alternative representations in literature need to be complemented by changes in approaches in the media, social sciences, and, ultimately, in the actual power relations at international and national levels.

Concluding Notes: Redefining "Culture" / Secularizing Analysis and Representation in Difficult Times

If Islamo*philia* is not a good and desirable strategy to address and counter Islamo*phobia*, what *is*? What conceptual tools and perspectives may help antiracist feminists articulate a voice and politics? What alternative notions of "culture" may help unleash it from its *a*historical and *im*material chains? Highly critical of the cultural*ism* of liberal multiculturalism, Davina Bhandar expresses her belief in the positive potentials of "cultural citizenship." She argues that cultural citizenship may help articulate demands for an inclusive public space, "invigorating civil society and expressing enacted forms of citizenship" (Bhandar 2010, 331). This, she suggests, could be possible when culture no longer functions as a disciplinary tool of governance, when [in the context of debates concerning Muslims] "the practice of the everyday realities of how people come to be identified as Muslim in multiple forms of signification and assemblage" might be given space within the public sphere" (2010, 341).

Like Bhandar, Gopal encourages a rethinking of the notion of culture as *living, lived* culture rather than a fixed, static "tradition" frozen in time and place. Rather than talking about "cultural practices" or "practice *of* culture," Gopal proposes that we think about culture *as* practice "When culture is conceptualized as a relation between selves or between selves and society, which carry within them the recurrent possibility of negotiation and transformation, it becomes possible to imagine change without ceding the terrain of belonging and shared history" (2013, 113). This perspective on culture, Gopal suggests, may help transcend the tensions between feminism and antiracism and anticolonialism. If culture *is* practice, culture is then constituted as much by critical ideas and struggles as it is with "tradition." This notion of culture as practice is entirely consistent with those articulated in critical anticolonial perspectives, such as Frantz Fanon's: "a national culture is not a folklore, *nor* an abstract populism that believes it can discover the people's true nature....a national culture is the whole body of efforts made by a people in the sphere of thought to describe, justify and praise the action through which that people has created itself and keeps itself in existence" (1963, 188).

As mentioned in the introduction, Edward Said's notions of secular criticism and secular humanism would prove to be very insightful in developing a sound analysis, forms of representation, and effective antiracist feminist political strategies. Said's secular criticism rejects unconditional belonging in, and unconditional acceptance of, any side of an issue or debate. It involves "a constant unsettling and an ongoing and never-ending effort at critique" (Mufti 2004, 3). Repudiating "the need for certainty, group solidarity, and a sense of communal belonging" (Said 1983, 290), secular criticism enables and encourages complex and paradoxical thinking. As much as Said's secularism is based in principles of universalism and humanism, it provides a perspective that can be "critical of humanism in the name of humanism" (2004, 10). Applied to the double bind faced by antiracist feminism, this position can help liberate the latter from the simplistic dichotomies of modernity versus tradition, universalism versus ethnic/religious difference, the West versus the East. It opens up space for a critique of all forms of domination regardless of their origin. This perspective also helps reveal the parochialism, contradictions, and limitations of some of the claims to universalism made in the West:

> Feminism is not incompatible with either antiracism or minority cultural practice but constitutive of them. As such it is a vitally regenerative means of rescuing both from the arid minimalism of certain kinds of identity politics and the assault they face from a parochial liberalism masquerading as the only acceptable source of universal values. Insofar as it calls upon both self and community to undertake critique and to acknowledge the complex texture of human existence, it cannot make "community" sacrosanct even as it draws on and contributes to its resources. While leaving open a space for faith and religiousity as human activities, feminism cannot and should not allow these to be the sole determinant of community. (Gopal 2013, 114)

As well intentioned as *Islamophilic* responses and gestures might be, they are not effective in countering *Islamophobic* attacks as they often help strengthen notions about the assumed absoluteness and incommensurability of cultural differences. As, or more importantly, *Islamophilia* affects Muslim communities and societies themselves, suppressing marginal and critical voices. Given these risks, an easier strategy of defensiveness about "culture" *as tradition* is not the right solution for antiracist feminism. As Himani Bannerji argues, "women in the service of traditional/cultural nationalism not only betray themselves and all other women, but all possibilities of social justice and political agencies" (2011, 126). The right strategy has to involve the difficult route of embracing complex identities. In order to avoid "becom[ing] the instruments of imperialism or of ethnic/cultural nationalism of the West or the East," feminists need to "work on an even-handed critique of all forms of domination" (Bannerji 2011, 125). "Feminists and antiracists must continue to insist on speaking from a place of difficulty even when the dominant rhetoric is that of siege and defense as much on the left as on the right. We abdicate this task at our peril" (Gopal

2013, 115). There is no question that reorienting and redefining "culture" in the directions suggested above—against cultural*ism*—involves enormous challenges in relation to struggles within minority communities as much as against the false and illusory claims to universalism made by dominant groups in society. There is also no question that in the process, there are serious difficulties in developing a voice, a critical voice that speaks *from* the community, and challenges the orthodoxy of the ethnic/religious culture, at the same time. One of the challenges in the latter is to make sure that the critical voices will not be "lost in translation" and be heard by the dominant group as the affirmation of the supremacy of their "Western culture" and (their) universalism. As nearly impossible as the challenge may appear to be, however, it is a project that needs to be undertaken as it is the only one that would liberate racialized, marginalized communities under siege and the dominant groups from their respective identitarian parochialisms and from their "clash of fundamentalisms."[5]

PART IV

“in there, together” / Land Intimacies

Deliberate Vulgarity

Performing the Demotic, Transforming Cultural Space?

/ PAMELA MORDECAI

> Indelibly, orality scores Negro poetry.
>
> —George Elliott Clarke, "Bring Da Noise"

These days I find myself saying
I am a poet masquerading
as a prose writer. In this poem,
I am playing mas as a "scholar."
(Playing mas not no joke, eh?
Ask any Trini, if you don't credit me!)

So what is this "deliberate vulgarity"?
A Jamdown thing, maybe,
a way of elevating

bad behave intentionally?
Make we agree is so for now.
This bad behave apparently involve,
"performing the demotic"
aka reading my poetry in patwa.
Patwa is Jamaican Creole.
My vernacular – how ordinary
people talk where I come from.

I know "perform" can mean plenty things.
A scholar name Elizabeth Bell –
she say performance is a key
contested word, "unstable, slippery."
Oh dear! Too highfalutin!
All I mean by performance
is reading my poetry, with feeling.

As for the "cultural space,"
I search the Internet
to find out how to say
what I mean by this space.
(Just like a Jamdowner to say
me going to talk bout someting
and don't know what it is!)
I come across a man name
Robert Maxwell Young.
Him say: "The most capacious space
within which we think about ourselves
is called culture." So look like when
we think about ourself,
that is the culture and the space.
Make sense to me.

How do I think reciting patwa poetry
might change the space?
When people hearken to other people

and hear them talk in their own tongue,
maybe they have a chance to make
a "convivial multicultural democracy"?
Is not me call it so. Is a scholar
name Paul Gilroy. (I don't know him
but I did know his late mama –
Guyanese British writer. A great lady.)
Right now we have a way to say
we have this multicultural democracy
in Canada, but is really not so it go.
Maybe the patwa poetry can give
a push to help it really go so.

On this safari, I going to take a trip
back down my life, a little tour
through the long time I writing *poetry*.
I know. The *little* and the *long* seem like
a contradiction. Howsomever
little and long can live together.
Everything don't have to fight down
whatever is different from itself.
If you open your mind, plenty
dissimilar things can live
in there, together, equally,
at the same time.
You know – like the
multicultural democracy!

Caribbean people good at that,
Jamaica folks for sure.
I say is a Caribbean cognitive style
and I make a name for it one time
long ago: "prismatic vision."
All the same, like civility,
what you call it don't signify
if is something you

understand and you live by.
One reason I touring you
through the poetry
is so I can recall and you can see
when it change from lying
on a page to riding air
and how it fare after that.

Now, from long time
people that study language
been insisting that one
is as good as another.
John McWorther V say
when young people use *totally*
and *like*, like that is not
bad English, like, is just
a different way to talk,
like, English. Like,
language is language.

But in life, if you say
a thing is so, that don't
necessarily make it so.
My Jamaican patwa –
is a "non-standard" tongue.
English is a "standard language."
No linguist's qualifications
can remove the bad reverb.

Sad thing is, plenty folks
that talk patwa and don't talk
nothing else, still think patwa
not good enough. When
Di Jamiekan Nyuu Testiment
did publish in 2012,
some Jamdowners say

is a disgrace to write
the Good News in patwa.
Like maybe God couldn't
understand it or talk it?
So what that have to do
with the price of poutine?

Well, for one thing
dialect poetry like spoken
word and slam and dub
can make a lot of noise
and for some literati
noisy poetry don't make
the cut as verse. Not only that,
but like I just say, patwa
is a disparaged code
making two strike against it.

But make we tour the poetry
and see, and when me done,
me going raise few question.

The Six Books

Journey Poem
When I publish my first book
I write mostly poems
that "fulfill themselves
on the page." (Poet Laureate
Emeritus, George Elliott Clarke,
refer to the condition
as "page-bound.")
Like, for example:

And as for you
Elizabeth
so wise
of the
slow eyelids
slower eyes
even now
secrets
grow mouldy
in your
store:
your small
foot
not quite
ready
gait
travels
with more
than I
can gather
yet we two
waxed
parallel
one heart
one head
fighting
about the
line drawn
down
the middle
of the
bed.

Such a poem is well behaved.
It not bawdy nor shrill.

But even in those long-time days
couple poems in *Journey Poem*
was begging to get up,
and like Trini critic
Gordon Rohlehr say,
assume the state
of "word in audible motion" –
in Yardie terms, make up noise.

Take "Last Lines":

This is the last line I draw.
Alright. Draw the last line.
But I tell you, yonder
is a next. No line never last
no death not forever.
You see this place? You see it?
All of it? Watch it good.
Not a jot nor a tittle
going lost. Every old
twist up man you see,
every hang-breast ooman,
every bang-belly pickney
...
every small gal-turn-ooman
that you crucify on the
cross of your sex
before her likl naseberry
start sweeten,
I swear to you
every last one shall live.

I read it at a con-celebration
of the life of the late Dudley Laws
and the people-dem clap.

Plus it end up in plenty anthology
so it must be a poem folks like –
better than the recumbent ones?

The poetry however take a turn
with my next book, *de Man*
a performance poem,
publish here by a Canadian
small press, the late Sister Vision
Black Women and Women
of Colour Press, of blessed memory.
From you hear the title, you know
something different
going on in this book.
No have no time to tell
the whole story now,
but is must God make it,
for I never think to do nothing so!
From the first line drop
out the sky on the page,
me know me just had
to follow my pen into patwa!
The poem is about
the crucifixion of Jesus.
Hear how it start out.

(Naomi, a maid that work
for Pilate's wife, is tackling
the rest of maids-dem
about whether them know Jesus.)

Oonu see mi dyin trial!
Dem people ya nuh easy.
A kill dem a go kill de man.
How yu mean "Which man?"

Nuh de man Jesus. Yu know –
De one dat preach? And
Tell story? Yu never hear
Him yet? Bwoy, me nuh
Understand oonu young
People. If oonu did stay at
Oonu yard, me would seh
Come. But oonu walk street
And ignorant same way.

de Man change my course as a poet.
After that I write in my heart language
as often as not – and me can't
stop tell story. (Is a Mennonite
gentleman name Dr Fehderau
come from Kitchener parts –
him dead and gone now –
did first tell me about "heart language" –
a term Bible translators use.)

Nobody hear *de Man* that don't love it.
It perform in Jamaica year in and year out.
Them put it on radio and don't tell
neither publisher nor me.
Some time is long after
that me hear bout how them
perform it on Good Friday
in this church or a next. Over here,
it perform in Newfoundland, Calgary,
Toronto, Kitchener – and not one
time neither. So it come
hard to me that it make no
appearance in the one book
me know about spirituality
in Jamaican poetry,

a book name *Soon Come...*
And Hugh Hodges that write it
include couple poem
of mine that cannot compare...

Me did think it well strange...

Certifiable and *The True Blue of Islands*
is the book-them that come next.
Me still telling story and me
writing in English about half the time.
The rest of the time is poem in patwa
or poem jumping from patwa to English
and back. Code-switching
them call it... code-sliding
sometimes. And I start to do
another thing new in those books.
I make up a tune to sing poems to.
Like, for example, a poem
name "Yellow Girl Blues..."
in *The True Blue of Islands.*

My mama she done told me
She tell me every day:
"No mind your skin is yellow
You're a nigger anyway."

Yellow Girl blues
Yellow Girl blues
I'm walking up the muddy road
in my sampata shoes.

True Blue also contain
the only dub poem me ever write:
"Everybody Get Flat – a Dub."

Where is the poem
that explains
what happens
to you when
they shoot your brother
and you hear
that his brains
spilled over the seat
to the back of the car
and you have to tell folks

"No, it wasn't a war
No, he wasn't
caught in crossfire.
No, it wasn't a fight...."

Yes it happen at night
but no, not in town –
out in the country
not a god soul around.

Now considering dub,
slam, spoken word,
performance poetry,
it may be that the livity,
aliveness of all poetry
that delight in disturbing
the air speak to more folks,
and more loudly
than the reclining kind?
Maybe that could be why so much
school pikni hate poetry,
so much teacher would
rather not teach it?

That is one of the things couple uni profs
that I ask bout attitudes to poetry
had to say...The poetry that dance
and sing is a more welcome thing
for students, especially the ones
as is undergraduate...

In the last two books, *Subversive Sonnets*
and *de book of Mary*, me find myself
doing yet another new thing –
using patwa in "traditional
poetic forms." I create
my version of sonnet
in *Subversive Sonnets*.
I write in what Elaine Savory
call "a casual Jamaican" and I do
the code sliding thing now and then.

This is from "Reading the Poets,"
the first part of a sonnet sequence
that I call "Reading at 4:00 a.m."

I read Walcott's *Omeros*, chapter six. Helen
chats with her friends down near to the sea wall.
She don't like when the tourist foreigners
put their hands on her ass and so she tell
the cashier he could keep the fucking job.
Is just a stupid waitress work, is all!
Only she now must find something to do
like how she pregnant and don't know for who.
For me her tale is poetry more than
"love songs fading over a firefly sea."
(chapter eleven). If ocean, hill and sky
can't hold this odyssey, what chance a page?
I set aside the book to search my face
for prudent lines to whisper to Helen.

Everybody love *Subversive Sonnets.*
Students at York buy out every copy
in the bookshop, make me sign book
till my hand nearly drop off. Sweet me you see!
Students at Wilfrid Laurier call the sonnets,
"spoken word!" I never really think
about it so, but since the Bard too
spoke his word, I figure I am
in good company.

Just like *de Man, de book of Mary*
is pure patwa – except perversely
for the titles of the poems.
This time the traditional English form
is triplets of anapestic feet –
da-da-dam, da-da-dam... Maybe
is because is two Bible story,
but folks love *de book of Mary*
like them love *de Man.*
Vancouver, Winnipeg, Ottawa,
Toronto, Kingston, Kitchener,
the other Kingston too!
And everybody always tell me,
"You must make a CD!"
Say it come clearer to them
when I read it.

Hear a piece of Mary book:

MARY, THINKING ON THINGS, REMEMBERS HER FRIEND ESTHER

Dat girl Es, she don't make
not one sound. She don't falter nor flinch
at de sight of a village of ravaging dogs

with de lust for fresh blood like a fire
up dem tail. Never drop till rock-stone
clap her head, topple her to her knees,

shub her flat pon her face. Esther girl,
look de number of time me warn you –
keep away from dat chap!

True is him scrape you up
de day you trip, tumble down,
bruck your nose and mash up

your top lip, almost dig out your eye.
True is him did run quick from centurion post,
snap your snout back in place

with a smart soldier hand –
dem can doctor real good, people have
it to say, apply ointment, poultice, tourniquet,

guide a babe on him way to de world
safe as any old crone.

So that make two sacred story
that I tell in noisy patwa poetry!

The six professorial persons
that I talk to say they love
performance poetry,
say it come full circle
from old tradition
including aboriginal,
where all poetry was oral
right back to the same
initial place.
Now though, to the nitty gritty.

Even though folks like the poems,
I get the feeling that, when it come
to brass facts, they are not good enough.
It's like, because the poems are noisy,
talk uncompromisingly,
this voiced, voluble quality
signify inferiority.

But maybe is something me imagine,
because me over-sensitive
and can't satisfy,
never mind how the cheering loud?

Me don't think so, though.
George Elliott Clarke say
in the "Percussive Conclusion"
of a chapter him call
"Bring Da Noise" in him
book of essays, *Directions Home* (2012):

"No matter...their absence from
the Eurocentric (white) anthologies...
Afro-Caribbean poets...refresh and renew
all of English-Canadian poetry.
They remind us that poetry
is also music...and that the lyric poem
is also a theatre – a one-woman
(or one-man) show, demanding...
all the resources of rhetoric
and drama... The rejection
of performance poetry –
or of *black* spoken word verse –
by the white aristocracy
of Academia is nothing
but a reactionary attack
upon the possibility

of a popular poetry
that articulates the deepest
feelings of its auditors."

Barbara Lalla,
Jamaican linguist and novelist –
she keep her gloves on,
and she talking about
the use of patwa
in both song and story,
but she not saying
nothing too different
if you consider the colour
composition of the academy.

"...literary Creole constitutes
a mechanism of resistance..."

"The persistent assumption
that Creole discourse
remains inherently oral
rather than literary
is simplistic
and somewhat paternalistic –
a view betraying a colonial mindset
even within academia itself...
that so maps orality
into our understanding of creole
as to obscure the extent
to which Creole participates
in literary discourse."

So, do we need to perform the demotic?
What is there about performance
that is going to enhance
a language's chance

of entering, let alone changing
how we think and talk about ourselves?
Why is this important?
Is there in fact a hierarchy in which dub,
spoken word, slam and performance poetry
come below contemporary poetry
that fulfills itself on the page?
Does orature, that-which-is-voluble,
have negative connotations
in life and in literature –
unless it is regarded as theatre –
another genre, different rules,
different criteria?

Are those who determine taste
on juries and in the academy
suspicious of the melody in poetry?
Given that students respond better
to poems whose words rejoice
in the state of audible motion,
should not more of them be included
in curricula at all levels?
Is it a matter of concern that some persons'
idea of themselves depends
on rejoicing in their volubility?

And, finally, for I must get
this book in, Christina Sharpe's
In the Wake: On Blackness and Being
is a text everybody should read.
Having explored the wake
as wake, ship, hold and weather,
Sharpe calls people of colour
who live in threat of being deprived
of their lives every walking minute
to the "wake work" of "aspiration" –

for brevity, "keeping breath
in the black body."
I am hoping this poem/paper
may contribute something
to that work of giving breath
to people of colour.
After all, it concerns language,
black vernacular speech,
and as Fanon says, "It is implicit
that to speak is to exist
absolutely for the other."

Perhaps if people of colour
are listened to more we will
all be murdered less.

"Making Things Right"

Black Settlement and the Politics of Urban Territory[1]

/ KARINA VERNON

> This is what makes people call you a radical. Understand?
> If you can abide things changing, they call that radicalism.
>
> —Wayde Compton, *Performance Bond*

Things have changed a lot in the culture and in Black and Indigenous studies since the 2017 Mikinaakominis / TransCanadas conference, and my mind has changed along with it. What it means for Black and Indigenous Peoples to be good relations to one another is different in 2021 than it was when I wrote the paper I gave in 2017. The worldwide #BlackLivesMatter actions—born of four hundred years of anti-Black brutality, racism, and injustice and catalyzed by the horrific murder of George Floyd by Minneapolis police—broke through public consciousness in a new way in 2020. While activists have always been resisting the violence inflicted on Black communities by the state and vigilantes, the video taken by Darnella Frasier showing the last nine-and-a-half minutes of Floyd's life laid bare in the most harrowing terms the fungibility of Black lives in white supremacist settler-colonial states. In Canada, the death of Afro-Indigenous woman Regis Korchinski-Paquet at the hands of police in the same month as Floyd, and Chantal Moore (Tla-o-qui-aht) on June 4, 2020, forcefully brought issues of policing and police abolition into the mainstream frame, which in turn has shifted how Black and Indigenous Peoples are approaching issues of land, relation, and responsibility.

Things have shifted in Black and Indigenous studies, too, with publications that offer new vocabularies and methodologies than were available to me in 2016–17. Robyn Maynard's *Policing Black Lives: State Violence in Canada from Slavery to the Present* (2017); Phanuel Antwi and David Chariandy's special issue of *Transitions*, "Writing Black Canadas" (2017); Eve Tuck and K. Wayne Yang's *Toward What Justice?: Describing Diverse Dreams of Justice in Education* (2018); Fred Moten and Stefano Harney's "Conversación Los Abajocomunes" (2018); Tiffany Lethabo King's *The Black Shoals: Offshore Formations of Black and Native Studies* (2019); Robyn Maynard's "Black Life and Death across the U.S.-Canada Border: Border Violence, Black Fugitive Belonging, and a Turtle Island View of Black Liberation" (2019); Nadine Chambers' "Sometimes Clocks Turn Back for Us to Move Forward" (2019); and Anthony Morgan's "Black People in Canada Are Not Settlers" (2019)—all these have put my thinking about Black and Indigenous relationality on a new path. Significant, too, are the fast-moving conversations in the public digital sphere among a younger generation of scholars, artists, and activists who are challenging collective understandings of Black, Indigenous, and Black-Indigenous identities. Especially important for me is the work of Erica Violet Lee (Nehiyaw), Joy Henderson (Black Lakota), and @IndigenousXca (Nehiyaw), which deconstructs the Native/settler and land/diaspora binaries that previously structured approaches to Black-Indigenous relationality and issues of responsibility. In an article called "Treaties beyond the State" (2021), Erica Violet Lee characterizes Black and Indigenous Peoples as "relations" to one another. If I understand her use of the term correctly, "relations" signifies expansively. "As a non-Black Cree who grew up on the west side of Saskatoon," Lee writes, "I am forever indebted to the history of Black resistance and thought that created frameworks of urban freedoms" (25 Apr. 2021). "Relations," she explains, means "We do not live on our own. We do not write on our own. Our movements are ancient and they are entangled" (25 Apr. 2021). Black and Indigenous Peoples have been organizing and resisting the genocidal and ecocidal conditions of empire together since our people met in the joint ruptures of colonization and chattel slavery on Turtle Island. We are "relations" because our past and ongoing resistance is "entangled." But as Lee elaborates the meaning of "relations," she expands it. She argues that Black and Indigenous Peoples are relations also because we structurally occupy the space feared and policed by the settler, what Himani Bannerji called "the dark side of the nation" (2000, 87). Lee writes, "Fear of Indigeneity is a fear of Blackness is a fear of the dark and all those left 'uncivilized' by assimilation" (25 Apr. 2021).

But Erica Violet Lee is also challenging the structures and discourses of anti-Blackness by joining others in a call to understand Blackness *as* Indigenous. On June 4, 2021, Lee wrote:

> NonBlack Natives need to stop policing Black & AfroIndigenous folks for smudging and using plant medicines.
>
> 1. Blackness is Indigenous!
> 2. Our kinships were devastated by colonization & antiBlackness. Plant medicines exist to help us repair & strengthen relations, not gatekeep (4 June 2021)

Similarly, a thinker with the Twitter handle @IndigenousXca writes: "Black people are Indigenous. African Americans, Afro-Caribbeans, Afro-Latino, African Canadians are all African Indigenous peoples that were displaced from their homelands and went through ethnogenesis to form new distinct cultures BASED IN THEIR AFRICAN INDIGENEITY" (2020). As I understand it, the argument that Black people are Indigenous is not advanced in an effort to erase the history of the middle passage, nor to supplant Indigenous peoples in their lands. In a recent conversation between Black studies scholars Fred Moten and Stefano Harney on the occasion of the Spanish translation of *The Undercommons*, they say that "Black people are indigenous people, doubly displaced—from the land and from the socius, in the land and in the socius. This displacement placed black people no place, but no place is not nowhere; it is the nonlocality of a general diffusion that is, at once, generative and genocidal" (2018). Like @IndigenousXca, Moten and Harney argue that "Against this world, this modernity, founded by this trade in and of the species-being that helped solidify the emergent monstrosity of the always already racialized human, black people *(re)create earth/flesh*, a social—though not human—collective life" (2018, emphasis added). The ideas that Black people forcibly "displanted" (Morgan 2019) in Indigenous lands during the transatlantic trade are Indigenous and have "(re)created earth/flesh" on Turtle Island utterly explode the settler/Native diaspora/land binaries that have heretofore structured understandings of Black-Indigenous relations in Canadian and Black Canadian literary studies. These ideas place my feet on another path forward. This path is new and at the same time very old. It rests on "(re)created earth/flesh" and I walk it in the hope that, as Erica Violet Lee states, while "[o]ur kinships were devastated by colonization & antiBlackness" (2021a), our mutual struggle for abolition and decolonization helps return us to one another with respect, kinship, and love.

These significant cultural and disciplinary shifts have quickly rendered the paper I gave at Mikinaakominis / TransCanadas historical. I can see now how difficult it was for me in 2016–17 to move beyond the discourses, binaries, and epistemologies that positioned Black people as "settlers of colour" even as I detail the problems involved in doing so. At the same time as my paper disavows "settlers of colour" discourses, my argumentation proceeds from the premise that Black people stand in the settler's house. We do not: we stand in another place created by what activist Ravyn Wngz calls "the technology of Blackness" (2020, n.p.). The name for this place might be Moten and Harney's "(re)created earth/flesh" (2018, n.p.). I would write a different paper today.

The conversation around Black-Indigenous solidarities is moving quickly, and what it means to "make things right" is thematized in the story I read by F. B. André (2007). As Eve Tuck and K. Wayne Yang write in their introduction to *Toward What Justice? Describing Diverse Dreams of Justice in Education*, "because abolition and decolonization are lodestars—stars which are used to guide our course—*and* practical, abolition and decolonization are not projects to be deferred for the next generation. They are happening next; they are happening now" (2018, 10). Tuck and Yang thus encourage us to "think of justice as an imperative, rather than as an end...to think and work "in the 'toward' of justice" (11). It is in this spirit that I offer both this new introduction and the revised paper that I gave in 2017. They show the path from there to here, both points in my thinking toward justice.

/ / /

This essay takes the moment that galvanized the related but also separate anticolonial movements of #Idle No More and #BlackLivesMatter as an opportunity to consider the possibilities that exist, as well as the barriers that prevent, Black Canada from intertwining its struggle with that of Indigenous nations as part of a larger decolonizing program.

Trinidadian-Albertan writer F. B. André's short story, "Is There Someone You Can Call?" from his short-story collection *What Belongs*, published in 2007, is a place from which to theorize the challenges of conjoining Black abolition and Indigenous decolonizing movements. In André's story, a Black couple in an unnamed suburban location attempts to move into a house they've recently bought, only to find it still occupied. The couple view the property during an open house and then, on second viewing, make an offer. But on the day they are to take possession, they discover a "problem":

> All the stuff from the previous owners is still here. Our new kitchen cupboards are full of their dishes....The closets in the master bedroom are full of his suits and her dresses, like an orderly crowd waiting their turn to get out. The *en suite* bathroom is stocked with towels, toilet paper and toothpaste. There is no sign of packing up. The only room that is even remotely close to empty is a spare bedroom. (2007, 132)

Reading the story in the context of my recovered archive,[2] an archive that is highly preoccupied with land-as-property as writers and orators turn time and again to histories of pioneering, of clearing the land and claiming ownership rights through their investment of sweat equity, André's story speaks volumes about the anxieties of Black people territorializing on lands that were not theirs by ancestral rights. In André's story, the perplexed narrator walks through the already-occupied house as the five-ton truck with his own family's belongings waits outside to be unloaded. This strange double-occupancy, mirrored in the image of the garage's double doors, leads to increasingly uncanny sensations:

> It takes a minute to find the switch that controls the garage door. It's got a neat feature: you can open one side at a time or both sides at once. I come around to the front of the house again. This time, I will turn the key, open the door, and presto! House empty! You are such a child, my wife would say if she were here. You can't just wish for things to go away. (133)

The narrator finds out from neighbours that the previous owners' names are Ross and Rita; readers learn little else about who they might be, or why their belongings remain inside a house that they themselves, presumably, have sold. As the day stretches on, it begins to snow, and the suburban landscape takes on the appearance first of farmers' fields and then of wilderness. The landscape seems to be reverting to its original uses. But, menacingly, the local Sheriff's Department takes the opportunity of the freshly falling snow to track and hunt deer.

> The windbreak of trees near the horizon stands in close for the forest that once was. The sheriff and his men are still trolling the neighbourhood, reluctant to abandon their annual hunt. How can they see in this weather? The Mazda is already covered by a coat of heavy snow. How long before it becomes a target? If I stay outside, I'll be game soon. But I'm reluctant to re-enter the house; I have this foolish feeling—not quite like I'm intruding, but as if I'm stepping on something. (137)

This evocative and intelligent story warns us that, when considering the politics of the territory in which the Black Prairies is implicated, it is too simplistic to merely slide Black Prairie people into the position of "settlers of colour," as initial analyses of Black-Indigenous relations did (see Lawrence and Dua 2005). Because of the specific intensity of the historical and contemporary disempowerment of Black people globally and especially as diasporic people in the Americas—forcibly transported from their homelands and enslaved in other peoples' nations—we cannot claim that Black people are true "settlers," even in situations like the Prairies when they became (unwanted) arrivals in the colonial nation-state. The Black Americans who came to the Prairies in the early part of the twentieth century would likely not have chosen this further dislocation if there had been other viable political options, for instance, if Oklahoma had become a Black state, as it almost did in the 1880s. But we know that between 1885 and 1930, there were at least 147 lynching deaths in Oklahoma alone (Everett n.d.); dozens more probably went unrecorded. Again, in January and February 2017, following the election of Donald Trump, there was a spike of migration to the Prairies from Somalian refugee communities in Minneapolis crossing the 49th parallel at Emerson, Manitoba—an unofficial land crossing—in order to circumvent Canada's third-party agreement with the United States.

In F. B. André's story, the narrator cannot continue standing in the snow outside the house. How long, he wonders, before he becomes a target? Yet, neither can he move inside this uncanny place. Despite the house being "officially" his, and despite the former homeowners' absence, they are not gone. He knows in his gut that moving into such a house is "stepping on something" (137).

Afua Cooper's keynote address at Mikinaakominis / TransCanadas, "Blackness Rejected: The Canadian Federal Government and the 1911 Order-in-Council Banning Black Migration to Canada," detailed what I have called the "second wave" of Black migration to the Canadian Prairies (see Vernon 2004, 2011, 2014, 2020). This was the period when Black farmers—mainly from Oklahoma, but also Kansas, Texas, and Missouri—responded to the Canadian government's immigration campaign to help "settle"—that is to say, colonize—the Canadian West. Clifford Sifton, Canada's minister of the interior, advertised that a farmer could get a title to a quarter section of land (160 acres), for just ten dollars if a farmer stayed on that land and "improved" it by clearing, planting, and building a house. The offer of land was a powerful incentive to African Americans. As one Oklahoman migrant, E. A. Cobbs, put it in his orature, "For our people, this was a goldmine. So they came" ("Alberta's Black Pioneer Heritage" 2012): African Americans moved by the hundreds to the Canadian Prairies; however, the Canadian campaign was never intended to attract Black people. When white Canadians envisioned Blacks "swarm[ing] by the tens of thousands" (Winks 2000, 309), they successfully pressured the federal government to pass Order-in-Council No. 1324 determining that "For a period of one year from and after the date hereof the landing in Canada shall be and the same is prohibited of any immigrants belonging to the Negro race, which is deemed unsuitable to the climate and requirements of Canada" (Government of Canada 1912).

But even as we rightly decry this history of anti-Blackness on the Canadian Prairies, we cannot disentangle it from the massive dispossessions suffered by Indigenous Peoples; it was the expropriation of Indigenous lands that made this Black migration to the Prairies possible in the first place. As Robyn Maynard notes,

> Black and Indigenous oppression are historically and currently connected. Indeed, recent writings by Black and Indigenous studies scholar Tiffany King (2013, 2014) argue that we cannot truly understand the conditions of Black life in settler societies without examining the relationship of anti-Blackness and slavery to settler colonialism and genocide...these were not isolated processes. 2017, 11)

The connectedness of anti-Black and genocidal processes is painfully apparent on the Prairies. After his re-election in 1878, Prime Minister John A. Macdonald orchestrated a state-sanctioned famine for Indigenous communities. Maynard recalls that "in one instance, in the spring of 1883, the government withheld food from nearly five thousand Indigenous people, who were then forcibly marched hundreds of kilometers to reserves in Battleford, Saskatchewan" 2017, 32). After the defeat of the 1885 Indigenous uprisings against these genocidal policies, Aboriginal peoples had little choice but to enter into alliances they understood to be agreements to "share" their lands with newcomers "in exchange for resources to establish new economies—education, medical assistance, and annuity payments" (Hildebrandt et al. 1996, i) but which the government representatives understood "more narrowly as a legal agreement, later interpreted to have been a land surrender" (Smith 1996, vii).[3] Kanai Elder Wilton Goodstriker (1996) argues, based on the oral histories of Blackfoot, Stoney, and Tsuut'ina Elders of Treaty 7, that the chiefs, headmen, medicine men, and spiritual leaders entered into negotiations with the government representatives with a specific agenda: "they wanted the encroachment of newcomers controlled, they wanted the buffalo protected, and they wanted the American traders controlled. These problems had resulted in tremendous hunger in the previous several years" (Hildebrandt et al. 1996, 25). Land "surrender" was not part of the leaders' conceptual understanding since, as Goodstriker notes, "There was no word for surrendering or relinquishing of title to land.

We are one with the land. Is it possible to give or relinquish part of oneself?" (Hildebrandt et al. 1996, 24). Instead, their understanding of the sacred alliance was that it would "benefit both sides in a substantial way" (Hildebrandt et al. 1996, 24). Thus, Treaty 6 was signed on August 23, 1876; Treaty 7 was signed on September 22, 1877; and, finally, Treaty 8 was signed in 1899 (Waiser 2005, 28–29). The second major wave of Black migrants began to arrive on the Prairies only six years after Treaty 8 was signed. In many instances Black farmers were the first arrivals on Indigenous lands, a sign that the promises made during treaty negotiations to protect the land and buffalo were already being broken.

As F. B. André's fiction makes clear, the complex story of what went on in the past—the intimate but also asymmetrical histories of Black and Indigenous dispossession on Turtle Island—unsettles a host of painful and difficult questions in the present. Given the complex histories of Black people—neither settlers nor immigrants on Turtle Island—how should we understand our social and legal relationship to Indigenous nations in the present? Should Black people, for instance, be understood within the framework offered by James Sa'ke'j Youngblood Henderson, who argues that "Canadian citizenship is the product of Aboriginal peoples' conditional permission, though the historical treaty process to the British sovereign to provide for the settlements" (2013, 116)? Are Black people, then, "treaty citizens"? But what does it mean that the people I am writing about in this chapter—those who arrived on the Prairies between 1905 and 1910—were not wanted by the Crown for the settlements made possible by treaty? As I have detailed, in 1911 the federal government banned Black people from crossing the international border and entering into those treaty relationships. If not as "treaty citizens," then how should Black people—especially those from the Oklahoma migration but also those who came after to suffer the anti-Black social order I describe below—understand our legal and ethical obligations to Indigenous peoples? What responsibilities do Black people have to make things right with Indigenous Peoples who are entitled to compensation for the promises made during treaty, which "have never properly been fulfilled" (Smith 1996, vii)?

To some Black Canadians, the idea that we, collectively, share a responsibility to "make things right" with Indigenous nations will be difficult—if not impossible—to hear. Some believe that because, as a whole, Black

Canada has not been permitted an equal share in the nation, its wealth, resources, and culture, it is wrong to ask Black people now to share in any process of making things right that involves forms of symbolic or material restitution. For instance, in October 2016 the United Nations' Committee on Economic, Social and Cultural Rights released a report, which garnered little media attention, that raised deep concerns about systemic anti-Black racism in Canada (Maynard 2017, 5). The report noted that Canada's history of anti-Black racism is "deeply entrenched," stretching back to the legacy of slavery in the sixteenth century and continuing into the present day: "History informs anti-Black racism and racial stereotypes that are so deeply entrenched in institutions, policies and practices, that its institutional and systemic forms are either functionally normalized or rendered invisible" (Canadian Press 2017, 7). The Committee highlighted the enormous racial inequalities with respect to income, housing, child welfare rates, access to quality education and health care, and the application of drug laws (United Nations, General Assembly 2017). The report was particularly concerned with the disproportionately high unemployment rates among African Canadians—11% for Black women as compared to 7% for the general population. "When employed," the report notes, "African Canadian women are making 37% less than white men and 15% less than their white female counterparts. Twenty-five percent of African Canadian women are living below the Canadian poverty line compared to 6% for white Canadian women. By extension their children are living in poverty at the unprecedented rate of 33% for children of Caribbean heritage and 47% for continental African children compared to 18% of white Canadian children living below the poverty line" (United Nations, General Assembly 2017, n.p.). The Working Group also noted the overrepresentation of Black Canadians in the criminal justice system. Whereas Black Canadians make up 3% of the population, we are 10% of the prison population. What is more, "There has been an alarming increase of 71.1% in the number of African Canadian detainees in federal corrections between 2005–2015" (2016, n.p). Finally, the report highlights the preponderance of "environmental racism" as a concern for Black Canadian communities. "Landfills, waste dump and other environmentally hazardous activities are disproportionately situated near neighborhoods of people of African descent, creating serious health risks. For example, the African Nova Scotian community of Lincolnville has been dealing with the social, economic and health effects of first and second-generation landfills since 1974" (2016, n.p.).

Given these stark economic and social realities facing Black Canada, it is not surprising that some believe they are not in a position to participate in a collective demand, along with other Canadians, to "give back" to Indigenous nations what they never had—land and money—in the first place. Indeed, many would argue that it is Black Canadians and others in the Black diaspora who are still owed restitution for unpaid labour during slavery and after. This issue of reparations, in fact, is one of the foci of the United Nations International Decade for People of African Descent (United Nations, General Assembly 2014). In addition to addressing the need for greater justice around racial profiling; fair and impartial trials; and addressing anti-Blackness in state institutions for Black people in the diaspora, the UN "Plan of Action" also argues that states—including Canada—should take further measures to ensure equality by:

> Acknowledging and profoundly regretting the untold suffering and evils inflicted on millions of men, women and children as a result of slavery, the slave trade, the transatlantic slave trade, colonialism, apartheid, genocide and past tragedies, noting that some States have taken the initiative to apologize and have paid reparation, where appropriate, for grave and massive violations committed, and calling on those that have not yet expressed remorse or presented apologies to find some way to contribute to the restoration of the dignity of victims. (2014, 7–8)

Despite Prime Minister Justin Trudeau's announcement in January 2018 that the government of Canada will recognize the International Decade for People of African Descent—already two years into the UN mandate—the government has not yet acknowledged, let alone compensated, Black Canadians for the injustices of the past, which continue to shape our realities in the present. Given the ongoing climate of anti-Black violence in Canada, and the "deeply entrenched" racism that shapes state institutions, many would argue that "making things right" necessarily means seeking justice for Black people, too.

In her plenary paper at Mikinaakominis / TransCanadas, "Recuperating Indigenous Narratives: Making Legible the Documenting of Injustices,"

Deanna Reder argues that "the study and teaching of Indigenous texts continues to require risky moves out of institutionalized and hierarchical disciplinary ways of knowing" (2017, n.p.). I would suggest that the study of Black Canadian texts similarly requires the willingness to shift toward a different, riskier conversation about rebalancing our relations. F. B. André's short story ends with just such a "risky" shift. With the truck full of his family's possessions still idling outside the occupied house, the narrator remains unsure of his next move. He calls his wife, who is impatient with him; to her mind, the situation is unjust. As a new homeowner, she feels she has done everything "right": "'I labeled all of my boxes,' she says. 'The movers were supposed to unload everything into the right rooms. That was our agreement. They won't get paid until it gets done right. They'll have to come back. They'll have to get it right'" (2007, 139). But to the narrator, what it means to "get it right" has by now shifted. In response to his partner's question about whether their "stuff is in the house," he becomes thoughtful. "I'm not sure," he says, "about a lot of stuff" (139). His focus now shifts away from their "stuff" in the truck toward the land outside. "There's a deer in our backyard," he says to her. "A big one." The story concludes, then, with the narrator still standing outside the house. It is an ending that could easily be read as pessimistic, especially since the narrator, despite his entitlement to the house and his legal citizenship, continues to stay on the threshold, unsettled.

But I read the closing image the story lingers on as hopeful, for it hints at the story's intersectional politics. The deer, being wild, depends on lands held in common—and kept uncultivated and unexploited—to survive. The deer is ultimately, as the title of André's short-story collection suggests, "what belongs." Rather than being about the arrival of third-wave (twenty-first century) Black homesteaders, then, this story interrupts that pioneer narrative and replaces it with a symbol of promise on the part of Black Canada to make no further claim on the land under the current terms of the liberal-democratic nation, and, as Larissa Lai puts it, to work to "return all animals to their proper land relations" (2021b). The narrator will not further divide up the land with fences; he will not cultivate the ground for profit. His refusal to step inside is a refutation of the legal principle of sweat equity upon which British property rights are based, and upon which the Black pioneers' title to their 160 acres of "free" prairie land were historically legitimated. The narrator's focus on the deer suggests a promise to protect Indigenous food sovereignty and economic rights.

But how, then, are we to imagine the future of André's narrator? Is he to be imagined as forever on the threshold of the settler-colonial nation, caught in the diasporic trap of deterritorializing but never arriving? André's story suggests a future in which Black diasporans commit to a juridical reframing of land and land rights from those of the British legal system and the current liberal democratic state to Indigenous traditions of governance in an effort to protect Indigenous self-determination in their homelands.

The idea of reframing Black-Indigenous relations in these ways will undoubtedly be met with resistance by some, for it involves a massive transformation not only of the institutions of the colonial society, institutions in which—after four hundred years, some Black Canadians are deeply invested, if not materially, then psychically—but also, most importantly, of ourselves and our political imaginations.

For instance, when Rinaldo Walcott said in his plenary talk at Mikinaakominis / TransCanadas that "Black people's enslavement remains out of the purview of the definition of colonization being used" (2017a), he made it clear that he sees such "risky moves" as the one I am proposing here as too risky. Such moves, to him, risk further decentring Blackness in Canada and Canadian literary studies. It was no accident, as I understand it, that Walcott's multiple interventions at that conference—his avowal to "quit CanLit" and his statement that he left the conference because no plenary session included Black women literary critics[4]—emerged at a conference that was framed around the central ethical issues of diasporic-Indigenous relations. To briefly recapitulate Walcott's stated arguments for "quitting CanLit," he said,

> CanLit fails to transform because it refuses to take seriously that Black literary expression and thus Black life is foundational to it. CanLit still appears surprised every single time by the appearance of Black literary expression and Black life. Because Black expression is reduced to surprise *there has been no sustained and ongoing serious consideration of Black work in CanLit*. You can write the same essay over and over again and no one will notice. (Walcott qtd. in Ballantyne et al. 2017, n.p.; emphasis added)

I will say more about this statement shortly. Yet, despite the feeling of crisis that was palpable at the conference, and in subsequent evaluations of the conference, for instance, that were published by Ballantyne et al. (2017) in *The Walrus*, which described the "Unbearable Whiteness of CanLit," I thought the conference constituted a highly successful—in fact, long overdue—shift in discussion. After all, the focus of the conference was, as stated in the Call for Papers, "to significantly advance Canadian/Turtle Island cultural and intellectual discussion on the relationship between Indigenous and non-Indigenous peoples" (Kamboureli and Lai 2016a).

All this is not to say that I don't see anti-Blackness shaping CanLit as a disciplinary formation; of course, I do. It is there in recently published literary histories, as well as in the public reception of them (see Rak 2017. It is there in the anonymous peer review reports Black scholars receive that more often than not assume we're white. It's there in the grant application feedback that both overtly and covertly devalues the scope and importance of Black Canadian literary studies as a field. It's there in the all-white prize committees and the all-white conference panels. It's there in the less-than-collegial peer reviews. I agree that we need to centre and support Black undergraduate and graduate students by teaching courses dedicated to Black Canadian literature so that students can see themselves, their histories and futures, reflected in the field. We need more Black scholars in the academy and in CanLit not only because representation is a good in and of itself, but also because the presence of Black literary scholars in English departments challenges and transforms the sedimented values of literary studies itself. In all this, I agree with Walcott (Ballantyne et. al. 2017).

But, truth be told, I don't think that it was (only) the issues that I've outlined above that provoked Walcott to make his interventions at the conference. After all, he did not attend the panel he was scheduled to chair at which I—a Black scholar—delivered my paper; nor did he acknowledge and amplify the work and presence of any of the other Black scholars—Lillian Allen, Michael Bucknor, David Chariandy, George Elliott Clarke, Afua Cooper, Jade Ferguson, Sonnet L'Abbé, Lucia Lorenzi, Suzette Mayr, and Katrina Leial Sellinger—who were also in the room. Moreover, there were a number of non-Black scholars who have dedicated their careers to the study and dissemination of Black Canadian literature, including Paul Barrett, Pilar Cuder-Domínguez, Belén Martín-Lucas, and Winfried Siemerling. (Other important scholars of Black Canadian literature, such as Ronald Cummings, Paula C. Madden, Linda Morra, and Maureen Moynagh, to name only a few, were not in attendance at this particular conference.) By naming these scholars it is not my intention to try to recuperate CanLit with respect to Blackness; CanLit is a disciplinary formation I regard with a high degree of double consciousness—all the more so now in the wake of UBCAccountable and the #metoo movement. Neither is it my intention to suggest that all or even any of the other Black scholars agree with my "take" on the conference. There is a diversity of opinions regarding both the field of CanLit, its engagement with Blackness, and Walcott's tactics.[5] What I *am* seeking to do by naming these scholars is to nuance Walcott's assertion that "there has been *no sustained and ongoing* serious consideration of Black work in CanLit" Ballantyne et.al. 2017). The work produced by these scholars over the last twenty years has helped to transform not just the authors, literary texts, and histories that form the contested corpus of CanLit; but also, crucially, their work has helped to transform the methodologies by which we produce knowledge about literature, history, and subjectivity—now more hemispheric, diasporic, and transnational. Significantly, these scholars' engagements over the years with Walcott's own scholarship has been a crucial part of what has produced the transformation of what CanLit is and means today.

It is telling that in all of Walcott's statements at the conference, his tweets, and in the private and public narratives that were shared after the conference, the central focus of Mikinaaḳominis / TransCanadas—Indigenous relation and justice—went missing. This is especially apparent in *The Walrus* article by Ballantyne, Barrett, Isaacs, and Singh, where all mention of the Indigenous—and with it questions of justice and relation—are evacuated. This is a sign that it is not just whiteness in CanLit that is "unbearable"; what is unbearable also is the difficult, necessary, painful work of thinking Blackness in relation to Indigenous peoples and their lands.

I agree with Walcott that "writing Blackness is difficult work" (1997, xi)—now, more than ever. But to those in my scholarly communities who continue to feel resistant to doing the work of entwining Black with Indigenous anticolonial struggles, I echo what Walcott himself has long said: the liberal-democratic nation as it is currently structured has failed us. The signs of that failure are everywhere: in the abominable poverty rates of our communities; in the state-sanctioned murders of Black citizens; in the "justice" and carceral systems that ensure our continuing unfreedom. In the face of such injustices, it becomes easier to imagine a future in which we try not to further integrate ourselves into Canada's "settler" framework, including its cultural and literary ones, but rather to try further to "unsettle" ourselves. Seeking to rebalance relations with Indigenous peoples is not only a matter of justice for Indigenous peoples, then. It is a matter of committing ourselves now fully to the seductive story of Blackness in the Americas, which story is powerful precisely because it is about the restless quest for freedom, self-ownership, and political sovereignty that we see Indigenous artists and activists fighting for today. Let us now dream the greater, more revolutionary, dream.

Listing Waters

The Poetics of Solidarity in Mahmoud Darwish and Rita Wong

/ DINA AL-KASSIM

Digging up Echo's Bones

Invited to contribute to this volume, which names coalition as a guiding aim in a project to shift a national literature from its moorings in cultural appropriation, I want to thank editors Smaro Kamboureli and Larissa Lai for taking the chance to include a comparatist for whom national literature is not an informing framework. This chapter has origins in a project on the different accounts of solidarity that can be found in literary reflections on liberatory politics. Beginning with the figure of adherence and anticolonial "love" in Jean Genet's political writings, tracking solidarities has taken me from the poetry of Mahmoud Darwish and Rita Wong to a series of Arab, French, and Bengali leftists reading Greek tales for fables of responsibility and alternative agencies. My aim here is to follow the water in activist poetics in order to offer a concise reflection on a discrete formal technique that I prefer to call simply "listing." Listing encompasses the anticatalogue, antiepic, and nonlyric index of a material world dematerialized by colonial occupation and neoliberal erasure of lived environment, which ruins watershed while shifting population. It is precisely these changed worlds—ruined watersheds and shifting populations—that are materialized in the poetics of Darwish and Wong. My intention is to trace the scenes of solidarity that bind these two poets in historical, poetic, and affective terms, starting with Darwish's 1992 tribute to Chief Seattle of the Duwamish and Suquamish in what is now Washington State, and ending with Wong's *undercurrent* (2015), a manifesto, field guide, organizing handbook, and notes for a revolution for our shared interdependence in water.

Darwish and Wong share a love for lists of names, objects, persons, places, scientific terms, waterways, weather, even celestial bodies; unlike Homer and his catalogues, neither Darwish nor Wong inventory possessions, nor do they seek to record might. Listing for Darwish and Wong renders the new world of the dispossessed into the symbolic register of a language outfitted for this precarious world transformed by colonial violence and the capitalism it ushers in. Neither depicting a realism that equals the properties of an incremental loss happening in real time, nor offering a survey of the damage incurred, listing is a provisional practice that makes figural language for the persons who are unmade and remade by ongoing colonial settler violence and the polluted landscapes we inhabit without having the language of their measure. Listing recalls the past and names the present; it is a political and symbolic strategy that uses poetic echo as a way to locate solidarity across time and land, between animal and element, beyond catastrophe and toward renewal. Repetitions, refrains, reiterations, strings of names: these are the means of listing, a poetic struggle to rematerialize a vanishing world, to conserve it but also to communicate it, the better to infect us with memory that will catalyze the agency of social processes grounded in responsiveness. In Darwish and Wong, water thematizes a forgotten history of Canadian literature, specifically the confluence of different streams of solidarity. Darwish, whom Wong cites as an inspiration, represented the Palestinian delegation to the 1976 United Nations Habitat Vancouver conference, the precursor to the establishment of the UN Commission on Human Settlement and Sustainability. This historic event also marked the meeting of Lee Maracle and Darwish, and became the source of decades of solidarity between them.[1] Wong inherits this connection, and repeats Maracle's dictum that no one owns the water, that "*water owns itself*" (Maracle, epigraph cited in Wong 2015), in *perpetual* and *undercurrent*, her two books on ecological crisis, water protection, and activist solidarities, the former an illustrated book of poems, comics, and essays, the latter a poetry collection.

While I was pursuing this literary history and the fragile thread of literary solidarities, I was startled when I, like other readers in Canada, was confronted with the responses to an exemplary case of failed solidarity and extreme literary narcissism passed off as an affirmation of the universality of human imagination. Two weeks before the Mikinaakominis / TransCanadas conference in May 2017, where I was to address an audience of Canadian literature specialists, *Write*, the trade journal of the Writers' Union of Canada (TWUC), ran a special issue devoted to emergent Indigenous writers edited by Hal Niedzviecki. Niedzviecki's introduction, titled "Winning the Appropriation Prize," began with a line that announced that "I don't believe in cultural appropriation" and continued with the instruction to "Write what you don't know...Relentlessly explore the lives of people who aren't like you, who you didn't grow up with" (2017, 8).[2] Deliberately playing on the colonial harm of words like "explore," the author exhorted readers to "Set your sights on the big goal: Win the Appropriation Prize" because "there's not even anything preventing us from incorporating a culture's myths, legends, oral histories, and sacred practices in our own works" (8). Going on to praise Indigenous writers for showing "courage" and "boldness," values often associated with the figure of the "noble savage" in colonial literatures, the editor extolled the virtues of "truth telling" as the universal value and sovereign power of literary imagination.

Niedzviecki's provocation drew international attention, with the *Guardian UK* citing amply from his statement, including his proposal that appropriation could help "Canadian literature shed its "exhaustingly white and middle class" subject matter (Niedzviecki 2017, 8).[3] The publication was followed by a Twitter feast in which major Canadian cultural figures offered to raise funds for the proposed appropriation prize and exchanged vulgar quips to public outrage. Within days Niedzviecki had resigned amid a cascade of criticism, including from the TWUC's Equity Task Force. In fact, the TWUC's Equity Task Force issued a strong denunciation, writing that "much Indigenous knowledge has been either erased from the historical record or has already been appropriated without attribution," and that Niedzviecki's call for an appropriation prize "partakes of a long-debunked false universalism" (TWUC, Equity 2017). The TWUC's Equity Task Force's response included a nine-point platform for change, some of which the TWUC has already instituted.

As the organ of TWUC, *Write* does not represent the views of individual members; it also represents the views of its entire membership; further, its editor has a responsibility to represent the values of its constituents, and institutional structures should be in place to hold rogues accountable. As evidence of a problem of racial and gendered inequity, the very existence of a TWUC Equity Task Force speaks to an ongoing and perceived problem of exclusion of Indigenous and other racialized writers both in the pages of *Write* and in the cultural leadership that TWUC exercises at a national level. Within a week of the scandal, CBC News invited the network's culture critic Jesse Wente (Ojibwa) to comment on Niedzviecki's editorial and the response it had elicited. Wente appeared alongside Jonathan Kay, editor of *The Walrus* at the time, who defended appropriation as a right of "artists to imagine other cultures." In response, Wente declared that cultural institutions needed to be reinvented entirely, and referenced the fact that his own community had been without running water for fifteen years without any media outcry, let alone outrage to the extent of that elicited in defence of Niedzviecki.[4]

Their interaction was a spectacle that replayed the racist script Smaro Kamboureli critiqued at the turn of the century when she traced the rise of media narratives that established multiculturalism as yet another word for divisive conflict that blames the ethnoracial subject: "Because it tends to employ stereotypes without necessarily considering the history that produced them, multiculturalism as a media-manufactured scandal circumvents the systemic structures of which it is both symptom and effect (2000, 89). As if taking dictation from Kamboureli's dissection of multiculturalism, Niedzviecki and Kay disavowed the racism of their positions by "turning diversity into the familiar sign of use value" (Kamboureli 2000, 89), thus assuming that "there are no epistemologically privileged subjects in Canada" (Kamboureli 2000, 86). They did this through a simultaneous elevation and debasement of Indigenous writing. First, claiming that "Indigenous writing is the most vital and compelling force in writing and publishing in Canada today," Niedzviecki announced its elevation of what in the next phrase he reduced to "writing from what they [Indigenous writers] don't know" (2017, 8), by which he means, quite literally, a lack of knowledge understood as object. The use value of Indigenous writing secured, praise is given only on condition that it is undermined in the same breath. Kay went a step further on CBC when he protested Niedzviecki's debasement on social media, saying that he had been treated "as a sort of hate criminal" when "there is a legitimate debate to be had about...the rights of artists to imagine other cultures" (Nathoo 2017), thus arguing that appropriation is an aesthetic right that must balance "the rights of those other cultures to avoid appropriation" (Nathoo 2017). Two days later, in conversation with *Metro Morning*'s Matt Galloway, Wente emphasized the difficulty of creating "fundamental change" in large cultural institutions when Indigenous communities are forced to "re-argue for our value as human beings" and when emotion is miscast "as weakness." Wente diagnosed a racial repetition compulsion as the refusal of cultural institutions to change such that once again, the difference of racialized subjects was positioned as the trouble's cause. (Nathoo 2017). Clearly, the spectacle that ensued from this controversy pitted a culture of rights against a culture of responsibility.

This controversy forced me to follow a different path in my consideration of Darwish, Maracle, and Wong on protecting water and surviving colonial violence. This path has taken its bearings from the signal failure of ethical responsibility exemplified by Niedzviecki's editorial, a failure that demands a response through the feminist, queer, antiracist, and anticolonial work of the last forty-plus years—I am counting somewhat arbitrarily from the publication of *Orientalism*—that has provided resources for potential cultural change. Repetition is our lot. I can only echo Jesse Wente's charge that the appropriation scandal lays bare the need for a complete change of cultural institutions, if Canadian institutional culture is to renew its credibility (Wente 2017; qtd. in Nahoo 2017). I speak as a fish out of water, or, as I have learned to say by reading Asian Canadian poets, as an "unsettled guest" on Indigenous land.

Like a listing boat still able to move but threatening to capsize, the white CanLit establishment risks its own irrelevance if it does not confront its need to see its idealized image reflected in its own generous acts of including "others," acts to which it has been reconciled but not converted. This is one definition of liberal multiculturalism. When a boat heels without wind, we suspect improper loading or a hull full of filthy bilge water. As far as a diagnosis of the "appropriation prize" is concerned, what transpired invites critical reflection both on the dominance of prize culture in Canada and the racialized masculinism transfixed by narcissism that characterized the debates. Questions of responsibility, authorship, and authenticity are raised in this context of liberal multiculturalism, yet the discussion proceeds asymmetrically. Just as Narcissus knows nothing of the lake that returns his gaze, but falls captive to his own aesthetic pleasure given back to him as "self-knowledge," so the *sovereign* imagination knows nothing of the complex ecology surrounding it, and cannot be reduced to intentions, good or bad. In this version of Narcissus's story, Echo remains unheard and unremarked.

In 1981, Gayatri Spivak returned to Ovid's tale of Echo and Narcissus to stage an intervention in psychoanalysis, and, surprisingly, found the basis of an ethical theory in her reading of Echo's bones. Spivak notes Freud's speculation that a narcissistic woman compensates herself for her lack of social power by shifting her self-image and satisfaction into the image of her son. In this account, the female narcissist enjoys a capacity to transfer sideways, which might be analogous to the imagined appropriation prize, fixated as it was on intentional knowledge of the other. This is knowledge that can be gathered, assessed, and calculated and, through the ruse of consultation or what Niedzviecki symptomatically referred to as "responsibility," authenticated, even if by no means authentic. This is knowledge imagined as an object such as one finds reflected in the glassy surface of a lake. One of the goals of Spivak's recourse to the tale of Echo and Narcissus is to question a version of knowledge as object of evidence, given in a static image that can be memorized, which is very different from the kind of knowing that might echo through histories of dispossession and also very different from the skill of reading the surface of a lake for the movement of currents or fish below. Narcissistic knowledge is embodied but only as "self-knowledge" (Spivak 2012a, 234). Meanwhile, Echo, as another figure of knowledge, is foreclosed in readings of Ovid that interpret her fate as a warning against idle talk (the girl Echo is punished for being a chatterbox who annoyed a powerful woman, Juno), condemned as she is to repeat fragments of another's speech. Such a foreclosure extends even to contemporary European feminists eager to retrieve from the classics an equal share in sovereign subjectivity. Spivak, instead, hears Echo's repetition of the other's speech as a figure for criticism itself; her reading strategy salvages Echo's desire to speak, along with her performance "dispersed into absolute chance rather than an obstinate choice" (2012a, 228). Here chance becomes another name for the chancy and inventive reuse of broken fragments of histories and language that cannot be reconstituted as wholes. Limited to fragmentary repetition rather than sovereign invention, Echo is an ambiguous figure for the critical drive, not the least because in pining after Narcissus, she wastes away leaving only scattered bones and the resounding repetition of voices. Echo's "risk of response...has no identity proper to itself" (Spivak 2012a, 228); as a response to another, risk becomes the ground of ethics, prompting the question, "what ethical instantiation does this interpretation of Echo offer 'us'—the worldwide collectivity of conscientized feminists of colour from bourgeois origins or in passive capitalist relations?" (2012a, 229).

Against a liberal multiculturalism that offers to include racial others on the condition that, as Spivak puts it, we learn to "remain-fixated-in-cultural-difference, simulate what is really pathogenic repression in the form of questioning the European universalist superego" (2012a, 229), Echo's bones become newly resonant, allowing us to play them "as the instrument of the possibility of a truth not dependent upon intention, a reward uncoupled from, indeed set free from, the recipient" (226).[5] This is another way Spivak calls on us to develop a capacity for understanding anew that "ethics are not a problem of knowledge but a call of relationship" (233). Or put another way, the change of cultural institutions begins in critical responsiveness to the fact that truth and intention are no longer and never have been coupled.

As a figure of non-knowledge, openness to contingency and learning through imitation and critical recitation, Echo resists appropriation by and translation into neoliberal forms of commercial subjectivity. For an editorial of a special issue devoted to Indigenous writing to reduce cultural differences to a problem of knowledge and an occasion for the assertion of subjective sovereignty in imagination, racial difference must have already been appropriated as datum rather than relation. Spivak calls this lesson in relation an "aesthetic education" (2012a)[6] which necessarily supplements the rights talk of access and inclusion, lest the latter be revealed as yet another abstraction of capital.

Against this constriction of knowledge to data, Spivak invokes a "planetary" thinking as another version of responsibility found in pre-capitalist cultural sources but crucially for her in Islam and Indigeneity. "The more ecological practice of living, where the opposition between the human and the natural is made indeterminate, is, of course, the Aboriginal" (Spivak 2012b, 341); that is to say, Indigenous cultures labour to understand the relation of humans to land and life but do so through the notion that we are born into responsibility for the other. Though writing in the early 1990s, Spivak's suggestion that the "precapitalist mindset" (2012b, 342)—even though touched by capitalism, can still echo a culture of responsibility within our discourses of rights—is relevant to what we call in Canada Indigenous pedagogy. As she says,

> This developed postcapitalist structure must once again be filled with the more robust imperative to responsibility which capitalist social productivity was obliged to destroy. And, to repeat, the imperative must be understood and valued (an aesthetic education!) as *defective for capitalism* rather than necessarily *pre*-capitalist on an interested sequential evolutionary model. (2012b, 344)

Spivak's insight into the entangled logic of narcissism, aesthetics, and capital also invites us to revisit European transnational attempts to defect *from* capital because they offer us a history of thinking aesthetics into political solidarity among writers, artists, communities, and revolutionaries. Kristin Ross's (2016) study of the 1871 Paris Commune excavates a workers' fellowship that was made possible only through the exercise of poetry and arts. In nineteenth-century anarchist tracts, it is literature's responsibility to gather the gestures of relationality and correspondence as the necessary conditions of and for solidarity. Comparing William Morris (now considered a founding voice in socialist ecology), Élisée Reclus (anarchist ecologist and anticolonial geographer), and the Russian anarchist, Peter Kropotkin, Ross shows that these three writers attempted to build the "context" for social change through a rethinking of "what Reclus called solidarity, Morris called 'fellowship,' and Kropotkin 'mutual aid,' not as a moral or ethical sensibility, but as political strategy" (2016, 7). Today, as we are caught up even against our will in debates that were vital in the 1990s—appropriation, identity politics, antiracism/anticolonialism, feminism, and aesthetics—it strikes me as imperative to recall the rich discourse of solidarity, which in Europe is connected to an embattled workers' resistance to the pollution of life and environment. These writings belong to a tradition that could be usefully brought into a conversation already framed at the outset by Indigenous resurgence. The legacy of what many people insist on calling "Western" aesthetic theory is a contested one that includes a steady stream of resistant critique and ecological awareness and that can be useful in attempts to "change cultural institutions" by imagining political solutions (Wente 2017). This is to say that the history of socialist ecological thinking is a history of thinking solidarity and interdependence with environment and literature in an explicitly anti-capitalist mode.

In this vein, George Bataille launched one of the most instructive critiques of the ideology of narcissistic aesthetic sovereignty, and especially of writers who mistake themselves for the vanguard. In 1929 Bataille castigated the surrealists for enacting nothing more than oedipal family dramas in the place of a necessary betrayal of their social class followed by an identification with the "old mole" ("vielle taupe") of proletarian struggle. Elaborating Marx's figure of the subterranean proletariat, the mole, for Bataille (1985b), figures the heterogeneity of community freed to pursue itself beyond the "light" of reason and exalted values. The mole does not need to exhibit his abjection for he suffers oppression in earthly communion with an intermittent, only sometimes possible, emergence. Neither the figure of sovereignty nor the emblem of a messianic triumph, the mole digs his hollows and tunnels persistently, incorporating both the psychological struggle of subjectivities dominated by normative order and proletarian consciousness emergent in the worker's revolutions of the early twentieth century. The task of the bourgeois anti-capitalist is nothing more nor less than that of bearing witness to the mole's eventual revolution.

Bataille's writing has been fundamental for the entire discourse on mastery and subjectivity in French theory and beyond since the 1920s but constitutes a lost genealogy in the sketch of "Western" subjectivity that reappears in contemporary assertions of artistic autonomy and unlimited imagination, despite having been thoroughly critiqued in the "anti-racist cultural gatherings of the 1980's and 1990's" (Lai 2014, 213). The conclusion to Larissa Lai's *Slanting I, Imagining We* details this story of a thinly disguised white backlash against racial coalition-building in the public cultural sphere, which used the keywords of that public sphere to quell or displace difference. Uncannily resonant with today's cascade of CanLit outrages, that 1980s era of Thatcherite neoliberalism hatching out rebellion across the Middle East and North Africa—and not only there—found a footing in revamped frontier notions of individual freedom primed for poetry, a misrepresentation of European struggles that theorize and forge international cross-classed solidarities. These strata of culture work were—and remain—an accessible storehouse of literary and philosophical images ready to be reimagined.

As witness to the revolution of the other, Bataille's attention to the mole enacts solidarity as attentive relation rather than as identification (the latter always deriving from internalization or consumption) or property in common. Standing in different relation to a common problem, mixed agencies will find their form in the singular solidarity they forge. The witness to the other's revolutions is called upon to respect but not to self-censor, perhaps to be silent but not be silenced, as a path to active listening rather than knowledge production. Sticking with the mole, we come to understand agency as echo.[7]

Solidarity: Eleven Planets and an Undercurrent

Darwish and Wong exemplify a literary practice of symbolic materialization that connects Indigenous and allied poetics. Listing, as I said earlier, is practised by Darwish and Wong as a means to create the images, and organize the fragments, of traditions into a symbolic language that speaks the reality of a dispossessed people who have never lived the present and so have few symbolic resources to inhabit it. Water protectors and refugees share this situation. Indigenous activists and their allies share this predicament. And though I have been arguing that anarchist, activist, and literary sources of critical engagement and refusal of sovereign aesthetics exist and could provide models of analysis, Darwish and Wong face the challenge of materializing the reality of relation through poetic means.

While serving as founding member of the Palestinian National Council, formed in 1988 at the beginning of the first Intifada, Darwish revisited a moment of Turtle Island's Indigenous history in his poem "The 'Red Indian's' Penultimate Speech to the White Man." (2009, 69–77) Part of the longer work "Eleven Planets" (2009a), which is included in his collection *If I Were Another* (2009b), the poem revives the voice of Chief Seattle, whom he cites in the epigraph. "Penultimate Speech" is perhaps most famous as Darwish's poem recited and enacted by George Aquilar in Jean-Luc Godard's *Notre Musique*, a film in which Darwish appears playing himself. In stark contrast to the version of aesthetic appropriation as sovereign right defended by the proponents of the "appropriation prize," Darwish does not appropriate the story of "other cultures"; instead, he weaves together elements of Chief Seattle's speech with material realities of colonial violence, several histories of conquest, and the contours of the Duwamish River in Washington State. That is, the poet explicitly ties the chief's speech to the land and does so out of an intimate knowledge of that relation, thus echoing one Indigenous voice with his own Indigenous voice in a masterful defence of land as a site and repository of memory. Care for ecology marks all Darwish's writing, but comes into greater historical focus in "Eleven Planets" as it builds on the theme of land begun narratively in his memoir about the siege of Beirut, *Memory for Forgetfulness: August, Beirut 1982* (1995), where he offers 112 words for water transcribed in the early eleventh century by the Andalusian lexicographer Ibn Sidah. As we will see, numbers and lists of plants, animals, aspects of terrain. and landscape accrue mounting significance in the years after the loss of Beirut.

Chief Seattle's oration of 1854 is held to be a prescient and early ecological manifesto as well as a carefully encoded speech of anticolonial resistance hidden in the language of defeat and concession. The text of the speech has been the subject of much editorial variation; the Suquamish community site favours the 1887 *Seattle Star* version:

> And when the last Red Man shall have perished, and the memory of my tribe shall have become a myth among the White Men, these shores will swarm with the invisible dead of my tribe...At night, when the streets of your cities and villages are silent and you think them deserted, they will throng with the returning hosts that once filled and still love this beautiful land. The White Man will never be alone.
>
> Let him be just and deal kindly with my people, for the dead are not powerless. Dead, did I say? There is no death, only a change of worlds. (Chief Seattle)[8]

A short distance to the north of the traditional Duwamish/Suquamish wintering ground, Vancouver-based Chinese Canadian poet, Rita Wong, marks her affinity with Darwish's poems, citing in *forage*, her award-winning collection coincidentally published the year of Darwish's death, the influence of his translated collection, *Unfortunately, It was Paradise. undercurrent*, one of the terms for water highlighted in Darwish's antiquarian catalogue of water in *Memory* (see below), is the title of Wong's 2015 poetic treatise on the despoliation of our water supply and the needfulness of solidarity with the keepers of the water, and especially the Hatchet Lake Denesuline (Wong 2015, 72), the Keepers of the Athabasca and Northlands Dene First Nation (2015, 68). The poet's connections are lived, committed, and exhibited in three years of healing walks along waterlines endangered or befouled in the tar sands. Listing provides much of the structure and cohesion of *undercurrent*, underlining the work's refusal of epic and lyric forms in a self-conscious style reminiscent of Wong's previous work with foodways in *forage*, where the poet bids farewell to Whitman's legacy of cataloguing the "Song of Myself" by footnoting him in verse. I single out Wong's *undercurrent* because it asserts, tracks, and elaborates our interdependence in and through water while offering a model of engaged participation with Indigenous water keepers at ceremonies, vigils, protests, and healing walks, all narrated as fragments of story in the poetry.[9] Inheriting many lineages, poetic and political, *undercurrent* is exemplary as an expression of the aesthetic, ethical, and practical solidarity with the elemental, the planetary, as well as with community partners intent to inaugurate a new history of what seems so often impossible. No solitary poet surveying his worlds in Wong; no chief charged to speak in the voice of a sovereign people. Instead, we are often informed that the writing is itself convoked from ties of affiliation. For example, *perpetual*, written by Wong and illustrated by Cindy Mochizuki, is framed as a "response to Dorothy Christian's call to protect sacred water" (2015) while Christian herself appears in Wong's narrative, which comprises comic, found poetry, and panel discussion. In Wong and Darwish we find demonstrations of the possible impossibilities—that we will save the waters, that the people will return—which are enabled by a time out of "clock time" (2015, 3).

Darwish's "Penultimate Speech" (2009b, 69–77) takes up a range of figures for lost sovereignty, from ancient Canaan and al-Andalus to North America and Iraq, whose autonomy was violated in the first Gulf War before being definitively lost in the second. Epic scenes of land loss and exile told in the antiepic and impersonal lyric style of Darwish's innovative free verse complicate the temporalities of narrative and observation. Anchoring the whole are a set of interlocking techniques of repetition and refrain, lists and ellipses, that reject the sovereign subjectivity of the national epic in the lyrical free verse inherited from Whitman, whose translated poetry has long become a common reference for modern Arabic poetics. Sometimes expanding to become the main body of the poem, often contracted to short, additive phrases, the list is central to Darwish's poetics. Darwish unfurls the list as a deliberate refusal of the state power of epic while simultaneously subordinating the narcissism of Whitman's catalogues to the necessary task of creating words and images for the expulsion and colonization of his people. Wong and Darwish share the technique of long and short lists that bind their poetic line to the politico-aesthetic project of impossible possibilities manifest in the link between Darwish's lexicographic moments and Wong's habit of sending us searching in encyclopedias, community archives, and environmental reports. This learning from our reality links the politics of resistance to the politics of poetic form evident in their refusal of epic and a complex negotiation undoing lyric sovereignty. I propose to call their inventories, repetitions, technical terms, lexicons, and refrains simply a poetics of lists to avoid the pitfalls of the Homeric dominance and to underline that solidarity in these poetic practices is not a tactical choice but responds to the vanishing present with naming[10] and to underline that solidarity in these poetic practices is not a tactical choice but responds to the vanishing present with naming.

"Eleven Planets" is also an allegory of this doubled relation of possible and impossible, present and absent. It references the Qur'anic story of Yusef/Joseph, whose prophetic vision of eleven stars, plus the sun and the moon, came true after many travails, beginning with his attempted murder by eleven envious brothers who pushed him into a dry well. On its surface, Yusef's tale of enslavement and dispossession serves as an allegory of the perils of beauty and Palestinian land coveted by others. "Eleven Planets," however, folds another narrative into its lists. When Darwish wrote "Eleven Planets" there were still nine in our solar system. From 1807 to 1845, there were, indeed, eleven planets. Since 2006 we have only eight as Pluto is now understood as entirely other. Impossible possibility and transformed reality are crucial indices for Darwish's liberatory poetics, which is bound up in scenes of setback, impasse, and lost sovereignty while the change of worlds is shown to be a less terminal figure. As the epigraph to "Penultimate Speech" reads:

> *Did I say, The Dead?*
> *There is no Death here,*
> *there is only a change of worlds.*
>
> —Duwamish Chief Seattle (Darwish 2009b, 69)

undercurrent also begins with an Indigenous epigraph in the words of Coast Salish author, Lee Maracle, long-time ally of the Palestinian people and friend of Darwish, which read: "*We do not own the water. The water owns itself*" (in Wong 2015, 3). The Lees multiply on the first page as the second epigraph repeats Bruce Lee's maxim, now an internet meme, "Be water my friend."[11] Between the Lees, the Indigenous water rights talk enters the poems of the Chinese Canadian experience, and no one owns the story. Being and having open *undercurrent* to two water-related impossibilities that are exposed throughout the text as the twin conditions of interdependence through water. Into this flow consider: Lee Maracle and Mahmoud Darwish first met in 1976 when the latter represented the Palestinian delegation at the UN Habitat conference on human settlement in Vancouver. During that visit Maracle read Darwish in English while he recited himself in Arabic (see Ditmars 2013).

What is the significance, then, of the 1976 UN Habitat conference? It laid the groundwork for the establishment of the UN Commission on Human Settlements and Sustainability with the mandate to improve sustainable access to safe drinking water and basic sanitation. The following December, the UN General Assembly passed resolutions 32:162, which established the Commission on Human Settlements, and, on the same day and in the same chamber, 32:161. Resolution 32:161 exhibits a similar concern for water and declares the "permanent" sovereignty of the Arab states and peoples over natural resources against the "aggression of the occupying Power" (United Nations, General Assembly, "Permanent Sovereignty" n.d.). The resolution does not name the occupied people. In 1976, like Pluto prior to 1930, Palestine and its people did not exist; rather, Clause 161 recalls

> its previous resolutions on permanent sovereignty over natural resources, particularly their provisions supporting resolutely the efforts of the developing countries and the peoples of the territories under colonial and racial domination and foreign occupation in their struggle to regain effective control over their natural and all other resources, wealth and economic activities. (United Nations, General Assembly, "Permanent Sovereignty" 1977)

The text of the resolution describes the illegality of the occupier's "repeated Israeli aggression and continued occupation of their territories," and urges UN member states to resist their attempts "to effect any changes in the demographic composition or geographic character or institutional structure of those territories" (United Nations, General Assembly, "Permanent Sovereignty" n.d.). The establishment of the UN Habitat reflects the consciousness that these problems require international co-operation, and charges UN member nations to find solutions "based on equity, justice and solidarity, especially among the developing countries" (United Nations, General Assembly, "Permanent Sovereignty" n.d.). Maracle's and Darwish's readings in 1976 consolidated a parallel solidarity between colonized subjects pursuing their duty to the land, people, and water through ecological engagements that we now call sustainability in acknowledgement of the unsustainable. This is another figure of the impossible possibility of now eleven, now nine, now eight planets.

Affinities with Native land loss and moments of *Nakba* (Catastrophe) taken up in "Eleven Planets" provide the historical and transglobal coordinates of shared but not identical experience, which in turn builds up a genealogy of survivance,[12] which is to say, a set of skills. On this continent, these skills are sometimes called Indigenous pedagogy. At other times and places, they have had other coordinates and contents.[13] In the link between Palestinian and Indigenous, attested by the circuit of poems in the late 1970s between Maracle, Darwish, and others (see Salaita 2016), land and rights are unassailably linked, though the knowledges derived from them are incommensurate.

Despite playing a key role in the drafting of the Palestinian charter and other founding documents that attempted to recentre Palestine from revolution to territorial technocracy, Darwish quit the Palestinian National

Council in 1996 as a result of the Oslo Accord, which brought only immiseration by other means, one of which has been the militarized appropriation of water to match theft of land and cultural erasure. By dint of the Oslo Accord, Israel owns and controls all water and its circulation in the Occupied Palestinian Territories, Gaza, Golan, and beyond. "Beyond" is a nebulous territory as Israel's actions have led directly to the depletion of aquifers and their pollution by improper or, in some cases, nonexistent water treatment (when the level falls, dirty water enters the aquifer). Sovereignty over water in the region bears the responsibility for the health of the living, the land, and also time. In the concrete sense of planning for the future replenishment of aquifer, the present is the future and the future is dreamed on the model of the past, yet there is no time but crisis. According to sources as varied as the International Monetary Fund and UNESCO, Israel practises a policy of expulsion through engineered water scarcity while cornering the world market in innovating desalination processes through nanotechnology in research partnerships with University of California–Los Angeles, University of Southern California, University of British Columbia, and other "cultural institutions" in North America. For Palestinians in the Occupied Territories the choices come down to one: buying water from the occupier as UN plans for new desalination plants are always already halted. Today in Gaza, a place-based knowledge of Palestinians, includes the knowledge that, because 80–85 percent of groundwater in the Occupied Territories is used by Israel while only 10 percent of Palestinians in Gaza have access to potable water, most must decide how to divide desalinated and boiled water into its different waters: one for bathing, one for cooking, another for plants and animals, yet another for flushing, and drinking—drinking only plastic bottled water sold to them by the colonial settler state.

In May 2017, when Jesse Wente was invited to speak on CBC about the appropriation prize, he shifted our attention to the absence of drinking water in Indigenous communities. In 2016, Human Rights Watch, citing the 134 water advisories in eighty-five First Nations reserves (ninety of them in Ontario), concluded that the Canadian government has failed in its duty to provide safe water for First Nations communities.[14] This negligence is fed by the regulatory and funding problems that derive from the continued existence of the 1877 Indian Act, which grants jurisdiction over reserves to the federal government while not requiring it to adequately fund communities. As a result, First Nations have faced decades of damage due to water scarcity in a country of immense water wastage.

The violence of colonial predation is felt not only as "disavowal of a politics of difference" (Kamboureli 2000, 86) but also in the survival of the epistemic supremacy that claims the right to own and raze everything from Indigenous towns to the very land itself. For Darwish and Wong, naming, repetition, information, and lists offer the poetic coordinates of imagination in ongoing transcommunity/transterritorial crisis. In Darwish, listing also becomes a way of multiplying time and memory so as to blur the deathly certainties of colonial settler futurity. We see this at work in the malediction in "Penultimate Speech" when the speaker promises that "My nation will return as air and light and water" (Darwish 2009b, 75) and, "through everything / that besieges you, white ones, we will look, as dying dead, as dead / who live, dead who return… / so leave, you guests of the place, / some vacant seats for your hosts" (2009b, 76–77). Detailing ecological catastrophe, the penultimate and sixth section of the poem suggests that after the time of "the new Rome, the Sparta of technology / and the ideology / of madness" (2009b, 76) will come another time. The poem argues that, in an uncertain season, the same land will be newly occupied by those who, returning, remember *and* by those who carried the place away. This double occupancy will necessitate new terms of a new peace to be dictated by the dead risen again. Thus the "Penultimate Speech" is not the last speech, for that will take place when the newly restored speak again. Complicating a simple narrative of return, the hard task of navigating the waters of colonial settler ecological demolition—bridges and buildings, minerals and mining index the activities of the poem's "white man"—sets the hope of planetary restoration in the poison taken up as the unwilled ethical instantiation of responsibility. Here are Echo's bones, resounding in the compass of Indigenous life loss and violation of what only water owns; here responsibility repeats with ethical purpose but not in the mode of scripted self-knowledge. Readers unattuned to the costs of inclusion in the pathogenic repression we know as the sovereign self will censure the poem for dwelling on the dead and for daring to translate Chief Seattle's oration for Palestinian ears. "Eleven Planets" reminds us that the dead are also the figure conditioning the negotiation of the new world after colonial settler domination ceases, as it must. No paradise at the end of imperial days.

undercurrent provides us some relief from this grim reality by inhabiting the grey waters of a negotiation with discrepant futures. Naming the real material conditions of our shared substance, Wong doubles down on the Darwishian imperative to write the poetry of this condition. Conditions of impossibility are always also conditions of possibility: this is the Derridean ethic that opens Spivak's reading of Echo as lever. "Flush," one of the poems in *undercurrent*, follows the flow of water from distant source through the pipes and showerhead and once more down the drain. This presence in absence, what Jacques Derrida and Gerald Vizenor call survivance, structures the "flow" that runs through *undercurrent* and which Darwish mobilizes defensively in his memoir.

Darwish's *Memory for Forgetfulness: August, Beirut 1982* recounts, at a three-year remove, the events of August 6, 1982, not coincidentally also Hiroshima Day (1995). That summer Israel laid siege to the city for eighty-eight days, cutting off water, supplies, movement, and subjecting the population to constant bombardment, including the Israel Defense Forces' use of vacuum bombs, prohibited by the UN: "from 13 June to 12 August with two short intervals of about a week each at the end of June and in the middle of July. During that period it [Beirut] was subjected to air raids, naval bombardment, heavy artillery barrages (155 mm guns and 121 mm howitzers), and fire from tanks, mortars and rocket launchers" (Gilmour 1983, 166).

Through reflections on everyday language, the impossibility of quotidian acts, restriction on movement, the silencing of poetry, or its reduction to scream or screed, Darwish's poetic memoir "writ[es] my silence" in extreme crisis (1995, 61). With the everydayness of poetry and life thrown into the event of siege, all is suspended—on the brink and not yet achieved. The resulting testimony divides the event and its recollection to show that oblivion conditions the everyday while memory does not belong solely to the event.

An involuntary refusal of poetry *in extremis*, the turn to prose and the everyday (e.g., walking in the street, making coffee, recalling literary fragments, dreaming, listening for a silenced radio, engaging in political and literary disputes), allows the poet to reproduce the poetic imagination after catastrophe disarticulates symbolic language to embargo verse. The state of siege, clearly demarcated as extremity in *Memory*, is also the state of suspended identity within which Darwish as a Palestinian has always worked, and thus a heightened condition of the ordinary. While his poetry decants the extension of siege into the elemental phrase "huna la hunaka / hunaka la huna / here is not there, there is not here" (1995, passim), Darwish's poetic practice both before and after August 6, 1982, finds its collective purpose and voice not in the personal but in the question of the subject as present absence, a figure that locates its lyric potentiality suspended by Zionist dispossession of people and place.

The memoir invites its reader into the perplexing incertitude of a text that offers neither the political realism of historical recollection nor the poetry of resistance and nationalist loss. The state of siege suspends the poet's practice and forces him to "writ[e] my silence" (1995, 61), a refrain that encodes a condition of symbolic precarity in war, which degrades language by exposing all to danger:

> It is for the killer to kill, the fighter to fight, and the bird to sing. As for me, I halt my quest for figurative language. I bring my search for meaning to a complete stop because the essence of war is to degrade symbols and bring human relations, space, time, and the elements back to a state of nature, making us rejoice over water gushing on the road from a broken pipe. (Darwish 1995, 9)

Reduced to a state of exposure and privation, the poet is exiled from his language by the event that bleeds over into the new routines of survival of which the temporary abandonment of figurative language is one. Siege disfigures poetic language; when he finds his tongue again, he incorporates listing as a way of writing that degradation of symbols into a new form.

The particularity of Palestinian exile as a passion and identity finds its most concise expression in one of Darwish's final poems, "Like a Hand Tattoo in the Jahili Poet's Ode":

> I said: where are you taking me?
> He said: toward the beginning, where you were born
> Right here, you and your name
> ...no one told me this place is called a country,
> and that behind the country there were borders, and behind
> the borders a place called wandering and exile

> for us. I wasn't yet in need of identity...
> but those who reached us aboard
> their combat tanks were transferring the place
> in truckloads swiftly away.
> Place is the passion. (2009b, 171, 173)

Dispossession teaches new words: identity, country, border, exile, and dispersion. It alienates the subject from his name and the place from its place while the poet must gather the traces of past presence into a language that can be held in common, though it does not yet exist in common:

> Bread sprang from the soil and water gushed from the rocks. Their rockets dug wells for us, and the language of their killing tempted us to sing, "We will not leave!" We saw our faces on foreign screens boiling with great promise and breaking through the siege with unwavering victory signs. From now on we have nothing to lose, so long as Beirut is here and *we're here in Beirut as names for a different homeland, where meanings will find their words again in the midst of this sea and on the edge of this desert. For here, where we are, is the tent for wandering meanings and words gone astray and the orphaned light, scattered and banished from the center.* (Darwish 1995, 11; emphasis added)

This passage situates two operations of the politics of dispossession and occupation that is the Palestinian fate: in the first move, we learn that the name is other and elsewhere meanings have lost their words. A shade of difference separates this displacement from a poetics of exile that might embrace difference. Here, the present absent is enforced by the law of the mighty and the exposure of the victim.

In the second moment or operation place is itself deracinated and made a tent for wandering meanings and words gone astray: "For here, where we are, is the tent...for the orphaned light" (Darwish 1995, 11). This second point—that place has been translated or scattered—occasions a third operation of the memoir and indeed of all Darwish's post-1982 poetic practice. This temporal operation of the text is legible in the chiastic reversal of the memoir's original title: *Al-Makan: Ab, Al-Zaman: Beyrut (The Place: August, The Time: Beirut).*[15] The three moments or operations taken together and which can be assembled as the present absent, the place as time and the time as place, are tethered by a network of reference and citation drawn from the Arabic poetic tradition and, crucially, through ample citation of pre-Islamic *QaSida* (ode) and classical *nashid* (lyric), as well as a globalized storehouse of poetry that includes Garcia Lorca, Seamus Heaney, Derrick Walcott, and Aimé Césaire, among others. Poetry makes sense of these displaced senses.

Darwish famously refused the insistent reading of his work and self as "poet of resistance" and saw himself as the Palestinian national poet whose obligation was to record the altered reality of his people with poetic accuracy. Committed to the task of innovating the Arabic poetic tradition and the Arabic language, which expresses the collective predicament of Palestinians dispossessed by history and all states, including the one that exile had taught us to dream, Darwish crafts a new language from the storehouse of Jahili (pre-Islamic) poets and the Adab tradition of belle-lettres to render the particularity of Arabic metre and rhyme structures into a modernist reduction that speaks in the new language of the present absent.

Darwish's innovation engages tradition through direct citation, use of classical topoi, and revision of well-known passages applied to the new material of everyday Palestinian life:

> For me, and others like me who have burned with the wounds of water, Ibn Sida has set out the names of water and its attributes. What follows is only a drop from that flood:
>
>> water, waters, waterfall, rapids, cataract, cascade, snow, ice, hail, backwater, backwash, aqueduct, canal, droplet, drop, drizzle, cloudburst, rain, shower, torrent, soaker, spate, flood, deluge, mist, dew, steam, condensation, humidity, moisture, vapor, evaporation, aquifer, aquiclude, reservoir, freshet, brook, runnel, rill, rivulet, stream, creek, river, tributary, confluence, inlet, reach, slough, swamp, marsh, fen, puddle, pond, pool, tarn, lake, lagoon, cove, current, wave, eddy, whirlpool, *undercurrent*, billow, ripple, chop, surge, swell, spray, spurt, spout, squirt, splash, gurgle, gush, run, flow, meander, drip, ooze, seep, percolate, trickle, drop, leak, soak, drench, douse, dunk, dribble, inundate, saturate, irrigate, sprinkle, slosh, wash, dunk, dive, plunge, submerge, splatter, immerse,

> freeze, thaw, damp, wet, sodden, sopping, hydrous, aquatic, aqueous, watery. (Darwish 1995, 6; my emphasis)

"Burned with the wounds of water" performs rhetorically the same figure as "present absent" but leads to a flood of alternatives for the lost object. And this quenching flood of possibilities recalls other supplies of water for, if the symbolic field is destitute of resources or risks manifesting as dispossession, the task of the poet is to reassemble the inventory of the possible and thereby expose that gesture of recollection as the everyday practice of a poetic retrieval not of the ideal but of the newly, again symbolizable existence.

"The 'Red Indian's' Penultimate Speech to the White Man" in "Eleven Planets" follows closely the named world—trees, grass, land—and the malediction of Chief Seattle's oration, which in all the versions extant, threatens to return along with the resurgent flora and fauna. In contrast, the white man addressed in the poem and the speech faces the very end of land, both as the Western continental terminus and as utterly depleted and exhausted through extraction and other indifferent economies.

By the poem's end Darwish's use of lists becomes a means to rematerialize the reality of what remains in the reality of words remaining. This poetic strategy, theorized in his writing and interviews, is not a meta or extra poetic theory; rather, it is the reflection of the material conditions of Palestinian life wherein its landed basis remains but at a ghostly remove. The colonial hope to *make* vanish fails to accomplish itself such that the life of the colonized is relegated to waiting—"king of waiting," as he says in "Eleven Planets" (2009b, 62).

Rebalancing Relation

Neither Darwish nor Wong engage in the project of liberal multiculturalism aiming to "include" the Indigenous and racialized other as yet another version of the self-owning subject seeking better living under capital. Each in their own way attests to and materializes, via imagery, sound, and rhythm, the unprecedented, incalculable gift of responsibility, rather than something we learn by rote or apply as paradigm. We "learn to learn"[16] how to teach from the historical and cultural ground of our landing in an active relationship among writers and teachers (Spivak 2012b, 347). Borrowing from Antonio Gramsci, Spivak reminds us that "'The environment reacts back...and imposes on [the writer] a continual process of self-criticism. It is the 'teacher'" that prepares the writer to realize "'that his personality is not limited to himself as a physical individual but is an active social relationship of modification of the cultural environment" (2012c; 9).

Nineteenth-century European socialist ecologists pursued a politics of social change dependent upon fellowship and mutual association that cut across classed belonging and argued that moral or ethical approaches could condition but not substitute for solidarity. Anarchist thinking (see Ross 2016), to which I refer above, responds to the ruin of nature, urban life, and the culture of responsibility that preceded that of rights. In today's climate of reconciliation as national obligation, inclusion or recognition proceeds from cultural institutions that have never made the transit across difference; they resist what Spivak (2012a) calls "aesthetic education" and cannot accede to an ethics of responsibility except as rote memory. In the liberal calculus of today, institutions cannot foster the deconstructive responsibility Spivak envisions, for it is drawn from the situation, the terrain, the text, and what surrounds it.

And so, following Kamboureli, we can see that the violence of scandal perpetually secures a structure of secondariness and repetition as rote—as story committed to memory—to undergird the transcendence of the dominant's identification with itself. So embedded is this mechanism that reflection becomes projection, and Echo "stands" accused of identity for failing to be "universal" enough for Narcissus. As amalgam of the narcissist's fascination with surface and rote learning of rights, this form of appropriation carries forward an imaginary construction of genius as autonomous and without supports. Spivak dives down on this error of our present moment to show that embedded in Echo's tale is the deeply held overvaluation of the singular genius, locked in an identificatory embrace with his own image of beauty and knowledge as self-knowledge. Echo's more studied repetitions can never, according to this fable, break open the subordination of critical reflection to the self-reflection of originary genius.

Here is where Wong's poetic practice shifts the ground of solidarity under our feet by liquifying it. In *undercurrent* the pileup of matter and a flood of listed detail that refuses all subordinating system teaches that all penetrates all. Figures of flow and saturation, seeping damp and gushing showers, these drive home the simple fact that "we" are multiply inhabited and contaminated by water, nutrients, toxins, microbes, and more. Even the form of the page is invaded by scrawled notations, footnotes and drawings, quotes and blots; no clear system organizes the detritus; sense is made from a persistent assertion of surface and flow rather than surface and depth. And the most consistent rhetorical and poetic tactic is the list.

In the poem "The Wonders of Being Several" listing meets excavation to take us one step beyond the limits of vanguardism. Telescoping into the body, everybody's body, to dwell on the microbial life within, this poem undoes metaphors of lyric subjectivity to provide another set of images, waters, and metaphors for connectivity, relation, and solidarity that may renew conditions of political coalition. Quotations from Louis Pasteur and Wes Nahanee float inside shadowed waves doodled at the bottom of the page. No one's word is more valuable than another's while the authority of the poetry itself is undermined by the literal undercurrent drawn in the footer. Within the poem, the sovereign subject is humbled by the poem's habit of multiplying interior beings and cycles of renewal in lists of viscera and biome; these invite connection while containing the engulfing force of identification. The plot line of the poem follows the human digestive tract through scenes of strip mining and devastated landscapes to argue that no particle of life or inert matter escapes the violence of colonial capital. Thus, in "The Wonders of Being Several" appropriation becomes expropriation in division and multiplication; this translates key terms like "water," "I," "border," and "gold" from possession to properties of the many. "Being several" ramifies separation but from the inside out with the inner multitude—literally our gut biome—cast as "the great decomposers," who will inevitably remetabolize the poison hatched by extractive capital. The line "unsettlers excavate like there's no tomorrow" is echoed elsewhere by "unsettled" guest (Wong 2015, 13), a term Wong deploys occasionally to underline immigrant allyship with Indigenous political resistance. This pliable term moves from the unsettled to the unsettlers, whose digging is both appropriation and extraction and who, insofar as the history of industrial capital depended upon colonial extraction from afar, may be the distant relations of those European working-class moles acknowledged by Bataille. As a poetic tactic, Wong's listing becomes a way of metabolizing the violence of extractive capital and shares with Darwish the capacity to resymbolize what has been erased and dematerialized. "The Wonders of Being Several" does this with economy:

> so much short-term gold, long-term arsenic
> short-term bitumen, long-term cancer
> short-term packaging, long-term polyethylene
> for germs to reorganize (Wong 2015, 13)

Here the undercurrent liquifies even the mine-blighted land as microbes and bacteria digest detritus both within and surrounding us. This motif is repeated throughout to underscore, by undermining, "our" belief in our own mastery: "*We are undercurrent, overburden, the rolling earth*" (2015, 47). Thinking we are sovereign masters responsible for pollution as for wealth, we repeat arrogant error and disavow our subordination to large forces of earthly metabolism where the only universality is the action of gut biome and the slow time of decomposition.

undercurrent echoes themes already pursued in "Ethical Waters: Reflections on the Healing Walk in the Tar Sands" (see Wong 2013). an essay that Wong opens by acknowledging solidarity from the four cardinal directions, including the Indigenous Amazon. The work centres ecology yet retains a focus on Indigenous rights to build from this foundation. Peace Walks and the writing that surrounds them constitute acts of solidarity that express an awareness that the author is witness to another's revolution. As witness participant in eco-preservation, Wong writes that "we walk through the desecration, we are trying to reconnect to the spirit of the land" that in her telling has been "exploited beyond human recognition" (136). The poet writes in the wake of direct actions, camps, and Peace Walks, without herself being able to take up the position of "speaking for." Instead, she witnesses a struggle, one she participates in without appropriating it for explanatory mediation or representation. It is here that a formal technique practised in poetry becomes inseparable from the political, ethical, and lived relations that allowed it to surface in the first place. Listing, then, supplies the poetic device that mediates between a long tradition of speaking for and a present commitment to a different set of relations, which we struggle to name when we use words like "ally," "coalition," and "solidarity." We have resources for thinking this through in the language of anarchist mutual aid, as I indicate above, but to rely too heavily on that leftist tradition (without the critiques of sovereign mastery produced by Bataille and Spivak) risks losing the nuance that both Darwish and Wong are at pains to communicate when they opt for the list, for example, Darwish offering a list of names for water, rather than a catalogue of possessions. The distance that Bataille and Spivak preserves by thinking and phrasing solidarity as a gap, an echo or a restrained witness to the mole's revolving is preciously developed in Darwish's imagining of Chief Joseph's penultimate rather than ultimate speech and in Wong's practice of studding her poetry with the names of the Indigenous Elders and activists she encounters. The list also enacts a form of respect for things lost and precarious, including the water that connects all these threads together.

The urgent call for "Asserting Peace," as Wong writes in her contribution to this volume, echoes through Karina Vernon's own call to "rebalance relations with Indigenous peoples" (p. 252). Vernon draws our attention to the archive of Black "anxieties" about "territorializing on lands that were not theirs by ancestral rights" (p. 241) and the obstacles to solidarity between Black Canadians and Indigenous Peoples that emerge from this anxiety, but, as she argues, achieving peace need not entail a forgetting of Black Canadian lives as is sometimes alleged. According to her analysis, conditions for political coalition can be established by recalling, relearning and incorporating histories of Black and Indigenous affiliation and living together, especially where state categories like "citizenship" were established without the mediation of a white colonial settler mandate. A buried history excavated in Vernon's ongoing work shows that Black communities escaping slavery in the United States were granted rights and citizenship under Treaty 8 sovereignty by Indigenous decision and eventually by custom. Specifically, Vernon's contribution to this volume reminds us that Treaty 8 was signed in 1899 and preceded the second wave of Black migrants by six years; in this way, Treaty 8 peoples accorded Black migrants citizen status enacted, as Vernon writes citing James (Sa'ke'j) Youngblood Henderson, through "aboriginals' permission, through the historical treaty process," or "treaty citizenship" (p. 245). By returning to this historical strata of negotiated difference and cohabitation on Indigenous lands, Vernon tunnels down into foundations that the settler state prefers to forget, and echoes Wong's prophetic assertion, "another world is not only possible, she is already here, carrying / on underneath our feet" (2015, 26).

Wong shifts away from "solidarity" by reframing it as undercurrent while Vernon calls for rebalancing relations with Indigeneity. These moves are portable beyond Canadian borders and can be followed through the relays and chains of association pursued by the authors I have gathered together in this chapter. Following this "protocol" of the tunnelling mole's errant movements, we produce neither a system nor a science of influence but perhaps a method of tracking that resists turning all relation and reality into what Spivak notices is only self-knowledge. To remember the Darwish/Maracle encounter through the figure of Echo in Wong's citational practice, this relay can serve as a reminder that affective rebalance need not become appropriation nor another foreclosure of Blackness, as Rinaldo Walcott, in this volume, fears. Learning to be Echo and to avoid the lure of Narcissus is the path to those structures of feeling and relation "deformative for capital" that I gestured toward at the outset. As I have hoped to show, water solidarity in Canadian poetry has its roots in the 1976 Vancouver meeting of Darwish and Maracle, a meeting of two Indigenous poets who forged a bond between Palestine and North American Indigenous Peoples. In 1976 UN language had not yet adopted the term "security" as the sole bulwark against neoliberal predation. Today we think nothing of using "food security" as Wong does in *undercurrent* to refer to peoples' right to eat. But, as Maracle reminds us, no one owns the water and thus the water, like food, should not be property to be secured. The transport of a term like "security" to come to mean "freedom from want," as in contemporary UN language for sustainability, has its own sad history traceable in the details of the language we use to name what we desire for our collectivity. Preserved from harm, conserved for wise use, restored to us all: ecological preservation efforts cannot be severed from an interdependence on Indigenous land sovereignty where the latter entails more than possession. This observation is borne out today by the prominence of Indigenous activists in the 2019 Climate Summit. If water solidarity and protection has been a project of Canadian poetry for half a century, it is because this connection between the fight for land rights and ecological restoration has been made obvious and clear through Indigenous struggle and through actions of solidarity between Indigenous poets in North American and Indigenous poets globally, including Palestinians. Without the specificity of Indigenous action—and, in other sites, refugee action—the difference or gap of solidarity cannot emerge; it is only because "reconciliation with the people of the land is... reconciliation with the land itself" (Behn 2016), that the rest of us, enmired in capital, have a chance of solidarity. Poetry attests to the struggle without appropriating it and so conserves the struggle itself to be transmitted well beyond the confines of identity.

Living on Unceded Indigenous Territories

Vancouver as a Site of Conflict in Building Alliance and Autonomy in Decolonial Struggles[1]

/ SOPHIE McCALL

The city of Vancouver, straddling multiple arteries of the Fraser River delta, and traversed by a network of bridges, tunnels, highways, railways, pipelines, and tanker routes, is a central subject in the work of Marie Clements, a Métis Dene playwright, filmmaker, and producer, and Wayde Compton, a Black Canadian poet, short-story writer, essayist, and turntablist. Both of these writers have reflected deeply upon the question of how to live and work on the unceded, ancestral, and traditional territories of the xʷməθkʷəy̓əm (Musqueam), Skwxwú7mesh (Squamish), and Səl̓ílwəta (Tsleil-Waututh) Nations, and how to build meaningful alliances with antiracist coalitions in the city. While they both powerfully assert the presence of Black and Indigenous people in the city, they also explore the possibilities of urban land stewardship in mixed cultural contexts against the forces of gentrification.

Recent discussions have drawn attention to both the fault lines and the points of connection between Indigenous decolonization and Black social justice movements. Efforts have been made to reveal how the making of the Americas and the establishment of a settler-colonial social order have depended upon both the expropriation of land on the one hand, and the appropriation of labour, bodies, and lives on the other. In this volume, Karina Vernon discusses "the possibilities that exist, as well as the barriers that prevent, Black Canada from intertwining its struggle with that of Indigenous nations as part of a larger decolonizing program" (p. 241).[2] While conversations about place, belonging, and embodiment have unfolded very differently in Black and Indigenous studies to date, the cultural production in question, like that of Clements and Compton, continues to attest to these intersecting histories. Yet the challenge to build viable critical frameworks that compare histories of occupation and resistance remains an urgently needed and relatively underthematized thread in critical discussions. Moreover, the stakes of these comparative endeavours often remain unarticulated: why and how do comparative frameworks matter? For whom do they matter? Under what sets of debates and in what arenas? Struggles over land, Indigenous rights, and sovereignty remain a key part of this dialogue. Land is central to the discussion. But if the goal is decolonizing social relations, there needs to be an understanding of the complexities of land, as well as a reckoning with what other goals look like for various communities.

In this chapter, I want to think about "the sometimes conflicted relationship between *alliance* and *autonomy*"[3] in debates around decolonization, antiracist coalition-building, and social justice movements through the multigenre works of Marie Clements and Wayde Compton. Clements, in the four versions of the musical documentary, *The Road Forward*, the first three as live productions (2010, 2013, 2015) and the last as a film (2017b), has documented the civil rights work of the Native Brotherhood in British Columbia while fiercely contesting public discourses that render invisible the precarious lives of Indigenous women in the city. While prioritizing Indigenous perspectives on sovereignty, Clements deliberately builds relationships across cultural differences in mixed, urban contexts in order to draw attention to shared histories of resistance. The hallmarks of

Clements's work are its extraordinary poetics of movement, its unwavering assertion of Indigenous presence in the city, and its engagement with the city as a gendered space.

Compton's work usually is discussed within a framework of Black studies, emphasizing Black presence in British Columbia. He has pursued intensive archival projects to unearth denied and forgotten Black histories of Vancouver, and, through his close involvement with the Hogan's Alley Memorial Project (HAMP), has sought to tether those histories to a neighbourhood that has been erased as a physical presence. What is less talked about in critical discussions of his work is how he wrestles with the ethics of portraying the city on unceded Indigenous territories. More than his other texts, his short-story collection *The Outer Harbour* (2015a) recentres Black histories in the context of acknowledging how uninvited guests are implicated in the ongoing occupation of Indigenous lands. At the same time, Compton underlines how Black lives are themselves subjected to occupation, containment, displacement, and forgetting. In finding common ground between Black and Indigenous lives, Compton searches for ways to mobilize communities to act upon a sense of solidarity across cultures, histories, and places.

A striking point of connection between these two Vancouver-based writers is how they combine documentary and speculative genres, self-consciously drawing attention to the limits and possibilities of each in social justice projects, while drawing attention to the reader's own positionality in determining the line between fact and fiction. Mobilizing by turns the modes of documentary, pseudo-documentary, and fantasy, these artists expose the narrative and conceptual frames of their works. By shifting, altering, and even shattering those frames, Clements and Compton draw attention to their own roles, and trace the impact of the shifts across genre, discipline, and media on their audiences.

In reading works of Indigenous and Black Canadian literary and film production I am necessarily mobilizing comparative approaches. I am indebted to many scholars who have crafted, and remain vigilant about the pitfalls in crafting, comparative or intersectional methods in Indigenous, Black, and diasporic literary studies.[4] In spite of the evident importance of inclusivity, to be included within dominant institutional structures can be a stifling embrace. Chickasaw scholar Chadwick Allen asserts that the academy is "ground zero" in "attacks on all forms of Indigenous intellectual autonomy" (2014, 377), further arguing that comparative frameworks are particularly implicated in a type of forced inclusion.[5] Similarly, approaches to Canadian "multicultural literature" have long functioned to appropriate and subsume differences, and to disavow a diversity of currents within particular fields of study, like Indigenous studies or Black studies. Phanuel Antwi and David Chariandy have argued that Black Canadian writers "confront[] a white and multicultural elite occasionally prepared to entertain token gestures of 'diversity' but unwilling to attend critically to the cultural and political specificity of blackness" (2017, 34). Likewise, Rinaldo Walcott in this volume rejects "multicultural recognition politics" (p. 108) and the "language of inclusion" (p. 107), arguing that these policies and rhetorics, both in the Canadian context and beyond, function more often as strategies of containment for Black people.

Scholars of Indigenous literary studies, like Glen Coulthard, Leanne Betasamosake Simpson, and other theorists of Indigenous resurgence, also reject the colonial politics of recognition (to evoke the subtitle of Coulthard's book, *Red Skin, White Masks*) associated with both multiculturalism and liberal approaches to Indigenous politics. Instead, Simpson argues for a refocusing of energies to "a flourishment of the *Indigenous* inside" (2011, 17). Both Coulthard and Simpson have modelled readings of Indigenous cultural production from within specific cultural contexts—be they nation-centred, urban, or pan-tribal—and beyond colonial thought and practice. As Simpson writes, "To do so, we need to engage in *Indigenous* processes," and "we need to do this on our own terms, without the sanction, permission or engagement of the state, western theory or the opinions of Canadians" (2011, 17). *Resurgence, autonomy, sovereignty,* and *self-determination* continue to be keywords in Indigenous studies, and they are strongly centred on Indigenous-led projects that reflect deeply on cultural and political specificities. That said, a notable feature of these theories is a consistent attention to relationality and kinship ties. Focusing on relationality is a very different conceptual starting point than focusing on inclusion. When Simpson asked Elder Gidigaa Migizi (Doug Williams) about what words or concepts in Anishinaabemowin best capture the idea of "nation," "sovereignty," or "self-determination," he stated, "the place where we all live and work together" (Simpson 2015, 18). This description highlights the importance of place, while at its core, the statement is "about relationships—relationships with each other and with plant and animal nations, with our lands and waters and with the spiritual world" (18). Simpson is talking about Anishinaabe-centred relationships primarily. But how might such a focus on place and relationships help build relations of affiliation between and among different communities, while upholding Indigenous sovereignty? The history of this place has been constituted by the original Nations building diplomatic relations with one another to share land, food, and resources while respecting one another's autonomy; yet critical frameworks have lagged behind in articulating this sense of affiliation and confederacy.[6] The challenge is to build comparative methods that grapple with intersectional histories of resistance, and that capture the complexities of the urban, unceded, ancestral Coast Salish territories like those in Vancouver.

White settler critics like me sometimes imagine ourselves in a place of objectivity in facilitating comparisons between works that are labelled "multicultural," "postcolonial," "diasporic," or "Indigenous." The artists I discuss in this chapter both defy *and* hold up a mirror to my own assumptions. They ask me to engage in a process of (un)learning settler narratives and complacent assumptions about the place where I live. They articulate the difficult questions of how to act responsibly in relation to others in profoundly racialized and colonial contexts while contending with the mixed, urban spaces of Vancouver. They challenge me to examine my own positionality as a Scottish-descended settler whose white skin confers upon me unearned privileges in settler-colonial society. Whiteness is often constructed as the unmarked, dominant norm that plays the "god trick" (Haraway 1988, 581) of seeing without being seen, while retaining the unmerited licence to label and racialize "others." As a mother of mixed-race kids, I am aware of what Compton has called the "pheneticizing" gaze that shapes my kids' experiences in the streets of Vancouver in ways that I do not experience. As I endeavour to trace a conversation between the work of artists whose cultural politics, debates, and communities are marked by significant differences, I am mindful of my responsibility to acknowledge the horizons of my knowledge, to heed Kwakwaka'wakw scholar Sarah Hunt's call to "foster[] a commitment to mobilize ourselves" (2018, 2), and to remain aware of the interpretive codes I use while reading texts and the worlds I encounter.

Marie Clements: Dreamscapes Grounded in Place, Land, History

In creating *The Road Forward*, Clements said she wanted to "reimagin[e] BC's history" and "to do something that was very specific to where I was, and where I grew up" (qtd. in Dickinson 2015, 37). The opening scene of the film version of *The Road Forward* depicts Clements walking into the offices of the Native Brotherhood of British Columbia (NBBC), located in North Vancouver, where she grew up. The NBBC, formed in 1931 when it was illegal for Indigenous Nations to initiate legal disputes relating to land,[7] holds the archives for the newspaper, the *Native Voice*. The scene's emphasis is on a layering of reflective surfaces: Clements walks into a glass sound booth and looks at a printed page, whose lettering reflects backwards onto the glass window. She sits down at a desk and begins reading the headlines from the first issue of the newspaper, published in 1946: "As president of the Native Brotherhood of BC I most urgently appeal to all Native people to give their full support to the NATIVE VOICE. We have established ourselves and will go forward. Through our NATIVE VOICE we will continue to the best of our ability to bind closer together the many tribes whom we represent into that solid NATIVE VOICE. ALL POWER TO THE NATIVE VOICE." This opening scene shows Clements positioning herself and reflecting upon her own role in formulating this story. The glass around her is simultaneously a window, through which Clements looks to gain insight into the past, and a mirror, reflecting back her own image. This is a key aspect of her ethics in which she interweaves embodied, positioned knowledge with an attention to the land upon which she is standing (see Figure 1).

At the heart of *The Road Forward*, in Clements's words, is "a fusion of ink and voice," a play on the newspaper's title. In the 1940s (and onwards into the 1960s and 1970s), the *Voice* was one of the few venues where Indigenous writers could publish their writings and organize politically. Interviewees in the film talk about how the newspaper enabled communication among coastal Indigenous communities. Edwin Newman (Heiltsuk), president of the Native Brotherhood for eleven years, notes that because Native people were prohibited from gathering as a group before the 1960s, they had to create the pretense of meeting as "Christian Soldiers." The *Voice*, like other Native publications of the time such as the *National Indian*, *Indian Record*, and *Nesika*, became a virtual meeting place that transmitted a wide diversity

Figure 1. Opening shot of *The Road Forward*, showing Clements's reflection. Marie Clements, *The Road Forward*, 2017 ©National Film Board of Canada. Reproduced with permission.

of information, including announcements of community events, political gatherings, marriages, birthdays, recipes, stories, and poems (Armstrong 2001, xvii). Similarly, *The Road Forward*, with its four versions—from ten-minute multimedia installation at the Aboriginal Pavilion during the Vancouver 2010 Cultural Olympiad, to full-length theatrical concerts in 2013 and 2015, to documentary film rock musical in 2017—moves across generic categories, connecting a wide variety of social and artistic issues, and bringing together new combinations of people, places, and media.

As deeply grounded as Clements's work is, it refuses to stay still. In all of her work, the action begins in a particular place and time, and then spirals out, creating an intricate network of connections across diverse histories, cultures, languages, and places. Intertribal and interracial relations provide the backbone of *The Road Forward*. Working with lead Tuscorora composer and musical director Jennifer Kreisberg, Clements used the headlines from the *Native Voice* as the basis for writing a series of nineteen songs, and then collaborated with fourteen Indigenous and Black musicians from different Nations and musical traditions, including blues, rock, and hip hop, and traditional singing and drumming, to generate the songs. *The Road Forward* emphasizes the role that the NBBC played in building a civil rights movement in British Columbia that connects stories of resistance across cultures and histories. In an interview, Clements states, "It's pretty hard not to be ignited by George Manuel and to try to grasp what he actually did, and his vision, and what he was saying over thirty years ago....When I first saw the speech it was like seeing Martin Luther King" (Mack 2017, para. 3). In naming this time period as part of a "long tradition of civil rights" in British Columbia, and invoking the figure of Martin Luther King Jr., Clements is connecting stories of resistance across the Americas, particularly between Indigenous and Black histories of struggle.

The Road Forward is about the struggle to *include* Indigenous rights in constitutional rights, but also a critique of the *forced inclusion* within dominant institutional and governmental structures. The film remembers and honours activists such as Secwepemc George Manuel, who pressed for the recognition of Indigenous rights in the 1970s and 1980s. Manuel, renowned author of *The Fourth World*, first published in 1974, played a leading role in the national organizing against Pierre Trudeau's efforts to terminate Indigenous rights, participated in the creation of the UN Declaration on the Rights of Indigenous Peoples, and was one of the central organizers of the Constitution Express in 1980, which was instrumental in ensuring that Aboriginal rights were "recognized and affirmed" in the amended Constitution in 1982 (Couture 2015, 48). At the same time, Manuel was highly critical of the forced inclusion that sometimes accompanies a politics of recognition, as Yellowknives Dene political theorist Glen Coulthard has definitively shown. One of the most powerful scenes in *The Road Forward* is of hip-hop artist, Ronnie Dean Harris (a.k.a. Ostwelve) performing the song, "If You Really Believe," whose lyrics borrow from one of Manuel's speeches calling for direct action: "If you really believe we are the First People....that we have our own Nations....Our own Indian Law.... that we have been here forever. If you really believe. You don't ask for it. You take it. My message to you is, you don't ask for it. You take it." Defying, in Coulthard's phrase, a "colonial politics of recognition," phrase, Manuel's words and Ostwelve's performance forcefully assert Indigenous rights in a resurgent politics of self-determination.

Clements also draws the audience's attention to less well-known women activists. While researching the Native Brotherhood, Clements discovered the formative impact that the Native Sisterhood played throughout this history. According to one headline from the *Voice*, the Haida Native Sisterhood was founded in February 1933. Kwakwaka'wakw Elder and former president of Native Sisterhood, Vera Newman, remembers that her own grandmother was a part of the Sisterhood in the 1940s. Women activists were deeply involved in writing, editing, and publishing the *Native Voice*. Welsh journalist and outspoken advocate of Indigenous issues, Maisie Hurley, played a key role in launching the newspaper and, as publisher and director, kept it going for many years. Kitty Carpenter (Heiltsuk), former president of the Native Sisterhood, contributed columns about the group's ongoing projects. Jimalee Burton, a Cherokee poet and graphic artist, was the editor for fifteen years (red diva n.d., para. 5).

Yet by layering footage from the Constitutional Express with images of murdered and missing women and the Highway of Tears in the 2015 theatrical production of *The Road Forward*, Clements intervenes in debates over the struggle for Indigenous rights by highlighting the high cost paid by Indigenous women who were "disappeared" in raced and sexualized encounters of violence (Dean 2015, 25–26). Juxtaposing iconic images from Constitutional Express with the absent-presence of the women's photographs, many of which come from the Vancouver Police posters, Clements confronts the viewer with the misrecognition of missing women. Sarah Hunt argues that the phrase "'the missing women' masks the brutal reality of how they become 'missing'" (qtd. in Dean 2015, xix). Hunt critiques the euphemistic turn of phrase, which conceals violence and ascribes accountability to the women themselves for their own disappearance. Gender studies scholar Amber Dean builds on this critique by deconstructing the disturbing assumptions that animate the police posters. *The Road Forward* challenges both the imagery and language of "missing women," particularly through the vibrancy of song. The song "My Girl" recounts a mother driving on the Highway of Tears looking for her young daughter. She ends up stopping and walking into the woods. In Clements's words: "In this moment her daughter is able to hear her mother from the spirit world. They are brought together through the music" (2017a). This much-missed daughter is no longer a "missing woman" but, crucially, part of a larger, collective voice.

Clements's description of *The Road Forward* as "a fusion of ink and voice" refers not only to the newspaper's title, the *Native Voice*, but also to the dialectic she creates between the projected newspaper pages and the songs as expressions of felt, embodied expressions of sovereignty. Further, the act of singing implicates the audience: "*The Road Forward* was and is an opportunity to create something that can sing inside an audience—the possibility to place this little known history inside our collective voice...not just so we get to know it, but so that we get to understand it is a part of ourselves" (Clements, qtd. in Couture 2015, 45). In the film version of *The Road Forward*, the searching mother and missing daughter harmonize together but are separated into two sound booths with glass walls reinforced with steel wiring. In a similar manner to the opening scene of the film, the emphasis is on both reflections and transparency. The glass becomes both an inaccessible perimeter and a fluid point of transmission between life and death, between knowing and not knowing, between unanswered questions and inadequate answers. The mother and daughter almost, but not quite, overcome this demarcation in order to access what appears to be a portal through which they might touch and hold each other again.

I agree with Selena Couture that the "focus on the women's voices... underscores the intention of honouring women activists and community members," including the Native Sisterhood, and "memorializing missing and murdered Indigenous women" (2015, 47). Yet *The Road Forward* does not permit us as audience members to rest comfortably with "honouring" and "memorializing" Indigenous women without reckoning with our own implication in this history as "a part of ourselves." Dean argues that the social injustice of disappeared Indigenous women demands, on the one hand, a recognition of the proximity of these tragedies to our own lives, and, on the other, a repudiation of that universalizing imperative (2015, xxvii). To put it another way, in a settler-colonial regime whose wealth is built upon the displacement and impoverishment of Indigenous peoples, as well as the simultaneous appropriation and erasure of racialized bodies and labour, the security of privileged citizens is obtained by rendering others precarious. As Stó:lō scholar Dylan Robinson argues, there is an urgent need for settlers to reflect upon our implication in what he calls the "intergenerational responsibility" of inheriting privileges in a settler-colonial society. Robinson expects from settler individuals, as well as settler society as a whole, a much greater degree of accountability as beneficiaries and perpetrators of settler colonial dispossession than has been shown to date (2016, 47). Part of this responsibility is accomplished through a concerted effort on the part of settlers to resist the tendency to disavow responsibility in the production and maintenance of material conditions of inequality in settler colonial society.

Electronic Mediations

The critique of settler colonial society from a gendered perspective drives another play by Clements, *The Unnatural and Accidental Women*. The starting point of the play was Clements's anger in finding in the newspaper, the *Province*, a two-page spread article on serial killer Gilbert Paul Jordan, while the women that he killed were described simply as "middle aged Native women" whose deaths were deemed by the coroner to be "unnatural and accidental." For a mainstream BC newspaper like the *Province*, convicting Jordan of murder is a triumphant story of justice; for Clements, the story itself marginalizes the women's lives and experiences. In contrast to the media coverage at the time, Clements does not focus on the killer; rather, she animates the emotional lives of the women. As Creek Métis Michelle LaFlamme points out, Clements does not represent the murder of the women on stage; rather, she shows slide projections of the coroner's reports. Only one murder is shown on stage, and that is the murder of the killer (2010b, 113).

As a way of interrogating and defamiliarizing the media's overemphasis on the killer, Clements highlights the indecipherable static in electronic media communications. Clements is one of the most innovative theatre artists working in Canada, highlighting the language of performance, theatre, and film in her multimedia productions, which often include music, video, projections, new media, radio, photography, and television. In the play, Rose is a switchboard operator who is supposed to facilitate communication between individuals, but more often intercepts messages from the murdered women in a surreal zone of the afterlife. Erin Wunker notes that, though as operator she is meant to connect people, Rose often misunderstands what people are saying (2010, 174). The play becomes a series of imperfectly overheard conversations mediated through multiple channels whose crossed signals have created a background of distortions and static. This background of "white noise" points to the role of media in silencing the stories of Indigenous women in Vancouver. The audience is not permitted to forget that all is electronically mediated, since the sounds of feedback, static, and tuning intrude throughout.

Imperfectly overheard conversations are also a theme in the play, *Burning Vision* (Clements 2002). Characters who are located thousands of miles away from one another in various locations in the Northwest Territories, the United States, and Japan hear fragments of one another's conversations across the permeable distances of time and space. More than any other work by Clements, *Burning Vision* is an extraordinary exploration of interconnectedness across histories, cultures, languages, and places. The play is a powerful engagement with the violence and premise of relation, foregrounding relations between Asian, Asian diasporic, and Indigenous peoples—although the relations between Asian diasporas and indigeneity are just one set of cultural and historical interconnections that animate the four movements in Clements's play.[8] The play traces several intertwined historical trajectories, especially those violently brought together through the mining, displacement, and explosion of uranium originating from Sahtu Dene territory near Port Radium, Northwest Territories. Through a series of repeated images that move in a circular pattern around the stage, as well as through a recurring soundscape made up of clicks, coughs, footsteps, heartbeats, radio static, radar frequencies, drums, and explosions, the play confronts its audience with a "burning vision" of intergenerational correspondence that demands both a response and an acceptance of historical responsibility.

The theatrical elements in *Burning Vision* play an important role in how Clements draws connections between disparate histories. For example, for the premiere performance in Vancouver, BC, in 2002, the stage was divided into four quadrants like a clock, tracing the journey of uranium through four locations, in four nations, and through the four elements: from the lands belonging to the Sahtu Dene Nation; to the fires in the refineries in Port Hope, Ontario; across the waters in ships to Los Alamos, New Mexico; and finally into the air above Hiroshima and Nagasaki in 1945. Each leg of this traverse implicates the people who live there and connects them to one another, whether they are aware of this connection or not.

One of the correlations that the play draws is the spiking rates of cancer in regions traversed by the uranium. Clements's own family history is deeply connected to the history of uranium. Not only do her Métis and Dene relatives come from the region around Port Radium, but also many of her family members worked in the mines and on the transport boats. In Clements's words: "Everything is innocent on the table but when you put it together, it can cause a lethal reaction." She adds, "when you look at uranium, you look at world events. Uranium had always been in the centre of the Dene world...when it was exposed, it created a domino effect" (Clements

2009). The domino effect is the cumulative effects of radioactive waste and its high levels of interactivity with living beings.

By writing characters and storylines as overlapping and even mutating into one another, Clements draws attention to intertwined historical relations and how individuals are positioned within these histories. The importance of shared responsibility is reinforced powerfully when the Dene See-er, played by the late Dene Elder George Blondin in the 2002 Vancouver production, announces that "The people they dropped this burning on, [they] looked like us, the Dene" (Clements 2002, 119). The play uses this moment of (mis)recognition to raise provocative questions about how we are implicated within and responsible for each other's histories. While the play emphasizes the danger of powerful detonations by staging the atomic blast no less than five times, it also suggests the potential transformation that becomes possible in explosive mixings of cultures, languages, nations, and communities. This doubled sense of correlation—as the fear of deadly contamination and as the hope for a renewed sense of collectivity based on the community's understanding of their cultural and philosophical inheritance—remains an insoluble tension in the play.

The dangers and transformative potential of cultural mixing is an enduring tension in Clements's work. While concerned with building relationality and connections across differences, she writes against historical dislocation and the silencing of Indigenous voices. She immerses her audience in a series of layered performances that are grounded in place, land, and history, while at the same time exploring the fluidity of dreamscapes to move surrealistically through time and space. She works collaboratively across media and professions, highlighting the mediating role of communication technologies, with the ultimate purpose of building a sovereign Indigenous practice of theatrical and film production. In virtually all of her projects, Clements acts not only as writer, but also as director, producer, and founder of Indigenous production houses, thereby maintaining control over content, process, and working team. She has worked extensively as a teacher and mentor, particularly in her capacity as co-director of Frog Girl Films, co-artistic director of red diva projects, and former founding artistic director and producer of urban ink productions (2001–07). As such, in LaFlamme's words, Clements has "played a foundational role in the development of Aboriginal theatre in Canada" (2010a, xxviii). Her ceaseless exploration of new methods, her intergenerational engagement, and her commitment to creative autonomy has helped to build a sovereign Indigenous theatrical practice.

Vancouver is a key touchstone in Clements's work, to which she returns again and again as she grapples with legacies of denial in intersectional histories. Likewise, in Wayde Compton's work, the city of Vancouver becomes a site of both conflict and coalition-building across communities, a flashpoint in struggles over access, space, and recognition of erased histories. As in Clements's work, Compton too employs music, soundscapes, and the static of electronic communications as ways of drawing attention to the role of language in shaping notions of identity, history, and place. Both writers move restlessly between genres and disciplines, incorporating soundscapes, graphic elements, and multimedia, pushing the limits of documentary into the realm of the speculative in order to illuminate the audience's own role in creating visions of reality. Both foreground the struggle for Indigenous sovereignty over land and water, while contending with the mixed cultural, geographical, and social transformations of the cityscape. Yet there are also significant discontinuities between how Clements treats the (literally) explosive history in *Burning Vision* and what Compton imagines in his collection of stories, *The Outer Harbour*, premised as it is upon the volcanic emergence of new land and with it new possibilities of building relationships across differences. Clements emphasizes the sheer power of Indigenous presence through song, voice, and words. Compton, on the other hand, finds a certain agency in the elusiveness of an indefinable Black presence through his layered, multigenre creations. These represent significant differences not only between their respective projects of articulating Indigenous and Black presence, but also reflecting broader disarticulations between Indigenous and Black critical paradigms—tensions that scholars need to articulate with a rigorous awareness of their own positioned and partial perspectives, along with their reliance on particular codes of intelligibility in reading and interpreting texts.

Wayde Compton's Retro-spec(ula)tions

Scholars such as Peter Hudson, Bertrand Bickersteth, and Joanne Leow have situated Compton's work in the context of Black studies, emphasizing the long history of Black presence in British Columbia, the neglected archive of Black writing, and the ongoing forces of erasure, colonial violence, and permanent displacement. In a similar manner to Clements's assertion of Indigenous presence, Compton grounds his writing and activism in a passionate declaration of Black presence in the city of Vancouver.[9] In particular, he has focused his efforts on documenting the historic Black neighbourhood of Hogan's Alley, which was evacuated and dismantled in order to make way for the Georgia Street viaduct in 1970. Both Compton and Clements take a close, critical look at the prejudices and excisions from mainstream media reports, and have sought out alternative media to give a fairer picture of Black and Indigenous histories. In both Compton's and Clements's work, the action is grounded in a specific place and time, but quickly radiates out as both writers refuse to remain bounded by time, space, or notions of realism. Another key connection to Clements's writing is Compton's self-conscious investigation into his own desire to find verifiable proof of a long and rich Black history of the city; when asked what he expected to find in what was Hogan's Alley, Compton realized the only way to answer that question "would be to create images of my own latent romantic pseudo black-nationalist desires" (2005, 114). Compton often juxtaposes documentary with speculative forms, bending one into the other in order to comment mindfully upon his own desires for a more complete record of the Black community.

In his long poem "Rune" in *Performance Bond*, Compton's challenge to White settler narratives of the city involves not only documenting but also rewriting and outright fabricating media reports of the past. In the absence of finding a seven-decade archive of community-specific newspaper articles like those in the *Native Voice*, as Clements did, Compton must reinvent and retro-speculate Black voices and representations into existence. The form and method of "retro-speculative verse" could be described as a paradoxical return to what was never there, combined with speculations about possible futures that may never come to be (2005, 109).[10] In "Seven Routes to Hogan's Alley," Compton curates over a century of mainstream newspaper headlines from the *Province* and *Vancouver Sun*, exposing how these newspapers prefigure the community's uprooting with headlines such as "Local Slums a Disgrace" (1940) or "Hogan's Alley No More" (1963) (Compton 2010, 135, 137). At the same time, in "Rune," Compton also retro-speculatively imagines alternative media outlets like "*The Far Cry Weekly: Voice of the Negro*

Northwest (since 1957)" (2004b, 127). In confabulating a newspaper like *The Far Cry*, Compton both identifies and redresses the barriers that the Black community faced when looking for publishing venues.

Compton wrestles with the paradox that commemorating a neighbourhood community that is no longer there threatens to fortify an existing discourse of disappearance in White settler narratives of the city. Compton's "Rune" is filled with spectres that blink in and out of view as manifestations of this paradox. In the poem "Ghetto Fabulous Ozymandias," the narrator only sees "Rev. Oz.," also known as "Reverend Oz, Revenant Oz, Revolutionary Oz, Revisitor Oz, Revisionist Oz, The Reinvented Oz, Revanchist Oz and Oz Reversed" (2004b, 155), through the viewfinder of his camera: "When he lowered the camera, the man was gone. / When he looked through the viewfinder again, the man was there" (153). By holding "the camera up to his face" he can "keep the individual from evanescing" (153). "Evanescing," defined in the OED as "pass[ing] out of sight, memory, or existence," is an important word in Compton's writing, capturing both the pain of erasure and the exhilaration of evading definition or detention. The narrator senses an ethical imperative to hold up the camera to provide this representational frame. However, Rev. Oz. is legible only through the narrator's tunnel vision produced by the camera's viewfinder. It could be argued that Rev. Oz. is a concoction of the narrator's desiring gaze. Yet it is equally arguable that his mysterious disappearances and appearances—his powers to vanish and rematerialize—evade the narrator's attempts to impose limiting definitions or frameworks upon him. The paradox of "evanescing" as a site of both freedom and obliteration is a recurring theme in Compton's work.

Through the narrator, Compton critically reflects upon his own in role in generating commemorative initiatives for Hogan's Alley. Since 2002, Compton has been committed to anchoring the many stories of the community to the site through his activist work with HAMP. In 2017, the City of Vancouver voted to remove the Georgia Street viaduct. The Hogan's Alley Working Group is advocating for the building of a Black cultural centre and a transfer of the city-owned lands to a community land trust, which will enable members of the collective to act as stewards of the land. Ultimately, HAMP is determined to re-story the city's landscape and ground Black history in the land.

What If…?

Several of the stories in the linked short-story collection, *The Outer Harbour*, hinge upon the retro-speculative question: What if a volcanic explosion under the Burrard Inlet gave birth to a new island?[11] Like the continuously replaying nuclear explosions in Clements's *Burning Vision*, the volcano in Compton's short story forces a volatile fusion of unlike things, histories, peoples, and places. On the one hand, the catastrophe prompts the imposition of an authoritarian regime of social control; on the other, a detonation of this force potentially revolutionizes existing narratives about the place and sweeps away rigid, exclusionary discourses of un-belonging. *The Outer Harbour* is distinctive among Compton's texts in how it engages with Black histories in relation to Indigenous histories in Vancouver. While emphasizing how Black subjects often must contend with a sense of homelessness and statelessness, his goal is to find ways for his mixed-race characters of multiple and often unknown origins to find one another and affirm their common experiences. His ultimate aim is to craft relations of affiliation and solidarity between his Black and Indigenous characters so that they might find ways to build new communities grounded in a sense of belonging in the land.

The story "The Lost Island," which magnificently imagines an entirely new island being pushed up through the waters of the Burrard Inlet, is rich with intertextual references and ironic doublings. The story intersects with the land's natural history in the sense that, as Musqueam Elder Larry Grant in Elle-Máijá Tailfeathers's film, *c̓əsnaʔəm: The City before the City* (2017), points out, the city of Richmond, which was once a series of twenty-six islands, has engulfed twelve other "lost islands." In other words, through a process of dredging the waterways, filling in wetlands, and building transportation routes, the city of Richmond is now made up of fourteen islands. In Compton's story, the city of Vancouver dubs the newly formed land mass "Pauline Johnson Island." By naming it Pauline Johnson Island, Compton is referencing Johnson's story with the same title in her collection, *Legends of Vancouver* from 1911. Emily Pauline Johnson, also known as Tekahionwake, is a Mohawk writer who was born on the Six Nations Reserve near Brantford, Ontario, and moved to Vancouver in 1909. *Legends of Vancouver* is based on the stories told to her by Squamish storytellers Chief Joe Capilano (Sahp-luk) and Mary Agnes Capilano (Lixwelut) (Shield 2018, 111).[12] In Joe Capilano's version, the island disappeared from the north arm of the Fraser River sometime during his grandfather's lifetime. Compton's story with the same title retro-speculatively goes "back to the future" to conjure that lost island. In naming the island after Johnson (and *not* after Joe or Mary Capilano), Compton is exposing the long history in Vancouver of emptying the city of xʷməθkʷəy̓əm (Musqueam), Skwxwú7mesh (Squamish), and Səl'ílwəta (Tsleil-Waututh) peoples and symbols of their presence, and replacing this presence with Indigenous symbols from other places, such as the totem poles from nonlocal Indigenous Nations in Stanley Park.[13] Johnson herself is precisely such a symbol: for decades, she delighted audiences with her culturally hybrid poetry recitals, in which she would wear clothes inspired by her Mohawk heritage for the first half of her performance, and change into English Victorian dress for the second half. And yet she remained the best-known, even the only, Indigenous writer "from" Vancouver. Stanley Park contains a plaque that honours her, and yet remains virtually silent on how the original peoples and caretakers of the land since time immemorial were forced out of the area.

In Compton's story, as soon as the island emerges from the waters, it is immediately claimed by the authorities as "a protected zone, a national site for research" (2015a, 34) that only scientists are permitted to access. Scientists become the explorers, soldiers, police officers, and government agents of the settler-colonial regime. When five activists of Indigenous and Black heritage take a boat to the island to stage the "Liberation of the New Pan-Indigenous Territory," their purpose is to provoke the authorities and to get the media to photograph their banner, which reads: "UNCEDED NATIVE LAND" (2015a, 44). Even though the media helicopters finally arrive, they do nothing to stop the police from shooting dead one of the Indigenous activists, Fletcher. As Compton repeatedly underlines in his work, the media do not expose injustice but rather complacently accept and sensationalize violence against Indigenous and Black bodies. Fletcher joins other Indigenous and Black people like Dudley George, Trayvon Martin, Helen Betty Osbourne, Michael Brown, Coulton Boushie, and Sandra Bland, who were killed simply for "being there—standing, walking, waiting, thinking, peopling it [a place]. Being people where they shouldn't be" (2015a, 43). Being on the land that the authorities deem out of bounds—as research site, national park, site of industry, or private property—is a life-threatening risk. Being on the land even if it is *not* officially a restricted area can prompt harassment, harm, even death.

The graphic story "The Boom" is composed as a series of posters following the death of Fletcher that demonstrate how acts of commemoration selectively champion certain versions of history, while at the same time facilitating the forgetting of other versions (see figures 2, 3 and 4).

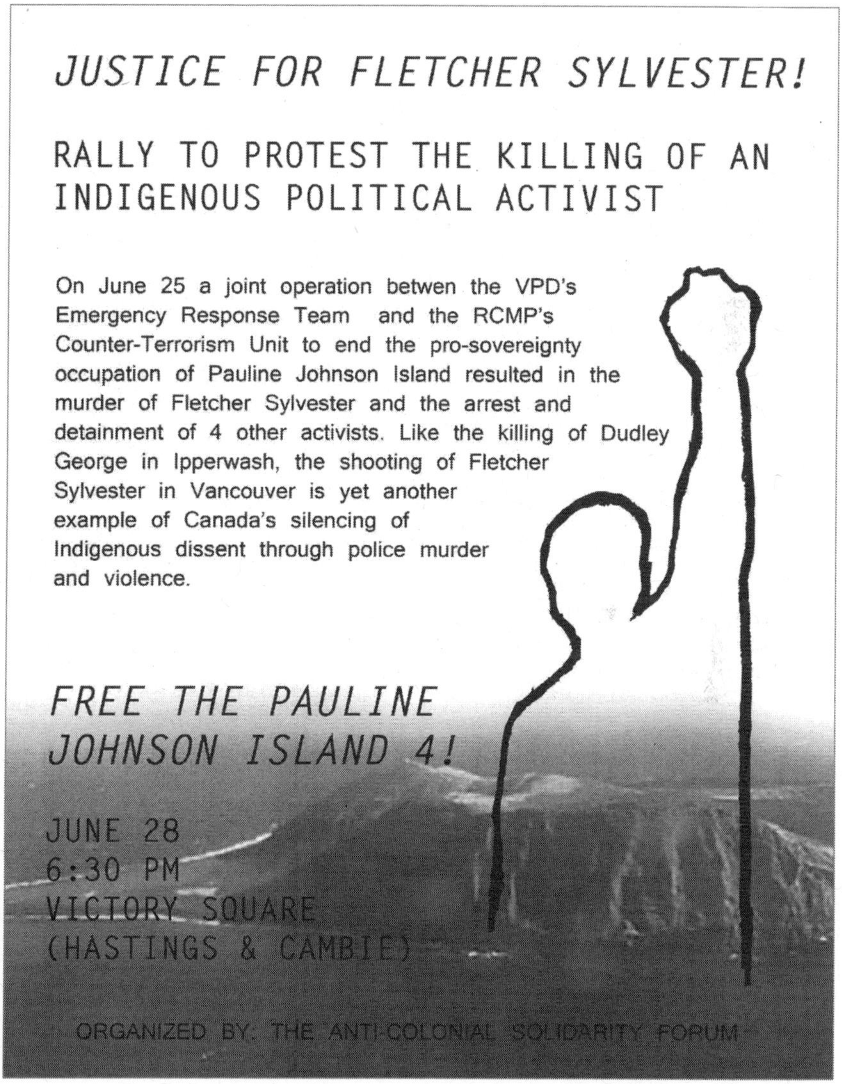

Figure 2. Wayde Compton's "The Boom," *The Outer Harbour* (Arsenal Pulp Press, 2014), p. 103. Visual art by April dela Noche Milne. Reproduced with permission.

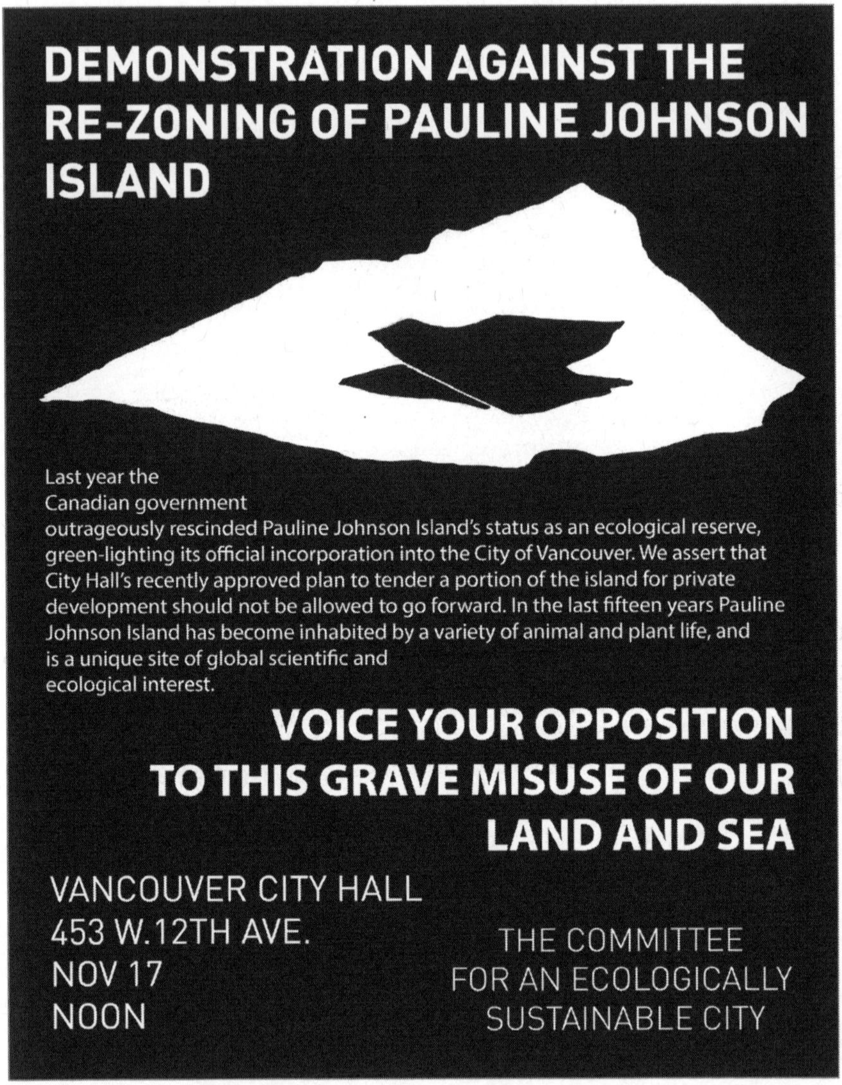

Figure 3. Wayde Compton's "The Boom," *The Outer Harbour* (Arsenal Pulp Press, 2014), p. 107. Visual art by April dela Noche Milne. Reproduced with permission.

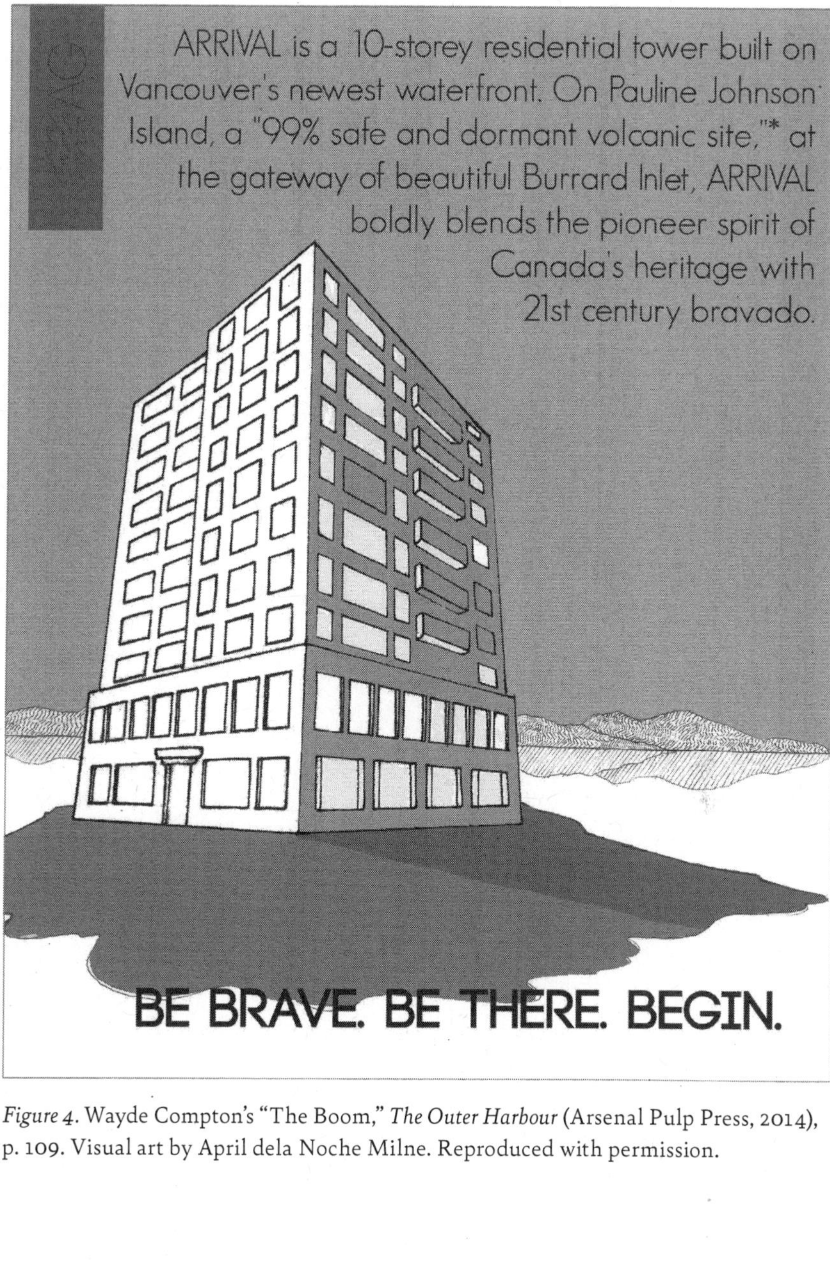

Figure 4. Wayde Compton's "The Boom," *The Outer Harbour* (Arsenal Pulp Press, 2014), p. 109. Visual art by April dela Noche Milne. Reproduced with permission.

The posters, created over a period of about thirty years, are an archive of how Pauline Johnson Island has been used to create and bolster shifting narratives of belonging and un-belonging. While the first poster, "JUSTICE FOR FLETCHER SYLVESTER!," is a call to action "to protest the killing of an Indigenous political activist" (103), the next poster, "THE PAULINE JOHNSON ISLAND OCCUPATION: FIVE YEARS LATER: A RETROSPECTIVE EVENT," makes no mention of the "pro-sovereignty" agenda of the activists. The tone of this commemorative event is reverent and nostalgic. Although the event promises to provide "information on new directions for Indigenous struggle in this area," the events of five years ago are relegated to the past. The third poster, "DEMONSTRATION AGAINST THE RE-ZONING OF PAULINE JOHNSON ISLAND," focuses exclusively on the latest "crisis": the federal government's rescinding of "Pauline Johnson Island's status as an ecological reserve" (107). In other words, an environmental concern for the island has effaced and written over the Indigenous land rights that Fletcher and the other activists were committed to defending. Ironically, Pauline Johnson Island now is described as a "unique site of global scientific and ecological interest," romanticizing its status as an object of scientific study (107). The fourth poster, a real estate advertisement for ARRIVAL, "an exclusive 10-storey residential tower built on Vancouver's newest waterfront," marks a shift to gentrification and a renewal of settler ideologies of the adventurous "pioneer spirit of Canada's heritage" (109). The final incarnation of Pauline Johnson Island, as we learn in the story "The Outer Harbour," is as a detention centre for illegal migrants. The posters document how Pauline Johnson Island has become a mirror for larger social and ideological shifts. Demands for justice about one set of issues, Indigenous land rights, can become redirected to other issues, environmental rights, and then become entirely forgotten through a process of gentrification and a reassertion of state authority.

Flowing between the multiple appropriations, co-optations, and "e/racing"[14] of histories, people, and places in *The Outer Harbour* is an underground current of alternative stories, in which Indigenous, Black, and migrant characters encounter one another and attempt to overcome the state's tactics of silencing and surveillance. This appearing and disappearing stream of alternative stories coalesces in the closing story, "The Outer Harbour," a genre-defying combination of film review, graphic illustration, maps, interview, report, and first- and third-person narratives, set in the year 2025. A group of migrants arrive by boat without papers, known origins, or an identified language. The authorities apprehend them but are confounded by the migrants' powers to suddenly evanesce, transgressing prison walls and reappearing a short distance away. This blinking in and out of place is a weapon of elusiveness for the migrants, who cannot be locked up. Like the figure of Rev. Oz. in Compton's long poem, "Rune," the migrants evade those who wish to both define and confine them.

Throughout the story collection, the ever-changing struggle over Pauline Johnson Island leads to many unexpected encounters between different groups and the building of alliances across differences. Several Indigenous and Black characters join solidarity movements to protest the injustices of the state, or to produce art that reveal the correlations between histories of resistance. The original activists include Fletcher Sylvester, with Snohomish heritage from his mother and "a local father from a band unknown to Fletcher or anyone else who might tell him," and Jean Martin, a Black woman whose motivation to go to the island is "a kind of retort to the Vancouver she has known:...all the where-are-you-froms and all the where-are-you-really-froms; being looked at or looked through, depending, but being summed up, appraised, pre-emptively estranged" (2015a, 37). This quotation illustrates Compton's neologism, "pheneticizing," from his book of essays *After Canaan*, which shifts the onus onto the perceiver of racial difference, rather than the perceived (2010, 22).[15] The other three Indigenous activists, Alison, Rob, and Marc, have roots that trace to the islands in the Salish Sea (2015a, 45). Jean promises to Dara, the daughter of Alison and Rob, that: "This new island is yours. You've never had it, but we're going to give it back to you" (2015a, 39). The bending of the past into the future underlines the urgency of redressing land thefts of the past, the effects of which continue into the present. In "The Outer Harbour," Jean and Fletcher's daughter, Suhaima Sylvester Martin, now in her early twenties, creates a series of drawings, "*Expropriatus*," using "condo map icons, redrawn and formed into hieroglyph-like or vèvè-like lines" (Compton 2015b). Suhaima's code-writings are a play on the idea of writing as a way forward in response to power. Compton comments, "Part of the hope of the book is that Suhaima is continuing to think through these things in 2025 as the book is closing—of lost languages and revivals of the imagination" (2015b).

Her drawings are juxtaposed with a series of maps of Burrard Inlet, produced by one of the detainees on the island, a young girl referred to as "Jane Doe 39" (2015a, 165). When the unnamed girl dies, her ghost connects with the ghost of Fletcher on the island, and then connects with the composite, a holographic image made up of the features of Riel Graham, a Black artist and activist, and Veršajna, who deliberately refuses to answer the "pheneticizing" questions of those she encounters (Compton 2010, 22). Although the composite is produced as a "pacification tool" by a security company to impede the activists' efforts to disrupt the G25 meetings of the global elite (2015a, 180), a system error leads to the composite becoming an autonomous being (189). Together, the ghosts of Fletcher, the young migrant girl, and the composite become the promise of an alternative social order as they "make plans to rendezvous with those yet to come. They will discuss what it means to regroup" (2015a, 194). These concluding sentences act as an ethical call to action to the reader, who is asked to reflect upon her responsibilities to "foster a commitment to mobilize ourselves" (Hunt 2018, 2), and to act in solidarity with sovereignty movements in the context of building alliances across differences.

Conclusion: Sites of Autonomy and Alliance

Recent conversations in public and academic arenas, including the contributors to this volume, aim to show how the legacies of slavery and the legacies of land takeover have combined in the making of the Americas. Scholars and artists have illuminated the simultaneous appropriation and erasure of Indigenous and Black voices, bodies, and labour in experiences of settler colonialism, as well as the shared histories of resistance among Black, Indigenous, and Black-Indigenous communities. Connecting together decolonization movements and coalitions of antiracist activism has tremendous potential in rewriting the history of the city. But crafting comparative methods and frameworks comes with pitfalls. For one thing, comparative methods historically have reasserted the centrality, yet the invisibility, of the white settler scholar who often facilitates that comparison, and yet erases her presence in that comparison. Work by Marie Clements and Wayde Compton offers readers a means of approaching these issues from a different angle by uncovering what are often underrecognized interconnections between Black and Indigenous histories. Their work asks readers to realign familiar comparative frameworks of analysis by drawing attention to the reader's own blind spots as she looks through her particular viewfinder.

In crossing genre and disciplinary borders—particularly in shifting between documentary and speculative modes, layering graphic, sonic, and textual media, and experimenting with form and language—Clements and Compton expose and shatter the frames of their works. In closing this chapter I want to consider a (self-)portrait of Clements, one that is clearly a work of self-representation; yet it defiantly asks the viewer to think carefully about how, by whose point of view, and through what lens her image becomes readable and consumed. The image is from the cover of *The Edward Curtis Project,* a coauthored book by Clements and photojournalist Rita Leistner, who together retraced late-nineteenth-century American photographer Edward Curtis's routes up and down the Pacific Northwest Coast. Leistner took the photograph, yet Clements is at the same time reflecting that image back to her collaborator with her own camera. Leistner took photographs of descendants of the subjects of Curtis's images, which included some of Clements's Métis and Dene relatives, but in these photographs, the subjects name and dress themselves, thereby redressing the staged anonymity of "Vanishing Indians" in Curtis's work. Instead of being the "subject" of Curtis's romantic portraits of a world that never was, Clements is now holding the camera, playing with the idea of the framer now framed by her own lens. The window frames she looks through highlights the multiple mediations that her work always engages with. Yet the glass within the frames is broken, as if Clements's iconoclastic vision has shattered the edging. This image powerfully recalls the politics of seeing and framing evident in Compton's work, in which the probing, desiring gaze of the investigator only "captures" retro-speculative confabulations through the limits of a camera's viewfinder; the subject ultimately evades that gaze by evanescing. In these ways the works by Clements and Compton warn the viewer to proceed cautiously in creating interpretive and comparative frameworks, reminding that what one sees is as much a reflection as it is a window.

Landsensing

Body, Territory, Relation

/ WARREN CARIOU

I am strongly influenced by the thinkers, artists, and activists of the Indigenous resurgence that we can see happening all around us now—Christi Belcourt, Leanne Simpson, Glen Coulthard, Winona LaDuke, Dylan Miner, and many more. These people have showed us how to avoid being caught up in counterproductive struggles when the terms of those struggles are dictated by colonial authority, and how to focus instead on the most crucial things in our communities: relationships, humility, creativity, the importance of giving back, and the teachings that are held within the land itself. In *Dancing on Our Turtle's Back*, Leanne Simpson describes a group of Nishnaabeg walking in a procession down the main street of Nogojiwanong, also known as Peterborough. "This was not a protest," she writes. "This was not a demonstration. This was a quiet, collective act of resurgence" (2011, 11). In the spirit of Simpson's story, I want to begin by stating that, despite recent events in Canadian literature and media, this chapter is not a protest. Instead, I would like you to think of it as a walk on the land—a walk with eyes and ears open, with our skin and our nostrils and even our taste buds attuned to *where we are*. This is an homage to

Jeannette Armstrong's great essay, "Landspeaking" (1998), which I have come to regard as a friend and companion over the years. It is also my attempt to explain why, and how, I always carry with me the soil and the stories of my homeland in northern Saskatchewan.

The image reproduced here is a photograph I made using bitumen gathered from the banks of the Athabasca River, not far from my home. This bitumen is the same material that is extracted in the nearby tar sands strip mines, and processed into the gasoline, diesel, and petrochemicals that underwrite the conditions of modern life. I call these images petrographs, and the practice of petrography is my attempt to divert some of this bitumen out of the capitalist conduit of petroleum usage and toward the creative purpose of revealing what is being done to the land of the Athabasca region and the people who are intimately connected to it. As I worked on this photographic project, I came to understand in a deeper way that I was using the land itself to signify, and that the process of petrography involved negotiating an unexpected relationship with that land—one that is mediated

Figure 1. Warren Cariou, "Suncor Structures Viewed from the Athabasca River." An 8" × 10" bitumen photograph on polished aluminum.

through the senses, especially the sense of smell. My thinking in this chapter has been influenced by this intimate and sometimes difficult sensory relationship with the bitumen of my petrographs, a material that is undeniably messy, toxic, and extremely smelly, yet one that also enables a sensory visual experience that is different from any other representational medium I'm aware of. The bitumen is one aromatic element of the land that I call home, an element that I believe communicates to us through scent, as well as through its other properties. I'm interested in the ways that parts of the land itself can have what Dylan Robinson calls "sensory agency" (2016, 46), and the ways we can amplify or collaborate with that agency through art.

Toward the end of this chapter I will return to a discussion of my petrography process and what it has taught me about my homeland and my place on it, but first I want to examine in more detail the resurgence movements I mentioned earlier, and the ways that many Indigenous people are asserting their relationships to the land as a way of reconnecting with their heritage, their teachings, their nourishment, and their responsibilities. At the same time as they are doing this, many of these same Indigenous people are also doing their utmost to stop environmentally destructive capitalist developments such as clearcuts, pipelines, and energy-extraction megaprojects. One example of this is Unist'ot'en Camp, where an organized group of Wet'suwet'en people have formed a community on their territory, right where a Chevron pipeline is proposed to be built underneath a creek. The people of Unist'ot'en Camp are practising traditional Wet'suwet'en lifeways, living off the land, and also defending the land against the incursions of corporate extractivism. They bring together resurgence and resistance in a seamless way: the practice of their traditional culture *is* their mode of resisting the incursion of a foreign and environmentally damaging influence onto their unceded and sovereign territory.

I am interested in the embodied and land-based aspects of this kind of resurgence/resistance, which we have also seen in other Indigenous communities, including Standing Rock, Grassy Narrows, Elsipogtog, and Madii Lii. One crucial aspect of these movements is the way in which the participants connect with and learn from their surroundings. I'm referring to particular skills of "sensing" the land, which were very highly developed among Indigenous people before colonization, but which been affected by colonial interventions in various ways. I think the activists, artists, Elders, and community members who are involved in activities of resurgence/resistance are trying to relearn and enhance those skills of sensing the land because these skills are still crucial for survival, and also because a deep and nuanced attentiveness to the land is what motivates their resistance in the first place.

I was first led toward this line of thinking at a presentation at the 2015 States of Extraction conference at Simon Fraser University by the Wet'suwet'en hereditary chief, Toghestiy, Warner Naziel, who is a member of the Unist'ot'en Camp. Toghestiy explained the philosophy and politics of Unist'ot'en Camp in a way that resonated powerfully for me, describing how the people of Unist'ot'en have committed to living in their traditional way, nourishing themselves through hunting and gathering on the land they are protecting. This is not a protest; it is a way of life. It is also a profoundly philosophical engagement, one that nourishes the body and also at the same time reinforces the connections between humans and the land. Toghestiy discusses the importance of

> going out there and just getting a chance to enjoy the land and be a part of it, to taste the land. Because the land has a flavour, and you cannot connect with the land unless you've actually tasted it. And we do that now, that's what we do, we live in the territory, we hunt, fish, and trap out there. The majority of the food that we set at the table comes from the land that we're protecting (2015).[1]

In this explanation, Toghestiy shows how the traditional practices he learned from his grandparents are connected to the guiding principles of the Unist'ot'en Camp's land-based form of resistance. And he also demonstrates that these traditional practices have a philosophy that is deeply engaged with the senses. His statement that "the land has a flavour, and you cannot connect with the land unless you've actually tasted it" resonates for me because I have experienced this myself in a small and underdeveloped way. I grew up fishing and hunting and picking berries on the land that I still think of as home. I return there every year, drawn by a kind of hunger, a need to soak up that place, to fish and pick berries and wander among the spruce trees, breathing their spiced air. When I heard Toghestiy speak, I realized that my connection to my homeland is more through flavour and scent than anything else—more, even, than story. I had always known this without really understanding it. And I recognized also that many other Indigenous people know it in a much deeper, more nuanced way than I do because they spend much of their lives on the land, tasting it, paying intimate sensory attention to it, being a part of it. I wanted to learn more about this idea, this sensory philosophy of belonging. I wondered if it was possible to articulate a politics, an aesthetics, an ethics, of tasting the land.

One question that continued to echo for me in the days after Toghestiy's talk was: How did I know about this sensory connection without knowing it? How could I have forgotten? One answer is that colonialism and extractive capitalism have brought with them an ideology of separation from the land and commodification of it. In this context, most people have become unable to sense the land with the nuance and intimacy that Indigenous people were able to feel it before colonization, and that some are still able to do today. I don't think this is because of any essential quality of Indigeneity, but rather because many Indigenous people have retained some of those skills of sensing the land that have been crucial to their survival for generation after generation. As I mentioned, many of these Indigenous people are now returning to those teachings, going back and spending time learning from the land in activities of cultural resurgence. And the sensory skills that these people learn, their fine-tuned abilities to pay close attention to the land, are also what enable them to recognize the magnitude of the damage that extractivism, agriculture, and urbanization are doing to the land. This is how the resurgence and the resistance come together, in the realm of the sensorium.

In her book *Braiding Sweetgrass*, Potawotami scholar Robin Wall Kimmerer writes about the connection of land, memory, spirituality, and sensation through the action of a sacred plant:

> Our stories say that of all the plants, wiingaashk, or sweetgrass, was the very first to grow on the earth, its fragrance a sweet memory of Skywoman's hand. Accordingly, it is honored as one of the four sacred plants of my people. Breathe in its scent and you start to remember things you didn't know you'd forgotten. Our elders say that ceremonies are the way we "remember to remember," and so sweetgrass is a powerful ceremonial plant cherished by many indigenous nations. (2015, 4–5)

Here, sweetgrass is discussed as an active, energetic plant that gives a gift of memory, connecting humans to the beginning of everything and to Skywoman herself. In other words, it enables a memory beyond what an individual human life might hold; it embodies an extraordinarily intimate connection to the deeper past and to a relationship with something beyond the narrow individual self, to the "things you didn't know you'd forgotten." And as Kimmerer describes sweetgrass in the book, it is the relationship with this plant that informs an entire ethics and set of teachings and ceremonial practices within her community. Many of these modes of relationship are focused on learning from the sweetgrass through the senses, as if its teachings come embedded within the fragrance itself. Even the process of searching for sweetgrass is one of paying minute attention to sensing the land. She writes,

> You can smell it before you see it, a sweetgrass meadow on a summer day. The scent flickers on the breeze, you sniff like a dog on a scent, and then it's gone, replaced by the boggy tang of wet ground. And then it's back, the sweet vanilla fragrance, beckoning. (2015, 156)

Thus, it is almost as if the sweetgrass teaches us how to find it by sending out its scent to us like a message, like a story that draws us closer. The plant itself shows us how we are related to it, through that most intimate form of communication: sensation.

But in contrast to this intimate, energized sensory relationship with the land that Kimmerer writes about, there are forces moving in the other direction, toward deadening our senses, numbing our abilities to distinguish the nuances and the teachings of the land. In our modern extractivist world, we have been persistently blinding ourselves to the consequences of our collective actions. We know intellectually that tar sands mines and other environmental sacrifice zones are *out there* beyond our immediate view, and that we are connected to them in some way, but we don't want to know, we don't want to see, we don't want to *sense* that connection. This state of wilful not seeing, not sensing, is a pervasive aspect of modern life. Much of our dominant culture is directed toward the deadening and denial of our connectedness to the natural world because such denial is the only thing that enables us, psychologically, to continue on with the unsustainable actions that we take part in as citizens of "states of extraction." This reminds me of the concept of "percepticide," which Diana Taylor (1997) identifies in her book *Disappearing Acts*. Taylor writes about the state-orchestrated "disappearances" of thousands of people during Argentina's Dirty War, and she shows that these disappearances were often shockingly public. The intended function of these public spectacles of state violence, she argues, was to make the people enforce a kind of self-censorship upon their very senses, so that they are no longer able or willing to sense the violence that is happening around them. She writes, "To see, without being able to do, disempowers absolutely. But seeing, without even admitting that one is seeing, further turns the violence on oneself. Percepticide blinds, maims, kills through the senses" (1997, 124).

The separation that many people feel from the natural world today is not exactly the same as Taylor's description of vicious state-sponsored perceptual warfare, but it is closer than it might at first seem. Most members of the dominant society in North America have already been long conditioned by the ideologies of capitalism and individualism to regard the land from a distance, as a thing to be manipulated rather than a living entity we are utterly dependent upon. So in a sense, these people do not "need" to be subjected to violence in order to shock them into a state of percepticide that will enable the status quo of environmental disaster to continue. They have already absorbed this lesson through cultural indoctrination. But there is another broad and diverse group of people whose cultures do *not* predispose them to accept this kind of belief system: Indigenous people. And I believe this is one more reason why Indigenous people have been targeted for cultural genocide throughout the history of colonialism in North America. Indigenous people's view of the land as a relative, a living being whom we connect with in the most intimate ways, is anathema to the prevailing values of the dominant capitalist colonial system, and thus it is not surprising that state authorities, and their corporate beneficiaries, have sought to suppress Indigenous lifeways. I think it is no coincidence that at the same time as the environmental degradation of Turtle Island accelerated in the late nineteenth century, Canada and the United States began to be more and more invested in eliminating Indigenous cultures altogether. Indigenous modes of relating to the land represented political, and I would also say sensory, threats to burgeoning carbon-based modernity.

As with other percepticidal mechanisms of state violence such as the ones Taylor writes about, the system of Indian residential schools in Canada tried to interrupt Indigenous people's ability to *sense* their surroundings. The residential school system used violence, humiliation, and physical separation in an attempt to interrupt not only language, culture, and family bonds, but also Indigenous people's intimate, sensory connection to the land. This kind of percepticide operated at brutally physical levels as well as symbolic ones, and I would like to spend a bit of time discussing this because I feel it is one aspect of the Indian residential school history that has so far received relatively little attention.[2]

Many of the stories in the Truth and Reconciliation Commission's (2015b) volume of personal testimony, *The Survivors Speak*, reference the residential schools' targeting of the *senses* of Indigenous children, especially the senses of taste and smell. Survivors talk about not only the lack of nutrition but also the numbing blandness and revolting flavour of the food served in these institutions. Survivor Daisy Diamond says, "When I was going to Shingwauk, the food didn't taste very good, because we didn't have our traditional food there, our moose meat, our bannock, and our berries. Those were the things that we had back home, and we were very lonely without those berries" (2015b, 69). Like Daisy, many of the other survivors also remembered fondly, and with vivid sensual detail, the tastes and scents and healing attributes of their homelands. Mabel Brown remembers the teachings of her father, who showed her

> how to tell what kind of trees are what and what the different kind of things you take off the gum, and things like that; what it's used for and you know, chew and my mom and dad used to dig up roots from the ground and I used to just love that roots. Chew on it and all those things are medicine for our bodies too. And I still, I still, can't eat just store-bought foods. I have to have caribou or fish or moose meat or something like that and to, to feel full; to feel satisfied. (2015b, 6)

Other survivors talk about having "bush foods" and other items from their homelands confiscated by school authorities. I believe this was not just arbitrary meanness but in fact part of the schools' mandate of breaking children's connection to their home territories. The "success" of this aspect of the residential school project can perhaps be measured in the degree to which Indigenous peoples lost their bushcraft skills when they were taken away. Survivor Raphael Victor Paul gives his father's assessment of the knowledge base of kids who returned from the school:

> He said, "You know you guys that went to residential school are useless, because you don't know how to survive like they did."...So, the people that went back had to relearn how to survive. And at that time, survival was fishing, hunting, and trapping. To this day, I don't know how to hunt. (2015b, 107)

This robbing of Indigenous people's connection to the land and of their survival skills is one of the most insidious and damaging aspects of the residential school system. The fact that dietary diseases such as diabetes are rampant among Indigenous people today is very likely connected to the loss of bushcraft skills, and the lack of any healthy food options for purchase in most of our Indigenous communities.

I want to focus on one more residential school story that symbolizes for me the connection between the senses and Indigenous concepts of belonging. In Richard Wagamese's (2012) *Indian Horse*, there is an extraordinary scene where the children in the residential school discover an unexpected gift from the land, even within the confines of the residential school grounds. The children notice that the creek behind the school is "a sucker creek" (53), where suckers run in the spring, and the children go down to the bank holding burlap bags:

> We could see the fish pushing up that water. It was thrilling. So much life, so much desperation, so much energy. We stood for a long time and just watched. Then some of us cut saplings and bent them around the inside lip of those sacks. We lowered the sacks into the water and pulled them up dripping and filled with fish. We watched the silvery, brown flash as they flopped out onto the bank, their puckered mouths flapping like wet kisses from fat aunties, their tails flipping and slapping against the ground. We pushed them back into the water and pulled up another sack. We did that four times. The fourth time we stood quietly, each of us lost in our thoughts, as the fish struggled for air, for life, for freedom. When we bent finally and took the fish in our hands to set them back into the water, most of us were crying. (2012, 53)

These children are not only sensing the aliveness and rich possibilities of the land there on the residential school grounds, but they are also practising bushcraft skills that the narrator, Saul, has learned from his grandmother earlier in the story. However, the kids are interrupted in this process, prevented from tasting the land and reconnecting to it in that most intimate manner. What is left is a scene of powerful affect and loss, as the children suddenly understand the symbolism of the situation.

However, I think this scene is not solely a representation of cultural loss and percepticide because despite the interruption of their traditional fishing practices, and their inability to prepare and consume the fish, the children are still marked afterward by a powerful sensory connection to the fish through smell:

> We turned as a group and began the long, sloping walk back up the ridge to the school. We walked with our hands cupped around our noses, breathing in the smell of those fish, pushing the slime of them around on our faces. We had no knives to clean them, flay them. We had no fire to smoke them over. We had no place to store them, no way to keep them. When they lay gasping on the grass, it was ourselves we saw fighting for air. We were Indian kids and all we had was the smell of those fish on our hands. We fell asleep that night with our noses pressed to our hands and as the days went by and the smell of those suckers faded, there wasn't a one of us that didn't cry for the loss of the life we'd known before. (2012, 53–54)

As in Kimmerer's representation of the scent of sweetgrass, this fish scent seems to be almost an active thing, embodying the energy and connectedness of the fish themselves. And the children's repeated action of catching the fish and then releasing them four times might be seen as a kind of ceremony, a performance of intimacy with the land that helps the children to, as Kimmerer says, "remember to remember." In addition, the scent of the fish is a connection that will remain with them, and that might help them to reconnect with the land in the future—as the narrator Saul does near the end of the book.

In addition to the residential schools, the state has used other tactics that attempt to interrupt Indigenous people's connections with the land, and one of the most common of these tactics is forced removal. There are many examples of this in Canada's history, and virtually all of them have been disasters for the Indigenous people who have been removed from their traditional home territory and moved to places where they are not intimately familiar with the land. In this context, I want to discuss an oral story by the Omushkego Cree Elder Louis Bird that gestures toward the cultural, bodily, and sensory legacies of such displacement—though he does so through the somewhat unexpected genre of the joke, rather than tragedy. Elder Bird told this story at a gathering of Cree writers and storytellers in Winnipeg in 2010, and he has generously given permission for me to publish a transcribed version of the story here. A transcription is a poor substitute for the embodied experience of the story itself, but it still carries many of the teachings that are embedded in the story, and I am very grateful to Elder Bird for his willingness to share it in this form.

He introduced the story by telling the audience that it was an old man's entry in a joke-telling contest that was held in an unnamed northern community, where the people had gathered near their traditional homeland after being displaced from it many years before. The prize for the best joke in this contest is fifty gallons of gas. After everyone else in the gathering has told their jokes, the old man and his wife are the last ones left who haven't spoken. The story continues as follows:[3]

> There was an old couple sitting right in front there, right in front of the moderator, whatever you call him, okay? And he says to the old man, "What about you, nimoshom?" It means, our grandpa. "What about you nimoshom, do you have any joke to tell?"
>
> And he was smoking with a pipe...."Who? Me?"
>
> "Yes, you...to give us a joke?"
>
> "No, no," he says, "I can't tell you a joke because I'm so sad about home. I'm so sad, sometimes we don't know what to do with ourselves." His wife is sitting beside him. "One day," he said, "we were *so* sad, in the afternoon, in the evening—grocery stores were almost closed, and we decided to camp a little ways from here. There's a creek out there that's famous for putting gillnets. Let's go spend the night there, we said, in memory of our home. To be just the two of us.
>
> "So we agree. So she went to buy some little groceries that we can use for the one night, and I prepared the canoe, and the tent and the stove, and my gun and all that, in case I see something.

"So we're ready to go, finally we push off, and I had my six-horsepower behind, and we took off, towards that little creek. Across the lake. And as we went there, the formation of the clouds was getting to be like a rainy evening. There was thunderclouds forming, and my wife says, 'We better get there fast, before this thing gets in our way.' So we traveled there and we reached there, and then we got close to that creek and we stopped.

"And that's when my wife begins—she forgot her groceries! The bag she packed for our groceries, it was behind. And...we have a net, yes, and I have my gun. And then we decide, it's too far away, it's too late to go back—and also it's starting to rain.

"And so we decided to camp right there, and then we'll put the net later, because it started to rain, and the cloud was very thick. So we made a camp first and we said 'Let's set up the tent first, and then the stove, then our blanket, and then we'll come back after the rain and we'll set the net. Also set the rabbit snares.

"On our way into that place, we had seen a duck, and I was ready to shoot it, and I had put two shots in my gun. I was ready to shoot...but I didn't. The duck was gone. So I still had the shotgun shells in my barrel, and I just left it in the bow of my canoe.

"So we got stuck in our tipi because it's starting heavy rain. And so we were sorry now that we never put the net out. We talked to each other: 'How are we going to eat, then?' And so she says, 'Oh, we're going to try to find a rabbit somehow, after the rain stops—or whether it stops or not.'

"So we're just sitting there waiting, and the thunder was getting louder, and lightning and everything! And we started to get so mad at that thing. Why does it have to happen? And so finally, my wife says, you know, 'Why don't you just turn the canoe over. And bring your gun in—you forgot your gun there!' So I went down to where we had beached our canoe. I went there, and I picked up my gun. There's a shell in there, I remembered, so I pop open my double-barrel.

"At *that* moment...that moment, the BIG thunder of lightning flashes on me, and I jump. I just popped my gun barrel back, and I'm so mad at this, I'm just cursing at this thunder and everything, and I just let go with the double barrels into the air, where the thunder sound. And I was cursing, and *mad*.

"I walked over to my little tent where my wife was. She says 'What did you shoot?'

"I said, 'Nothing. I was just accidentally shooting up there, I was so mad!' So anyway, 'What's the idea?' she says.

"Then we sat down. Quite a while later...quite a while later...we just sit there quietly, thinking about my canoe—I still forgot to turn it over. All of a sudden we hear something—thunk!—something heavy falls down a little ways towards my canoe, you know? And she said 'What IS that? Tree fall down? Maybe lightning struck it?' And my wife says 'Why don't you go down and take a look, what is falling down?'

"I go outside there, and look around where I hear something fall. As I walk around through a little bit of small grass and a little bit of rose bush...And *there* sticks two feet! Feet sticks out, like claws...like an eagle... eagle feet, okay? But big! And I went there, and sneak in, and see what it is. I was so sure that it's an eagle! When I got closer it gets larger, and larger, and I look at it....

"*There lies the Thunderbird!* I have shot the Thunderbird...accidentally!

"And then I thought, what am I going to do with this? So...then I pick it up anyway, grab the neck and drag it to my tipi, show it to my wife. She says, 'What was it?' and I said 'Well, here it is. This is what fell down.'

"And then she was all scared and wondered what to say. Nothing to say, she just opened her mouth. And we said 'It's a Thunderbird. Yeah...' And then we talked about 'What are we going to do with it?'

"And then she says, 'What do you mean? We don't have a thing to eat!'

"And I said to my wife, 'Well, pluck it, pluck at least part of it. We'll have our supper. At least we can have a soup, you know? Thunderbird soup!'

"So my wife started to pluck the leg part and then cut it in pieces and make a stew. And it was really good! Almost like a goose. In our little stove, okay, our little wood stove. And then it boiled and boiled and she prepared it real nice. And she said, 'It should be cooked by now.'

"And 'Okay, let's eat, I'm starving,' I said. So we sit down and eat this food—It really tasted good. We really stuff ourself. Couldn't stop anyway, just keep on eating until we were...*really* full.

"So we lay down to relax. My wife do the same thing, both sides of the stove, she lays there and I lay beside, and this is the back end of the tent.

> And later on, maybe half hour later, we begin to feel as if we have a gas in our stomachs—really blow up, eh? Getting big stomach.
>
> "I asked my wife, I says 'Do you feel something?' She says 'Yeah, yeah, I feel like I have gas.' And then I said 'Me too...it's really hurting.' And then I thought, I wonder if it's the Thunderbird that does that?
>
> "So we sat down there and forgot all about it...and then all of a sudden, I couldn't hold it. I couldn't hold it, it just had to let go. And then finally as I let it go...a big loud sound came out from behind...a blue flame came out from there!"
>
> That's the end of the story. (Bird 2018, n.p.)

This narrative may initially seem like light entertainment, but to me it is suffused with sadness and loss despite the comic tone, and it contains some profound teachings about affect, sensory awareness, and traditional Cree knowledge of the land. The old man begins the story by focusing on the community's loss, and the affective experience of displacement. He says, "I can't tell you a joke because I'm so sad about home," and when he starts telling the story, it is not clear that it is a joke at all. The couple decide to go out on the land as an act of memorialization, saying "Let's go spend the night there...in memory of our home." But the plan begins to go awry when they realize they have forgotten their groceries. In their attempt to memorialize their relationship to their home, they are faced with the fact that colonial intervention has taken a toll on their land-based memories. In this unexpected situation, they are going to have to survive on the land like they used to do, but this is a problem because they have not only forgotten the groceries; they have also forgotten their bushcraft. First, the old man is going to shoot the duck, but then inexplicably he doesn't. Then he leaves his gun out in the rain, and neglects to turn the canoe upside-down. They delay setting their nets, deciding to wait until the rain is over. If we think of hunting and gathering as processes of embodied, sensory interpretation of the land, the old couple seems to have lost the skills of *sensing* it in that way. They have also become accustomed to a certain kind of comfort, not wanting to be out in the rain even though that means they will go hungry. Furthermore, their lack of sensory engagement with the land goes well beyond the realm of simply nourishing themselves—it is also an ethical lapse, one that leads to an enormous mistake. The old man's frustration at the weather and at his own loss of bush survival skills is what leads him to lash out. He doesn't pay attention to the signs that the land is giving him, especially through the sound of the thunder. Thunder means something in this story, but he doesn't realize that until he has already made his fateful skyward shot.

The old man's inattention does not excuse his action of shooting at the sky; in fact, this lapse *is* his transgression. The old couple have been affected by their community's removal, and they appear to have adopted some Western ideologies of separation from the land that lead the old man to make his dangerous mistake. He doesn't "remember to remember" (2015, 5), as Kimmerer says—doesn't remember the importance of sensing the land, and also the teachings associated with the creatures of the land. The result of not paying attention to the land is that he unthinkingly commits an act of violence against the most sacred creature in the Omushkego Cree tradition. He shoots the Thunderbird, and even though he doesn't react as if this is a terrifying thing, any Omushkego Cree listener would know that it *should* be terrifying. As Louis Bird later confirmed to me, the old man has committed an act of *pastahowin*, or what Louis elsewhere calls "a sin against nature."[4]

In many stories about *pastahowin*, the transgression against nature has very serious consequences indeed, usually the withholding of nature's bounty from the offending person and his or her community, which often leads to starvation. However, in the context of this comedic situation, it seems as if the old man and his wife are exempted from this punishment since they are able to feed themselves from the man's accidental hunting after all. By eating the Thunderbird, they can pretend that they still have their survival skills, that they are still able to live on the land. In the description of their meal, we see a parody of what Toghestiy talked about: this old couple ends up "tasting the land," but at the same time they are committing a sacrilege. Note the storyteller's focus on the taste of their meal: "It tasted *really* good...almost like a goose." But despite its good taste, the Thunderbird soup brings explosive consequences; it is not good nourishment at all, but rather something that rebounds against the old couple in a painful, embarrassing, and, most likely, very smelly way. And that blue flame of flatulence at the end of the story makes manifest the decolonial and antiextractive theme that has been implicit throughout: the old couple's intestinal gas is an echo of the fifty gallons of gas that the old man stands to win in the contest if his joke is the best one. Petroleum might seem like a prize of sorts for

Indigenous communities as for any other community—enabling mobility and insulation from the extremes of the environment—but instead, here it is associated with the killing and eating of the Thunderbird, and we come to understand that the story is an allegory of separation from the land, and the implicit role of colonial energy politics in that separation. Those of us who have lost our ability to sense the land through colonial intervention or cultural indoctrination are like the old couple. We may *believe* that we are nourishing ourselves with what we violently and thoughtlessly extract from the land, and we may even think that it tastes good, but our senses have been fooled, and soon we will have to face the gaseous consequences. If you kill and consume the most sacred being, you will not be able to survive on that meat for long.

So what are we to do now, when so many of us may find ourselves in a situation like that of the old couple, our collective bellies already full of ill-gotten nourishment that is making us and our whole world very sick? We need to find ways to reestablish an intimacy with the land, ways to improve our skills of sensing our environment—and I mean this not just in a technological way through improved instruments and measurement regimes, though scientific documentation of environmental damage is extremely important as well, and it too is now under threat in unprecedented ways. But I'm talking about something more personal, more rooted in affect. We need to find better ways to *feel* our connection to the environment, and to the sources of our energy, so that we understand at a deep bodily level what is at stake in our relationships with the world. And I believe that the ongoing projects of resurgence/resistance that are taking place throughout Turtle Island are providing pathways toward that kind of learning and commitment.

This brings me back to my own messy dabbling with petroleum in the bitumen photographs I make. As I mentioned, my petrography process is extremely smelly, and the bitumen is probably toxic, so I take precautions by wearing a respirator when I work closely with it. I have to treat it with respect. Its very scent advertises its dangers. But at the same time, that smell carries a memory for me that will probably seem strange to most people. It reminds me of the place where I gathered the bitumen, a place that was not at all what I had expected. While searching along the riverbank for a source of bitumen that I could use in my petrography, I made a discovery about the place of this substance within the natural environment. After travelling by boat through the most devastated landscape I have ever seen—miles and miles of completely stripped hillsides, suffused in horrible toxic odours and drifting smoke—we turned a couple of corners and suddenly came to a very different landscape. It was one of the most lush and beautiful places I have ever experienced in the boreal region. Here, the mining companies had not come to disturb the surface, and the bitumen was there as it has always been, as part of the natural ecosystem. And the smell there was wonderful. We could sense the bitumen, but it was beautifully mingled with the other scents of fresh rain, new spring growth, and blooming wild roses. And now when I smell the raw, unprocessed bitumen in my petrography studio, I remember the gorgeous place it came from, and I think about the Indigenous people of the Athabasca region who, according to legend, used bitumen for generation after generation to seal their birchbark canoes and other vessels. And in that smell, I think I can sense a possibility of a different relationship with this material, which has been treated with such disrespect for more than a century. I even imagine that the bitumen might be used for healing purposes, if we can learn the sensory skills and the teachings that the material has to give us.

Notes

Introduction

1 This important project, chaired by the Honourable Justice Murray Sinclair, was an opportunity for those affected by the Indian residential schools to share their stories and experiences. Between 2007 and 2015, the commission travelled across the country and heard from sixty-five hundred witnesses. It hosted seven national events to educate people about the history and legacy of residential schools. For more, see rcaanccirnac.gc.ca/eng/1450124405592/1529106060525.com and trc.ca/assets/pdf/Calls_to_Action_English2.pdf. While the TRC was a necessary step in creating discussion between Indigenous and settler peoples on Turtle Island north of the 49th parallel, it is key that we understand it as an opening, and not a closing in the making of better relationships.

2 For more, see blacklivesmatter.ca and Diverlus et al. (2020).

3 This incident began with an article in *Maclean's* entitled "Too Asian: Some Frosh Don't Want to Study at an Asian University," which suggested that white students avoid certain universities because of their high enrolment of Asian and Asian Canadian students. For analysis, see Heer (2012).

4 See Lederman (2016). There is a plethora of further material available on the web for readers interested in further details.

5 See Barrera (2016). This is just one piece among many published on the topic in such venues as the *Globe and Mail*, CBC, the *Toronto Star*, the *National Post*, and *The Walrus*, among others.

6 See the dialogue that follows this introduction for more on this.

7 Held in 1992 and organized by Daniel David Moses and Lenore Keeshig.

8 Held in 1994 and organized by a large and disparate committee that included, at various times, Roy Miki, Michelle LaFlamme, Peter Hudson, Scott Toguri McFarlane, Joy Hall, C. Allyson, and myself.

9 Held in 1993 and organized by Lillian Allen, Shirley Bear, Marrie Mumford, Gloria Eshibok, Zool Suleman, Sherazad Jamal, Monika Kin Gagnon, David Woods, Paul Wong, Dana Claxton, and Cheryl L'Hirondelle.

10 The term "people of colour" and its more recent iteration "Black, Indigenous, and people of colour" is falling out of favour currently because it doesn't address the specificity of Black, Indigenous, and Asian histories and experience, and tends to lump those it refers to together, as though the histories and experiences of all those it refers to are the same in their specificity and intensity. I agree with this critique, but still sometimes use the term "BIPOC" to describe a broad and uneven coalition of people working toward a future together in which we retain our histories, experiences, and differences. I use it because of the meanings and community attachments it has accrued over time, in all their productivity and all their fraughtness. In order to remain on this journey, the difference, unevenness, and contestation within the term need to be addressed. This book contributes to that work. I recognize, however, that the term's meanings will necessarily shift over time, and that it may fall out of use, as so many other contingent terms have, after it has served its purposes.

11 This laying out of identity terms makes more clear some lines of difference within a frame that was historically identified in Canada as "non-white" or "visible minorities," later reclaimed as "people of colour" to steer away from the negation of "non-white" and the false and marginalizing descriptor "minority," and still later revalenced as "BIPOC" to make Black and Indigenous locations distinct from "people of colour" ones in light of the specificities of Black and Indigenous experience. To my mind, none of these terms are fully accurate because they don't lay out differences internal to any one term, and further, they reproduce colonial categories, albeit for the purposes of empowerment and liberation. This is a paradox of living inside a managerial state with a long and complex history of colonization that remains ongoing, and needs to be able to speak to the experience of being colonized and managed, as well as of relationships with others who inhabit the experience of being colonized and managed differently from oneself, but within the same regime. Further, because the history of being colonized and managed is so long, a sense of one's own being is caught up in this language. The need for the language remains. I expect it will continue to evolve as the self-understanding and self-location of communities evolves.

12 When speaking of the combined practices and effects of official state Multiculturalism and popularly received multiculturalism, that is, insufficiently critical understanding that lumps together people historically designated as "visible minorities" or "non-White," this book uses the term "M/multiculturalism."

I recognize a certain awkwardness here, but nevertheless, the term references a specific phenomenon.

13 Smaro Kamboureli has written about these difficulties in another volume with origins in the conference: "Literary Solidarities: Should I Be Here?" (2020). Larissa Lai has written about them in "Insurgent Utopias: How to Recognize the Knock at the Door" (2018). See also Larissa Lai, Neil Surkan, and Joshua Whitehead, "Counterclockwise," special issue of *Canada and Beyond: A Journal of Canadian Literary and Cultural Studies* (2019).

14 For more, see Monika Kin Gagnon (2000) and Carol Tator et al. (1998).

15 For me, recognizing that the land is sovereign means that anything Asian Canadian people do or did to fight for their rights within the bounds of the Canadian state—including the Japanese Canadian Redress movement and the Chinese Canadian Head Tax Redress movement—because they reinforce the state, in fact, work counter to Indigenous sovereignty. This doesn't make our agitation for rights wrong or bad, but it does cast a light on the structural ways in which, in this instance, Indigenous and Asian Canadian interests are cast in opposition to each other. I wonder if Asian Canadian acts of self-empowerment have to be settler acts, that is, acts against Indigenous sovereignty, and, at the time of writing, I am working on a book that thinks about this problem and finds other ways of self-empowering in relation to Black and Indigenous friends and colleagues. Sometimes those other ways involve addressing my own accountability and critiques of the state. Sometimes they involve avenues of relation that circumvent or exceed the state. Ideal or utopian relations may or may not be possible; in any case, it is necessary to be accountable for the ways in which one has already reinforced and benefited from the state, and to resist both reinforcement and benefit. To think about these issues more deeply, I hope will be useful to help at least some people think about and actually be in relationships differently. I use the term "Asian Canadian" here in part to recognize a long-fought-for identity claim, in part because a discipline of that name is currently under formation, and in part to recognize Asian Canadian attachments for both better and worse to the state. In other moments in this introduction, where it makes more contextual sense to simply say "Asian," I do that, as in when describing it in its (always problematic) racial valences, or in relation to Blackness and Indigeneity, or when I'm referring to it as a racial condition in a global field. If there is apparent inconsistency here, it is because identity terms are not stable or selfsame from one historical or discursive moment to the next. For more on this, see *Slanting I, Imagining We* (2014).

16 Afua Cooper addresses this powerfully in *The Hanging of Angelique* (2011).

17 Their works are infinitely more complex than this, of course. Each in their own way illustrates the agented centrality of their characters and subjects.

18 I have written more extensively about this issue in an essay entitled "Bone to Bone, Spirit to Spirit: Sovereign Matriarchy, Asian/Indigenous Relations, and the Work of Directed Re-membering" (2021a).

19 Abel plays with spelling in his work. As I understand it, "Nisga'a" names the traditional people and culture he is disenfranchised from, while "Nishga" names the partially and creatively recovered contemporary culture he creates and inhabits through his critical and experimental poetry practice. The shift in spelling designates both a loss and a gain. As this work is new in my moment of writing, I expect these understandings to move and shift as criticism on Abel's work develops.

20 I'm borrowing from Judith Butler's *Bodies That Matter* here. She writes: "'race' is partially produced as an effect of the history of racism...its boundaries and meanings are constructed over time not only in the service of racism, but also in the service of the construction of racism" (1993, 18).

21 This is something that Smaro Kamboureli recognized in the earliest book to come out of the TransCanada Project, *Trans.Can.Lit: Resituating the Study of Canadian Literature* (2007). She writes:

> The body literary does not always have a symmetrical relationship to the body politic; the literary is inflected and infected by the political in oblique and manifest ways, at the same time that it asserts its unassimilability...From the belated and gradual fashion in which it has entered the curriculum of Canadian English departments to the ways it has become a popular field of study, from the various critical debates as to how it should be read to the professional and disciplinary determinants that influence its teaching and study, CanLit has reached a certain deadendedness; yet is also displays a resistance to being entirely subsumed by the very processes and institutions that influence its course. (2007, viii–ix)

22 The Appropriate Voice conference in 1992, the International Dub Festival in 1993, and Writing Thru Race in 1994 are examples of such struggle.

23 I note that Canadian literature's original project was to make space for Canadian writers and writing against the impositions of British and American literatures. Though colonial and exclusionary, its stated purpose was to make space for silenced voices. The voices it privileged and foregrounded, however, were white voices.

24 I have written about this phenomenon before in *Slanting I, Imagining We* (2014) with regard to the institutionalization of Asian Canadian literatures.

25 See Ina Batzke et al. (2018).

26 We express our appreciation to the four anonymous readers who generously gave us feedback on the original manuscript and suggested that an introduction might make this book more accessible to a general audience. We had originally intended our dialogue to be the introductory frame, to begin with a more collaborative form of writing, in the spirit of Mikinaakominis / TransCanadas and the TransCanada project broadly.

27 An earlier, working title for this book was *Re-Storying Land*.

28 See, for instance, Alicia Elliott (2017) and Jen Sookfong Lee (2017). To be clear, these are important essays that rightly call out unbearable injustices in Canadian literature, injustices that must be made right. The critiques are profoundly important. What L'Abbé is asking us to consider is the dynamics that unfold behind the scenes in relation to them: which senior practitioners try to take the reins and to what ends; how the industry and the press try to capitalize on scandal; and how even her speaker, who can see what's going on, can't break free from "guilty ogre-fathers."

29 See youtube.com/watch?v=dy4ZYnJ6jQk&ab_channel=UniversityofCalgary.

30 Here the incapacities of Canadian literature as an industry undermine the more nuanced and productive capacities of Canadian literature as critical cultural practice and academic discipline.

The TransCanada Project and CanLit

1 I am not speaking here on Roy Miki's behalf but sharing my collective understanding; Roy may very well recollect the many conversations we had in different terms.

2 For information about the TransCanada One conference, see smarokamboureli.ca/transcanada-institute-archive/conferences/transcanada-1-2005/. For the TransCanada Two conference, see smarokamboureli.ca/transcanada-institute-archive/conferences/transcanada-two-2007/. For the TransCanada Three, see smarokamboureli.ca/transcanada-institute-archive/conferences/transcanada-three-2009/.

3 The workshop resulted in the collection *Retooling the Humanities* (Coleman and Kamboureli 2011).

4 For an account of the Japanese Canadian Redress movement and its outcomes, see Miki (2004).

5 TIA House is sponsored by Larissa Lai's Canada Research Chair in Creative Writing at the University of Calgary. See tiahouse.ca/about/.

6 For readers interested in finding out more on emergent insurgency, see Lai (2018).

Back to the Future

1 See the CFP: britishassociationforcanadianstudies.files.wordpress.com/2017/08/canada-150.pdf.

Neoliberal Gothic, Settler Social Imaginaries, and the Case for Decolonization on Two Fronts

1 Thanks to Clint Burnham, Amy Chamberlin, Ian Cummins, Keith Denny, Stacy Douglas, Zoe Druick, Margery Fee, Dalie Giroux, Heather Howard, Eva Mackey,

Jody Mason, Susie O'Brien, and Cheryl Suzack for engagement with these ideas, and to audiences at Maladies of the Soul, September 2016, Mikinaakominis/TransCanadas, May 2017, and Cultures of Capitalism, December 2017 for their feedback.

2 On news-media construction of a public memory of residential schools, see Matt James (2017) and Jennifer Henderson (2015).

3 "Don't Call Me Resilient" is the title of a podcast by Vinita Srivastava. See especially Episode 6, "Indigenous land defenders."

4 See Jennifer Henderson (2013) and Angel and Wakeham (2016).

5 In the context of my reading of *Going Home Star—Truth and Reconciliation* as a cultural text participating in the construction of a reductive settler-public imaginary of residential schooling, it is pertinent to observe that the story for the ballet was written by Joseph Boyden. Boyden's willy-nilly acceptance of his mainstream-media promotion to the position of representative Indigenous person, on the basis of vague identity claims, is not unrelated to the work of cultural erasure done by residential schools. My thanks to an anonymous reader for reminding me of this connection.

6 It is pertinent that Barnaby grew up on the Listuguj Mi'kmaq reserve in eastern Quebec. As J. R. Miller observes, "[r]eliance on 'reserve' day schools and travelling missions," not residential schools, was the pattern of Roman Catholic schooling initiatives in Quebec, with the "grand experiment" of assimilative residential school education "effectively dead by the 1680s" (1996, 55).

7 My observations about the anti-Catholicism of the British Gothic novel should not be taken as a defence of the Catholic orders whose dioceses ran many of the residential schools. The Final Report of the TRC includes the call for a resumation of efforts on the part of Roman Catholic churches in Canada to fulfill their Indian Residential Schools Settlement Agreement fundraising obligations in support of Indigenous healing, efforts which were abandoned in 2015.

8 *Restoring Dignity*, a 2000 report of the Law Commission of Canada, included residential schools among institutions in which "children were placed for their education, welfare, rehabilitation or even protection" only to be subjected to abuse by adults bearing institutional authority and to forms of dehumanization associated with "the very nature of institutional life" (2000, 1–2).

9 TallBear is writing about the "genomic rearticulation of indigenous life as the rightful patrimony of global society" (2017, 183), but I am extending her insights to the resourcing of what is called Indigenous resilience.

10 Of course, settler state powers have been, and continue to be, monstrous for Indigenous peoples. On the Indigenous experience of the Canadian welfare state, see Tester and Kulchyski (1994), Shewell (2004), and the autobiography of Maria Campbell, *Halfbreed* (1973). Rather than offering a naive or nostalgic defence of the settler state, I am describing a historical conjuncture in which decolonial critique and neoliberal caricature of state power to some degree coincide, posing

conceptual and practical challenges for serious redress, just redistribution, and restitution of lands.

11 Like the imagery of the residential school, the imagery of the closed prison risks seeming to announce the end of a condition that is very much ongoing, as the statistics on the wildly disproportionate incarceration of Indigenous and Black, compared to white, populations attest. For an example of closed prison tours, see kingstonpentour.com.

12 Erving Goffman's essay "Characteristics of Total Institutions" was published in his book, *Asylums* (1961). He described the "social world of the hospital inmate" as a crystallization of the regime aspired to by institutions in general (4). In his analysis, the institution erected an absolute barrier against the outside world, producing a self systematically "disinfected of identifications," and a form of social organization incompatible with the life of the family (19, 16). The essay helped to mobilize demands based on the rights of the vulnerable to freedom, autonomy, and self-determination.

13 On deinstitutionalization and increased incarceration, see Alison Howell and Jijian Veronka (2012) and Ian Cummins (2016). Unsurprisingly, since the project to dismantle institutional care and empower "stakeholders" in the voluntary sector has been conducted in contexts of government austerity, female relatives have carried a disproportionate burden of the care now renaturalized as a "private" or "domestic" responsibility. Racialized and minoritized populations, especially, have been undersupported, sometimes according to culturalist expectations of a special extended-family caregiving capacity (Langan 1990) offered as justification for the costs of austerity being borne disproportionately, as always, by those already living precarious lives.

Re-storying and Restoring the Buffalo to the Indigenous Plains

1 I have expanded on this argument in "Buffalo Genocide in 19th Century North America: 'Kill, Skin, and Sell'" (Hubbard 2014).

2 See buffalotreaty.com.

Federal State, Feral Culture

1 I am grateful to Smaro Kamboureli and Larissa Lai for feedback on an earlier, much longer, version of this intervention, and to Alison Calder, Warren Cariou, and Jessica McDonald for very helpful conversations about the state of CanLit.

2 See Hayday and Blake (2016).

3 See the section "The Durham Effect" in Blodgett (2004).

4 Le Refus global was a manifesto issued on August 9, 1948, that challenged Quebec's traditional values. Signed by fifteen members of the Automatistes Group, its main text was written by painter Paul-Émile Borduas.

5 Taylor is quoting from Lipsius, *Six Bookes of Politickes*, translated by William Jones (London 1594), 17, quoted in Hale (1995, 360).

Between Empire and Nation

1 I would like to thank Smaro Kamboureli, Larissa Lai, and the organizers of Mikinaakominis/TransCanadas for the opportunity to present an earlier version of this essay and their support throughout the revision process. I would also like to thank my co-panelists—Margery Fee, Sophie McCall, Pauline Wakeham, and Rinaldo Walcott—for conversations and papers that helped clarify my arguments.

2 For an extended discussion of this problem, see Miki (1998, 2004).

3 Two prime examples of this critique are Cho (2010) and Kamboureli (2000).

4 For a discussion of these issues, see Kim and Lee (2015).

5 Karl borrows the notion of global totality from Fredric Jameson and insists that it not be understood as interchangeable with the universal (as in the Hegelian universalizing of the nation-state).

6 I elaborate this point further in my previous study *The Semblance of Identity* (2012).

7 See McKeown (2008). Radhika Mongia (1999) cogently argues that the crisis occasioned by the exclusion of the *Komagata Maru* in 1914 led to the institution of passports and other forms of border control in the British Commonwealth/Empire.

8 For a discussion of Kang Youwei's activities in Canada, including the founding of the Empire Reform Association, see Chen (2014).

9 The Chinese title of *The Chinese Times* is 大漢公報, which literally renders China as the "Great Han." Feng himself wrote later that one of primary goals of the newspapers was to "oppose the Qing and restore the Han." For more information about this newspaper, see Xu and Wu (2021).

10 Chung-shan (Zhongshan) County was renamed in honour of Sun after his death. In Chinese, Sun Yat-sen is usually rendered as Sun Zhongshan.

11 From what I have been able to gather, this story was widely circulated among old-timers, although Chang's interview is the only written version that I have come across.

12 Yee, of course, is one of the most well-known writers of Chinese Canadian historical fiction, particularly for young readers. *Curses* was his second published work, after the groundbreaking *Teach Me to Fly, Skyfighter and Other Stories* (1983). It should be noted that very few works of published fiction for any age group dealing with Chinese Canadian experiences were available at that time.

13 Because the novella takes place over several months, this is likely a reference to Sun's 1910 visit, although the exact timing is unclear.

14 Here and elsewhere in this section, I am indebted to Lauren Cross for her insights on Yee's treatment of Chinese nationalism from a transnational perspective.

15 It should be noted here that the number of Chinese Canadian families in Vancouver at that time was exceedingly small, a result of immigration measures such as the Chinese Head Tax, which resulted in an overwhelmingly male labourer population. At one point, Yee writes: "There weren't many children or women living in Chinatown because of the travel costs and the special head tax that Chinese immigrants had to pay when they came into Canada" (1986, 34). Moreover, the so-called "Sojourner" mentality meant that returning to China was a common trajectory for many migrants.

16 See Zarrow (2012). For some reformers, the Manchu origins of the Qing was not a problem per se. But even in Yee's text, which more or less reproduces the revolutionary position, there is some slippage between an ethnonationalism that excludes Manchus and a recognition that the state or empire was still a polity to which all "Chinese" had a stake. The embrace of racial ideologies also provided a means to place China within a world structured along racial hierarchies, whereby the "yellow" races were being oppressed by the "white races." As Tsu notes, some fin-de-siècle writers would create speculative tales in which the Chinese emerged in the future as a dominant race that showed benevolence to previously oppressed "black" and "red" races (2006, 251–52).

Diplomacy *before* Reconciliation

1 My eternal thanks to Sneja Gunew, Helen Hoy, Asha Varadharajan, the anonymous reviewers, and the editors of this volume for their comments. Remaining oversights or overgeneralizations are mine alone.

2 He expands on this terse comment in his book, *Canadian Law and Indigenous Self-Determination*.

3 Jennifer Henderson and Pauline Wakeham's collection situates the TRC in a wider culture of redress.

4 The expressions "worldview" and "neoliberal capitalism" suggest codified and bounded entities that, of course, can only gesture to the workings of dynamic social discourses.

5 Many disciplines embed colonial assumptions: consider that historians and politics scholars until recently studied mainly Eurowestern cultures and anthropologists study the rest. See Viswanathan (1989) for the origins of the study of English literature in colonial India.

6 Some important Indigenous anthologies of literary criticism are *Looking at the Words of Our People: First Nations Analysis of Literature* (Armstrong 1993); *(Ad)dressing Our Words: Aboriginal Perspectives on Aboriginal Literature* (Ruffo 2001); *Introduction to Indigenous Literary Criticism in Canada* (Macfarlane and Ruffo 2016); and *Learn, Teach, Challenge: Approaching Indigenous Literatures* (Reder and Morra 2016).

7 Several contributors to *Braiding Legal Orders: Implementing the United Nations Declaration on the Rights of Indigenous Peoples* have difficulty with limitations in the wording of section 35 (Borrows 2019, 5–7). This collection suggests "braiding" Indigenous legal orders with national and international law.

8 One outcome of this failure to negotiate was a 500-page coroner's report determining that the policeman was killed in an armed exchange by an unidentifiable Mohawk defender. The report was strongly critical of the initial unnecessary police action. See *Windspeaker* (1995).

9 Manitoba's Aboriginal Justice Implementation Commission (Aboriginal Justice Inquiry 1991) "was established in 1988 in response to two specific incidents: the 1987 trial of two men for the 1971 murder of Helen Betty Osborne, and the 1988 shooting death of J. J. Harper following an encounter with a Winnipeg police officer. These two events raised serious questions as to whether the justice system was failing Aboriginal people" (Aboriginal Justice Inquiry 1991, ch. 1, n.p.). The Public Inquiry Commission on Relations between Indigenous Peoples and Certain Public Services in Québec (Viens Commission 2019) was sparked by Indigenous women in Val d'Or reporting police violence and sexual assault (Quebec 2019).

10 The CBC, "Beyond 94," and the Yellowhead Institute (see Jewell and Mosby 2019) are tracking progress on the TRC Calls to Action.

11 Bill C-15 (2020) was introduced as a private member's bill by then-NDP MP Romeo Saganash (Cree), blocked by the Senate, and died on the order paper when the 2019 election was called. It was reintroduced by the Liberal government in December 2020 and passed in June 2021 as United Nations Declaration on the Rights of Indigenous Peoples Act (S.C. 2021, c. 14).

12 See "Implementing the United Nations Declaration on the Rights of Indigenous Peoples in Canada: Myths and Misrepresentations" (2020). Note that Amnesty International is a member of the Coalition for the Human Rights of Indigenous Peoples. Joseph Slaughter argues that Amnesty's focus on individual prisoners rather than the collective movements they represent is symptomatic of a wider shift to a focus on individual human rights (felt to be nonpartisan) as opposed to support for entire groups under siege by nation-states.

13 See Forrester (2020) for an overview of reactions to the bill; for White Paper 2.0, see Indigenous Activists Network, "UNDRIP Bill C-15 is Deeply Flawed and Must be Rejected," idlenomore.ca/indigenous-networks-and-land-defenders-call-to-reject-bill-c-15. Regarding the framework, Joyce Green comments that it "does not refer to Indigenous nations as governments, instead describing them as legal entities likened to 'natural persons,' a legal term with the potential for the corporatization of Aboriginal and treaty rights" (2019, n.p.). See also Ladner (2001); King and Pasternak (2018); McFarlane and Shabus (2017).

14 Indigenous worldviews share similarities, but they do vary across nations. Although these worldviews permeate all Indigenous cultural production, a

few Indigenous writers have laid out their nation's worldview in detail. See, for example, Atleo (Nuu-chah-nulth) (2004), Bastien (Blackfoot/Siksika) (2004) and Sioui (Huron-Wendat) (1999).

15 For comment on conciliation before reconciliation, see Amagoalik (2012).

16 Who belongs to the "public" in this expression is, of course, always at issue. However, sewage outfalls (Musqueam Indian Reserve), highways, railway lines, oil pipelines (Joeyaska Indian Reserve), and dam floodplains (the Cheslatta Carrier village was flooded for the Kitimat-Kemano aluminium project, 1952) tend to be sited on or through reserves or traditional territories. Coastal Gaslink, Site C dam, the James Bay hydroelectric project, the St. Lawrence Seaway, the Oldman River Dam—the list of these and other major development projects that have impinged on Indigenous territories is long.

17 Even religion: the oath sworn by all government officials requires mention of the Queen, but now individuals may opt out of any mention of (any) God.

18 Treaties cover most, but not all, of Canada. The Government of Canada recognizes seventy historical treaties signed between 1701 and 1923. Modern treaties (sometimes called comprehensive land claims) began to be negotiated after the Supreme Court decision in *Calder et al. v. Attorney General of British Columbia* (1973) recognized Aboriginal title.

19 For example, a recent survey in BC "found 84 per cent of Indigenous respondents reported discrimination in health care, with Indigenous women and girls disproportionately affected. Among Indigenous health-care workers, 52 per cent reported experiencing racial prejudice at work, largely through discriminatory comments by colleagues" (DeRosa 2020, n.p.). See timescolonist.com/local-news/report-finds-systemic-racism-in-bcs-health-care-system-but-no-evidence-of-alcohol-game-4685899.

20 Examining two recently negotiated treaties, the one that formed Nunavut (1999) and the Tsawassen First Nation Final Agreement (2009), Lightfoot notes that these agreements are based on fee-simple or corporate collective land ownership (2016, 184, 190).

21 Two UBC students in what was then called First Nations Studies, Amy Perreault and Karrmen Crey (2018), made a twenty-minute video, *What I Learned in Class Today*. Their research project laid bare some unhappy experiences of their Indigenous classmates at UBC. This video has subsequently been made into the centrepiece of an ongoing project, "How Do You Talk about Indigenous Issues in the Classroom?" The original video makes a very good first assignment for class discussion.

22 This summary is inadequate. The Cree concept of "wahkohtowin" has received considerable attention. Matthew Wildcat gives a good overview of the concept. See Armstrong (2009) on "en'owkin." See also Atleo (2004), Bastien (2004), and Sioui (1999).

From Islamo*phobia* to Islamo*philia*?

1 Please see Kundnani (2015) and some chapters in Kumar (2012). Even though it has been more than two decades since the "clash of civilizations" thesis has been popularized and used specifically against Muslims, it seems that anti-Muslim sentiments, rather than diminishing, might be on the rise in different countries. See also, for example, Bangstad (2014).

2 As Lama Abu-Odeh observes, it is highly curious, for example, that Saba Mahmood's "post-secular" book, *The Politics of Piety*, has enjoyed enormous popularity in Euro-American academia while it remains untranslated into Arabic (2019, 1).

3 A number of people, including Ayaan Hirsi Ali, Irshad Manji, and Azar Nafisi, have acquired international status and fame as "public intellectuals" in this period. For an excellent critical discussion of the work of Azar Nafisi as a "native informer," see Dabashi (2006).

4 See Razack's (2007) references to Talal Asad's critique of secularism.

5 The term is from the title of Tariq Ali's (2002) book.

"Making Things Right"

1 I would like to thank Larissa Lai and Suzette Mayr for creating a space at "Black Lives Out West" (UCalgary November 2017) where I could think through the issues that I wrote about in the original paper. Gratitude to Erica Violet Lee who offered valuable feedback on an earlier draft. Sincerest thanks to Smaro Kamboureli and Larissa Lai for giving me time and for helping me to map a way through my shifting thoughts on Black and Indigenous relations.

2 See *The Black Prairie Archives: An Anthology* (2020).

3 Kanai Elder Wilton Goodstriker notes that there is no word in Blackfoot for "treaty." "The event is simply referred to as '*istsist aokhotspi*' or *iitsinnaihtsiiyo'pi* (the time we made a sacred alliance)."

4 In an email to Smaro Kamboureli, which she read at the conference; see Walcott (2017b).

5 I use "tactics" here in the sense Michel de Certeau developed in *The Practice of Everyday Life* (2011) to distinguish between the "strategies" of the powerful and the "tactics" used to resist those strategies.

Listing Waters

1 For more on Palestinian/Indigenous connections, see Steven Salaita's "Palestinians in Native Poetry," a 2015 talk delivered at the University of Toronto complit.utoronto.ca/events/professor-steven-salaitas-public-lecture-palestine-in-native-american-poetry/) and his *Inter/Nationalism: Decolonizing Native America and Palestine* (2016).

2 See also Anna Maria Tremonti speaking with Niedzviecki, cbc.ca/radio/thecurrent/the-current-for-may-15-2017-1.4112604/i-invoked-cultural-appropriation-in-the-context-of-literature-and-writing-only-hal-niedzviecki-1.4112618.

3 See "Canadian Journalists Support 'Appropriation Prize' after Online Furore," theguardian.com/world/2017/may/13/canadian-journalists-appropriation-prize.

4 See Jesse Wente and Jonathan Kay, "Appropriation vs Artistic Freedom," cbc.ca/player/play/943249475957.

5 Liberal multiculturalism is a major concern in Spivak's *An Aesthetic Education in the Era of Globalization* (2012a), and in particular in "Echo," an essay that, so the "Preface" tells us, began as a response in 1981 to gender inequity in Christopher Lasche's *The Culture of Narcissism*. While "multiculturalism" in Spivak is not limited to the version that became official state culture in Canada, the similarity between official culture and her examination of an ideology that appropriates immigrants but leaves out or ambiguously positions Indigenous, Black, and mixed-race Latinx populations are resonant today. See Spivak's chapter "Teaching for the Times" in the same book (2012a, 137–57), especially page 154.

6 See Spivak's "Introduction" to *An Aesthetic Education* (2012a).

7 Bataille diagnoses the oedipal structure of leftist vanguardism by reference to Ovid's tale of Icarus and the figure of the mole. For a short discussion of this development as a resource for activism today, see my "For Solidarity. Witnessing the Other's Revolution" (2017), *Camera Austria International*, "Sincerity" 139.

8 "Chief Seattle's 1854 Oration"-ver.1 at Suquamish.nsn.us/home/about-us/chief-seattle-speech/

9 Wong has long supported Indigenous activism by serving as reporter as in her contributions to many newsletters and online journals; see, for instance, "Water is All of Us" (2011).

10 A Canadian critic, when writing on catalogues in poetry, insists that the practice is entailed in oral traditions as mnemonic because oral poetry has simple metres. Such conclusions can only be the result of intellectual isolation and lack of acquaintance with poetic traditions of Asia and the Middle East to say the least. It is impossible to judge how such an opinion, were it modified as applying only to Anglo-Saxon and Greek poetry, two traditions noticed by the text, could be produced by reading such texts in transcription. See Northrop Frye, *On Canada* (2003).

11 See "Bruce Lee: A Warrior's Journey" (Little 2000). This quotation is from the documentary and not his poem as quoted by John Little, his biographer.

12 I learned this term from Jacques Derrida before learning it from George Vizenor. For the most sustained consideration of survivance as living in death, see Derrida (2017) and Vizenor (1999).

13 Indigenous stories, knowledge of land, and technologies of living on it, are unique but also shared—these being the skills of survival that enable a people

to adapt to water abuse while also retaining precapitalist lexicons and not as relics of an earlier evolutionary period. Questions of the spirit, cosmology, and religious institution I leave for another occasion and an engagement with Talal Asad's work on agency with which he frames alternatives to secular fundamentalism and as a bridge between faith and secularism within the same social space, family, community, nation. See Asad (2003).

14 See hrw.org/report/2016/06/07/make-it-safe/canadas-obligation-end-first-nations-water-crisis.

15 Translation mine for the purposes of this volume.

16 Spivak takes this phrase from Gregory Bateson's 1972 *Steps to an Ecology of Mind* (Chicago: University of Chicago Press, 2000), p.272.

Living on Unceded Indigenous Territories

1 My deepest thanks are due to several readers who graciously took the time to offer invaluable suggestions on an earlier draft of this paper: Phanuel Antwi, David Chariandy, Wayde Compton, Christine Kim, Sam McKegney, and Deanna Reder. Remaining infelicities are entirely mine.

2 See Walcott and Vernon in this volume for important cautions against simplistically applying the term "settler" in speaking about Black history, especially when reckoning with the ongoing occupation of Indigenous lands. Walcott emphasizes how Black people have acted and spoken out "in defense of our lives against brutal, anti-Black states" (see page 110), while Vernon convincingly argues that the term "settlers of colour" applied to Black people in the Prairies risks bracketing how Black people were "forcibly transported from their homelands and enslaved in other peoples' nations" (see page 242).

3 I am quoting from the Indigenous Literary Studies Association's (2016, n.p.) Program for their Annual Gathering in Calgary, Alberta, in 2016.

4 Writers from this volume have offered creative and critical insights on how to do both intersectional and comparative analyses, specifically Vernon, Walcott, Al-Kassim, Allen, and Moure. Beyond these contributors, there are several models for comparative work that have helped me in writing this chapter, including Allen (2014), Justice (2008), and Wakeham (2017a) in Indigenous literary studies; Cornum (2017), NourbeSe Philip (2017), and Vigil and Miles (2014) in Black and Indigenous studies; and Coleman (2015), Eigenbrod (2012), Fachinger (2014), Lai (2017), and Wong and Christian (2017) in Indigenous and diasporic studies.

5 In thinking about forms of ongoing colonial violence, scholars in Indigenous studies have noted that while Indigenous people are often *excluded* from full participation in Canadian institutions and citizenship rights, a more insidious form of *forced inclusion* also perpetuates colonial relations of domination. An example of forced inclusion is enfranchisement, "a legal process for terminating

a person's Indian status and conferring full Canadian citizenship" (Crey 2009, par. 1). Though this section of the Indian Act was amended in 1951 and 1985, other assimilative practices, laws, and policies continued for decades more, their effects continuing today.

6 See Simpson, "The Place" (2015, 19) and *Dancing* (2011, 86–95) on how Indigenous Nations have built and continue to build relations on shared or overlapping territories.

7 In 1951, certain sections of the Indian Act were repealed that enabled Indigenous peoples to access the legal system in prescribed ways, though formidable institutional barriers persisted well into the late twentieth century, and arguably continue today.

8 There is a substantial and ever-growing body of scholarship on relations between Asian, Asian diasporic, and Indigenous peoples. To name only a few, see Wong (2008), Wong and Christian (2017), Lai (2017), Lew (2017), and Mawani (2009). For a fascinating film on Chinese-Musqueam relations in Vancouver, see director Alejandro Yoshizawa's *All Our Father's Relations* (2016).

9 See Peter Hudson (2000, 2007, 2018), Bertrand Bickersteth (2015), and Joanne Leow (2012).

10 I am paraphrasing Giorgio Caproni's poem, "The Last Homecoming," which Compton uses as the epigraph to his essay, "Hogan's Alley and Retro-speculative Verse" (2005, 109). The first lines read: "I returned there / where I have never been. / Nothing has changed from how it was not."

11 The story is an example of speculative fiction, but it is also a reimagining of the past. Volcanic activity in what is called the Cascadia region of the Pacific Northwest over the past 37 million years, and as recently as 2,350 years ago, contributed to the shaping of the coastline of the Salish Sea, including its islands, mountains, and waterways (De Ruydts 2017).

12 Settler scholar Alix Shield (2018) explains that it is not well known that Mary Capilano narrated many stories to Johnson because when these stories were first published in the *Province;* the narrator was misidentified as Chief Capilano exclusively. I am indebted to Shield, who has done extensive research in uncovering the relationships that are misrepresented in the many versions of Johnson's published stories.

13 Stanley Park displays poles from several Pacific Northwest Coast Nations, but until recently had no poles from Musqueam, Squamish, and Tsleil-Waututh Nations. The most recent pole, by Squamish carver Robert Yelton, was raised in 2009. Another notable piece is a post-and-beam structure by Musqueam artist Susan Point.

14 I borrow "e/racing" from Marlene NourbeSe Philip's article, "Black W/Holes," which carefully compares the "e/racing of the First Nations presence" (2017, 125) with the "erac[ing of] the black presence" (131) in "this space that is canada" (131).

15 "Pheneticizing" is Compton's neologism to describe the act of perceiving racial difference. He argues that pheneticizing is often a more accurate term than "passing." "Passing" is based on the assumption that the racialized subject is deliberately performing an identity while "grammatically absent[ing] the person who reads someone's race" (2010, 22). Yet, the racialized individual is often not doing anything; rather, it is the perceiver who is seeking to categorize and determine that individual's identity.

Landsensing

1 This speech was made during the Roundtable on Indigenous Rights, Land, and Alternatives at Simon Fraser University on March 29, 2015. A video of the panel was available at the conference website (statesofextraction.org), but unfortunately the site is no longer active. I verified the text of this transcription against the video.

2 My argument here is indebted to Dylan Robinson's article "Intergenerational Sense, Intergenerational Responsibility" (2016), which I gestured toward earlier, as well as to Clint Burnham's "Is the TRC a Text?" (2019).

3 Story and transcription copyright 2018, Louis Bird. Anyone wanting to reproduce or quote from the story should seek Mr. Bird's permission.

4 See my article "Wastewest: A State of Mind," in which I discuss Elder Bird's teachings about *pastahowin* (2015, 28–31).

Works Cited

"A Legal Analysis of Genocide: Supplementary Report." National Inquiry into Missing and Murdered Indigenous Women and Girls, Government of Canada, 2019, mmiwg-ffada.ca/wp-content/uploads/2019/06/Supplementary-Report_Genocide.pdf.

Abbas, Sadia. "The Echo Chamber of Freedom: The Muslim Women and the Pretext of Agency." *Boundary* 2, vol. 40, no. 1, 2013, pp. 155–89.

Abel, Jordan. *The Place of Scraps*. Talonbooks, 2013.

Aboriginal Justice Inquiry. *Aboriginal Justice Implementation Commission Final Report*. Aboriginal Justice Implementation Commission, Manitoba, 1991, ajic.mb.ca/reports/ final_ch01.html.

Abraham, Nicolas, and Maria Torok. *The Shell and the Kernel: Renewals of Psychoanalysis*. Edited and translated by Nicholas T. Rand, U of Chicago P, 1994.

Abu-Odeh, Lama. "Post Secularism and the Woman Question." *Georgetown University Law Centre*, 2019, pp. 1-7. scholarship.law.georgetown.edu/cgi/viewcontent .cgi?article=3160&context=facpub.

Adcock, Fleur. "The Limitations of the Current International Human Rights Law System in Regard to Monitoring of Rights. Does it Encourage 'Rights Ritualism?'" International Expert Group Meeting, "Dialogue on an optional protocol to the United Nations Declaration on the Rights of Indigenous Peoples," 27–29 Jan. 2015. ncis.anu.edu.au/_lib/doc/Adcock_Limitations_of_International_Human_Rights_law_sytsem.pdf.

Agamben, Giorgio. "The Thing Itself." In *Potentialities: Collected Essays in Philosophy* by Giorgio Agamben, edited and translated by Daniel Heller-Roazen, Stanford UP, 1999, pp. 27–38.

———. *The Use of Bodies*. Trans. Adam Kotsko. Stanford UP, 2016.

Ahmed, Sarah. "Complaint!" Courageous Conversations Series, 22 Mar. 2021, University of Calgary, youtube.com/watch?v=dy4ZYnJ6jQk&ab_channel=UniversityofCalgary.

Ajzenstat, Janet, et al. *Canada's Founding Debates*, U of Toronto P, 2003.

Al-Azmeh, Aziz. "'Postmodern Obscurantism and 'The Muslim Question.'" *Socialist Register*, no. 39, 2003, pp. 28–50.

Al-Kassim, Dina. "Resistance Terminable and Interminable." In *Derrida/Deleuze/Psychoanalysis*, edited by Gaby Schwab, Columbia UP, 2007, pp. 105–41.

———. "For Solidarity: Witnessing the Revolution of the Other," *Camera Austria*, "Sincerity" 139. 2017. https://camera-austria.at/en/zeitschrift/139-2017-2/. Accessed May 18, 2022.

"Alberta's Black Pioneer Heritage." *Alberta Source*, Dec. 2012, wayback.archive-it.org/2217/20101208160345/http://www.albertasource.ca/Blackpioneers//index.html.

Ali, Tariq. *The Clash of Fundamentalisms: Crusades, Jihads and Modernity*. Verso, 2002.

Allen, Chadwick. "Decolonizing Comparison: Toward a *Trans-Indigenous* Literary Studies." In *The Oxford Handbook of Indigenous American Literature*, edited by James H. Cox and Daniel Heath Justice, Oxford UP, 2014, pp. 377–94.

Almonte, Richard. Introduction. *A Narrative of Thomas Smallwood (Coloured Man)* by Thomas Smallwood, edited by Richard Almonte, Mercury P, 2000, pp. 9–23.

Altamirano-Jiménez, Isabel. *Indigenous Encounters with Neoliberalism: Place, Women and the Environment in Canada and Mexico*. U of British Columbia P, 2013.

Althusser, Louis. 1971. "Ideology and Ideological State Apparatuses (Notes towards an Investigation) (January-April 1969)." In *Lenin and Philosophy and Other Essays*, trans. by Ben Brewster. New York: Monthly Review Press, pp. 127–86.

Amagoalik, John. "Reconciliation or Conciliation? An Inuit Perspective." In *"Speaking My Truth": Reflections on Reconciliation and Residential School*, edited by Shelagh Rogers et al., Aboriginal Healing Foundation, 2012, pp. 37–45.

André, F. B. *What Belongs: Stories*. Ronsdale, 2007.

Angel, Naomi, and Pauline Wakeham. "Witnessing In Camera: Photographic Reflections on Truth and Reconciliation." In *Arts of Engagement: Taking Aesthetic Action in and beyond the Truth and Reconciliation Commission of Canada*, edited by Dylan Robinson and Keavy Martin, Wilfrid Laurier UP, 2016, pp. 93–134.

Anielski, Mark, and Colin Soskolne. "Genuine Progress Indicator (GPI) Accounting: Relating Ecological Integrity to Human Health and Well-Being." In *Environmental Ethics: Divergence and Convergence*, edited by Susan Armstrong and Richard Botzler, McGraw-Hill, 2004, pp. 537–46.

Anker, Elizabeth S., and Rita Felski, eds. *Critique and Postcritique*. Duke UP, 2017.

Antwi, Phanuel, and David Chariandy. Introduction. *Writing Black Canadas*, special issue of *Transition*, edited by Phanuel Antwi and David Chariandy, no. 124, 2017, pp. 31–37.

Arat-Koç, Sedef. "Invisibilized, Individualized, and Culturalized: Paradoxical Invisibility and Hyper-visibility of Gender in Policy Making and Policy Discourse in Neoliberal Canada." *Canadian Woman Studies/Les cahiers de la femme*, vol. 29, no. 3 (Spring/Summer), 2012, pp. 6–17.

———. 2014. "Dance of Orientalisms and Waves of Catastrophes: Culturalism and Pragmatism in Imperial Approaches to Islam and the Middle East." *Third World Quarterly*, vol. 35, no. 9, 2014, pp. 1656–71.

Armstrong, Jeannette. *Slash*. Theytus Books, 1985.

———, ed. *Looking at the Words of Our People: First Nations Analysis of Literature*. Theytus Books, 1993.

———. "Land Speaking." In *Speaking for the Generations: Native Writers on Writing*, edited by Simon J. Ortiz, Arizona UP, 1998, 175–94.

———. "Four Decades: An Anthology of Canadian Native Poetry from 1960 to 2000." In *Native Poetry in Canada: A Contemporary Anthology*, edited by Jeannette Armstrong and Lally Grauer, Broadview, 2001, x–xx.

———. "En'owkin: What It Means to a Sustainable Community." Center for Ecoliteracy, 25 Oct 2009. ecoliteracy.org/article/enowkin-what-it-means-sustainable-community.

Asad, Talal. *Formations of the Secular: Christianity, Islam, Modernity*. Stanford UP, 2003.

Atleo, E. Richard (Umeek). *Tsawalk: A Nuu-Chah-Nulth Worldview*. U of British Columbia P, 2004.

Austin, David. *Fear of a Black Nation: Race, Sex, and Security in Sixties Montreal*. Montreal: Between the Lines, 2013.

Bakhtin, M. M. *The Dialogic Imagination: Four Essays*. Translated by Caryl Emerson and Michael Holquist, edited by Michael Holquist, U of Texas P, 1981.

Ballantyne, Darcy, Paul Barrett, Camille Isaacs and Kris Singh. "The Unbearable Whiteness of CanLit." *The Walrus*. 26 July 2017, thewalrus.ca/the-unbearable-whiteness-of-canlit/.

Balibar, Étienne. *Secularisms and Cosmopolitanism: Critical Hypotheses on Religion and Politics*. Translated by G. M. Goshgarian, Columbia UP, 2018.

Bangstad, Sindre. "The Weight of Words: The Freedom of Expression Debate in Norway." *Race and Class*, vol. 55, no. 4, 2014, pp. 8–28.

Bannerji, Himani. *The Dark Side of the Nation: Essays on Multiculturalism, Nationalism and Gender*. Canadian Scholars' P, 2000.

———. *Demography and Democracy: Essays on Nationalism, Gender and Democracy.* Canadian Scholars' P, 2011.

Barbeau, Marius. *Totem Poles.* 2 volumes. National Museum of Canada, 1950.

Barman, Jean. *The West Beyond the West: A History of British Columbia.* 3rd ed., U of Toronto P, 2007.

Barnaby, Jeff, director. *Rhymes for Young Ghouls.* Prospector Films, 2013.

———. Audio commentary, *Rhymes for Young Ghouls*, Entertainment One Films Canada, 2014.

Barrera, Jorge. "Author Joseph Boyden's shape-shifting Indigenous identity," *APTN National News*, 23 Dec. 2016, aptnnews.ca/national-news/author-joseph-boydens-shape-shifting-indigenous-identity.

Bassel, Leah. "Silencing to Protect: The Debate Over Women's Rights in France and Canada." In *Silencing Human Rights: Critical Engagements with a Contested Project*, edited by Gurminder K. Bhambra and Robbie Shilliam, Palgrave Macmillan, 2009, pp. 166–83.

Bastien, Betty. *Blackfoot Ways of Knowing: The Worldview of the Siksikaitsakapi.* U of Calgary P, 2004.

Bataille, Georges. "The Language of Flowers." In *Visions of Excess: Selected Writings, 1927–1939*, translated by Allan Stoekl, Carl L. Lovitt, and Donald M. Leslie Jr., edited by Allan Stoekl, U of Minnesota P, 1985, pp. 10–14.

———. "The Old Mole and the Prefix Sur in the Words Surhomme and Surrealist." In *Visions of Excess: Selected Writings, 1927–1939*, translated by Allan Stoekl, Carl L. Lovitt, and Donald M. Leslie Jr., edited by Allan Stoekl, University of Minnesota P, 1985, 32–44.

———. "The Practice of Joy Before Death." In *Visions of Excess: Selected Writings, 1927–1939*, translated by Allan Stoekl, Carl L. Lovitt, and Donald M. Leslie Jr., edited by Allan Stoekl, 1985, pp. 235–39.

Bateson, Gregory. *Steps to an Ecology of Mind.* U of Chicago P, 2000.

Battiste, Marie, and James (Sa'ke'j) Youngblood Henderson. *Protecting Indigenous Knowledge and Heritage: A Global Challenge.* Purich, 2000.

Batzke, Ina, Eric C. Erbacher, Linda M. Heß, and Corinna Lenhardt, eds. *Exploring the Fantastic: Genre, Ideology, and Popular Culture.* Transcript Verlag, 2018.

Bauman, Zygmunt. *Wasted Lives: Modernity and Its Outcasts.* Polity, 2003.

Behn, Caleb. "Site C Dam Project Betrays Trudeau's Commitment to First Nations, Say Critics." Interview by Robyn Bresnahan. *CBC Radio*, 24 Aug. 2016. cbc.ca/radio/thecurrent/the-current-for-august-24-2016-1.3733551/site-c-dam-project-betrays-trudeau-s-commitment-to-first-nations-say-critics-1.3733566.

Beier, J. Marshall, ed. *Indigenous Diplomacies.* Palgrave Macmillan, 2009.

Berlant, Lauren. *Queen of America Goes to Washington City: Essays on Sex and Citizenship*. Duke UP, 1997.

———. *Cruel Optimism*. Duke UP, 2011.

"Beyond 94." Canadian Broadcasting Corporation. newsinteractives.cbc.ca/longform-single/beyond-94?&cta=1.

Bhandar, Davina. "Cultural Politics: Disciplining Citizenship." *Citizenship Studies*, vol. 14, no. 3, 2010, pp. 331–43.

Bickersteth, Bertrand. "Bordering on African American: Wayde Compton and the Readability of Blackness." *University of Toronto Quarterly*, vol. 84, no. 1, 2015, pp. 55–77.

"Bill C-15." House of Commons of Canada. parl.ca/DocumentViewer/en/43-2/bill/C-15/first-reading.

Bird, Louis. "Story of the Man Who Shot Thunderbird." Oral story. Cree Stories Event, 10 Aug. 2018, Aqua Books, Winnipeg.

Blackstock, Cindy. "Canadians Must Stop Normalizing Inequality for Indigenous People." *Maclean's Magazine*, 9 Dec. 2019, macleans.ca/opinion/canada-must-stop-normalizing-inequality-for-indigenous-people.

Blodgett, E. D. "Francophone writing." In *The Cambridge Companion to Canadian Literature*, edited by Eva-Marie Kröller, Cambridge UP, 2004, pp. 49–69.

Blühdorn, Ingolfur. "Post-Ecologist Governmentality: Post-Democracy, Post-Politics and the Politics of Unsustainability." In *The Post-Political and Its Discontents: Spaces of Depoliticisation, Spectres of Radical Politics*, edited by Japhy Wilson and Erik Swyngedouw, Edinburgh UP, 2015, pp. 146–66.

Borrows, John. *Recovering Canada: The Resurgence of Indigenous Law*. U of Toronto P, 2002.

———. "Introduction." In *Braiding Legal Orders: Implementing the United Nations Declaration on the Rights of Indigenous Peoples*, edited by John Borrows et al., McGill-Queen's UP, 2019, pp. 1-9.

Bourdieu, Pierre. *On the State: Lectures at the College de France, 1989–1992*. Translated by David Fernbach, edited by Patrick Champagne et al., Polity, 2014.

Brand, Dionne. *Bread Out of Stone: Recollections, Sex, Recognitions, Race, Dreaming, Politics*. Coach House P, 1994.

———. *Map to the Door of No Return*. Vintage, 2002.

———. *What We All Long For*. Knopf, 2005.

Brown, Rosemary. *Being Brown*. Random House, 1989.

Burnham, Clint. "Is the TRC a Text?" 2019. Unpublished Paper.

Butler, Judith. *Bodies That Matter: On the Discursive Limits of "Sex."* Routledge, 1993.

Byrd, Jodi. *Transit of Empire: Indigenous Critiques of Colonialism*. U of Minnesota P, 2011.

Cadena, Marisol de la . *Earth Beings: Ecologies of Practice across Andean Worlds.* Duke UP, 2015.

Cajete, G. *Look to the mountain: An ecology of Indigenous education.* Kivakí P, 1994.

Calder et al. v. Attorney General of British Columbia. SCR 313, Supreme Court of Canada.

Campbell, Maria. *Half-Breed.* Formac Publishing, 1973.

———. *Halfbreed.* 1973. Penguin Random House, 2019.

Canada, Department of Justice. "Implementing the United Nations Declaration on the Rights of Indigenous Peoples in Canada." n.d. justice.gc.ca/eng/declaration/index.html.

Cariou, Warren. "Wastewest: A State of Mind." In *Sustaining the West: Cultural Responses to Canadian Environments*, edited by Liza Piper and Lisa Szabo-Jones, Wilfrid Laurier UP, 2015, pp. 23–32.

Carolino, Bernise. "Bill C-15 to Affirm UNDRIP as Human Rights Instrument Applicable to Canadian Law." *Canadian Lawyer*, Dec. 2020, canadianlawyermag.com/practice-areas/indigenous/bill-c-15-to-affirm-undrip-as-human-rights-instrument-applicable-to-canadian-law/336059.

Castro-Gómez, Santiago. "The Missing Chapter of Empire: Postmodern Reorganization of Coloniality and Post-Fordist Capitalism." *Cultural Studies*, vol. 21, no. 2–3, 2007, 428–48.

Certeau, Michel de. *The Practice of Everyday Life.* Translated by Steven Rendall. U of California P, 2011.

Chambers, Nadine. "Sometimes Clocks Turn Back for Us to Move Forward: Reflections on Black and Indigenous Geographies." *Canada and Beyond*, no. 8, 2019, uhu.es/publicaciones/ojs/index.php/CanadaBeyond/article/view/4566.

Chandler, David, and Julian Reid. "Being in Being: Contesting the Ontopolitics of Indigeneity." *The European Legacy: Toward New Paradigms*, vol. 23, no. 3, 2018, pp. 251–68.

Chariandy, David. *Soucouyant.* Arsenal Pulp, 2007.

Chen, Zhongping. "Kang Youwei's Activities in Canada and the Reformist Movement Among the Global Chinese Diaspora, 1899–1909." *Twentieth Century China*, vol. 39, no. 1, 2014, pp. 3–23.

Cho, Lily. *Eating Chinese: Culture on the Menu in Small Town Canada.* U of Toronto P, 2010.

Christian, Barbara. "Fixing Methodologies: *Beloved.*" *Cultural Critique*, no. 24, Spring 1993, pp. 5–15.

Christie, Gordon. *Canadian Law and Indigenous Self-Determination: A Naturalist Analysis.* U of Toronto P, 2019.

———. "How Can the Canadian Jurisprudence on Section 35 be Decolonized?" *Peter A. Allard School of Law*, allard.ubc.ca/about-us/our-people/gordon-christie. n.d

Clarke, George Elliott. *George and Rue*. Harper Perennial, 2005.

———. *Whylah Falls*. Polestar, 2011.

———. "Bring Da Noise: The Poetics of Performance, chez d'bi.young and Oni Joseph." *Directions Home: Approaches to African-Canadian Literature*, U of Toronto P, 2012, pp. 176–89.

Clements, Marie. *Burning Vision*. Talonbooks, 2002.

———. *The Unnatural and Accidental Women*. Talonbooks, 2005.

———. Reading and Talk at Simon Fraser University. 26 Nov. 2009, Simon Fraser U, Burnaby. Talk.

———. "Interview: *The Road Forward*: An Innovative Documentary Explores Indigenous Activism through Songs." Interview by Tom Power. CBC, 26 Apr. 2017. cbc.ca/radio/q/ wednesday-april-26-2017-bob-mankoff-marie-clements-and-more-1.4082549/the-road-forward-an-innovative-documentary-explores-indigenous-activism-through-songs-1.4082561.

———. director. *The Road Forward*. Produced by Shirley Vercruysse, music by Wayne Lavallee, National Film Board of Canada, 2017.

Coleman, Daniel. *White Civility: The Literary Project of English Canada*. U of Toronto P, 2006.

———. "Indigenous Place and Diaspora Space: of Literalism and Abstraction." *Settler Colonial Studies*, vol. 6, no. 1, 2015, pp. 1–16.

Coleman, Daniel, and Smaro Kamboureli, eds. *Retooling the Humanities: The Culture of Research in Canadian Universities*. U of Alberta P, 2011.

Compton, Wayde. *Performance Bond*. Arsenal Pulp, 2004.

———. "Rune." *Performance Bond*. Arsenal Pulp, 2004, pp. 111-56.

———. "Hogan's Alley and Retro-speculative Verse." *West Coast Line*, vol. 39, no. 2, 2005, pp. 109-15.

———. *After Canaan: Essays on Race, Writing, and Region*. Arsenal Pulp, 2010.

———. *The Outer Harbour: Stories*. Arsenal Pulp, 2015.

———. Personal communication. 5 Mar. 2015. Email.

Cooper, Afua. *The Hanging of Angelique*. Harper Collins, 2006.

Cooper-Bolam, Trina. "On the Call for a Residential Schools National Monument." *Journal of Canadian Studies*, vol. 52, no. 1, Winter 2018, pp. 57–81.

Copley, John. "Lebret Residential School Petroglyphs on Display at SNAP Gallery in Edmonton." *Alberta Native News*, 24 Jan. 2016, albertanativenews.com/lebret-residential-petroglyphs-on-display-at-snap-gallery-in-edmonton.

Cornum, Lou. "The Space NDN's Star Map." In *Read, Listen, Tell: Indigenous Stories from Turtle Island*, edited by Sophie McCall, Deanna Reder, David Gaertner, and Gabrielle L'Hirondelle Hill, Wilfrid Laurier UP, 2017, pp. 364–71.

Coulthard, Glen Sean. "Subjects of Empire: Indigenous Politics and the 'Politics of Recognition' in Canada." *Contemporary Political Theory*, no. 6, 2007, pp. 437–60.

———. *Red Skin White Masks: Rejecting the Colonial Politics of Recognition*. U of Minnesota P, 2014.

Couture, Selena. "Theatrical Activism in Vancouver: From the Native Brotherhood and Sisterhood of BC to Marie Clements's The Road Forward and Back..." *Canadian Theatre Review*, no. 164, 2015, pp. 44–50.

Craddock, Andrea, Mary Madsen, Rita Wong, et al. "An Open Letter from NDP Members about Site C." *The Tyee*, 2 Feb. 2018, thetyee.ca/Opinion/2018/02/02/Open-Letter-NDP-Site-C/.

Crey, Karrmen. "Enfranchisement." In *Indigenous Foundations*. First Nations Studies Program, UBC, 2009, indigenousfoundations.arts.ubc.ca/enfranchisement/.

Crey, Karrmen, and Erin Hanson. "Indian Status." n.d. indigenousfoundations.arts.ubc.ca/indian_status/.

Crosby, Andy. "The Truth about Treaties: Internal Government Documents Reveal Canada's Position at the Negotiating Table." *Briarpatch*, 30 June 2017, briarpatchmagazine.com/ articles/view/truth-about-treaties.

Culhane, Dara. *The Pleasure of the Crown: Anthropology, Law and First Nations*. Talonbooks, 1997.

Cummins, Ian. "Deinstitutionalization: Mental Health Services in the Age of Neoliberalism." *Social Policy and Social Work in Transition*, vol. 1, no. 2, 2010, pp. 55–74.

———. *Mental Health and the Criminal Justice System: A Social Work Perspective*. Critical Publishing, 2016.

Dabashi, Hamid. "Native Informers and the Making of American Empire." *Al Ahram Weekly*, 1 June. 2006, weekly.ahram.org.eg/2006/797/special.htm

Darwish, Mahmoud. "Eleven Planets." In *If I Were Another*. Translated by Fady Joudah, Farrar Straus & Giroux, 2009, pp. 57–98.

———. *If I Were Another*. Translated by Fady Joudah, Farrar Straus & Giroux, 2009.

———. "The 'Red Indian's' Penultimate Speech to the White Man Kivakí." *"If I touch the depths of your heart": The Human Promise of Poetry in Memories of Mahmoud Darwish*, special issue of *Human Architecture: Journal of the Sociology of Self-Knowledge*, no. 7, 2009, pp. 19–25.

———. "'Exile Is So Strong Within Me, I May Bring It to the Land': A Landmark 1996 Interview with Mahmoud Darwish." Interview by Helit Yeshurun. *Journal of Palestine Studies*, vol. 42, no. 1, Autumn 2012, pp. 46–70.

De Ruydts, Francois-Xavier. "Lava Land: The Story of Canada's Volcanic Past Is Written in the Mountains of the Pacific Northwest." *Canada's History*, 14 Jan. 2017, canadashistory ca/explore/environment/lava-land.

Dean, Amber. *Remembering Vancouver's Disappeared Women: Settler Colonialism and the Difficulty of Inheritance*. U of Toronto P, 2015.

Dean, Mitchell, and Kaspar Villadsen. *State Phobia and Civil Society: The Political Legacy of Michel Foucault*. Stanford UP, 2016.

Deen, Ishara. *God Smites and Other Muslim Girl Problems: Asiya Haque Mystery #1*. Deeya, 2016.

DeRosa, Katie. "Report Finds Systemic Racism in BC's Health Care System," *Victoria Times Colonist*, 30 Nov. 2020, n.p.

Derrida, Jacques. *Specters of Marx: The State of the Debt, the Work of Mourning and the New International*. Translated by Peggy Kamuf. Routledge, 1994.

———. "The Beast and the Sovereign." Vol. 2, *The Seminars of Jacques Derrida*, translated by Geoffrey Bennington, U of Chicago P, 2017.

Dhawan, Nikita. "Coercive Cosmopolitanism and Impossible Solidarities." *Qui Parle: Critical Humanities and Social Sciences*, vol. 22, no. 1, 2013, pp. 139–66.

Ditmars, Hadani. "Palestinians and Canadian Natives Join Hands to Protest Colonization." *Israel News*, 29 Jan. 2013, hadaniditmars.com/articles/haaretz/palestinians_and_canadian_natives_join_hands_to_protest_colonization_haaretz_by_hadani_ditmars.pdf.

Diverlus, Rodney, Sandy Hudson, and Syrus Marcus Ware. *Until We Are Free: Reflections on Black Lives Matter Canada*. U of Regina P, 2020.

Dobrowolsky, Alexandra. "Interrogating 'Invisibilization' and 'Instrumentalization': Women and Current Citizenship Trends in Canada." *Citizenship Studies*, vol. 12, no. 5, 2008, 465–79.

Doctor, Farzana. *Six Meters of Pavement*. Dundurn, 2001.

———. *Stealing Nasreen*. Inanna Publications and Education, 2007.

———. *Seven*. Toronto: Dundurn, 2020.

Dubois, Sophie. *Refus Global: Histoire d'une réception partielle*. Presse universitaire de L'Université de Montréal, 2017.

Dyck, Erika. "Dismantling the Asylum and Charting New Pathways into the Community: Mental Health Care in Twentieth Century Canada." *Histoire sociale/Social History*, vol. 44, no. 88, 2011, pp. 181–96.

Eigenbrod, Renate. "Diasporic Longings: (Re)Figurations of Home and Homelessness in Richard Wagamese's Work." In *Cultural Grammars of Nation, Diaspora, and Indigeneity in Canada*, edited by Christine Kim, Sophie McCall, and Melina Baum Singer, Wilfrid Laurier UP, 2012, pp. 135–51.

Elliott, Alicia. "CanLit Is a Raging Dumpster Fire." *Open Book*, 17 Sept. 2017, open-book.ca/Columnists/CanLit-is-a-Raging-Dumpster-Fire.

———. "CanLit Is a Raging Dumpster Fire." In *Refuse: CanLit in Ruins*, edited by Hannah McGregor, Julie Rak, and Erin Wunker, Book*hug, 2018, pp. 93–98.

Enright, Robert. "RWB's Going Home Star—Truth and Reconciliation Is Inspired and Inspiring." *CBC News*, 2 Oct. 2014, cbc.ca/news/canada/manitoba/rwb-s-going-home-star-truth-and-reconciliation-is-inspired-and-inspiring-1.2785096.

Everett, Dianna. "Lynching." *Oklahoma Historical Society*, In *The Encyclopedia of Oklahoma History and Culture*, Oklahoma Historical Society, n.d. okhistory.org/publications/enc/entry.php?entry=LY001.

Fachinger, Petra. "Intersections of Diaspora and Indigeneity: The Standoff at Kahnesatake in Lee Maracle's *Sundogs* and Tessa McWatt's *Out of My Skin*." *Canadian Literature*, no. 220, 2014, pp. 74–91.

Fagan, Kristina R. "Tewatatha:Wi: Aboriginal Nationalism in Taiaiake Alfred's *Peace, Power, Righteousness: An Indigenous Manifesto*." *American Indian Quarterly*, vol. 28, no. 1, 2004, pp. 12–29.

Fanon, Frantz. *The Wretched of the Earth*. Translated by Constance Farrington, Grove P, 1963.

Fatona, Andrea. *Where Outreach Meets Outrage: Racial Equity at the Canada Council for the Arts (1989-1999)*. 2011. U of Toronto, PhD dissertation. *T Space*, tspace.library.utoronto.ca/handle/1807/31747

Foggo, Cheryl. *Pourin' Down Rain: A Black Woman Claims her Place in the Canadian West*. Brush Education, 1990.

———. director. *John Ware Reclaimed*. National Film Board of Canada, 2020.

Forrester, Brett. "Battle Brewing over UNDRIP: A Primer on Government Bill C-15." APTN (Aboriginal Peoples Television Network), 15 Dec. 2020, aptnnews.ca/national-news/battle-brewing-over-undrip-a-primer-on-government-bill-c-15/

Foster, Cecil. *A Place Called Heaven: The Meaning of Being Black in Canada*. HarperCollins, 2002.

Foucault, Michel. "Governmentality." In *The Foucault Effect: Studies in Governmentality*, edited by Graham Burchell, Colin Gordon, and Peter Miller, U of Chicago P, 1991, pp. 87–104.

Freire, Paulo. *Pedagogy of the Oppressed*. Continuum, 2005.

Frye, Northrop. *On Canada*, Vol. 12. Edited by Jean O'Grady and David Staines, U of Toronto P, 2003.

Gagnon, Monika Kin. *Other Conundrums: Race, Culture and Canadian Art*. Arsenal Pulp, Artspeak and Kamloops Art Gallery, 2000.

Gago, Verónica, and Sandro Mezzadra. "A Critique of the Extractive Operations of Capital: Toward an Expanded Concept of Extractivism." *Rethinking Marxism*, vol. 29, no. 4, 2017, pp. 574–91.

Gaikezheyongai, Sally. *The Seven Fires: An Ojibway Prophecy*. Sister Vision P, 1994.

Garneau, David. "Imaginary Spaces of Conciliation and Reconciliation: Art, Curation, and Healing." In *Arts of Engagement: Taking Aesthetic Action in and Beyond the Truth and Reconciliation Commission*, edited by Dylan Robinson and Keavy Martin, Wilfrid Laurier UP, 2016, pp. 21–41.

Gilmour, David. *Lebanon: The Fractured Country*. St. Martin's P, 1983.

Gilroy, Paul. *There Ain't No Black in the Union Jack the Cultural Politics of Race and Nation*. Unwin Hyman, 1987.

———. *Small Acts: Thoughts and Politics of Black Culture*. Serpent's Tail, 1993.

Glissant, Édouard. *Poetics of Relation*. Translated by Betsy Wing, U of Michigan P, 1997.

Goffman, Erving. *Asylums: Essays on the Social Situation of Mental Patients and Other Inmates*. Anchor, 1961.

Goldberg, David Theo. "Racial Europeanization." *Ethnic and Racial Studies*, vol. 29, no. 2, 2006, pp. 331–64.

Goodstriker, Wilton. "Otsistsi Pakssaisstoyiih Pi (the Year When the Winter Was Open and Cold)." In *The True Spirit and Original Intent of Treaty 7*, edited by Walter Hildebrandt, Sarah Carter, Dorothy First Rider, and Treaty 7 Tribal Council. McGill-Queen's UP, 1996, pp. 3–64.

Gopal, Priyamvada. "Speaking with Difficulty: Feminism and Antiracism in Britain after 9/11." *Feminist Studies*, vol. 39, no. 1, 2013, pp. 98–118.

Gordon, Avery. *Ghostly Matters: Haunting and the Sociological Imagination*. U of Minnesota P, 1997.

Government of Canada. 1912. *Order-in-Council No. 1324*.

———. "Overview of a Recognition and Implementation of Indigenous Rights Framework." Crown-Indigenous Relations and Northern Affairs, n.d. rcaanc-cirnac.gc.ca/eng/1536350959665/1539959903708.

Gray, Charlotte. "It's Our Party and We'll Complain If We Want to: Why Canada's Sesquicentennial Failed to Live up to the Hype." *Globe and Mail*, 30 Dec. 2017, pp. O1, 4.

Green, Joyce. "It's Time for a Recognition of Wrongs Framework" *Policy Options*, 26 Sept. 2019, policyoptions.irpp.org/magazines/september-2019/its-time-for-a-recognition-of-wrongs-framework/.

Guerin v. The Queen. 2 SCR 335, Supreme Court of Canada, 1984, scc-csc.lexum.com/scc-csc/scc-csc/en/item/2495/index.do.

Habib, Samra. *We Have Always Been Here: A Queer Muslim Memoir*. Viking, 2019.
Hamilton, Sylvia. *And I Alone Escaped to Tell You*. Gaspereau, 2014.
Hanson, Erin. "The Marginalization of Indigenous Women." In *Indigenous Foundations*, Critical Indigenous Studies, University of British Columbia, n.d. indigenousfoundations.arts.ubc.ca /marginalization_of_aboriginal_women/.
Haraway, Donna. "Situated Knowledges: The Science Question in Feminism and the Privilege of Partial Perspective." *Feminist Studies*, vol. 14, no. 3, 1988, pp. 575–99.
Harootunian, Harry. *Marx After Marx: History and Time in the Expansion of Capitalism*. Columbia UP, 2015.
Hayday, Matthew, and Raymond B. Blake, eds. *Celebrating Canada*. Vol. 1, *Holidays, National Days, and the Crafting of Identities*. U of Toronto P, 2016.
Heer, Jeet. *"Too Asian?": Racism, Privilege, and Post-Secondary Education*. Between the Lines, 2012.
Henderson, James (Sa'ke'j) Youngblood. *Indigenous Diplomacy and the Rights of Peoples: Achieving UN Recognition*. Purich, 2008.
———. "Incomprehensible Canada." In *Reconciling Canada: Critical Perspectives on the Culture of Redress*, edited by Jennifer Henderson and Pauline Wakeham, U of Toronto P, 2013, pp. 115–28.
Henderson, Jennifer. "Transparency, Spectatorship, Accountability: Indigenous Families in Settler-State 'Post-Democracies.'" *English Studies in Canada*, vol. 38, no. 3-4, 2012, pp. 299–330.
———. "The Camp, the School, and the Child: Discursive Exchanges and (Neo) liberal Axioms in the Culture of Redress." In *Reconciling Canada: Critical Perspectives on the Culture of Redress*, edited by Jennifer Henderson and Pauline Wakeham, U of Toronto P, 2013, pp. 63–83.
———. "Residential Schools and Opinion-Making in the Era of Traumatized Subjects and Taxpayer Citizens." *Journal of Canadian Studies*, vol. 49, no. 1, 2015, pp. 5–43.
Henderson, Jennifer, and Keith Denny. "The Resilient Child, Human Development, and the 'Post-Democracy.'" *Biosocieties*, vol. 10, no. 3, 2015, pp. 352–78.
Henderson, Jennifer, and Pauline Wakeham, eds. *Reconciling Canada: Critical Perspectives on the Culture of Redress*. U of Toronto P, 2013.
Hildebrandt, Walter, Dorothy First Rider, Sarah Carter, and Treaty 7 Tribal Council, eds. *The True Spirit and Original Intent of Treaty 7*. McGill-Queen's UP, 1996.
Hill, Lawrence. *The Book of Negroes*. Harper Collins, 2011.
Howard, Heather. "Historification, Healing, and the Precarity of Being Well: 'How We Remember, Teaches Us How to Live.'" Keynote address at the Memory at

the Intersection of Mass Violence and Socioeconomic Inequality Workshop, 14 Apr. 2018, Saint Paul U, Ottawa. Keynote Address.

Howell, Alison, and Jijian Veronka. "Introduction: The Politics of Resilience and Recovery in Mental Health Care." *Studies in Social Justice*, vol. 6, no. 1, 2012, pp. 1–7.

Hubbard, Tasha, director. *Buffalo Calling*. Buffalo Song Productions Inc. and the Banff Centre of the Arts, 2013.

———. "Buffalo Genocide in 19th Century North America: 'Kill, Skin, and Sell.'" In *Colonial Genocide and Indigenous North America*, edited by Andrew Woolford, Jeff Benvuto, and Alex Hinton, Duke UP, 2014, pp. 292–305.

Hudson, Peter. "The Lost Tribe of a Lost Tribe: Black British Columbia and the Poetics of Space." In *Black Geographies and the Politics of Place*, edited by Katherine McKittrick and Clyde Woods, Between the Lines P, 2007, pp. 154–76.

Hunt, Sarah. "The Past Names Nothing Anyplace: Wayde Compton, C.S. Giscombe, and the Poetics of Black British Columbia." *Canadian Review of American Studies*, vol. 30, no. 2, 2000, pp. 229–36.

———. "Rupturing Colonialscapes: Politicizing the Relational Sites and Scales of Indigenous Resurgence." 16 Jan. 2018, Simon Fraser U.

———. "Violence, Law and the Everyday Politics of Recognition: Comments on Glen Coulthard's *Red Skin, White Masks*." Conference presentation at Native American and Indigenous Studies Association (NAISA), 28 Feb. 2018, Washington, DC.

Huntington, Samuel. *Clash of Civilizations and the Remaking of World Order*. Simon and Schuster, 1996.

Hussain, Saima. *The Muslimah Who Fell to Earth: Personal Stories by Canadian Muslim Women*. Mawenzi House Publishers, 2016.

"Implementing the United Nations Declaration on the Rights of Indigenous Peoples in Canada: Myths and Misrepresentations." Coalition for the Human Rights of Indigenous Peoples, 2020, afn.ca/wp-content/uploads/2020/11/UNDRIP_Implementation_ENG.pdf

Indigenous Activists Networks, et al. "On 50th Anniversary of the 1969 White Paper on Indian Policy Indigenous Activist Networks Condemn the Trudeau Government's Termination Legislation." *Indigenous Policy Journal*, vol. 30, no. 3, 2019, indigenouspolicy.org/ index.php/ipj/article/view/647/629.

Indigenous Literary Studies Association. "Storying Solidarities: Sites of Autonomy and Alliance in Indigenous Literary Arts." Indigenous Literary Studies Association (ILSA) Program, Mohkinstsis / Calgary, 28–29 May 2016.

IndigenousXca. [@IndigenousXca]. "Black People Are Indigenous." *Twitter*, 18 June 2020, twitter.com/ indigenousxca/status/1273692394047909891.

Itter, Carole, and Daphne Marlatt. *Opening Doors: Vancouver's East End*. Harbour Publishing, 1979.

Jacobs, Madelaine Christine. *Assimilation through Incarceration: The Geographic Imposition of Canadian Law over Indigenous Peoples*. 2012. Queen's University, PhD dissertation.

Jalaluddin, Uzma. *Ayesha At Last*. Harper Avenue Publishing, 2018.

James, Matt. "Changing the Subject: The TRC, Its National Events, and the Displacement of Substantive Reconciliation in Canadian Media Representations." *Journal of Canadian Studies*, vol. 51, no. 2, 2017, pp. 362–97.

Jameson, Fredric. *The Political Unconscious: Narrative as a Socially Symbolic Act*. Cornell UP, 1981.

Jewell, Eva, and Ian Mosby. "Calls to Action Accountability: A Status Update on Reconciliation." Yellowhead Institute, 2019, yellowheadinstitute.org/2019/12/17/calls-to-action-accountability-a-status-update-on-reconciliation/.

"John Horgan Announces Site C Decision." *Global News*. 11 Dec. 2017, globalnews.ca/video/3909966/john-horgan-announces-site-c-decision.

Johnson, E. Pauline. "A Red Girl's Reasoning." In *Tekahionwake: E. Pauline Johnson's Writings on Native North America*, edited by Margery Fee and Dory Nason, Broadview, 2016, pp. 163–78.

Jordan, June. "The Craft That the Politics Requires: An Interview with June Jordan." Interview by Margaret Christakos. *Fireweed*, no. 36, Summer 1992, pp. 26–39.

Justice, Daniel Heath. *Our Fire Survives the Storm*. U of Minnesota P, 2006.

———. "'Go Away, Water!' Kinship Criticism and the Decolonization Imperative." In *Reasoning Together*, edited by Craig S. Womack, Daniel Heath Justice, and Christopher B. Teuton, Native Critics Collective, U of Oklahoma P, 2008, pp. 147–68.

———. *Why Indigenous Literatures Matter*. Wilfrid Laurier UP, 2018.

Kamboureli, Smaro. *Scandalous Bodies: Diasporic Literature in English Canada*. Oxford UP, 2000.

———. "Preface." *Trans.Can.Lit: Resituating the Study of Canadian Literature*, edited by Smaro Kamboureli and Roy Miki, Wilfrid Laurier UP, 2007, pp. vii–xv.

———. "Introduction: Shifting the Ground of a Discipline: Emergence and Canadian Literary Studies in English." In *Shifting the Ground of Canadian Literary Studies*, edited by Smaro Kamboureli and Robert Zacharias, Wilfrid Laurier UP, 2012, pp. 1-36.

———. *Literary Solidarities / Critical Diversities: A Mikinaakominis / TransCanadas*, special issue of *University of Toronto Quarterly*, edited by Smaro Kamboureli and Tania Aguila-Way, vol. 89, no. 1, Winter 2020, pp 1–22.

———. TransCanada Institute. n.d. smarokamboureli.ca/transcanada-institute-archive.

Kamboureli, Smaro, and Larissa Lai. Second Call for Papers, Mikinaakominis / TransCanadas: Literature, Justice, Relation, 2016. smarokamboureli.ca/wp-content/uploads/2016/05/CFP-Mikinaakominis-May-20-2016.pdf.

———. Mikinaakominis / TransCanadas: Literature, Justice, Relation. Conference Program, 24 May. 2016, smarokamboureli.ca/transcanada-institute-archive/conferences/transcanada2017/

Karl, Rebecca. *Staging the World: Chinese Nationalism at the Turn of the Twentieth Century*. Duke UP, 2002.

Kay, Jonathan. "Worst National Birthday, Ever: Why the Country's Intellectual Class Decided to Celebrate Canada with an Orgy of Shame." *National Post in the Star Phoenix*, 30 Dec. 2017, pp. 1–2.

Kim, Christine, and Christopher Lee. "Editorial: Asian Canadian Critique Beyond the Nation." *Canadian Literature*, no. 227, 2015, pp. 6–14.

Kimmerer, Robin Wall. *Braiding Sweetgrass: Indigenous Wisdom, Scientific Knowledge, and Teachings of Plants*. Milkweed Editions, 2015.

King, Hayden. "The Erasure of Indigenous Thought in Foreign Policy." *Open Canada*, 31 July 2017. opencanada.org/erasure-indigenous-thought-foreign-policy/.

———. "First Nations Crisis is About Land. We Need a New Settlement." *Globe and Mail*, 10 Feb 2015. theglobeandmail.com/globe-debate/hayden-king-first-nations-crisis-is-about-land-we-need-a-new-settlement/article22887364/.

King, Hayden, and Shiri Pasternak. *Canada's Emerging Indigenous Rights Framework: A Critical Analysis*. Yellowhead Institute, 2018.

King, Tiffany Lethabo. *The Black Shoals: Offshore Formations of Black and Native Studies*. Duke UP, 2019.

Kiyooka, Roy K. *TransCanada Letters*. Edited by Smaro Kamboureli, NeWest P, 2005a.

———. "We Asian North Americanos: An Unhistorical 'Take' on Growing up Yellow in a White World." In *Pacific Rim Letters* by Roy K. Kiyooka, edited, with an afterword, by Smaro Kamboureli, NeWest P, 2005b, pp. 108–10.

Kumar, Deepa. *Islamophobia and the Politics of Empire*. Haymarket Books, 2012.

Kundnani, Arun. *The Muslims Are Coming! Islamophobia, Extremism, and the Domestic War on Terror*. Verso, 2015.

Kuokkanen, Rauna. "From Indigenous Economies to Market-Based Self-Governance: A Feminist Political Economy Analysis." *Canadian Journal of Political Science*, vol. 44, no. 2, 2011, pp. 275–97.

Lackenbauer, P. Whitney, and Andrew F. Cooper. "The Achilles Heel of Canadian International Citizenship: Indigenous Diplomacies and State Responses." *Canadian Foreign Policy*, vol. 13, no. 3, 2011, pp. 99–119.

Laclau, Ernesto. *On Populist Reason*. Verso, 2005.

Ladner, Kiera L. "Negotiated Inferiority: The Royal Commission on Aboriginal People's Vision of a Renewed Relationship." *American Review of Canadian Studies*, no, 31, 2001, pp. 241–64.

Ladner, Keira L. and Myra J. Tait, eds. *Surviving Canada: Indigenous Peoples Celebrate 150 Years of Betrayal*. Arbeiter Ring P, 2017.

LaFlamme, Michelle. "Speaking up, Speaking out, or Speaking back: The Signposts Are in the Right Direction." *Theatre Research in Canada*, vol. 31, no. 2, 2010a, pp. xxvii–xxx.

———. "Theatrical Medicine: Aboriginal Performance, Ritual, and Commemoration." *Theatre Research in Canada*, vol. 31, no. 2, 2010b, pp. 107–17.

Lai, Larissa. Slanting I, Imagining We: Asian Canadian Literary Production in the 1980s and 1990s. Wilfrid Laurier UP, 2014.

———. "Saturate/Dissolve: Water for Itself, Un-Settler Responsibilities." *Downstream: Reimagining Water*, edited by Dorothy Christian and Rita Wong, Wilfrid Laurier UP, 2017, pp. 259–69.

———. "Insurgent Utopias: How to Recognize the Knock at the Door." *Exploring the Fantastic: Genre, Ideology, and Popular Culture*, edited by Ina Batzke et al., Transcript Verlag, 2018, pp. 91–118.

———. "Bone to Bone, Spirit to Spirit: Sovereign Matriarchy, Asian/Indigenous Relations, and the Work of Directed Re-membering." In *Ideology in Postcolonial Texts and Contexts*, edited by Katja Sarkowsky and Mark U. Stein, Brill Rodopi, 2021a, pp. 223–58.

———. "Editorial feedback to author [Karina Vernon]," 15 June 2021b.

Lai, Larissa, Neil Surkan, and Joshua Whitehead, eds. *Counterclockwise*, special issue of *Canada and Beyond: A Journal of Canadian Literary and Cultural Studies*, vol. 8, no. 1, 2019.

Lai, Larissa, and Rita Wong. *Sybil Unrest*. New Star Books, 2013.

Langan, Mary. "Community Care in the 1990s: The Community Care White Paper, 'Caring for People.'" *Critical Social Policy*, vol. 10, no. 29, 1990, pp. 58–70.

Lavery, Jonathan, and Louis Groarke. "Introduction: Genre as a Tool of Philosophical Interpretation and Analysis." In *Literary Form, Philosophical*

Content: Historical Studies of Philosophical Genres, edited by Jonathan Lavery and Louis Groarke, Fairleigh Dickinson UP, 2010, pp. 13–40.

Law Commission of Canada. *Restoring Dignity: Responding to Child Abuse in Canadian Institutions*. Minister of Public Works and Government Services, 2000.

Lawrence, Bonita. *"Real" Indians and Others: Mixed-Blood Urban and Native Peoples and Indigenous Nationhood*. Nebraska UP, 2004.

Lawrence, Bonita, and Enakshi Dua. "Decolonizing Antiracism." *Social Justice*, vol. 32, no. 4, 2005, pp. 120–43.

Lederman, Marsha. "Author Steven Galloway Fired from UBC after Investigation of 'Serious Allegations.'" *Globe and Mail*, 22 June 2016, theglobeandmail.com/news/british-columbia/author-steven-galloway-fired-from-ubc-after-investigation-of-serious-allegations/article30557345/.

Lee, Christopher. *The Semblance of Identity: Aesthetic Mediation in Asian American Literature*. Stanford UP, 2012.

———. "The World(liness) of Chinese Canadian Literature." Plenary Two: Literature and Relation, Mikinaakominis/TransCanadas: Literature, Justice, Relation Conference, 25 May 2017, University of Toronto. Plenary Presentation.

Lee, Erica Violet. "Treaties beyond the State: Honouring Our Responsibilities to Each Other." *CBC News*, 25 Apr. 2021, cbc.ca/news/canada/saskatchewan/black-on-the-prairies-treaties-beyond-the-state-1.5986994.

———. [@ericavioletlee]. "NonBlack Natives Need to Stop Policing Black & AfroIndigenous Folks." *Twitter*, 4 June 2021. https://twitter.com/ericavioletlee/status/1401008924422115329.

Lee, Jen Sookfong. "Open Letters and Closed Doors: How the Steven Galloway Open Letter Dumpster Fire Forced Me to Acknowledge the Racism and Entitlement at the Heart of CanLit." *Humber Literary Review*, 2017, humberliteraryreview.com/jen-sookfong-lee-essay-open-letters-and-closed-doors.

Lee Tung-hai. *Jianada Huaqiao Shi* [A History of Chinese in Canada]. Zhonghua Dadian Biandianhui, 1967.

Lentin, Alana. "Post-Race, Post-Politics: The Paradoxical Rise of Culture After Multiculturalism." *Ethnic and Racial Studies*, vol. 37, no. 8, 2014, pp. 1268–85.

Leow, Joanne. "Mis-Mappings and Mis-Duplications: Interdiscursivity and the Poetry of Wayde Compton." *Canadian Literature*, no. 214, 2012, pp. 47–66.

Lew, Janey. "A Politics of Meeting: Reading Intersectional Indigenous Feminist Praxis in Lee Maracle's *Sojourners and Sundogs*." *Frontiers*, vol. 38, no. 1, 2017, pp. 225–59.

Lightfoot, Sheryl. *Global Indigenous Politics: A Subtle Revolution*. Routledge, 2016.

Lindberg, Tracey. "The Doctrine of Discovery in Canada." In *Discovering Indigenous Lands: The Doctrine of Discovery in the English Colonies*, edited by Robert J. Miller et al., Oxford UP, 2010, pp. 89–167.

Little, John. *Bruce Lee: A Warrior's Journey.* Warner Home Video, 2000.

Little Bear, Leroy. "Aboriginal Relationships to the Land and Resources." In *Sacred Lands: Aboriginal World Views, Claims, and Conflicts*, edited by Jill Oakes et al., Canadian Circumpolar Institute, 1998, pp. 15–20.

———. "National Bison Day." 1 Nov. 2014, Bozeman, Montana. Keynote Address.

Locke, John. *Second Treatise on Civil Government.* U of Adelaide Library, 2014.

Lorde, Audre. "The Master's Tools Will Never Dismantle the Master's House." In *Sister Outsider*, Sister Visions P, 1979, pp. 110–13.

Lowe, Lisa. *The Intimacies of Four Continents.* Duke UP, 2015.

Macfarlane, Heather, and Armand Garnet Ruffo, eds. *Introduction to Indigenous Literary Criticism in Canada.* Broadview P, 2016.

Mack, Adrian. "DOXA Looks to The Road Forward." *Georgia Strait*, 3 May 2017, straight.com/movies/904116/doxa-looks-road-forward.

Mackey, Eva. *Unsettled Expectations: Uncertainty, Land and Settler Decolonization.* Fernwood, 2016.

Macklin, Audrey. "Particularized Citizenship: Encultured Women and the Public Sphere." In *Migrations and Mobilities: Citizenship, Borders, and Gender*, edited by Seyla Benhabib and Judith Resnik, New York UP, 2009, pp. 276–303.

Maclear, Kyo. *The Letter Opener.* Harper Collins, 2007.

Mahmood, Saba. *Politics of Piety: The Islamic Revival and the Feminist Subject.* Princeton UP, 2005.

Malik, Kenan. *Multiculturalism and Its Discontents.* Seagull Books, 2013.

Mamdani, Mahmood. *Good Muslim, Bad Muslim: America, The Cold War and the Roots of Terror.* Pantheon Books, 2004.

———. "Political Identity, Citizenship and Ethnicity in Post-Colonial Africa." Arusha Conference, New Frontiers of Social Policy, 12–15 Dec. 2005, Keynote Address.

———. Define and Rule: Native as Political Identity. Harvard UP, 2012. Manuel, George. *The Fourth World: An Indian Reality.* 1974. U of Minnesota P, 2019.

Maracle, Lee. *Memory Serves: Oratories.* Edited by Smaro Kamboureli, NeWest P, 2015.

———. "Voices of Elders: The Reconciliation Movement." 22 Apr. 2016, Queen Elizabeth Theatre, Vancouver, facebook.com/events/1118669788164225/. Public talk.

Marshall, Alison. *The Way of the Bachelor: Early Chinese Settlement in Manitoba.* U of British Columbia P, 2011.

Mawani, Renisa. *Colonial Proximities: Crossracial Encounters and Juridical Truths in British Columbia, 1871–1921*. U of British Columbia P, 2009.
Maynard, Robyn. *Policing Black Lives: State Violence in Canada from Slavery to the Present*. Fernwood, 2017.
———. "Black Life and Death across the U.S.-Canada Border: Border Violence, Black Fugitive Belonging, and a Turtle Island View of Black Liberation." *Journal of the Critical Ethnic Studies Association*, vol. 5, no. 1–2, 2019, pp. 124–51.
McFarlane, Peter, and Nicole Shabus, editors. *Whose Land Is It Anyway: A Manual for Decolonization*. Federation of Post-secondary Educators of BC, 2017, fpse.ca/sites/ default/files/news_files/Decolonization%20Handbook.pdf.
McFarlane, Scott. "The Haunt of Race: Canada's *Multiculturalism Act*, the Politics of Incorporation, and Writing Thru Race." *Fuse Magazine*, vol. 18, no. 3, 1995, pp. 18–31.
McGregor, Hannah, Julie Rak, and Erin Wunker, editors. *Refuse: CanLit in Ruins*. Book*hug, 2018.
McGuire, Patricia. "Exploring Resilience and Indigenous Ways of Knowing." *Pimatisiwin: A Journal of Aboriginal and Indigenous Community Health*, vol. 8, no. 2, 2010, pp. 117–31.
McKeown, Adam. *Melancholy Order: Asian Migration and the Globalization of Borders*. Columbia UP, 2008.
Mignolo, Walter D., and Catherine E. Walsh. *On Decoloniality*. Duke UP, 2018.
Miki, Roy. "Inter-Face: Roy Kiyooka's Writing, A Commentary/Interview." *Roy Kiyooka* by Roy Kiyooka. Artspeak Gallery; Or Gallery, 1991, pp. 41–54.
———. "Asiancy." In *Broken Entries: Race Subjectivity Writing*. Mercury P, 1998, pp. 101–24.
———. *Redress: Inside the Japanese Canadian Call for Justice*. Raincoast, 2004.
———. *In Flux: Transnational Shifts in Asian Canadian Writing*. NeWest P, 2011.
———. "Inter-Face: Roy Kiyooka's Writing, A Commentary/Interview." *Roy Kiyooka* by Roy Kiyooka. Artspeak Gallery; Or Gallery, 1991, pp. 41–54.
Miller, J. R. *Shingwauk's Vision: A History of Native Residential Schools*. U of Toronto P, 1996.
Million, Dian. *Therapeutic Nations: Healing in an Age of Indigenous Human Rights*. U of Arizona P, 2013.
Mongia, Radhika. "Race, Nationality, Mobility: A History of the Passport." *Public Culture*, vol. 11, no. 3, 1999, pp. 527–55.
Mordecai, Pamela. *Journey Poem*. Sandberry, 1989.
———. *De Man: A Performance Poem*. Sister Vision, 1995.
———. *Certifiable*. Goose Lane Editions, 2001.

———. *The True Blue of Islands*. Sandberry, 2005

———. *Subversive Sonnets*. TSAR, 2012.

———. *De book of Mary*. Mawenzi, 2015.

Morgan, Anthony. "Black People in Canada Are Not Settlers." *Ricochet*, 12 Mar. 2019. ricochet.media/en/2538/black-people-in-canada-are-not-settlers.

Moten, Fred, and Stefano Harney. "Conversación Los Abajocomunes." *The New Inquiry*, 5 Sept. 2018, thenewinquiry.com/conversacion-los-abajocomunes/.

Moylan, Tom. *Demand the Impossible: Science Fiction and the Utopian Imagination*. Methuen, 1986.

Mufti, Aamir. "Critical Secularism: A Reintroduction for Perilous Times." *Boundary* 2, vol. 31, no. 2, 2004, pp. 1–9.

Narayan, Uma. "Essence of Culture and a Sense of History: A Feminist Critique of Cultural Essentialism." *Hypatia*, vol. 13, no. 2, Spring 1998, pp. 86–106.

———. "Undoing the 'Package Picture' of Cultures." *Signs*, vol. 25, no. 4, Summer 2000, pp. 1083–86.

Nathoo, Zulekha. "Cultural Appropriation vs. Artistic Licence: How Far Have We Really Come?" *CBC News*, 13 May. 2017, cbc.ca/news/entertainment/cultural-appropriation-media-1.4114158.

National Inquiry into Missing and Murdered Indigenous Women and Girls. 2019. "A Legal Analysis of Genocide: Supplementary Report." Government of Canada. mmiwg-ffada.ca/wp-content/uploads/2019/06/Supplementary-Report_Genocide.pdf.

Niedzviecki, Hal. "Writer's Prompt: Winning the Appropriation Prize." *Write: The Magazine of the Writer's Union of Canada*, vol. 38, no. 1, 2017, p. 8.

Ninh, erin Khuê. "Affect/Family/Filialty." *The Routledge Companion to Asian American and Pacific Islander Literature*. Ed. Rachel C. Lee. London: Routledge, 2014, pp. 46–55.

Ontario Black History Society. 2007. *Ontario Black Heritage Exhibit*, 15-20 Jan. 2007, The Diversity, Equity, & Human Rights Office, George Brown College, Toronto.

Pasternak, Shiri. "The Fiscal Body of Sovereignty: To 'Make Live' in Indian Country." *Settler Colonial Studies*, vol. 6, no. 4, 2016, pp. 317–38.

Peake, Linda, and Brian Ray. "Racializing the Canadian Landscape: Whiteness, Uneven Geographies and Social Justice." *Canadian Geographer*, vol. 45, no. 1, 2001, pp. 180–86.

Perreault, Amy, and Karrmen Crey. "How Do You Talk about Indigenous Issues in the Classroom?" *What I Learned in Class Today: Aboriginal Issues in the Classroom*, University of British Columbia, 2018, intheclass.arts.ubc.ca/.

Perry, Adele. *On the Edge of Empire: Gender, Race, and the Making of British Columbia 1849–1871*. U of Toronto P, 2001.

Public Inquiry Commission on Relations Between Indigenous Peoples and Certain Public Services in Québec: Listening, Reconciliation, and Progress, Final Report. Commission d'enquête sur les relations entre les Autochtones et certains services publics, Québec, 2019, cerp.gouv.qc.ca/fileadmin/ Fichiers_clients/Rapport/Final_report.pdf.

Philip, M. NourbeSe. *Frontiers: Selected Essays and Writings on Race and Culture, 1984–1992*. Mercury P, 1992.

———. "Black W/Holes: A History of Brief Time." *Writing Black Canadas*, special issue of *Transition*, no. 124, 2017, pp. 118–35.

Phung, Malissa. "Are People of Colour Settlers Too?" In *Cultivating Canada: Reconciliation through the Lens of Cultural* Diversity, edited by Ashok Mathur, Jonathan Dewar, and Mike DeGagné, Aboriginal Healing Foundation, 2011, pp. 291–98.

Powell, Enoch. "Enoch Powell Delivered His 'Water Tower' Speech." *The Health Foundation*. navigator.health.org.uk/theme/1/timeline?page=3#timeline-item-345.

Pratt, Mary Louise. *Imperial Eyes: Travel Writing and Transculturation*. Routledge, 1992.

Pratt, Richard H. "The Advantages of Mingling Indians with Whites." *Proceedings of the National Conference of Charities and Correction, at the Nineteenth Annual Session held in Denver, Col., June 23–29, 1892*, edited by Isabel C. Barrows, Geo. H. Ellis, 1892, pp. 45–49. carlisleindian.dickinson.edu/teach/kill-indian-him-and-save-man-r-h-pratt-education-native-americans.

Price, John. *Orienting Canada: Race, Empire and the Transpacific*. U of British Columbia P, 2011.

R. v. Van der Peet. 2 SCR 507, Supreme Court of Canada. scc-csc.lexum.com/scc-csc/scc-csc/en/item/1407/index.do.

Rajchman, John. "Diagram and Diagnosis." In *Becomings: Explorations in Time, Memory, Futures*, edited by Elizabeth Grosz, Cornell UP, 1999, pp. 42–54.

Rak, Julie. "Another Dumpster Fire: An Opinionated Review of *Arrival: The Story of CanLit* by Nick Mount." *Hook & Eye*, 16 Nov. 2017. hookandeye.ca/2017/11/16/guest-post-another-dumpster-fire-an-opinionated-review-of-arrival-the-story-of-canlit-by-nick-mount/.

Razack, Sherene. "Imperilled Muslim Women, Dangerous Muslim Men and Civilized Europeans: Legal and Social Responses to Forced Marriages." *Feminist Legal Studies*, no. 12, 2004, pp. 129–74.

———. "The 'Sharia Law Debate' in Ontario: The Modernity/Premodernity Distinction in Legal Efforts to Protect Women from Culture." *Feminist Legal Studies*, no. 15, 2007, pp. 3–32.

Readings, Bill. *The University in Ruins*. Harvard UP, 1996.

red diva projects. "History." In *The Road Forward*, n.d. reddiva.ca/history.

Reder, Deanna. "Recuperating Indigenous Narratives: Making Legible the Documenting of Injustices." Plenary presentation. Plenary Four: Literature and Justice, Mikinaakominis/TransCanadas: Literature, Justice, Relation Conference, 26 May 2017, University of Toronto. Plenary Presentation.

Reder, Deanna, and Linda M. Morra, eds. *Learn, Teach, Challenge: Approaching Indigenous Literatures*, Wilfrid Laurier UP, 2016.

Reder, Deanna, and Alix Shield. "'I Write This for All of You': Recovering the Unpublished RCMP 'Incident' in Maria Campbell's *Halfbreed* (1973)." *Canadian Literature*, no. 237, 2019, pp. 13–25.

Regan, Paulette. *Unsettling the Settler Within: Indian Residential Schools, Truth Telling, Reconciliation in Canada*. U of British Columbia P, 2010.

Retallack, Joan. *The Poethical Wager*. U of California P, 2004.

Richard, Nelly. *The Insubordination of Signs: Political Change, Cultural Transformation, and the Poetics of the Crisis*. Duke UP, 2004.

Robinson, Dylan. "Intergenerational Sense, Intergenerational Responsibility." In *Arts of Engagement: Taking Aesthetic Action In and Beyond the Truth and Reconciliation Commission of Canada*, edited by Dylan Robinson and Keavy Martin, Wilfrid Laurier UP, 2016, pp. 43–66.

Robinson, Dylan, and Keavy Martin, eds. *Arts of Engagement: Taking Aesthetic Action In and Beyond the Truth and Reconciliation Commission of Canada*. Wilfrid Laurier UP, 2016.

Rohlehr, Gordon. "The Folk in Caribbean Literature." *Tapia*, 17 Dec. 1972, pp. 7–8, 13–14.

Ross, Kristin. *Communal Luxury: The Political Imaginary of the Paris Commune*. Verso P, 2016.

Royal Commission on Aboriginal Peoples. "A Note about Terminology." In *Report of the Royal Commission on Aboriginal Peoples: Restructuring the Relationship*, vol. 2. Royal Commission on Aboriginal Peoples, Government of Canada, 1996. data2.archives.ca/e/e448/e011188230-02.pdf.

Ruffo, Armand Garnet, ed. *(Ad)dressing Our Words: Aboriginal Perspectives on Aboriginal Literatures*. Theytus Books, 2001.

Saghal, Gita. "The Return of the Grand Narrative: Relating Secularism to Racism and Belonging." In *Secularism, Racism and the Politics of Belonging*, edited by Nira Yuval-Davis and Philip Marfleet, Runnymede Perspectives, 2012, pp. 53–56.

Said, Edward. *The World, the Text, and the Critic*. Harvard UP, 1983.

———. Humanism and Democratic Criticism. Columbia UP, 2004.

Salaita, Steven. *Inter/Nationalism: Decolonizing Native America and Palestine*. U of Minnesota P, 2016.

Sangari, Kumkum. "Politics of Diversity: Religious Communities and Multiple Patriarchies (Section I)." *Economic and Political Weekly*, vol. 30, no. 51, 1995, pp. 3287–310.

Sedgwick, Eve Kosofsky. *Touching Feeling: Affect, Pedagogy, Performativity*, Duke UP, 2003, pp. 123–51.

Sharpe, Christina. *In the Wake: On Blackness and Being*. Duke UP, 2016.

Shelley, Percy. *A Defense of Poetry*. Edited by Albert S. Cook, Ginn & Company, 1891.

Shield, Alix. "Rethinking the Paratext: Digital Story-Mapping E. Pauline Johnson's and Chief Joe and Mary Capilano's *Legends of Vancouver* (1911)." *BC Studies*, no. 197, 2018, pp. 111–25.

Simpson, Leanne, ed. *Lighting the Eighth Fire: The Liberation, Resurgence and Protection of Indigenous Nations*. Arbeiter Ring P, 2008.

———. *Dancing on Our Turtle's Back: Stories of Nishnaabeg Re-Creation, Resurgence and a New Emergence*. Arbeiter Ring P, 2011.

———. "The Place Where We All Live and Work Together: A Gendered Analysis of 'Sovereignty.'" In *Native Studies Keywords*, edited by Stephanie Nohelani Teves, Andrea Smith, and Michelle H. Raheja, U Arizona P, 2015, pp. 18–24.

———, ed. *Lighting the Eighth Fire: The Liberation, Resurgence and Protection of Indigenous Nations*. Arbeiter Ring P, 2008.

Sioui, Georges E. *Huron-Wendat: The Heritage of the Circle*. Translated by Jane Brierley, U of British Columbia P, 1999.

Slaughter, Joseph R. "Hijacking Human Rights: Neoliberalism, the New Historiography and the End of the Third World." *Human Rights Quarterly*, no. 40, 2018, pp. 735–75.

Šlezić, Lana. "If These Walls Could Talk: The Physical Traces of Residential Schools." *The Walrus*, 17 Aug.2015. thewalrus.ca/if-these-walls-could-talk/.

Slomp, Jan. "Renegades Rewarded at Public Expense in Site C Dam Decision." *National Farmers Union*, 20 Dec.2017. nfu.ca/renegades-rewarded-at-public-expense-in-site-c-dam-decision/

Smith, Gregg C. "Foreword." In *The True Spirit and Original Intent of Treaty 7*, edited by Walter Hildebrandt, Sarah Carter, Dorothy First Rider, and Treaty 7 Tribal Council, McGill-Queen's UP, 1996, pp. vii–viii.

Spivak, Gayatri Chakravorty. *Outside in the Teaching Machine*. Routledge, 1993.

———. "Echo." In *An Aesthetic Education in the Era of Globalization*, Harvard UP, 2012, pp. 218–40.

———. 2012b. "Imperative to Re-Imagine the Planet." In *An Aesthetic Education in the Era of Globalization*, Harvard UP, 2012, pp. 335–50.

———. 2012c. "Introduction." In *An Aesthetic Education in the Era of Globalization*, Harvard UP, 2012, pp. 1-50.

Stone, Anne. *Delible*. Insomniac, 2007.

Strakosch, Elizabeth. *Neoliberal Indigenous Policy: Settler Colonialism and the "Post-Welfare" State*. Palgrave Macmillan, 2015.

Sutherland, David, and Jennifer Holness. *Speakers for the Dead*, National Film Board of Canada, 2000.

Suzuki, David. "David Suzuki Fires off from the 'Death Zone' at Trudeau, Weaver, and a Broken System." *National Observer*, 5 Mar. 2018, nationalobserver.com/2018/03/05/ news/david-suzuki-fires-death-zone-trudeau-weaver-and-broken-system.

Tailfeathers, Elle-Máijá, director. *C'əsnaʔəm: The City before the City*, produced by Musqueam First Nation / c'əsnaʔəm curatorial team, 2017.

TallBear, Kim. "Beyond the Life/Not-Life Binary: A Feminist-Indigenous Reading of Cryopreservation, Interspecies Thinking, and New Materialisms." In *Cryopolitics: Frozen Life in a Melting World*, edited by Joanna Radin and Emma Kowal, MIT P, 2017, pp. 181–202.

Tator, Carol, et al. *Challenging Racism in the Arts: Case Studies of Controversy and Conflict*. U of Toronto P, 1998.

Taylor, Charles. *Modern Social Imaginaries*. Duke UP, 2004.

Taylor, Diana. *Disappearing Acts: Spectacles of Gender and Nationalism in Argentina's "Dirty War."* Duke UP, 1997.

Tester, Frank, and Peter Kulchyski, *Tammarniit (Mistakes): Inuit Relocation in the Eastern Arctic, 1939–63.*, U of British Columbia P, 1994.

Toghestiy, Werner Naziel. "Roundtable on Indigenous Rights, Land, and Alternatives." Presentation at States of Extraction Conference, 29 Mar. 2015, Simon Fraser University, Vancouver. Presentation.

Truth and Reconciliation Commission of Canada. *Honouring the Truth, Reconciling for the Future. Summary of the Final Report of the Truth and Reconciliation Commission of Canada*. Truth and Reconciliation Commission of Canada, 2015.

———. *The Survivors Speak: A Report of the Truth and Reconciliation Commission of Canada*. Truth and Reconciliation Commission of Canada, 2015.

———. *What We Have Learned: Principles of Truth and Reconciliation*. Truth and Reconciliation Commission of Canada, 2015. publications.gc.ca/collections/collection_2015/TRC/IR4-6-2015-eng.pdf.

Tsu, Jing. "Extinction and Adventure on the Chinese Diasporic Frontier." *Journal of Chinese Overseas*, vol. 2, no. 2, 2006, pp. 247–68.

Tuck, Eve. "Suspending Damage: A Letter to Communities." *Harvard Educational Review*, vol. 79, no. 3, Fall 2009, pp. 409–27.

Tuck, Eve, and Ruben A. Gaztambide-Fernandez. "Curriculum, Replacement, and Settler Futurity." *Journal of Curriculum Theorizing*, vol. 29, no. 1, 2013, pp. 72–89.

Tuck, Eve, and K. Wayne Yang, eds. *Toward What Justice? Describing Diverse Dreams of Justice in Education*. Routledge, 2018.

TWUC, Equity. "Statement from the TWUC Equity Task Force in Response to Niedzviecki Editorial 'Winning the Appropriation Prize.'" 10 May 2017. tiahouse.ca/statement-twuc-equity-task-force-response-niedzviecki-editorial-winning-appropriation-prize/.

United Nations. "2015–2024 International Decade for People of African Descent: Access to Justice." n.d. un.org/en/events/africandescentdecade/justice.shtml.

United Nations, General Assembly. "Convention on the Prevention and Punishment of the Crime of Genocide," 9 Dec. 1948, un.org/en/genocideprevention/documents/atrocity-crimes/Doc.1_Convention%20on%20the%20Prevention%20and%20Punishment%20of%20the%20Crime%20of%20Genocide.pdf.

———. "Permanent Sovereignty Over National Resources in the Occupied Arab Territories," 19 Dec. 1977. digitallibrary.un.org/record/188042/files/A_RES_32_161-EN.pdf?ln=en

———. "Programme of activities for the implementation of the International Decade for People of African Descent," 2014, pp. 1–12.

———. Human Rights Council. "Report of the Working Group of Experts on People of African Descent on its mission to Canada," 2017, pp. 1–20.

Vanderhaeghe, Guy. "We're All Right." Fiction: The Story of Canada. *Globe and Mail*, 15 June 2017, pp. L1–3.

Vernon, Karina. "Writing a Home for Prairie Blackness: Addena Sumter Freitag's *Stay Black & Die* and Cheryl Foggo's Pourin' Down Rain." *Canadian Literature*, no. 182, Fall 2004, pp. 67–83.

———. "The First Black Prairie Novel: Chief Buffalo Child Long Lance's Autobiography and the Repression of Prairie Blackness." *Journal of Canadian Studies*, vol. 45, no. 2, Spring 2011, pp. 31–57.

———. "Black Civility: Grammars of Black Protest on the Canadian Prairies 1905–1950." *Black Canadian Thought*, special issue of CLR *James Journal*, vol. 20, no. 1/2, 2014, pp. 83–96.

———, ed. *The Black Prairie Archives: An Anthology*. Wilfrid Laurier UP, 2020.

Vigil, Kiara, and Tiya Miles. "At the Crossroads of Red/Black Literature." In *The Oxford Handbook of Indigenous American Literature,* edited by James H. Cox and Daniel Heath Justice, Oxford UP, 2014, pp. 31–49.

Viswanathan, Gauri. *Masks of Conquest: Literary Studies and British Rule in India.* Columbia UP, 1989.

Vizenor, Gerald. *Manifest Manners: Narratives on Postindian Survivance.* U of Nebraska P, 1999.

Vowel, Chelsea. "An Open Letter to 'Angry Settlers.'" *âpihtawikosisân,* 26 Feb. 2020. apihtawikosisan.com/2020/02/an-open-letter-to-angry-settlers/.

Wagamese, Richard. *Indian Horse.* Douglas & McIntyre, 2012.

Waiser, Bill. *Saskatchewan: A New History.* Fifth House, 2005.

Wakeham, Pauline. "Beyond Comparison: Reading Relations between Indigenous Nations." *Indigenous Literature and the Arts of Community,* special issue of *Canadian Literature,* no. 230/231, 2017, pp. 124–42.

———. "#Indigenous Reads and the Public Pedagogy of Reconciliation." Plenary presentation. Plenary Two: Mikinaakominis/TransCanadas: Literature, Justice, Relation, 25 May 2017, University of Toronto.

Walcott, Rinaldo. *Black Like Who: Writing Black Canada.* Insomniac P, 1997.

———. "The Problem of the Human: Black Ontologies and 'the Coloniality of Our Being.'" *Postcoloniality-Decoloniality-Black Critique: Joints and Fissures,* edited by Sabine Broeck and Carsten Junker, Campus Verlag, 2014, pp. 93–108.

———. "Black Gifts, Black People: 'Lament for a Nation' and Reading Canada in the Americas." Plenary presentation. Plenary Two: Literature and Relation, Mikinaakominis / TransCanadas: Literature, Justice, Relation Conference, 25 May 2017, University of Toronto.

———. Email to Smaro Kamboureli and Larissa Lai, 26 May 2017.

———. *On Property.* Biblioasis, 2021.

Weaver, Andrew. "Extremely disheartening decision by BC NDP to proceed with fiscally reckless Site C project." *Andrew Weaver MLA,* 11 Dec. 2017. andrewweavermla.ca /2017/12/11/ extremely-disheartening-decision-bc-ndp-proceed-fiscally-reckless-site-project/

Wente, Jesse. "An Emotional Jesse Wente on the 'Remarkable Arrogance' of an Appropriation." Interview by Matt Galloway. *CBC,* 15 May 2017., cbc.ca/news/canada/toronto/jesse-wente-appropriation-prize-1.4115293.

West, Cornel. "The New Cultural Politics of Difference." In *Out There: Marginalization and Contemporary Culture,* edited by Russell Ferguson and Trinh T. Minh-ha, MIT P, 1992, pp. 19–38.

Wickberg, Edgar. "Chinese and Canadian Influence on Chinese Politics in Vancouver, 1900–1947." *BC Studies*, no. 45, Spring 1980, pp. 37–55.

Wildcat, Matthew. "Wahkohtowin in Action." *Constitutional Forum / Forum constitutionnel*, 27, no. 1, 2019, pp. 13–24.

Williams, Gilda. "Introduction: How Deep Is Your Goth? Gothic Art in the Contemporary." *The Gothic: Documents of Contemporary Art*, edited by Gilda Williams. Whitechapel/MIT P, 2007. 12–19.

Windspeaker. "Report Finds Mohawk Warrior Responsible for Policeman's Death." *Windspeaker*, vol. 13, no. 5, 1995, ammsa.com/publications/windspeaker/report-finds-mohawk-warrior-responsible-policemans-death.

Winks, Robin. *The Blacks in Canada*. McGill-Queen's UP, 2000.

Wngz, Ravyn. "An Activism Manifesto." *CP24*, 21 July 2020. marksking.com/my-fabulous-disease/the-scorching-words-of-ravyn-wngz/.

Wolfe, Patrick. "Settler Colonialism and the Elimination of the Native." *Journal of Genocide Research*, vol. 8, no. 4, 2006, pp. 387–409.

Wong, Paul, ed. *Yellow Peril Reconsidered*. On Edge, 1990.

Wong, Rita. *monkeypuzzle*. Press Gang, 1998.

———. "Decolonizasian: Reading Asian and First Nations Relations in Literature." *Asian Canadian Studies*, no. 199, 2008, pp. 158–80.

———. "Water is All of Us". *The Dominion: News from the Grassroots* 79, 24 Aug. 2011. dominionpaper.ca/articles/4154

———. "Ethical Waters: Reflections on the Healing Walk in the Tar Sands." *Feminist Review*, no. 103, 2013, pp. 133–39.

———. *undercurrent*. Gibsons: Nightwood Editions, 2015. pp. 72.

Wong, Rita, and Dorothy Christian. "Introduction: Re-storying Waters, Re-storying Relations." In *Downstream: Reimagining Water*, edited by Dorothy Christian and Rita Wong, Wilfrid Laurier UP, 2017, pp. 1–25.

Wong, Rita, and Cindy Mochizuki. *perpetual*. Nightwood, 2015. nightwoodeditions.com/collections/bestsellers/products/9780889713130

Writers' Union of Canada. Writing Thru Race. Racial Minority Writers Committee, The Writers' Union of Canada. 30 June – 2 July 1994, smarokamboureli.ca/twenty-years-of-writing-thru-race/.

Wunker, Erin. "The. Women. The Subject(s) of *The Unnatural and Accidental Women* and *Unnatural and Accidental*." *Theatre Research in Canada*, vol. 31, no. 2, 2010, pp. 164–81.

Wynter, Sylvia. "On Disenchanting Discourse: 'Minority' Literary Criticism and Beyond." In *The Nature and Context of Minority Discourse*, edited by Abdul JanMohamed and David Lloyd, Oxford UP, 1990, pp. 432–70.

Xu, Xueqing, and Hua Laura Wu. "A Misconception: The Relationship between the Chinese-English Daily Newspaper and the Chinese Times." *BC Studies*, no. 209, Spring 2021, pp. 63–80.

Yee, Paul. *The Curses of Third Uncle.* James Lorimer, 1986.

———. *A Superior Man*. Arsenal Pulp P, 2015.

———. "The Lucky Seven Interview, with Paul Yee." *Open Book*, 18 Jan. 2016, open-book.ca/News/The-Lucky-Seven-Interview-with-Paul-Yee.

Yoshizawa, Alejandro, dir. *All Our Father's Relations*. Right Relations Productions, 2016.

Yu, Henry. "Refracting Pacific Canada: Seeing Our Uncommon Past." *BC Studies*, no. 156, Winter 2007/08, pp. 5–10.

Zarrow, Peter. *After Empire: The Conceptual Transformation of the Chinese State, 1885–1924*. Stanford UP, 2012.

Zuboff, Shoshana. *The Age of Surveillance Capitalism: The Fight for a Human Future at the New Frontier of Power.* PublicAffairs, 2019.

Contributors

Jordan Abel is a Nisga'a writer from Vancouver. He is the author of *The Place of Scraps* (2013), winner of the Dorothy Livesay Poetry Prize, *Un/inhabited* (2020), and *Injun* (2016), winner of the Griffin Poetry Prize. Abel's latest publication, *NISHGA* (2021), is a deeply personal and autobiographical book that addresses the complications of contemporary Indigenous existence and the often invisible intergenerational impact of residential schools. His poetry has been widely anthologized. Abel holds a PhD in English from Simon Fraser University. He is Assistant Professor in the Department of English and Film Studies at the University of Alberta, where he teaches Indigenous literatures and Creative Writing.

Dina Al-Kassim is a critical theorist who writes on contemporary political subjectivation, sexuality, and aesthetics in modernist and contemporary forms with reference to the Middle East and Africa, Europe, and the United States. An Associate Professor in the Department of English Language and Literatures at the University of British Columbia, she is the author of *On Pain of Speech: Fantasies of the First Order and the Literary Rant* (2010). Al-Kassim has been a Mellon Postdoctoral fellow at Stanford University, a Senior Seminar Fellow at Harvard University's Radcliffe Institute, and a Sawyer Seminar, Residency Fellow at the University of California, Humanities Research

Institute. Al-Kassim's publications have appeared in *Grey Room, International Journal of Middle East Studies, Interventions, Journal of Middle East Women's Studies, Public Culture, Cultural Dynamics, Camera Austria International*, and the volume *Islamicate Sexualities*. Her current project, *Exposures*, asks why and how exposure has come to be a condition of contemporary truth through selective soundings in literature and politics from Egypt, Lebanon, South Africa, and the United States.

Lillian Allen is Professor of Creative Writing at Ontario College of Art and Design University, where she spearheaded the establishment of an interdisciplinary, multimedia Creative Writing BFA program inspiring students to claim space for their dreams in the world and to use their creativity to make revolution. Acclaimed as a foremother of Canadian poetry by the League of Canadian Poets, she is a two-time Canadian Juno award winner for her albums *Revolutionary Tea Party* and *Conditions Critical*, and the author of *Women Do this Every Day* and *Psychic Unrest*, plus several books and recordings for children and young people. Allen is at the leading edge of dub poetry and spoken word, and has received many awards and citations, including the Toronto Cultural Champions Award, the William P. Hubbard Award for Race Relations, and an honourary doctorate from Wilfrid Laurier University for her contribution and impact on Canadian Letters. Allen's most recent book is *Make the World New: The Poetry of Lillian Allen* (2021), edited by Ronald Cummings.

Eileen Antone, Professor Emerita, University of Toronto, is a member of the Oneida of the Thames First Nation Turtle Clan. She is the past Director of the Aboriginal Studies/Centre for Aboriginal Initiatives at the University of Toronto, where she also served as a faculty member in the Department of Adult Education, Community Development, and Counselling Psychology as well as the Transitional Year Programme. Her research has focused on Aboriginal knowledge and traditional ways of being. Upon retirement she returned to her community, where she is a member of the Oneida Long Term Care Home Committee. She also serves on St. Paul's University College Indigenous Advisory Council, as well as the University of Toronto Indigenous Initiative Council and Elder's Circle. She is also Special Indigenous Advisor to the Dean of Arts and Science at the University of Toronto.

Sedef Arat-Koç teaches in the Department of Politics and Public Administration and the graduate program in Immigration and Settlement Studies at Toronto Metropolitan University (formerly Ryerson University). Her research and publications tackle questions of citizenship, migration, refugees, racialization, gender, colonialism, and imperialism, focusing specifically on Canada, Turkey, and the Middle East. Her work has appeared in several journals including *Third World Quarterly, Studies in Political Economy, Atlantis: A Women's Studies Journal, Social Justice, Journal of Middle East Women's Studies, Journal of Contemporary European Studies*, and *Studies in Social Justice*.

Warren Cariou has devoted much of his career to studying the storytelling traditions and the environmental politics of Indigenous communities in Canada, especially in Métis, Cree, and Anishinaabe territories. He was inspired to study Indigenous stories by the example of his late father Ray Cariou, a gifted Métis raconteur. He has published works of fiction and memoir, as well as critical writing about Indigenous storytelling, literature, and environmental philosophy. He has also created photography and video projects about Indigenous communities in western Canada's tar sands region, and has written numerous articles, stories, and poems about the energy politics of contemporary Indigenous cultures. He is Professor in the Department of English, Theatre, Film & Media at the University of Manitoba.

Margery Fee, FRSC, is Professor Emerita of English at the University of British Columbia. Recent publications are *Literary Land Claims: The "Indian Land Question" from Pontiac's War to Attawapiskat* (2015); *Tekahionwake: E. Pauline Johnson's Writings on Native North America* (2016), coedited with Dory Nason; *Polar Bear* (2019); and an edited collection of Jean Barman's essays, *On the Cusp of Contact: Gender, Space, and Race in the Colonization of British Columbia* (2020). With Daniel Heath Justice, she is co-investigator on the SSHRC-funded project The People and the Text, led by Deanna Reder (thepeopleandthetext.ca). Her current book project examines how mainstream beliefs about language, literacy and literature relate to Indigenous ways of thinking about these matters.

Len Findlay is Distinguished University Professor Emeritus, former Director of the Humanities Research Unit, founding member of the Indigenous

Humanities Group at the University of Saskatchewan, and past president of Academy One (Arts and Humanities) of the Royal Society of Canada. Trained in nineteenth-century European elite and radical cultural theory and production, his more recent Canadianist work engages with the Indigenous–settler interface, historically and currently, the distinctiveness and endangerment of the humanities in Canada, and with connections between academic freedom and Canadian politics. His pending publications include book chapters "Back to Anti-Racist Basics after the Gerald Stanley 'Verdict'" and "After 'English Canada': The Indigenous Humanities and the Feral/Federal State," and a book on academic freedom.

Jennifer Henderson is a settler scholar and Professor in the Department of English and the School of Indigenous and Canadian Studies at Carleton University, on unceded Algonquin territory. She is the coeditor of *Reconciling Canada: Critical Perspectives on the Culture of Redress* (2013) and the author of *Settler Feminism and Race Making in Canada* (2003), as well as numerous articles on governmentality, settler colonialism, and the family. Her recent work on genres of public discourse appears in *Biosocieties*, *Journal of Canadian Studies*, *English Studies in Canada*, and *American Indian Culture and Research Journal*.

Tasha Hubbard (Cree) is an award-winning filmmaker and Associate Professor in the Faculty of Native Studies at the University of Alberta. Hubbard won a Gemini Canada Award for her first solo project, *Two Worlds Colliding* (2004), an exposé of the infamous "starlight tours," whereby Saskatoon police were abandoning Indigenous men in freezing winter conditions. With her acclaimed 2017 documentary *Birth of a Family*, made in collaboration with journalist Betty Ann Adam, Hubbard parses the Sixties Scoop legacy, a practice that saw more than twenty thousand Indigenous babies removed from their birth families and placed in foster homes or adopted. Hubbard speaks and writes widely on racism and Indigenous media both in Canada and abroad.

Smaro Kamboureli is the Avie Bennett Chair in Canadian Literature at the University of Toronto. Her most recent publications include "Diaspora" in *The Oxford Encyclopedia of Literary Theory* (2022); "Literary Solidarities: 'Should I be here?'," her introduction to "Literary Solidarities/Critical

Accountability: *A* Mikinaakominis / TransCanadas Special Issue," in *University of Toronto Quarterly* (2020), which she coedited with Tania Aguila-Way; and the bilingual English/Italian edition of her poetry book, *in seconda persona* (2019). Other publications include *Scandalous Bodies: Diasporic Literature in English Canada* (2000), which won the Gabrielle Roy Prize for English Canadian literary criticism, and *On the Edge of Genre: The Contemporary Canadian Long Poem* (1991). She has also edited many books, including Lee Maracle's *Memory Serves: Oratories* (2015), winner of the 2016 Alberta Book Publishing Non-Fiction Book of the Year Award; Barbara Godard's *Canadian Literature at the Crossroads of Language and Culture* (2008); *Critical Collaborations: Indigeneity, Diaspora and Ecology in Canadian Literary Studies* (2014, with Christl Verduyn); *Editing as Cultural Practice in Canada* (2016, with Dean Irvine), a finalist for the Gabrielle Roy Prize; and *Producing Canadian Literature: Authors Speak on the Literary Marketplace* (2013, with Kit Dobson).

Sonnet L'Abbé is a Canadian poet and editor. They are the author of *A Strange Relief* (2001), *Killarnoe* (2007), and *Sonnet's Shakespeare* (2019). In 2014, they coedited the annual *Best Canadian Poetry in English* anthology. Their chapbook, *Anima Canadensis*, won the 2017 bp Nichol chapbook award. They teach Creative Writing and English at Vancouver Island University, and sit on the editorial board of Brick Books.

Larissa Lai has written four novels, *The Lost Century* (2022), *The Tiger Flu* (2018), *Salt Fish Girl* (2002), and *When Fox Is a Thousand* (1995); three poetry books, *Iron Goddess of Mercy* (2021), *Automaton Biographies* (2009), and *sybil unrest* (2008, with Rita Wong); and a critical book, *Slanting I, Imagining We: Asian Canadian Literary Production in the 1980s and 1990s* (2014). She is Professor of English at the University of Calgary, where she holds a Canada Research Chair Tier II in Creative Writing. In July 2023, she will become the Richard Charles Lee Chair in Chinese Canadian Studies at the University of Toronto.

Christopher Lee is Associate Professor of English and Director of the Asian Canadian and Asian Migration Studies Program at the University of British Columbia. He is the author of *The Semblance of Identity: Aesthetic Mediation in*

Asian American Literature (2012) and coeditor of *Tracing the Lines: Reflections on Contemporary Poetics and Cultural Politics in Honour of Roy Miki* (2012, with Maia Joseph, Christine Kim, and Larissa Lai). He recently coedited special issues of *Asian Diasporic Visual Cultures and the Americas* ("Beyond Canada 150: Asian Canadian Visual Cultures," 2018, with Glenn Deer and Marissa Largo) and *American Quarterly* ("From Anarchy to Chaos: Generations of Empire," 2022, with Melani McAlister). He is currently writing a book about race and capital in Chinese Canadian historical narratives.

Sophie McCall is a settler scholar whose main areas of research and teaching are Indigenous literatures in Canada and contemporary Canadian literature from the twentieth and twenty-first centuries. She is Professor in the Department of English at Simon Fraser University and Director of the Masters of Arts for Teachers of English (MATE) program with a specialization in Indigenous Literatures. She has published widely on topics such as textualizing oral history, the struggle for Indigenous rights, decolonization, resurgence, and reconciliation. Her book, *First Person Plural: Aboriginal Storytelling and the Ethics of Collaborative Authorship* (2011), was a finalist for the Gabrielle Roy Prize for English Canadian literary criticism and the Canada Prize from the Federation for the Humanities and Social Sciences for scholarly work in the Humanities. She has edited and coedited several collections of essays, stories, and visual arts, including *Read, Listen, Tell: Indigenous Stories from Turtle Island* (2017, with Deanna Reder, David Gaertner, and Gabrielle L'Hirondelle Hill) and the fiftieth anniversary special issue of *ARIEL: A Review of International English Literature* (2020, with Deanna Reder).

Pamela Mordecai writes poetry and fiction for adults and children, as well as the occasional critical article. A former teacher and teacher-trainer with a PhD in English, she was for many years Publications Officer in the Faculty of Education, University of West Indies, Mona, where she edited the *Caribbean Journal of Education* for over a decade. A prolific anthologist with a special interest in the writing of Caribbean women, she has published nine books of poetry, including *Up Tropic* (2021), *De Book of Mary* (2015), and *Subversive Sonnets* (2012). *Pink Icing* (2007), her collection of short fiction, was greeted with rave reviews, and her debut novel, *Red Jacket* (2015), was shortlisted for the Rogers Writers Trust Fiction Award. *A Fierce Green Place: New and*

Selected Poems and *De Book of Joseph* were published by New Directions and Mawenzi House, respectively, in 2022.

Erín Moure is a poet and translator of poetry who has published eighteen books of poetry, a coauthored book of poetry, a volume of essays, a book of articles on translation, a poetics, and two memoirs; she has translated or cotranslated twenty-one books of poetry and two of biopoetics from French, Spanish, Galician, Portuguese, and Ukrainian, by poets such as Nicole Brossard (with Robert Majzels), Andrés Ajens, Chantal Neveu, Rosalía de Castro, Chus Pato, Uxio Novoneyra, Lupe Gómez (with Rebeca Lema Martínez and on her own), Fernando Pessoa, and Yuri Izdryk (with Roman Ivashkiv). Three of her own books have appeared in translation, one each in German, Galician, and French. Her work has received the Governor General's Award twice, Pat Lowther Memorial Award, A. M. Klein Prize twice, and has been a three-time finalist for the Griffin Prize and two-time finalist in the USA for a Best Translated Book Award (Poetry). Her latest is *The Elements* (2019) and her next, *Theophylline*, will appear in 2023.

Karina Vernon is Associate Professor of English at the University of Toronto–Scarborough, where she teaches and researches in the areas of Canadian and Black Canadian literature, Black-Indigenous solidarities, and critical pedagogy. She is the editor of *The Black Prairie Archives: An Anthology* (2020), and a forthcoming companion volume, *Critical Readings in the Black Prairie Archives*. With Winfried Siemerling, she is working on a book project on the politics and aesthetics of relation of Black Canadian cultural achievement, including writing, music, film, and visual art.

Rinaldo Walcott is Professor and Chair of Africana and American Studies and the Carl V. Granger Chair in Africana and American Studies at the University of Buffalo (SUNY). He is also Director of Women and Gender Studies Institute and a member of the Graduate Program in Cinema Studies of Faculty of Arts and Science at the University of Toronto. His teaching and research are in the area of Black diaspora cultural studies and postcolonial studies with an emphasis on questions of sexuality, gender, nation, citizenship, and multiculturalism. Walcott is the author of *Black Like Who: Writing Black Canada* (1997; second revised edition in 2003), *Rude: Contemporary Black*

Canadian Cultural Criticism (2000), and *Black Life: Post-BLM and the Struggle for Freedom* (2019, with Idil Abdillahi). His most recent books are *On Property* (2021) and *The Long Emancipation* (2021).

Rita Wong is the coeditor of *Downstream: Reimagining Water* (2016; with Dorothy Christian). She teaches at Emily Carr University of Art and Design and has written six books of poetry: *Current, Climate* (2021), *beholden* (2018; with Fred Wah), *undercurrent* (2015), *sybil unrest* (2008, 2013; with Larissa Lai), *forage* (2007; winner of Canada Reads Poetry 2011 and the 2008 Dorothy Livesay Prize), and *monkeypuzzle* (1998), as well as a collection of graphic essays with Cindy Mochizuki called *perpetual* (2015). She was arrested in August 2018 and served time in prison for her principled opposition to the Trans Mountain Pipeline expansion. Wong is active in solidarity efforts to protect the Peace Valley from being destroyed by the Site C dam, as well as calling for British Columbia and the rest of Canada to respect Wet'suwet'en law and land.

Index

Page references in **bold** denote figures

Books in the TransCanada Series

Published by Wilfrid Laurier University Press

Smaro Kamboureli and Roy Miki, editors
Trans.Can.Lit: Resituating the Study of Canadian Literature
2007 / xviii + 234 pp. / ISBN 978-0-88920-513-0

Smaro Kamboureli
Scandalous Bodies: Diasporic Literature in English Canada
2009 / xviii + 270 pp. / ISBN 978-1-55458-064-4

Kit Dobson
Transnational Canadas: Anglo-Canadian Literature and Globalization
2009 / xviii + 240 pp. / ISBN 978-1-55458-063-7

Christine Kim, Sophie McCall, and Melina Baum Singer, editors
Cultural Grammars of Nation, Diaspora, and Indigeneity in Canada
2012 / viii + 276 pp. / ISBN 978-1-55458-336-2

Smaro Kamboureli and Robert Zacharias, editors
Shifting the Ground of Canadian Literary Studies
2012 / xviii + 350 pp. / ISBN 978-1-55458-365-2

Kit Dobson and Smaro Kamboureli
Producing Canadian Literature: Authors Speak on the Literary Marketplace
2013 / xii + 208 pp. / ISBN 978-1-55458-355-3

Eva C. Karpinski, Jennifer Henderson, Ian Sowton, and Ray Ellenwood, editors
Trans/acting Culture, Writing, and Memory
2013 / xxix + 364 pp. / ISBN 978-1-55458-839-8

Smaro Kamboureli and Christl Verduyn, editors
Critical Collaborations: Indigenity, Diaspora, and Ecology in Canadian Literary Studies
2014 / viii + 288 pp. / ISBN 978-1-55458-911-1

Larissa Lai
Slanting I, Imagining We: Asian Canadian Literary Production in the 1980s and 1990s
2014 / xii + 262 pp. / ISBN 978-1-77112-041-8

Bart Vautour, Erin Wunker, Travis V. Mason, and Christl Verduyn, editors
Public Poetics: Critical Issues in Canadian Poetry and Poetics
2015 / x + 366 pp. / ISBN 978-1-77112-047-0

Dean Irvine and Smaro Kamboureli, editors
Editing as Cultural Practice in Canada
2016 / x + 296 pp. / ISBN 978-1-77112-111-8

Smaro Kamboureli and Larissa Lai, editors
Land/Relations: Possibilities of Justice in Canadian Literatures
2023 / xvi + 392 pp. / ISBN 978-1-77112-510-9